Puerto Rico's Winter League

Puerto Rico's Winter League

A History of Major League Baseball's Launching Pad

by Thomas E. Van Hyning

with a foreword by EDUARDO VALERO

McFarland & Company, Inc., Publishers
Jefferson, North Carolina, and London

> The present work is a reprint of the library bound edition of Puerto Rico's Winter League: A History of Major League Baseball's Launching Pad, *first published in 1995 by McFarland.*

LIBRARY OF CONGRESS CATALOGUING-IN-PUBLICATION DATA

Van Hyning, Thomas E., 1954–
  Puerto Rico's Winter League : a history of major league baseball's lauching pad / by Thomas E. Van Hyning.
      p.   cm.
  Includes bibliographical references and index.

  ISBN 0-7864-1970-9 (softcover : 50# alkaline paper)

  1. Puerto Rico Winter League (Baseball league)—History.
I. Title.
GV875.P84V36   2004
796.357'097295—dc20   95-5914

British Library cataloguing data are available

©1995 Thomas E. Van Hyning. All rights reserved

No part of this book may be reproduced or transmitted in any form or by any means, electronic or mechanical, including photocopying or recording, or by any information storage and retrieval system, without permission in writing from the publisher.

On the cover: (foreground) Santurce catcher Roy Campanella, *(background)* 1944–45 Santurce Crabbers *(both photographs courtesy of Diana Zorrilla)*

Manufactured in the United States of America

McFarland & Company, Inc., Publishers
  Box 611, Jefferson, North Carolina 28640
      www.mcfarlandpub.com

To Rafael Costas (1938–1992),
founder and first president,
Puerto Rico Professional Baseball Hall of Fame

Contents

Acknowledgments		ix
Foreword (by Eduardo Valero)		1
Preface		3
1	THE LAUNCHING PAD	7
2	A WORKING VACATION	33
3	ROBERTO CLEMENTE #21	53
4	PIONEERS	73
5	STARS AND WORKHORSES	94
6	THEY PLAYED ON	117
7	IMPORTS	139
8	SKIPPERS	165
9	BEHIND THE SCENES	187
10	TEAMS FOR THE AGES	208
11	GAMES	220
12	FANS	234

Appendices: Puerto Rico Winter League Statistics

1 Team Standings: Wins-Losses, 1939–1995	241
2 All-Star Teams, Selected Seasons, 1939–1994	244
3 Single Season Records: Hitting and Pitching	247
4 Regular Season .400+ Hitters (100 or More at Bats)	247
5 Selected Puerto Rico Career Records, 1939–1995	248
6 Most Valuable Players, 1939–1995	255
7 Major League Titles and Awards, Puerto Rico League Players, 1950–1994	257
8 Puerto Rico Professional Baseball Hall of Fame Inductees	258

9 Puerto Rico Winter League Cooperstown Inductees	259
10 Puerto Rico Winter League Teams and Stadiums	259
Notes	261
Selected Bibliography	269
Index	273

ACKNOWLEDGMENTS

This endeavor was a team effort and my thanks go to everyone who helped.

Rafael Costas provided encouragement and information during the six months before he passed away. Héctor Díaz Salichs and Ismael Trabal Martell helped me contact ballplayers, umpires, team officials and sportswriters. Víctor Navarro, a tireless statistician, produced valuable hitting and pitching stats from his publications and research. Angel Armada, Panchicú Toste and Héctor Barea did as well.

Luis Alvelo helped with photos and information on Puerto Ricans who played in the Negro Leagues and the Americans from that era who came to Puerto Rico. Larry Lester, Research Director of the Negro Leagues Baseball Museum, shared his expertise.

Diana Zorrilla deserves special thanks for photos and information about her husband, Pedrín.

Angel Colón, an official with the Puerto Rico Professional Baseball Players Association, provided background information and photographs and facilitated contacts with some of the book's subjects. Rai García also came through with photos.

Benny Agosto, Executive Director of the Liga de Béisbol Profesional de Puerto Rico, authorized credentials for professional baseball stadiums throughout Puerto Rico during the 1991-92, 1992-93 and 1993-94 seasons. Benny gave me *Compilaciones oficiales* for the league with team records and batting and pitching leaders.

Eduardo Valero shared information on the "Romantic Period" in Puerto Rican baseball history, from approximately 1902 to 1938. His foreword speaks for itself.

Tony Menéndez, Puerto Rico correspondent for *USA Today Baseball Weekly*, had pertinent information from the 1990s.

The sports editors of Puerto Rico's three major newspapers—David Colón, *El Nuevo Día*; Luis Colón, *El Vocero*; and Marcos Pérez, *The San Juan Star*—provided assistance, as did sportswriters Eric Edwards and Gabrielle Paese of *The San Juan Star*.

Ubaldo Bernier mailed Puerto Rican baseball clippings from the late

1930s to late 1980s. Frank Otto also sent clippings on Puerto Rican baseball. Francisco Soto Respeto shared articles, as did Miguel J. Frau and Luis Romero Cuevas.

Carlos Costas, a Ponce fan, shared anecdotes about the Lions, as did Charles Ferrer, a lifelong Santurce fan. Ernesto Camacho and Luis Moux were two helpful San Juan fans. Luis Moux also provided photos.

Luis Rodríguez Mayoral was helpful in Puerto Rico and the U.S. as an official with the San Juan Metros and a public relations executive with the Texas Rangers. He introduced me to Roberto Clemente's widow, Vera.

Thanks to Doña Vera for her insights on Roberto Clemente and to Dra. María Angelica Bithorn, who graciously provided materials on her brother, Hiram Bithorn.

And thanks to Jorge Aranzamendi, Rafael Costas, Miguel Gaud, John Hennig, Mary Irizarry, Carlos Miranda, Carmen Iris Orellanes, Rudek Pérez, "Palillo" Santiago, Jorge Tirado, Jr., Luis Alvelo, Díaz Salichs, Víctor Navarro, Panchicú Toste and Trabal Martell for transportation assistance in Puerto Rico.

Mark Alvarez read my two sample chapters. Peter Bjarkman made key suggestions after reading some early drafts. John Holway provided a list of publishers and encouragement. Juan Vené was also a source of inspiration. Thanks to Lonnie Wheeler, who put me in touch with Bob Gibson and Mickey Owen.

Bill Deane, former Senior Researcher at the National Baseball Hall of Fame library, assisted me in locating back issues of *The Sporting News* and other publications. Tracey Barton, at the Library of Congress, delivered countless microfilm materials.

Major league public and media relations officials helped me secure credentials for major league and spring training games: Rob Antony, Minnesota Twins; John Blake, Texas Rangers; Jon Braude, Cincinnati Reds; Jeff Idelson, New York Yankees; Bob Miller, Baltimore Orioles; John Maroon, Cleveland Indians; Rob Matwick, Houston Astros; Chuck Pool, Florida Marlins; Ruth Ruiz, Los Angeles Dodgers; Jim Schultz, Atlanta Braves; Greg Shea, Detroit Tigers; Larry Shenk, Philadelphia Phillies; Howard Starkman, Toronto Blue Jays; Jim Trdinich, Pittsburgh Pirates; Dean Vogelaar, Kansas City Royals.

Minor league officials facilitated access to their clubhouses: Mike Cummings, Rick Muntean and Bill Terlecky of the Scranton/Wilkes-Barre Red Barons, Class AAA; Bill Blackwell of the Jackson Generals and R. C. Reuteman of the Binghamton Mets, Class AA; Sam Nader of the Oneonta Yankees and Brian Lindsay of the Elmira Pioneers, Class A. To these, my special thanks.

And my thanks to umpires Pete Celestino, Gerry Davis, Dale Ford,

Doug Harvey, Tim McClelland, Durwood Merrill, Dan Morrison, Kermit Schmidt and Waldemar Schmidt for their input.

Paula Van Hyning, my mother, receives kudos for her editing, word processing and printing and for compiling the index.

And finally, to the "stars of the show" who took time out to answer my questions, my great appreciation. There was not enough space to include all of your quotes. Your names are listed below.

Notes on Research

First-hand information from Puerto Rico League players and managers was obtained through face-to-face and telephone conversations and three mail surveys. League players and managers from the 1950s and 1980s received a one-page (front and back) questionnaire in January 1992. Players and managers from the 1960s and 1970s were sent the same questionnaire a year later. Issues of *The Sporting News* from the 1950s and 1960s and *Compilaciones oficiales* for the 1970s and 1980s were used to prepare team rosters prior to the mailings. Approximately 500 players and managers were sent a questionnaire. Of these, some 40 individuals had moved and left no forwarding address. The response rate was 50 percent for the 1950s, one third for the 1960s and 1970s and 20 percent for the 1980s. The aggregate response rate was 36.5 percent, based on 168 usable questionnaires out of the 460 received by potential respondents.

I placed follow-up phone calls to players and managers who provided their phone number on the questionnaire. This enabled players and managers to share anecdotes and recollections in addition to their written responses. Spring training trips to Florida in March 1992 and March 1993 enabled me to speak with current big league players and managers who had played or managed in Puerto Rico. Conversations at 15 spring training camps took place before or after Grapefruit League contests. Regular-season conversations were conducted in big league stadiums: Philadelphia's Veterans Stadium, September 14–15, 1991; Yankee Stadium, October 5, 1991; Baltimore's Camden Yards, May 19, June 30 and August 19, 1992, and August 4, 1993. Players and managers also spoke with me before and after minor league games in Scranton, Pennsylvania; Binghamton, New York; Jackson, Mississippi; and Oneonta and Elmira, New York, between August 1991 and May 1994. Other former league players were visited or called at their homes in Puerto Rico or the States. Conversations with players and managers were conducted in Spanish or English.

Research trips were made to Puerto Rico in October 1991, January 1992, January 1993 and December 1993. I covered the October 20, 1991, Puerto Rico Professional Baseball Hall of Fame Ceremonies during the first trip. Subsequent trips included conversations at stadiums, homes and offices throughout Puerto Rico.

Rafael Costas and Víctor Navarro shared statistical data from working papers in addition to their publications. Luis Alvelo and Angel Armada also shared data from their working papers. When Costas succumbed to cancer in January 1992, Navarro became the "pipeline" for a wealth of Puerto Rico League statistics. Ismael Trabal Martell, Héctor Díaz Salichs and Ubaldo Bernier provided various Don Q Baseball Cues which featured interesting statistical tidbits through the 1960s.

Library research centered on reviewing back copies of five Puerto Rican newspapers at the Library of Congress in Washington, D.C., between July 1991 and December 1993. Trips were made to the National Baseball Hall of Fame Library in Cooperstown, New York, between September 1991 and September 1992 to examine back issues of *The Sporting News* and *The Official Baseball Guide and Record Book*.

Here is the list of players and managers with whom I spoke and corresponded:

Kyle Abbott, Juan Agosto, Luis Aguayo, Luis Alicea, Marcial "Canenita" Allen, Gary Allenson, Jaime Almendro, Roberto Alomar, Sandy Alomar, Jr., Sandy Alomar, Sr., Felipe Alou, José Alvarez, Manolo Alvarez, Craig Anderson, Sparky Anderson, Bob Apodaca, Luis Aquino, Jorge Aranzamendi, Jim Archer, Luis "Tite" Arroyo, Ramón Avilés;

Carlos Baerga, Jay Baller, Ray Barker, Skeeter Barnes, Tom Barrett, Nica Bayrón, Jim Beauchamp, Fred Beene, Jay Bell, Gene Benson, Vern Benson, Alfred "Butch" Benton, Dave Bergman, Kurt Bevaqua, Wayne Blackburn, Paul Blair, Steve Blateric, Johnny Blatnik, Gary Blaylock, Mike Boddicker, Wade Boggs, Don Bollweg, Bobby Bonilla, Bob Boone, Rich Bordi, Bob Boyd, Dennis "Oil Can" Boyd, Glenn Braggs, Jackie Brandt, Cliff Brantley, Jeff Brantley, Sid Bream, Ken Brett, Rocky Bridges, Nelson Briles, Jim Brosnan, Bob Bruce, Tom Bruno, Don Buford, Jim Bunning, Tom Burgmeier, John Burgos, Ellis Burks, Pete Burnside, Brett Butler, Joe Buzas;

Iván Calderón, Mike Caldwell, Ken Caminiti, Dave Campbell, George Canale, Casey Candaele, John Candelaria, Tom Candiotti, John Cangelosi, Gary Caraballo, Jack Cassini, Danny Cater, Orlando Cepeda, Ron Cey, Wes Chamberlain, Chris Chambliss, Al Cihocki, Mike Clark, Ron Clark, Horace Clarke, Donn Clendenon, Frank Coímbre, Jr., Jim Colborn, Cristobal Colón, Marco Comas, Cefo Conde, Ramón "Guito" Conde, Joey Cora, Wilfredo Cordero, Pat Corrales, Edwin Correa, Henry Cotto, Harry Craft, Ray Crone, Terry Crowley, Jimmie Crutchfield, Cirilo "Tommy" Cruz, José "Cheo" Cruz, Mike Cuéllar, George Culver;

ACKNOWLEDGMENTS xiii

Danny Darwin, Doug Dascenzo, Ted Davidson, Chili Davis, Mark Davis, Piper Davis, Leon Day, Ken Dayley, Ellis "Cot" Deal, Iván de Jesús, José de Jesús, Mike de la Hoz, Pito Alvarez de la Vega, Luis "Mambo" de León, Félix "Felle" Delgado, Steve Demeter, Rick Dempsey, Mike Devereaux, Mario Díaz, Rob Dibble, Jack Dittmer, Moe Drabowsky, Bob Dustal;

Doc Edwards, Lee Elia, Cal Ermer, Nino Escalera, Rubén Escalera;

Junior Félix, Wilmer Fields, Ed Figueroa, Fernando Figueroa, Eddie Fisher, Gil Flores, Tim Foli, Tony Fossas, Eric Fox, Herman Franks, Roger Freed, Jim Fregosi, Todd Frohwirth;

Ron Gant, Manolo García, Omar García, Ronquito García, Phil Garner, Bob Geren, Bob Gibson, Russ Gibson, Bernard Gilkey, Dan Gladden, Leo Gómez, Orlando Gómez, Rubén Gómez, Javier González, Juan González, Rich Gossage, Bill Greason, Kip Gross, Juan Guilbe, José Guzmán, Chris Gwynn;

Harvey Haddix, Kevin Hagen, Larry Haney, Todd Haney, Erik Hanson, Charley Harmon, Brian Harper, Bill Harrell, Donald Harris, Lenny Harris, Jack Harshman, Bryan Harvey, Von Hayes, Rickey Henderson, Elrod Hendricks, Tom Henke, José Hernández, Roberto Hernández, Rudy Hernández, John Herrnstein, Earl Hersch, Tom Hilgendorf, Joe Hoerner, Chris Hoiles, Joel Horlen, Sam Horn, Ralph Houk, Frank Howard, Art Howe, Bill Howerton, Benny Huffman, Dick Hughes, Woody Huyke;

Pachy Irizarry, Monte Irvin, Luis Isaac;

Grant Jackson, Forrest Jacobs, Dion James, Ferguson Jenkins, Sam Jethroe, Jay Johnstone, Barry Jones, Doug Jones, Ricky Jordan, Howie Judson;

Mick Kelleher, Pat Kelly, Roberto Kelly, Kevin Kennedy, Joe Keough, Bruce Kison, Danny Kravitz, Chad Kreuter, John Kruk;

René Lachemann, Gary Lance, Jim Landis, Hobie Landrith, Tom Lasorda, Graig Lefferts, Charlie Leibrandt, Al Leiter, Buck Leonard, Dennis Leonard, Dave Leonhard, George Lerchen, Dennis Lewallyn, Nick Leyva, Don Liddle, Derek Lilliquist, Lou Limmer, José Lind, Orlando Lind, Paul Lindblad, Johnny Lipon, Johnny Logan, Jim Lonborg, Javier López, Steve Lyons;

Ernie McAnally, Tom McCraw, Shane Mack, Jack McKeon, Greg McMichael, Jerry McNertney, Mike Maddux, Rick Mahler, Candy Maldonado, Frank Malzone, Charley Manuel, Carmelo Martínez, Chito Martínez, Dennis Martínez, Edgar Martínez, Marty Martínez, Jon Matlack, Lee May, Milt May, Willie Mays, Luis "Torito" Meléndez, Mario Mendoza, Rudy Meoli, Orlando Mercado, Orlando Merced, Félix Millán, Ray Miller, Randy Milligan, Gino Minutelli, John Montague, Willie Montañez, Wally Moon, Balor Moore, Jerry Morales, José M.

Morales, Luis "Wito" Morales, Angel Morris, Jack Morris, Les Moss, Manny Mota, Pedro Muñoz;

Emilio "Millito" Navarro, Jaime Navarro, Julio Navarro, Denny Neagle, Al Newman, David Nied, Phil Niekro, Randy Niemann, Melvin Nieves, Otis Nixon, Jim Northrup, Ed Nottle;

Pete O'Brien, Bob Ojeda, Omar Olivares, Pochy Oliver, Francisco Javier Oliveras, Mako Oliveras, José Olmeda, Luis Olmo, Paul O'Neill, José "Polilla" Ortíz, Junior Ortíz, Claude Osteen, Mickey Owen;

Tom Pagnozzi, Rafael Palmeiro, Lance Parrish, Bob Patterson, Daryl Patterson, Tony Peña, Julián Pérez, Mike Pérez, Tany Pérez, Ron Perranoski, Gary Peters, Juan "Terín" Pizarro, Herb Plews, Bill Plummer, J. W. Porter, Vic Power, Jim Price;

Luis R. Quiñoñes, Jamie Quirk;

Luis Raven, Claude Raymond, Randy Ready, Jeff Reardon, Gary Redus, Win Remerswaal, Merv Rettenmund, Harold Reynolds, Dennis Ribant, Pete Richert, Steve Ridzik, Jim Riggleman, Cal Ripken, Jr., Ray Rippelmeyer, Florentino Rivera, Germán Rivera, Germán "Deportivo" Rivera, Jim Rivera, Luis Rivera, Quíque Rivera, Leon Roberts, Don Robinson, Frank Robinson, Boi Rodríguez, Ellie Rodríguez, Iván Rodríguez, Victor Rodríguez, Ed Roebuck, Cookie Rojas, Papo Rosado, Rico Rossy, Jerry Royster;

Joe Sambito, Ronnie Samford, Reggie Sanders, Benito Santiago, Carlos M. Santiago, José G. "Pantalones" Santiago, José R. "Palillo" Santiago, Ted Savage, Mike Schmidt, Barney Schultz, Dick Selma, Gordon Seyfried, Mike Sharperson, John Shelby, Sonny Siebert, Rubén Sierra, Mike Simms, Wayne Simpson, Ken Singleton, Tommie Sisk, Joel Skinner, Bill Skowron, Don Slaught, Bobby Gene Smith, Dwight Smith, Lonnie Smith, Robert G. Smith, Zane Smith, Van Snider, Dennis Springer, Marv Staehle, John Strohmayer;

Pat Tabler, Danny Tartabull, Ken Tatum, Charley Taylor, Tony Taylor, Gene Tenace, Frank Thomas, Jim Thome, Dickie Thon, Bob Thurman, Tom Timmerman, Tommy Toms, Félix Torres, Dick Tracewski, Quincy Trouppe, Bob Turley, Wayne Twitchell;

Corky Valentine, Fernando Valenzuela, Héctor Valle, Joe Van Durham, Otto Vélez, Frank Verdi, Héctor Villanueva, Luis "King Kong" Villodas, Bill Virdon, Ozzie Virgil, Sr.;

Bob Walk, Dave Wallace, Denny Walling, Dan Warthen, Ron Washington, Turk Wendell, Rick Wilkins, Jerry Willard, Bernie Williams, Gerald Williams, Artie Wilson, John Wockenfuss, Ed Wojna, Bill Wright, Ken Wright;

Gerald Young, Robin Yount;

Chris Zachary, Pat Zachry, Don Zimmer.

FOREWORD
by Eduardo Valero

There seems to be a general belief that baseball was first played in Puerto Rico upon the arrival of the American soldiers who were stationed there in 1898, at the conclusion of the Spanish American War. But Puerto Ricans played baseball before that.

The first game was played in San Juan in 1896, between the "Almendares" and "Borinquén" teams. Baseball was brought to Puerto Rico by the sons and nephews of a Spanish Army officer who had been detailed in Cuba prior to being assigned to Puerto Rico. But it was after the beginning of the twentieth century that baseball really developed in Puerto Rico. Government, private companies and public schools organized teams that participated in local and island-wide tournaments played on Sundays and holidays. Many players, inducted into the armed forces during World War I, held games in the army camps. They taught the fundamentals of baseball to many other inductees, who eventually became interested in baseball and spread it all through the Island.

After World War I, teams from the United States and Cuba were invited to Puerto Rico during their off-season. Among the best-known players were major leaguers Leon Cadore and Henry Zimmerman from the U.S. and Adolfo Luque from Cuba. Also from Cuba was José de la Caridad Méndez, who John McGraw called the greatest pitcher he ever saw.

Sportswriters also contributed to the popularity of the game, giving nicknames to the players, enhancing their image and arousing the interest of Puerto Ricans in the sport. Baseball rapidly became the number one recreational activity on the Island; teams were organized in every city and town, all participating in continuous tournaments.

Pedro Miguel Caratini, a great shortstop from Coamo, Puerto Rico, was instrumental in exporting baseball to the Dominican Republic, where this outstanding player is considered "the father of Dominican baseball." A mathematics and accounting wizard, Caratini had received a fabulous offer to teach that he couldn't decline; he introduced the sport to the Dominican Republic, where it spread rapidly. A few years later, he brought

Dominican teams to Puerto Rico, where the players participated with local teams, which also contained Cubans who had remained in Puerto Rico. During the 1920s and 1930s local promoters brought teams from Cuba, Mexico, Venezuela and the Dominican Republic, and from the minor leagues and the Negro leagues in the United States.

Puerto Ricans saw the top players of those years. Among the Cubans were Hall of Famer Martín Dihigo, Alejandro Oms, Ramón Bragaña, Lazaro Salazar, Manuel "Cocaína" García, Brujo Rosell, and Cristóbal Torriente—who outhit Babe Ruth a few times. Horacio Martínez, Fellito Guerra, Pedro Alejandro Sam and Juan E. "Tetelo" Vargas were stars from the Dominican Republic. One of the greatest teams ever assembled was the "Concordia" from Venezuela, with Hall of Famers Joshua Gibson, Satchel Paige and Martín Dihigo among other Latin stars like Tetelo Vargas from the Dominican Republic and Frank Coímbre and Emilio Navarro from Puerto Rico. Visiting minor league teams from York, Camden, Richmond, Hazleton and Norfolk had top players on their rosters who eventually became major leaguers, including Johnny Mize, George McQuinn, George Hockette, Al Vincent and Jimmy Jordan, among others, as well as Ted Norbert, an outstanding outfielder and batter in the Pacific Coast League. From the Negro leagues came the Brooklyn Eagles, the New York Black Yankees and the Lincoln Giants, among others. Satchel Paige, Joshua Gibson, Raymond Dandridge, Raymond Brown, Dick Seay, Rap Dixon, Leon Day, Bertrum Hunter, Terry McDuffie, Johnny Hayes and Showboat Thomas were some of the outstanding stars of the Negro leagues who became very popular and acquainted Puerto Ricans with high-quality baseball.

In 1936 the Cincinnati Reds became the first major league team to hold their spring training in Puerto Rico, playing several games against the Brooklyn Eagles as well as Almendares from Cuba, Azteca from Mexico and Ponce from Puerto Rico. Ponce had Hiram Bithorn, the pitcher who became the first Puerto Rican to play in the major leagues. Bithorn also pitched for the Brooklyn Eagles.

The ever-growing popularity of the sport and the players who participated led to the organization of the Puerto Rico Winter League in 1938. The actual circuit was originally called the Puerto Rico Semi-Pro League, affiliated with the National Baseball Congress presided over by Raymond Dumont. Six teams were organized at that time, in San Juan, Ponce, Mayagüez, Caguas, Humacao and Guayama.

EDUARDO VALERO, *President,*
Puerto Rico Professional Baseball Hall of Fame
Chairman, Latin America Committee,
Society for American Baseball Research
San Juan, Puerto Rico

Preface

This book took shape around 1991 after Ferguson Jenkins, Jim Palmer and Johnny Bench had been inducted into Cooperstown. This trio, like countless other players, had benefited from the Puerto Rico Winter League. Impetus was given to the project when I was named U.S. correspondent for the newly created Puerto Rico Professional Baseball Hall of Fame in August 1991. Among the reasons for this designation were my lifetime interest in winter league baseball, my fluency in Spanish, having grown up and lived in Puerto Rico for 25 years, and membership in the Society for American Baseball Research.

Between the summer of 1991 and the spring of 1994, I touched base with some 400 players and 40 managers involved in the Puerto Rico League. In-person and telephone conversations with the majority of these, supplemented by survey responses, resulted in valuable first-hand information. The conversations were held at baseball stadiums in Puerto Rico, spring training camps throughout Florida, major league and minor league stadiums, and homes and offices in Puerto Rico and the States.

Conversations with former and current Puerto Rico League team owners, sportswriters, general managers, coaches, trainers, umpires and league historians provided a behind-the-scenes perspective.

Johnny Bench played in Puerto Rico in the winter of 1967-68. He refined his skills there and became the 1968 National League Rookie of the Year. As a junior high student that winter, I saw Bench play against his future Cincinnati teammate Tany (Tony) Pérez when San Juan squared off against their archrivals, the Santurce Crabbers. The enthusiasm among the fans at San Juan–Santurce games was compared to the Brooklyn Dodgers–New York Giants matchups by former league players Rubén Gómez and Don Zimmer. Ex-Dodger pitcher Ed Roebuck and Negro league hurler Leon Day told me that fans in Puerto Rico and Cuba took baseball more seriously than U.S. fans.

When my father took me to Hiram Bithorn Municipal Stadium to see Santurce battle the Arecibo Wolves in a 1964-65 game, I enjoyed what most stateside residents miss—baseball played in the Caribbean. Tany Pérez sent the Santurce fans home in a happy mood with a game-winning homer. His long clout set off a reaction in the stands with the force of a tropical storm. The cheering continued for ten minutes after the symmetrically wound Wilson A1010 was deposited over the left-field fence. As the contest was being played, a Santurce cheerleader stood on top of the dugout to lead the crowd in various chants. Fans were betting on the outcome of an inning, how a player would fare in a given at-bat, and even on a pitch!

The Puerto Rican experience launched the careers of future stars (Chapter 1). It enabled numerous players to get over the "AAA hump" or get their big league careers back on track. From the early 1950s through the mid-1990s, Puerto Rican baseball was superior to AAA ball in the States. Former Negro leaguers, top major league prospects and a smattering of current big leaguers on Puerto Rican rosters made this a competitive league.

Puerto Rico was a "working vacation" (Chapter 2) for many "imports" from the states. The U.S. players commented on the hospitality of Puerto Ricans, the tasty food, the tropical weather and the beaches and recreational activities. They had fun while earning extra money during their "off-season."

I saw Roberto Clemente (Chapter 3) wear the San Juan uniform at Bithorn Stadium as a player and a manager. He played hard in Puerto Rico to please the local fans. He eventually received his due in the States after his 1971 World Series MVP performance. But the first "World Series" Roberto Clemente starred in took place in Caracas during February 1955, when Santurce earned the round-robin title after besting teams from Cuba, Panama and Venezuela.

"Pioneers" (Chapter 4) made the Puerto Rico League a viable winter circuit from its inception in 1938–39. These early players were primarily Negro leaguers, who played their positions at a high level of skill and inspired local players with their talent, goodwill and professionalism. Satchel Paige, Josh Gibson, Leon Day, Raymond Brown, Monte Irvin, Roy Campanella, Buck Leonard, Buster Clarkson, and Ray Dandridge were among these pioneers. Hiram Bithorn and Luis Olmo, the first two Puerto Rican ballplayers to reach the majors, were the most celebrated of the local pioneers, along with other players, managers and league officials.

Vic Power, Luis "Tite" Arroyo, Rubén Gómez and Orlando Cepeda were top Island "stars and workhorses" (Chapter 5) in the league between the late 1940s and the mid–1960s, and also had successful careers in the major leagues. Inspired by the Negro leaguers who came to Puerto Rico, they, in turn, made it possible for future players like José "Cheo" Cruz, Willie Montañez and Ed Figueroa to play competitive winter ball on their way to successful big league careers. Island stars Roberto Alomar, Juan González, Carlos Baerga, Edgar Martínez, Iván Rodríguez, Rubén Sierra and Javier López played in the league during the 1990s.

Chapter 6 focuses on more stars from both Puerto Rico and the U.S. Virgin Islands, who "played on" in the Winter League and provided excitement on Island diamonds regardless of their big league or minor league status. Luis "Canena" Márquez played during 20 Puerto Rico League seasons. Elrod Hendricks, José "Palillo" Santiago, José Manuel Morales, Juan Beníquez and Candy Maldonado did double duty in Puerto Rico and the majors.

The number of "imports" (Chapter 7) allowed per team in Puerto Rico ranged from zero during several World War II seasons to ten in the 1980s. Imports, for the most part, have been Americans. Cubans, Dominicans, Nicaraguans and Panamanians have also been imported for league play. In recent years, imports have usually played for only one winter, in contrast to earlier years, when they played in multiple seasons. Willard Brown, Bob Thurman, Wilmer Fields and Cot Deal were top American imports. Some valuable imports from other countries include Cookie Rojas (Cuba), Dennis Martínez (Nicaragua) and Chili Davis (Jamaica).

Quite a few big league managers (Chapter 8) got valuable experience in Puerto Rico. Skippers Frank Robinson, Sparky Anderson, Jim Fregosi, Rene Lachemann and Kevin Kennedy were among those I spoke with. These skippers agreed that Puerto Rico was a useful experience—handling Spanish-speaking players, gaining confidence, using strategy and working in a league characterized by aggressive baseball.

Behind-the-scenes personnel (Chapter 9) make this league work. Team owners, general managers, broadcasters, sportswriters, umpires and trainers have been instrumental in fostering a sense of continuity. Owners, general managers and managers created working agreements between the big leagues and Puerto Rican teams. Two such links were the New York/San Francisco Giants with the Santurce Crabbers, and the Boston/Milwaukee Braves with the Caguas Criollos.

Broadcasters include Buck Canel, Felo Ramírez and Miguel Angel Torres. Puerto Rico has also had colorful and dynamic sportswriters with a flair for the game, such as Rafael Pont Flores, Miguel J. Frau, Francisco Soto Respeto and Luis Romero Cuevas.

Top U.S. umpiring prospects have handled tough situations in Puerto Rico on their way to the big leagues. Feedback from Doug Harvey, Dale Ford, Tim McClelland, Durwood Merrill and others showed me there is more to winter ball than balls and strikes.

The 1954-55 Santurce Crabbers were one of Puerto Rico's "teams for the ages" (Chapter 10). Santurce featured Roberto Clemente, Willie Mays and the league's career home run leader, Bob Thurman, in the outfield. Satchel Paige and Perucho Cepeda paced the 1939-40 Guayama Witches to the league title. Ponce's 1946-47 team won four straight final-series contests after being down three games to none. The 1948-49 Mayagüez

Indians boasted some of the top Negro leaguers who played in Puerto Rico—Artie Wilson, Luke Easter, Wilmer Fields, Alonzo Perry and Johnny Davis. San Juan's 1994–95 "Dream Team" won the 1995 Caribbean Series.

Puerto Rico's teams have colorful nicknames. One nickname not translated into English throughout this book pertains to the Caguas Criollos. The term "Criollo" within the context of Puerto Rico refers to individuals who are natives of, and indigenous to, this Island. Within the context of winter baseball, native players who represent Spanish-speaking countries in Caribbean Series events have been called "criollos." Thus, this term is a source of pride. The Caguas Criollos have a tradition of producing top native talent so this nickname suits them well.

Every league has its share of memorable games, and Puerto Rico's is no exception. In Chapter 11 some of the regular-season, playoff, All-Star and Caribbean Series games will be highlighted. Winning has a high premium in Puerto Rico. Since 1970, the Puerto Rican champion has played the winners of the Dominican, Mexican and Venezuelan winter leagues in the Caribbean Series. From 1949 to 1960, Puerto Rico, Cuba, Panama and Venezuela vied for the Caribbean Series title. In the Interamerican Series, in place from 1961 to 1964, Puerto Rico, Venezuela, Nicaragua and Panama took turns hosting a round-robin tournament.

For Island fans (Chapter 12), the Puerto Rico League is *their* major league and they want to win. Puerto Rico's *fanáticos* appreciate imports who come to play. Fans have been known to do everything from lighting candles in the stands, where they simulate a wake, to inviting players home for dinner. They are quite knowledgeable and vocal.

This book cannot begin to cover all the excitement in other winter leagues such as the Dominican, Mexican, Venezuelan and Australian leagues, or those in Arizona and Hawaii. When appropriate, reference will be made to these and winter leagues no longer operational—Colombia, Cuba, Nicaragua and Panama. Cuba's league produced 7 of the 12 Caribbean Series champions from 1949 to 1960 and was rated a shade above Puerto Rico's at that time. But with more Puerto Ricans reaching the majors from the 1960s on, and the best American prospects being sent to Puerto Rico, Puerto Rico's league has become a force to be reckoned with.

The Puerto Rico Winter League, in continuous operation from 1938-39 to the present, is now the "grandfather" of current winter leagues. It has nurtured the best local and stateside talent. Many of Puerto Rico's top major leaguers opted to play the entire 1994-95 winter season. That Puerto Rico has made a major contribution to the national pastime must be recognized. Here, then, is the story of the "Liga de Béisbol Profesional de Puerto Rico."

1. THE LAUNCHING PAD

It provided experience in a high classification without major league pressure.
—Bob Gibson, former Santurce pitcher

When the first pitch was thrown in Puerto Rico's maiden 1938-39 semi-professional baseball season, featuring six teams and a 40-game schedule, little did the fans know that their league would play a pivotal role in launching major league careers. Only two native athletes on 1938-39 league rosters, San Juan's Hiram Bithorn and Caguas's Luis Olmo, made it to the majors. Raymond Brown, Jimmie Crutchfield, Clarence Palm and William Perkins—Negro league players earning extra money—never played in the big leagues.

But starting with Roy Campanella and Monte Irvin in the early 1940s, and continuing to Juan González and Carlos Baerga 50 years later, the Puerto Rico Winter League launched the big league careers of countless athletes. Johnny Logan, Jim Gilliam, Harvey Haddix, Hank Aaron, Bob Turley, Jack Harshman, Chuck Harmon, Willie Mays, Sandy Koufax and Maury Wills benefited from Puerto Rico League play in the 1950s. Mays was a star by the time he played in Puerto Rico, while Koufax still needed a few more years before he became a great pitcher.

Bob Gibson, Ferguson Jenkins, Denny McLain, Steve Carlton, Mike Cuéllar, Nelson Briles and Jim Palmer pitched in Puerto Rico during the 1960s. Frank Howard, Tony Pérez, Jim Northrup, Lee May, Willie Horton and Johnny Bench were league sluggers who went on to have outstanding major league careers. Reggie Jackson came to Puerto Rico in 1970-71 to work on his hitting. Mike Schmidt, Don Baylor, Dusty Baker, Ken Griffey, Dan Driessen, Robin Yount, Jack Morris and Lance Parrish contributed to their Puerto Rican teams during the 1970s. "Imports" who came to Puerto Rico in the 1980s included Rickey Henderson, Lee Smith, Wade Boggs, Cal Ripken, Don Mattingly, Tony Gwynn, Joe Carter and Terry Pendleton.

Puerto Rican players of the 1950s and 1960s, such as Clemente,

From left: Orlando Cepeda, Victor Pellot Power, Puerto Rico Senate President Miguel Hernández Agosto, Sandy Alomar, Jr., and Sandy Alomar, Sr., when the Puerto Rico Senate paid tribute to the current and former players in December 1991 (courtesy of Angel Colón).

Cepeda, Vic Power, Rubén Gómez, Juan "Terín" Pizarro and Luis "Tite" Arroyo, made for a dynamite league. As other Island players—Sandy Alomar, Sr., Ed Figueroa, Jerry Morales, Willie Montañez, Félix Millán, José "Cheo" Cruz, Dickie Thon, Rubén Sierra, Roberto Alomar, Edgar Martínez, Sandy Alomar, Jr., Carlos Baerga, Juan González, Iván Rodríguez and Javier López—came into the equation, the league remained explosive. Native talent coupled with imported players from the U.S., Cuba and other countries made the league an excellent training ground.

The League

The six original teams in the Puerto Rico League were the San Juan Senators (Senadores), the Ponce Lions (Leones), the Mayagüez Indians (Indios), the Caguas Criollos, the Humacao Oriental Grays (Grises Orientales) and the Guayama Witches (Brujos). The 1939-40 season welcomed two more teams, the Santurce Crabbers (Cangrejeros) and the Aguadilla Sharks (Tiburones).

From 1938 through 1941 the Puerto Rico League formed part of the

National Semi-Professional Baseball Congress, comprising teams from the 48 states and Puerto Rico, presided over by Raymond J. Dumont.[1] Thus, the Spanish title of the league was "Liga de Béisbol Semiprofesional." In the fall of 1939, and again in 1940, the champions from the U.S. contingent of the congress faced Guayama in a best-of-seven series. Guayama beefed itself up with native players from other squads for these events. The name change from Semi-Pro to Professional was proposed by Rafael Delgado Márquez on September 14, 1941.[2]

The idea of an organized league in Puerto Rico came from Enrique Huyke, a 30-year-old physical education instructor from Mayagüez. Huyke worked closely with Teofilo Maldonado, president of the Island's Commission on Sports and Recreation, to make the league a reality. Gabriel Castro assisted Huyke in bringing the factions together, and recalls that each of the six franchises had to pay $1,000 before being admitted into the fold. The Guayama Rotary Club was instrumental in raising the necessary funds for that town's team.

Professor Huyke was asked to manage the Mayagüez franchise by owner Alfonso Valdés, the India Brewery magnate. Valdés threatened to back out if Huyke did not accept his offer. Huyke agreed to manage the 1938-39 Mayagüez Indians. Puerto Rico's Department of Parks and Recreation was designated to administer the new league through Teofilo Maldonado, the new commissioner. Three weeks into the season, Huyke was fired by Valdés. He continued his teaching, coaching and civic career and passed away at age 76, but never received his due for his work creating the Semi-Pro League.[3]

From 1938-39 to 1947-48 the seasons were divided into halves, called *vueltas*. The winners of each half would square off in the finals. Ponce, however, won three titles outright, in 1941-42, 1943-44 and 1944-45, by winning both *vueltas*. A bone of contention was the number of teams making the playoffs. Since a team had to win one of the two *vueltas* to qualify for postseason play, there tended to be a loss of interest by fans whose teams were mathematically eliminated from winning the second-half title. This led to player turnover. Leon Day left Puerto Rico toward the end of the 1939-40 season to play in Venezuela, since his Aguadilla team stood no chance of making the playoffs.[4] It wasn't until 1948-49 that the top four teams were eligible for playoff competition.

Initially, each team was allowed three imports; the allotment was increased to five later in the decade. The impact of World War II curtailed the 1942-43 regular season to 36 games, with only four teams competing. The number of teams remained at four through 1945-46, but they played 48 games from 1943-44 to 1945-46. No imports were allowed during the 1942-43 and 1943-44 seasons.[5]

The league set deadlines for roster changes. In 1939-40, for example, any roster moves had to be completed and approved by January 3, 1940, at midnight.[6] This was meant to discourage player turnover during the second half of the season.

A 40- to 80-game season does not leave much margin for error. Eighty-game seasons were played from 1948-49 to 1953-54, and in 1961-62. A 72-game schedule was in place for three seasons. Several 64-game schedules were drawn up. The league scheduled 70 contests from 1962-63 through 1974-75, followed by a decade of 60-game seasons.[7] Anywhere from 48 to 60 games have been on the calendar from 1985-86 to the mid–1990s.[8]

A league All-Star Game has traditionally been held on Three Kings Day, January 6, but has recently taken place closer to Christmas. Its format has included "Natives" against "Imports," the Metro area teams (San Juan, Santurce, Caguas) versus Island clubs (Arecibo, Mayagüez, Ponce), and North Americans playing Latin Americans.

Special games have included the San Juan–Cuba game on December 1, 1993, and five contests between Island teams and the 1947 Yankees prior to the 1946-47 final series.

Since 1958-59, the top four teams have met in end-of-season playoffs. The lone exception was the 1960-61 split season. A semifinal and final series system was used through 1984-85, but in 1985-86 the league adopted a round-robin system, which leads to the top two teams squaring off in the finals. In recent years, the finals have been best-of-nine series.

League champions have participated in the Semi-Professional World Series, the Caribbean Series and the Interamerican Series. Guayama represented Puerto Rico in the 1939 and 1940 Semi-Pro events.[9] The four-country Caribbean Series has been held from 1949 through 1960, and 1970 to date. Puerto Rico and Venezuela have played in all events. Cuba and Panama were replaced by the Dominican Republic and Mexico in the second phase. The Interamerican Series, held from 1961 to 1964, grouped Puerto Rico, Venezuela, Panama and Nicaragua.[10]

Stadiums

A decade after league play began, the six teams were playing an 80-game schedule. By 1949-50 several new ballparks had been built, with lights for night games, and attendance had surpassed the 750,000 mark.[11] The new stadiums were Caguas's Solá Morales (6,744 capacity), Mayagüez's Isidoro García (6,718 capacity) and Ponce's Paquito Montaner (9,718 capacity).[12] The novelty of the new lighting systems spurred attendance. Caguas's dedication December 14, 1949, consisted of eight towers and 508 bulbs.[13]

San Juan and Santurce shared Sixto Escobar Stadium, named after

Puerto Rico's first world boxing champion, a bantamweight. Escobar is located near the Atlantic Ocean, a few bus stops from Old San Juan's cobblestone streets, historic forts and shops. José R. "Palillo" Santiago, a star pitcher for San Juan in the 1960s and early 1970s, compared the friendly confines of Escobar to Fenway Park, where he twirled for the Red Sox. The fans were very close to the action at Escobar and Santiago remembers accepting a variety of snacks from them before, during and after the games. Escobar's official seating capacity was 13,135, but over 15,000 could jam the stadium for playoff contests.[14]

Hiram Bithorn Municipal Stadium, with its 20,000 seating capacity, replaced Escobar for San Juan's and Santurce's home games beginning in the 1962-63 season. When the Arecibo Wolves came into the league in 1961-62, they played at Luis Rodríguez Olmo Stadium, which held approximately 6,000 fans.[15] These stadiums are named after the Island's first two big leaguers.

The league's other stadium during the late 1940s and early 1950s was Aguadilla's Parque Colón, located on the northwestern shore of Puerto Rico near where Columbus landed on November 19, 1493, during his second voyage to the New World. Seating only 2,500, it has the appearance of an American Legion ballpark.[16] But the fresh ocean breeze during the October to February season and the vendors selling crushed ice with syrup (*piraguas*), fruit and assorted goodies make for a pleasant atmosphere.

Much of the old-fashioned ambience of the Island's ballparks has been retained up to the present day. For example, until 1993 all league games were played on grass. In that year, artificial turf was installed in Ponce's Montaner Stadium. Caguas installed artificial turf in 1994-95.

Johnny Logan

It's a long way from Endicott, New York, to Aguadilla, Puerto Rico. Boston Braves prospect Johnny Logan, one of the young American stars with Aguadilla during the 1949-50 season and a future big league standout, was a Yankee fan who had watched Luis Olmo display his talent with Brooklyn. He played against Olmo that season. "We were idols to the fans in Aguadilla," recalls Logan. Although Aguadilla was a small town, "they figured we could compete with [other franchises in] the big cities. The first couple of weeks I ate rice and beans, then I found out about the Ramey [Air Force] base and I'd go there some days for hamburger, steak, potatoes, french fries. In the evenings we'd sit on benches on the town square, and watch all the girls go around."

Logan was aware that Alvin Dark was holding the fort at shortstop for the Braves, but "I was a nice, naive kid. ... I wanted to get recognized. I had a pretty good year in Puerto Rico. It was a stepping stone."

By the time Logan made his big league debut for the 1951 Braves, along with former Aguadilla teammate Luis "Canena" Márquez, the Aguadilla franchise had folded. Aguadilla never managed a .500 campaign or a single playoff berth in eight league seasons.

Harvey Haddix

A two-year Army hitch from 1950 to 1952 was one reason the St. Louis Cardinals wanted Harvey Haddix to work out the rust in Puerto Rico. St. Louis coach Johnny Riddle, hired to manage San Juan, received instructions that Haddix must return to the States by December 1, 1952. Setting up this kind of timetable for pitchers would become more prevalent in the 1980s.

The Puerto Rico experience came in handy—Haddix went on to have his only 20-win major league season for the 1953 St. Louis Cardinals. "I lost five years, including three in World War II and two in Korea," says Haddix. "Puerto Rico helped me get the feeling back for pro ball. I remember a hitter by the name of [Willard] Brown."

Hank Aaron

The Milwaukee Braves wanted Hank Aaron, Bob Buhl, Félix Mantilla and other prospects to shine in Puerto Rico. Aaron was a 19-year-old infielder who, in the words of Ozzie Virgil, Sr., was one Puerto Rico at-bat away from getting sent back to the States. Hank Aaron was not playing well at second base for the Caguas Criollos; his manager, Mickey Owen, decided to move him to right field early in the 1953-54 campaign. "I knew where I could get a better second baseman than Aaron, [but] he could sure hit," remembers Owen. "So one day I hit him a few flyballs and he went to it and got them easy, and he threw good. I said, you're not an infielder, you're an outfielder."

Mickey Owen secured Charley Neal to play second base, and the rest is history. Neal had been the second sacker for Newport News in the 1953 Piedmont League and Owen had gotten a good look at him while managing Norfolk to Piedmont's title. When Neal teamed with Aaron's buddy, shortstop Félix Mantilla, in the middle of Caguas's infield, Aaron went to right field.

Owen: "I never told Aaron how to do anything except once I told him to hit one to right field, and he hit a bullet there. Aaron said I helped him hit to right, but all I really did was urge him to hit the ball there."

Aaron served notice that he was for real by tying for the Puerto Rico home run title with teammate Jim Rivera. He finished third in the batting chase at .322, behind Island legend Canena Márquez and Cincinnati prospect Chuck Harmon.[17]

Hank Aaron saw major league pitching in Puerto Rico almost every day, and after moving to the outfield he began hitting it. Aaron has fond recollections of his two homers in the Puerto Rico All-Star Game and of being named its MVP. His first child was born in Puerto Rico, another reason Puerto Rico has sentimental value to the major league home run king.[18] "There's no question it was a stepping stone in my getting to the major leagues," Aaron later told a reporter. "It gave me confidence."[19]

Bob Turley

Bob Turley was throwing aspirin tablets for San Juan the winter Aaron played in Puerto Rico. Turley made waves of his own by striking out 17 Caguas batters on January 3, 1954, to tie Satchel Paige's mark, set for Guayama against Mayagüez on December 3, 1939.[20] Turley was coming off an MVP season in the Texas League, where he had earned $350 per month. In Puerto Rico, Turley received the princely monthly salary of $1,000 plus $350 for living expenses. He also endorsed a local fruit drink and received an extra $500. "That league had a lot of talent ... top AAA players, American players who had been in the bigs for a year, top native talent," recalls Turley. "You could tell Aaron had a major league stroke, the way he sprayed the ball to right and right-center."

Turley enjoyed the whole experience, noting that the hospitality in San Juan was outstanding. He lived over a grocery store and took a bus to Escobar with his uniform on. Upon returning from Escobar, he'd be greeted by patrons at the night club beside the apartment building.

Jack Harshman and Chuck Harmon

Jack Harshman teamed with Turley to give San Juan a strong one-two pitching duo. Harshman used his 15 league wins to claim a berth with the 1954 White Sox, while Turley had his first full big league season with the Orioles. Like Turley, Harshman, was awed by Aaron in Puerto Rico. "He had absolutely great hand-wrist action. I had him 0-2 once and threw him a high and inside fastball to force him away from the plate," says Harshman. "But he leaned back and hit it over the center field wall. Aaron had the best hands I've ever seen."

Chuck Harmon hit .311 in 1953 for Tulsa, the Cincinnati Reds' farm team in the Texas League, and caught the eye of Dallas hurler José G. "Pantalones" Santiago, star pitcher with Ponce. He tipped off the Ponce ownership about Harmon's abilities, and Ponce made the appropriate arrangements with the Cincinnati organization. "If you could cut it in Puerto Rico, you could be in the big leagues within a year," says Harmon. "That happened to me."

Steve Ridzik

Pitcher Steve Ridzik, a teammate of Chuck Harmon with the 1953-54 Ponce Lions, noted it was always tough winning in Puerto Rico. "You couldn't just walk in there and win," he says. "It was quality baseball." He worked on a palm ball and breaking stuff that winter. Ridzik and Bob Buhl agreed each league team had at least three major league or potential big league hurlers.

Ridzik returned to Puerto Rico in 1955-56 and was the league's top starter with Santurce. He was one of several New York Giants who came under the scrutiny of Carl Hubbell that winter. Hubbell, on assignment with the Giants, visited Puerto Rico to watch Rubén Gómez, Ridzik and Al Worthington pitch for Santurce.

After a stint in the Dominican Republic, Ridzik pitched for Mayagüez in 1957-58 under Mickey Owen. Ridzik lived in Mayagüez's Darlington Apartments, as did teammates Maury Wills and Pete Wojey. Many American managers and players lived in Darlington units located in San Juan, Ponce and Mayagüez during the 1950s and 1960s.

Maury Wills

Maury Wills was considering leaving Puerto Rico during the 1957-58 season. He had been mired in the minors for the previous five years and had a large family to support. Mickey Owen recalls the day when Wills visited him at his Mayagüez Darlington penthouse apartment. He showed Owen a telegram from Mrs. Wills asking him to come home. Owen felt Wills was Mayagüez's best player, but knew there were right-handed pitchers he just couldn't hit. "Maury, you're an intelligent guy and you should switch-hit," suggested Owen. "Sometimes you look so bad swinging at those pitches. They don't think you can hit at all. Why don't you come out in the morning and I'll pitch batting practice to you."

With Owen pitching extra batting practice to Wills in morning workouts, the diminutive shortstop made positive strides hitting from the left side. When Wills batted left for the first time, Owen remembers him getting a base hit on a topper over the pitcher's head in his initial at-bat.

Owen: "I'll take credit for Wills becoming a switch-hitter, but give Maury credit for being smart and working hard. He was a dandy shortstop and the best base stealer I ever saw. He was fast, and one of those fellows who gets a walking lead ... takes everything over and [you] can't throw 'em out. That was Maury Wills."

Sandy Koufax

Wills's future Dodger teammate Sandy Koufax also honed his skills in Puerto Rico during the 1950s. It was Koufax's only "minor league" experience, since the hard-throwing lefty went straight from the University of Cincinnati campus to Brooklyn. Koufax was sent to Puerto Rico to work on his control in the 1956-57 season. He left the Island when a rule went into effect on December 20, 1956, limiting each Puerto Rican team to three experienced major leaguers on active rosters, excluding natives.[21] Koufax was one of the Caguas club's big leaguers who returned to the States after roster changes.

Sandy Koufax may have needed some more seasoning, but he was held in high esteem by the hitters he faced. Mayagüez catcher J. W. Porter recalls hitting against Koufax in a 10 A.M. game on a Sunday. Team owners were concerned about the effect Sunday afternoon horse races were having on baseball attendance; one strategy was to schedule Sunday morning games. "The sun came up in center field. Not only were you facing Sandy, but you had the big, bright ball of sun right behind you," Porter recalls. "You had no chance whatsoever."

Bob Gibson

Hall of Famer Bob Gibson pitched in Puerto Rico during the 1961-62 season and felt it enhanced his big league career. He faced Roberto Clemente, José Págan, Frank Howard, Jim Rivera, Lee Maye and a host of others, without the inherent big league tension. "It provided experience in a high classification without major league pressure," says Gibson. "I got along well because I tried to learn and speak Spanish."

Gibson started 19 regular-season and six postseason games for Santurce that winter. All he did in the postseason was go 5-0 to help Santurce win the league playoffs and the Interamerican Series.[22]

Frank Howard

Frank Howard, a.k.a. "El Condominio" (the Condominium) for his 6'7" frame, played two seasons with Caguas after one winter with Escogido in the Dominican Republic. Howard is credited with the longest Puerto Rico League homer on record, a 536-foot shot (measured by an engineer at Escobar Stadium) off San Juan's Jack Fisher in the 1960-61 finals.[23] Those who were there assert this blast was closer to 600 feet. The real old-timers, however, remember a homer by Josh Gibson at Escobar that reached the ocean after clearing the wall. This one may have traveled over 600 feet. "You learned to hit in old Sixto Escobar Stadium when you faced

Bob Gibson, Juan Pizarro, Bob Bolin, Tite Arroyo," says Howard. "Every young player should play two to three years of winter league baseball to refine their skills. The Puerto Rico League kept me in the big leagues and toughened me up. It was better than AAA."

Howard emphasized there is no substitute for nine innings of baseball every day. The added game experience, learning a new language and the extra income were positive aspects of playing winter ball for Howard. For the next three decades, the Puerto Rico League continued to launch careers with the force of a Frank Howard tape-measure blast.

Ferguson Jenkins

The Philadelphia Phillies sent Ferguson Jenkins and other prospects, including Rick Wise and Grant Jackson, to Caguas in the mid–1960s. Cal McLish, the Phillies' pitching coach, monitored their progress. Jenkins had pitched two winters in Nicaragua but was still far from being the dominant 20-game winner he became for the Cubs starting in 1967. His 1964-65 and 1965-66 seasons with Caguas included a league-leading ERA the second winter.[24] "I was down there to learn how to pitch and increase my knowledge to basically earn a major league job with the Phillies," Jenkins remembers. "I didn't pitch that much in the minors, so Puerto Rico was useful, in that I learned how to throw a slider, conduct myself on the mound, throw pitches in certain situations to set the hitters up. I was down there to learn how to pitch."

Nino Escalera, a Caguas coach during both of Jenkins's seasons, noticed his continued improvement in Puerto Rico. He saw Jenkins carrying around an iron ball to strengthen his pitching arm. "The more he pitched, the better he got in Puerto Rico," says Escalera. "His control was very good, so he was on his way. That iron ball was always with him after a game or between starts."

Mike Cuéllar and Denny McLain

Mike Cuéllar and Denny McLain were the league's best pitchers during Jenkins's first Puerto Rico campaign. Both finished with 12-4 records, for the Arecibo Wolves and Mayagüez Indians, respectively.[25] Cuéllar went from the bullpen of the 1964 world champion St. Louis Cardinals to Arecibo's starting rotation. He had learned a screwball from Rubén Gómez while spending part of the previous summer with Jacksonville. "Rubén Gómez inspired me to use the screwball," says Cuéllar. "He didn't have me throw it his way, but gave me advice on using this pitch. It really helped me in winter ball and later with Baltimore."

Cuéllar had a storied winter league career in Cuba and Puerto Rico.

He was a teammate of Tom Lasorda, Art Fowler and Tony Taylor with the 1958-59 Almendares championship club of the Cuban League, and recalls Lasorda working with him on throwing curves. Mike Cuéllar would pitch in the Puerto Rico League until he was 45. He also served as a pitching coach in the league.

Denny McLain joined a number of hungry Detroit Tiger youngsters with the 1964-65 Mayagüez club. Willie Horton, Jim Northrup and Joe Sparma were up-and-coming Tigers who led Mayagüez into the finals against the eventual champion, Santurce. McLain showed his durability by pitching every fourth day and cracked Detroit's 1965 starting rotation.

Jim Northrup

Jim Northrup, McLain's Mayagüez and Detroit teammate, was bullish on the Puerto Rico League more than 25 years after he earned this loop's batting title in 1965-66. Northrup awakened the Detroit brass with his hitting in Puerto Rico. He had hit well in the minors, but it was his Puerto Rican performance that earned him a starting outfield position with the 1966 Tigers.

Northrup: "When I first came up with Detroit in 1964 and 1965, I struggled. In my first season with Mayagüez I lost the batting title to [Santurce's] Lou Johnson, but the next year [1965-66] I hit .353 and won it."

Northrup recalls earning $1,330 per month as a rookie with the 1965 Tigers. But he earned $1,500 a month with Mayagüez in 1964-65 and was given a raise the second winter. Northrup appreciated Babel Pérez and Pachy Irizarry, Mayagüez front office officials, for giving him the opportunity to exploit his talent and make some money doing it.

Luis Tiant

Luis Tiant pitched for three different clubs in Puerto Rico: Caguas in 1961-62, Ponce in 1964-65 and Santurce during the 1982-83 season. He played many winters in Venezuela and was a proponent of staying active on a year-round basis.

Tiant remembers that he first had injury problems after Cleveland would not allow him to pitch in winter ball following the 1968 big league season. "It wasn't like you were going to pitch every day. But they [the big league club] didn't understand."

Tiant considered Puerto Rico a very strong league. He got a lot out of his season with Caguas before he became a major league pitcher. And Tiant particularly remembers a 1–0 duel with Santurce's Pizarro in game seven of a semifinal series, in which a young first baseman named Martín

Beltrán took him deep for the game's only run. After the Santurce-Mayagüez final series, Tiant reinforced Mayagüez in the 1962 Interamerican Series.

The legendary Tiant played for Ponce in 1964-65 because of Ponce's working agreement with Cleveland. The starting rotation included a trio of Cleveland's best pitching prospects—Tiant, Sonny Siebert and Steve Hargan. Tiant appreciates what Ponce manager Johnny Lipon and other Latin players in the Cleveland organization did for him. "Lipon spoke pretty good Spanish—I first worked under him in the minors in 1962. When one comes to the U.S. without speaking English, it's very difficult, but Lipon did a lot for us."

By the time Tiant returned to Puerto Rico for his final tour of duty, in 1982-83, his major league career was over. Tiant joined fellow Cuban Tany (Tony) Pérez on the Santurce club, which won the regular-season pennant before bowing out in the playoffs.

Pat Tabler, a Santurce teammate of Tiant and Pérez that winter, remembers: "One of the most influential guys was Tony Pérez when I was there. Just his leadership demanded respect from everyone. And Luis Tiant was something else. I asked Luis one day, how do you pitch so well? What's your secret, no one knows how old you are?"

Tiant replied that he ate a rattlesnake mixture every day and offered him a powdery concoction. Tiant said, "Sprinkle it on your food, and play forever." But Tabler took one sniff of it, licked it and tasted it, and threw it out.

Luis Tiant warms up for Caguas in the 1961-62 season (courtesy of *El Nuevo Día*).

Tony Pérez

He is Tony Pérez to stateside fans, but to Puerto Rico fans it was Tany (short for Atanasio). Pérez went from the San Diego AAA club in 1964 to the 1964-65 Santurce Crabbers. "Puerto Rico was almost major league caliber in the 1960s," Pérez recalls. "The league attendance was good and I developed a great relationship with Cepeda, Terín [Pizarro] and Rubén [Gómez]."

The slugging of Cepeda and Pérez, plus the hurling of Pizarro and Gómez, spelled doom for the other five league clubs as Santurce won the title. Pérez's big league career took off several years later, shortly before stateside fans saw his game-winning homer in the 1967 major league All-Star Game. But Puerto Rico's fans knew all along that Pérez was a gamer who produced when it counted. They had seen him win the 1966-67 League batting title and MVP award.

Pérez: "I played winter ball for the last time in 1982-83. It was a farewell to the fans. I appreciate what Hiram Cuevas and Poto Paniagua [Santurce's owners] did for me. Puerto Rico truly helped me, and I am in debt to the Island and its fine people."

Nelson Briles

A St. Louis prospect, Nelson Briles garnered league pitching laurels for the 1966-67 Ponce Lions. Briles's only winter league endeavor was a productive one. "I had made it to the big leagues quickly from AA ball," says Briles, who came up in 1966. "So Puerto Rico gave me more experience and more time to hone my skills. It made me feel more comfortable. It also helped coming out of winter ball because you're already in shape, the arm and body are in shape, and there is not that much time off between winter ball and spring training."

Briles recalls a lot of enjoyable times with his teammates, who came from a variety of big league organizations, including St. Louis. Ponce's manager that winter was former Yankee reliever Tite Arroyo, and this helped account for Roy White and Horace Clarke being in the starting lineup as well as Pedro Ramos being on the mound. Briles has memories of a young, skinny rookie named José Cruz. An early-season episode on Ponce's first bus trip to San Juan was one Briles won't ever forget. These bus trips could take three hours in the days before the modern *autopista*, or expressway, was constructed, linking Ponce to San Juan in 75 minutes.

Briles: "Whoever honked first on those narrow roads going up the mountains had the right of way. After the game, we always stopped at the top of the mountain on the way back to Ponce. The native players had a tradition where we had to drink two shots of regular rum and two shots of

151 proof rum. I drank my shots, and at the same time an older, haggard-looking guy with one eye was doing the same thing, plus having four or five other shots. I'm the last one to get on the bus, and the bus driver was the guy sitting next to me! The one-eyed guy who had seven or eight shots of rum. I thought, you guys don't understand what you're doing, but they told me not to worry about a thing."

Steve Carlton

Steve Carlton took his spot alongside Briles in Ponce's starting rotation and won nine games. Carlton and Briles would pitch well for St. Louis in their 1967 championship season after leaving Puerto Rico. For Carlton, 1966-67 was his second winter with Ponce. According to his manager, Tite Arroyo, and team owner Yuyo González, he improved tremendously from one season to the next.

Tite Arroyo had traveled to St. Louis in August 1965 on a mission to sign imports for the 1965-66 Ponce Lions. He noticed a tall lefty warming up in the bullpen. It was Steve Carlton. Arroyo was intrigued with bringing Carlton to Puerto Rico, but the St. Louis brass were not, since he was a top prospect whom they wanted to shield from possible injuries in winter ball. Arroyo convinced St. Louis to send Carlton to Ponce and received permission to speak with the 20-year-old.[26] "Carlton frequently told me how much the Puerto Rico Winter League meant to him," Arroyo later recalled. "He didn't even know how to get ready on the mound with men on base. All the runners on first got to second easily. He didn't pivot properly. We worked on that."[27]

Johnny Bench

Johnny Bench was a 1967 AAA All-Star with Buffalo before putting on the San Juan uniform in the 1967-68 season. Palillo Santiago, San Juan's star pitcher, knew Bench was special. "He had it all, and could he throw!" Santiago later pitched to Thurman Munson, another great receiver with San Juan.

Opposing pitchers soon found out that Bench was a smart hitter as well as a fine catcher. Tom Timmerman had pitched against Bench in AAA as well as in Puerto Rico. "The line on him [Bench] was the only thing he could hit was fastballs, but when he got to Puerto Rico, he learned to hit to right field, and right-center, and hit most of them up the alley," recalls Timmerman. "Bench really matured in Puerto Rico and became a good, smart hitter after that."

Johnny Bench earned National League Rookie of the Year honors in 1968, after his winter in Puerto Rico, where he played on a team with big

Jim Palmer receives gifts for being named Player of the Week, 1968-69. League officials and members of the press look on (courtesy of Angel Colón).

league players—Lee May, Tony Taylor and Tony González, not to mention Roberto Clemente. Bench handled a variety of pitchers, from flame-throwers Pat Dobson, Palillo Santiago and Rick Wise to crafty veterans such as Orlando Peña. His line drives to the gap paid off and he tied Tany Pérez for the most league doubles, with 20.[28]

Jim Palmer

Unlike the young Bench, Jim Palmer was on the comeback trail in 1968-69. His big league career was in jeopardy because of injuries and he thought Puerto Rico might be the tonic to cure his ailments. Santurce owner Hiram Cuevas had hired Frank Robinson that winter to be his team's manager. Moreover, Cuevas was on excellent terms with Harry Dalton, Director of Player Development for the Baltimore Orioles. According to Cuevas, Dalton offered to cover Palmer's Puerto Rico salary while he remained on the inactive list in Puerto Rico, and Santurce was to chip in once Palmer was activated.

The 1968-69 Santurce squad was well stocked, with Elrod Hendricks, George Scott, Leo Cárdenas, Joe Foy, Julio Gotay, Dave May and Paul Blair, as well as starters Terín Pizarro, Rubén Gómez, Wally Bunker and Dave Leonhard. Palmer wasn't rushed into action, but when he did pitch, the results were excellent. He twirled a seven-inning no-hitter against the Mayagüez Indians and their versatile pitcher Ozzie Virgil, Sr.

Puerto Rico resurrected Palmer's career. There were no more rehab stints in Miami or Rochester. Nick Acosta, Santurce's trainer, recalls Palmer coming to Puerto Rico with an inflamed right rotator cuff. "We gave him first-class treatment in Puerto Rico. He recovered and became a Cy Young winner. Jim listened to me, and that was a plus. He is a very intelligent person and followed all the tips *al pie de la letra* [by the book]."

Reggie Jackson

Reggie Jackson slumped with Oakland in 1970. The A's owner, Charley Finley, suggested that Jackson play winter ball. Hiram Cuevas remembers Harry Dalton of Baltimore getting permission from Finley to contact Jackson about coming to Puerto Rico. At the time, most of Santurce's imported players came from Baltimore's organization. "Reggie got a salary of some $2,000 a month and calls me 'my Puerto Rican father,'" says Cuevas. "When I first brought him down, Reggie thought he'd hit more for average, but it wasn't until later in the season he started hitting homers. He wanted to improve in all aspects of the game. He played hard, slid hard, ran out ground balls, worked on his hitting stance, and stayed the whole season."

Jackson started out 1970-71 by striking out 14 times in the first week.[29] He was fitted for glasses on a week-long trip to the States around Thanksgiving and returned to Puerto Rico. His home run pace picked up and he ended with a league-best 20, the most since Willard Brown's 27 for Santurce in 1947-48.[30]

By mid–December 1970, Jackson was on a homer binge which included five in four games.[31] Santurce manager Frank Robinson had worked with Jackson on his hitting and was impressed. "He's just not striking out anymore," he said. "He's made up his mind just to make contact and with his power, the results have been something else."

Roger Freed, another Santurce slugger, was hitting for power when he injured his right arm about the time Jackson got hot. The young Orioles prospect played left, with Don Baylor in center and Jackson in right. Freed hit third in the lineup, with Jackson as the "cleanup" hitter. He remembers Jackson telling him, "Roger, you don't leave anyone on base for me to pick up."

Jackson acknowledges that Frank Robinson had always been his hero. It was an important winter for Reggie Jackson, as he later told a reporter: "I played in Puerto Rico for only three months, but I learned a lot about being a pro, about being a leader. As a man of great baseball knowledge, Frank showed me that I could mature a lot."[32]

In a 1970-71 postseason interview, Jackson commented how impressed he was by Robinson's winning attitude and said that he listened to what his manager was saying when he might have ignored the same advice from another person. The experience of playing winter ball made Jackson appreciate the major leagues. "After you play in these parks, where the fields aren't nearly as good as what we have in the States, or you ride a bus over the mountains to get to a game instead of flying first class, you begin to appreciate how good it really is in the majors."[33]

Jon Matlack and Bruce Kison

The 1971-72 San Juan Senators had a few talented New York Mets and Pittsburgh Pirates prospects on their roster. One of them was Jon Matlack. The lefty felt the Puerto Rican League was better than AAA. He struggled a bit early in the season and manager Bill Virdon put him in the bullpen for a spell to work out the kinks. "I had to rise to the next level if I was going to compete," says Matlack. "It was the next step up the ladder that helped me ease into the big leagues the following spring and an important cog in the machine that was my development as a pitcher. I know that Puerto Rico was an important piece of the puzzle that helped me become the pitcher I ended up being."

Bruce Kison went to Puerto Rico after the 1971 World Series. He pitched to Milt May, a teammate with the 1971 Pirates. Bob Johnson was another Pirate on the San Juan pitching staff. The experience was good for Kison. "Throughout the league you faced legitimate major league players with two to three years under their belts," he says. "It provided you with real good feedback from the organization's standpoint, in terms of facing major league caliber play—reassured me I could pitch well in the big leagues."

Mike Schmidt

Mike Schmidt felt the extra Puerto Rico at-bats over the course of the 1972-73 and 1973-74 seasons did a lot for his big league career. Schmidt was selected for the 1973-74 Puerto Rico League All-Star team along with Caguas teammate Jerry Morales. By the time his Caguas team captured the 1974 Caribbean Series in Hermosillo, Mexico, Schmidt was ready to put up Hall of Fame numbers with the Phillies. Morales once heard Schmidt comment that winning the 1974 Caribbean Series title was one of the highlights of his professional baseball career.

Schmidt's teammates with Caguas included Bob Boone, Roger Freed, Wayne Twitchell and Jay Johnstone, since the Phillies still sent players to this franchise.

Mike Schmidt (#20) and Jerry Morales (#4) pose with their 1973-74 league all-star trophies. Angel Colón, of the Puerto Rico Professional Baseball Players Association, is in the middle (courtesy of Angel Colón).

Robin Yount

When Robin Yount flew to Puerto Rico after his rookie season with the 1974 Milwaukee Brewers, he was coming off an injury which forced him to miss the final month. Yount made the most of the trip. "It was an opportunity for me to go down and make sure that I was healthy enough to start the season properly the next year," Yount recalls. "But also, more than that, I was gaining more playing experience. I was very young [19] at the time. A lot of the players who go to the Winter League are young players just trying to learn the game of baseball. I was very lucky to go down there and play for a great manager in Frank Robinson and I was able to learn a lot of things about playing the game."

Yount could count on veteran Santurce teammates for advice and guidance ranging from his double-play partner Sandy Alomar, Sr., to catcher Elrod Hendricks. Orlando Cepeda was playing his final winter for Santurce.

Yount: "Without a doubt, Sandy Alomar helped me quite a bit, and I was very lucky to be on a team with Alomar and Hendricks. Cepeda was like a hero of mine because I was a big Giant fan growing up."

Phil Garner

Phil Garner wore the red-and-black Ponce uniform in 1973-74. Garner missed about a third of the season because of an injury, but recovered in time to help Ponce reach the finals. It was a valuable winter. "It was part of my maturation process," says Garner. "I was getting better and getting more confident to face that better [big league] competition. You either get up to their level or you're out of the system. I felt like Puerto Rico was indispensable—couldn't have possibly gotten to the big leagues without it."

Mike Caldwell and Rich Gossage

Mike Caldwell, Garner's Ponce teammate, learned he had been traded to the San Francisco Giants from San Diego for Willie McCovey while listening to the radio in Puerto Rico. "Back then, everybody who played in Puerto Rico was a major league ballplayer or very close to being one," Caldwell recalls. "Everybody in our starting lineup played in the big leagues. The competition is the best you're going to find in the winter leagues. Some of the Puerto Rican players were superstars down there."

Rich Gossage pitched for Ponce the winters before and after Garner and Caldwell played for the Lions. Gossage echoed Garner's sentiments when he reiterated that the level of competition in Puerto Rico benefits the players. He became more comfortable both starting and relieving.

Gossage: "My first year, I didn't want to go, but the White Sox kind of forced me to go down there. The next time I went down to work on things and got a lot out of it. The more you play there, the more comfortable you become. I had to work on a breaking ball. That's really what I was down there for—work and get my slider down."

Lance Parrish and Jack Morris

As the 1970s drew to a close, Mayagüez continued bringing young Detroit Tiger prospects to Puerto Rico. Jack Morris and Lance Parrish were two more Tigers who used Puerto Rico to further their big league aspirations. Morris led the league in strikeouts and pitched Mayagüez into the finals.[34]

Lance Parrish had one year with Detroit under his belt when he formed one of Puerto Rico's best batteries with Morris.

Parrish: "For myself, to be able to play with Jack down there, it just kind of furthered our growth as pitcher and catcher in the Detroit organization. I caught him a couple of seasons in the minors, then had the opportunity to catch Jack in the Puerto Rico League, and then worked with him in the majors. It was another step in our progression as major leaguers."

Rickey Henderson

Major league teams continued sending their top prospects to Puerto Rico in the 1980s. Rickey Henderson split the 1979 season between Ogden and Oakland before joining Ponce for the 1979-80 winter campaign. José Pagán, Henderson's manager at Ogden, was Ponce's skipper. Pagan recommended that Henderson play on his Ponce team. "Pagán helped me in my career," says Henderson. "I was in the minors trying to get my way to the big leagues and went to winter ball with guys older than me. It showed me a lot of what it took to get to the big leagues and was good for my career."

Henderson returned to Ponce in 1980-81 and set the all-time single-season stolen base standard with 44, breaking the mark of 41 set by Carlos Bernier in 1949-50.[35] His defense improved in Puerto Rico, as attested by a 1981 American League Gold Glove.

Henderson: "I continued playing winter ball because it kept you sharp, kept you learning about pitcher's moves and what you're going to do on the basepaths. I went down there and stole many bases, and read the pitchers well."

Jeff Reardon and Mookie Wilson

The New York Mets sent Jeff Reardon and Mookie Wilson to Arecibo for the 1979-80 and 1980-81 seasons. Reardon's bullpen work and Wilson's play helped Arecibo qualify for the playoffs.

Reardon was called on to face quality hitters like José Cruz, Dickie Thon, Rickey Henderson and others when the game was on the line. This type of experience came in handy. "I had the chance to face big league ballplayers, and that gave me the confidence I could make it in the 'bigs,'" Reardon says. "I enjoyed Puerto Rico winter ball very much." Mookie Wilson led the league in steals his first winter, and made his big league debut in September 1980. Wilson's second winter season preceded a consistent big league career.

Wade Boggs

Wade Boggs had lived at Ramey Air Force Base in Puerto Rico, where Johnny Logan had gone for American food in the 1949-50 season. Boggs's father was stationed there for three years when the future ballplayer was a toddler. Boggs returned to Puerto Rico in October 1981, just as he was about to make the transition from Pawtucket to the Boston Red Sox.

Boggs hit .354 for the Bayamón Cowboys in the 1981-82 season.[36] But with too few official plate appearances, he was ineligible for the league batting title and his teammate Dickie Thon claimed the title at .333.[37] Thon recalls that Boggs was constantly working on perfecting his swing and fit in well on the Bayamón club.

For Boggs, "It was a stepping stone that I used. I went ahead and got more playing time and experience and used it to improve my ability. I was on the verge of playing in the major leagues when I got out of there. I had just come out of AAA, so I think when you raise your standards in terms of quality of play, it's got to help."

Cal Ripken

When Cal Ripken, Jr., first came to Puerto Rico in October 1980, he had completed a AA season with Charlotte. The makeup of his team provided an incentive to produce.

"We had a lot of big league players in Puerto Rico," recalls Ripken. "Our Caguas team—God, [it] had at least six to seven good big league players [José Cruz, Ed Figueroa, Jerry Morales, Willie Montañez, Dennis Martínez, Héctor Cruz, Ozzie Virgil, Jr.]. A lot of the pitching was AAA, so the level was between AAA and the big leagues. So coming out of AA, I had to compete at a higher level and learned quite a few things playing all those games."

Ripken, a two-time Caguas MVP, returned to the team in 1981-82 after a summer at AAA and a brief stint with Baltimore. He played in all 60 regular season games and led the league in RBIs.[38]

Ripken: "It allowed me to get to the big leagues before I was 21, and part of my goal in baseball was to reach the big leagues early and be able to play a long, long time and I don't think I'd be able to do it without Puerto Rico."

Cal Ripken at third base during a 1981-82 Caguas-Bayamón game (courtesy of Angel Colón).

Tony Gwynn, Don Mattingly and Brian Harper

Tony Gwynn and Don Mattingly produced in Puerto Rico on their way to major league stardom. Gwynn hit .368 in 1982-83, but lost out in the batting chase to Bayamón teammate Brian Harper who hit .378.[39] Harper, a six-year veteran of winter ball in Puerto Rico, the Dominican Republic and Venezuela, remembers the batting race. "To be honest with you, Tony Gwynn got hurt the final two weeks of 1982-83," Harper says. "He was getting hot. If he didn't get injured, he probably would have won the batting title and hit .400. The next winter we had a real good lineup, with Gwynn, Thon, Kevin McReynolds, Carmelo Martínez and Luis Aguayo."

Don Mattingly played first base for Caguas in 1983-84 and won the league batting title. His manager, Vic Power, knew a little about fielding, having won seven American League Gold Gloves. He worked with Mattingly on his fielding and developed a good rapport with him. Power tried to help Mattingly win the hitting crown. "Randy Ready of Mayagüez was challenging Mattingly for the batting title and wasn't playing a late-season game," Power remembers. "We were up against a tough lefty, and I suggested that he take the night off. If Mattingly goes hitless, he falls behind Ready. But Mattingly told me he wanted to play and went three-for-four."

Sid Bream and Terry Pendleton

Puerto Rico was still a AAA+ league in the mid–1980s. Sid Bream, who played for Mayagüez in 1983-84 and 1984-85, can vouch for the quality of play at the time. "Both years we had very good teams. At that stage in my career, I needed more consistency and Puerto Rico was able to give me that. You were seeing a better pitcher every night instead of every four or five nights. It made you work harder."

Terry Pendleton was Bream's Mayagüez teammate in 1984-85 and got in a lot of work before his rookie big league season with the 1985 St. Louis Cardinals. Other teammates with big league aspirations were Vince Coleman, Bobby Bonilla and John Cangelosi. "It was a great mixture of guys who liked to play the game," says Pendleton. "I was originally going to the Dominican Republic, but when [St. Louis third base coach] Nick Leyva got the job with Mayagüez, St. Louis felt it was better sending me to Puerto Rico."

Bobby Bonilla

Bobby Bonilla played as a league "native" by virtue of his Puerto Rican heritage. Bonilla first played in Puerto Rico for the 1983-84 San Juan club and saw limited duty, batting behind Gwynn, Harper and McReynolds. He was traded to Mayagüez in 1984-85, but he didn't become an everyday player until 1985-86. One of Bonilla's biggest boosters in Puerto Rico was Mako Oliveras, a coach with San Juan who later managed that club and Santurce.

Oliveras: "When Bobby first arrived in Puerto Rico, he had nowhere to stay. We took an immediate liking to each other. I spoke to my mother about his staying with her and it worked out fine. Bobby lived in our home for two seasons and loved the food. He became one of the family. Mom has a great deal of affection for Bobby and always will."

Bonilla is proud of his five years in the Puerto Rico League, during which time he helped Mayagüez to two league championships. He worked on all aspects of his game and recovered from various injuries. Bonilla's Puerto Rican heritage was important to him. "It meant a lot for me to play on the Island," said Bonilla. "We won some titles during my years in the league. I used it as quite a tool myself, to gain experience. Not having played that many games in high school baseball, due to the weather in New

Bobby Bonilla gets a hit during the 1988 Caribbean Series (courtesy of *El Nuevo Día*).

York City, made the winter season even more important. Plus, I never played AAA baseball in the States. No question it helped."

Bryan Harvey

Bobby Bonilla's final season in Puerto Rico, 1987-88, was the only time Bryan Harvey played winter ball. And he was a revelation for Mako Oliveras's San Juan club, saving 17 of the team's 25 wins[40] and becoming the league's MVP. Oliveras had managed Harvey in 1987 at AA Midland in the Angels' organization and brought him to San Juan. Harvey made it to the big leagues in 1988, after spending the first 12 days of the season at AAA. "Mako has done a lot of good things for me," Harvey says. "He just has a good idea on how the game is supposed to be played. He doesn't put a lot of pressure on the guys. If you go there and do well, you have a good chance of making the major league team next spring training."

Jay Bell

Little did Jay Bell know that his double play partner with Santurce in 1987-88, José "Chico" Lind, would turn plenty of twin killings with him as his Pittsburgh teammate. The play of Bell and Lind was instrumental in Santurce's run to the finals that season.

The high level of play on Island diamonds helped Bell improve his game. So did the substandard field conditions, caused in part by the constant rainfall and lack of maintenance. This negative became a positive for Bell, since it forced him to concentrate more on the defensive aspects of his game. "It was a comfortable place to live and a super place to play," says Bell. "There were a few too many [round-robin playoff] games at the end, but it was a great experience."

Rob Dibble

Rob Dibble was throwing strikes for Caguas in 1987-88 and saved ten games.[41] He insists Puerto Rico got him over the hump and into the big leagues. "I didn't get a lot of pitching experience in the minors," says Dibble. "They didn't use me like I thought they should. But down in Puerto Rico, [Caguas manager Terry] Bevington told me, 'You're going to be my closer.'"

Dibble spent a lot of his time studying hitters and found out that the older players in the league took more pitches than the younger guys. He didn't have to go home and get a winter job, since he earned between $3,000 and $3,500 per month his first winter and a little more in 1988-89.

Dibble: "I've always been a student of the game and would pick the brains of Caguas teammates Carmelo Martínez, Ron Gant and Sam Horn. These are the type of hitters I face when the game is on the line. I have all the appreciation and love in the world for the people of Puerto Rico; they're excellent. It is definitely a great way to come up in baseball and learn about the game. It was a turning point in my career."

Lonnie Smith

San Juan's Lonnie Smith proved he could still play during his 1988-89 MVP season. Smith led the league in batting average and steals, and tied for the RBI title.[42] This showing propelled Smith into the 1989 Atlanta starting lineup.

Smith: "Puerto Rico gave me the opportunity to keep physically fit. It was very enjoyable. The native players instructed me how to get around the Island. It's a great league, and I proved to people I could still play. I wanted to come back the next year, but a league rule said I had too many big league at-bats."

Smith had over 250 at-bats with Atlanta in 1989. Imports with more than 250 big league at-bats and 125 innings pitched in the previous season are ineligible to play in the Puerto Rico League.

Mark Lemke, David Nied and Greg McMichael

Atlanta sent some top prospects to Puerto Rico in the early 1990s. Mark Lemke put in time with Santurce in 1990-91. David Nied pitched for Santurce a year later. Greg McMichael had a banner winter for Ponce in 1992-93. "Puerto Rico was real helpful overall," says Lemke. "I had an ankle injury in the States and my game got better."

Nied felt Puerto Rico compared favorably to his AAA experience at Richmond in 1992. But he discovered what Bob Gibson had found out 30 years earlier: there's not as much pressure. "Over there [Puerto Rico] you can work on things," says Nied. "In the U.S., it's your job."

Greg McMichael pitched superbly for Ponce while recording the most league strikeouts. He took this momentum into spring training and became Atlanta's closer during the 1993 season. "I enjoyed it a lot and played as well as I could," says McMichael. "It was kind of a laid-back league and not as intense as the majors."

Catchers, infielders, outfielders, starting pitchers and closers have used Puerto Rico as a launching pad for beginning or continuing their big league careers. Utility players to future Hall of Famers have made their presence felt. They have enhanced the league's level of play. Major league organizations have shown their confidence in Puerto Rico by sending their best prospects down. For most, the Puerto Rico Winter League has been the right tonic.

2. A Working Vacation

Where else can you "work" in a vacation paradise, meet great people and play against great ballplayers?
—John Strohmayer, former Caguas, Ponce and San Juan pitcher

Chris Zachary hooked up with the Ponce Lions in 1971-72 after being one of the pitching stars for the Dominican champion Licey Tigers in the 1971 Caribbean Series hosted by Puerto Rico. Zachary was one of the cogs in Ponce's championship season, which culminated in a 1972 Caribbean Series title. If anyone knew winter ball dynamics, it was Zachary. He had drawn one opening-day starting assignment against Luis Tiant in the Venezuelan League, before a packed house and guards with submachine guns. The owner of his Dominican League team had given Zachary a gold-and-silver combination Rolex watch for winning a key game.

And Zachary still couldn't get over the setup in Puerto Rico. "I was making about $2,500 a month, but they paid you in hundred-dollar bills," Zachary recalls. "They furnished me with a car, normally a little old VW or Toyota. It wasn't much, but it got you around. Heck, it was like a big paid vacation for me. Being a pitcher, you might pitch once a week. If the team was going across the mountains and I had to pitch the next day, I didn't have to go unless I wanted to. I'd just go to the ballpark and do a little running. It was great."

Zachary thrived on winter ball. He enjoyed himself on and off the field. The right-hander gave fans their money's worth, but kept the winter season in proper perspective.

Sun, Fun and Rain

There have been many ballplayers who put in their work and found time to enjoy themselves in Puerto Rico. During the formative years of the

Puerto Rico League, the Negro leaguers especially enjoyed the Island's hospitality. Players had plenty of time for fishing, socializing in town plazas and dinner at the homes of teammates, fans and team officials. It was a common sight to see players mingling with fans in restaurants, bars and movie theaters.

In the mid–1950s, one might spot Willie Mays and Bob Thurman, of the 1954-55 Santurce Crabbers, playing a hand of dominoes in the Mayagüez town plaza. Mayagüez sportswriter Rafael Soler Rivas recalls one day when rain was pouring down in Mayagüez and Mays and Thurman challenged Soler Rivas and a partner in dominoes, one of Puerto Rico's favorite pastimes. Rivas remembers Mays jumping up and down after he and Thurman won a hand. "It was something to see ballplayers like Mays act so spontaneously off the field. They gave it their all on the field, and to see them mingle with us the way they did was special."

Mays's Santurce teammate Rubén Gómez would often invite imports with Santurce or even archrival San Juan to go fishing. San Juan's Danny Kravitz remembers fishing with Gómez during the mid–1950s. Every now and then Gómez would take a teammate in his car to an away game. Gómez got carsick if he rode in the team bus, so he had permission from the Santurce management to travel on his own. Billy Hunter, Santurce's shortstop the first half of the 1952-53 season, has vivid memories of the time Gómez gave him a ride to a night game. To Hunter, Gómez's driving through the mountains was like an Indianapolis 500 competitor. Even scarier were the crosses at the roadside marking the sites of fatal accidents. Hunter was very relieved when they arrived in Mayagüez.

Hunter, originally slated for the Almendares club in Cuba, was sent to Puerto Rico by the Dodgers, who wanted him and Jim Gilliam to work together as a double-play combination. This was a most enjoyable winter for Hunter. He worked well with Gilliam, but had plenty of time for lounging at the pool and playing beach volleyball.

While Hunter was on his Puerto Rico "working vacation," he and his wife Bev were eating breakfast one morning at the Condado Beach Hotel—one of the Island's classiest hotels—when they saw a headline in the New York *Daily News* that read, "Billy Hunter Sold to St. Louis Browns." Hunter thought this was a trick, and asked his wife for the *New York Times*. Alas, it had the same news. When Hunter returned to his Gallardo apartment his phone was ringing. It was Bill Veeck. "We want you to come home," said Veeck. "I can't," responded Hunter. "I'm making more money—$1,200 a month—than at any time in my life."

Veeck arranged to increase Hunter's 1953 salary by $1,000, with $1,000 bonus for returning to the States. Veeck had already discussed this matter with Santurce owner Pedrín Zorrilla, and two days later Hunter returned home.

2. A WORKING VACATION					35

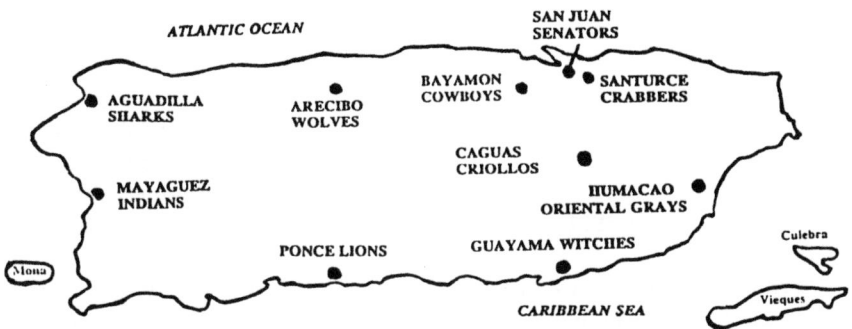

Map of Puerto Rico showing location of league teams.

Geography

The mountains referred to by Hunter and Nelson Briles comprise Puerto Rico's Cordillera Central (Central Mountain Range). The Island's highest peaks, ranging from 3,900 to 4,400 feet, are found in the municipalities of Jayuya, Adjuntas, Orocovis and Ciales.[1] It is not the height of the mountains but the narrow curves, that can wreak havoc on the nerves of ballplayers and tourists. A copy of the 1993 winter *Qué Pasa (What's Happening)* tourist guide for Puerto Rico advises mountain drivers to keep well to the right and blow the horn on curves. It describes the Panoramic Route, a complex, 165-mile network of 40 roads connecting the Island's east coast and west coast via the Cordillera Central.[2]

Puerto Rico is small—35 by 100 miles—and densely populated, with some 3.5 million inhabitants. Eighty miles east of Santo Domingo, 40 miles west of the U.S. Virgin Islands and about 1,000 miles southeast of Miami, it is the easternmost of the Caribbean's Greater Antilles. Puerto Rico's average annual temperature is 78 degrees fahrenheit. Roughly 70 inches of rainfall on Puerto Rico annually, with the rain forest (part of the Caribbean National Forest) getting much more precipitation.[3] Southern Puerto Rico gets the least rainfall.

Many league baseball contests are postponed due to rain during November and December, or subjected to long rain delays. Rainouts can be a nightmare for the schedule makers, who have to fit in makeup games and doubleheaders. In some cases, rain has affected pitching depth come playoff time. Hurricanes, however, tend not to be a problem during the baseball season. August and September are usually the prime months for hurricanes to hit the Caribbean.

A Modern Island

Puerto Rico transformed itself from an agricultural to an industrial-based economy in the 1950s. Its infrastructure was modernized and by 1955 imports (both trade goods and ballplayers) could arrive at the new $13 million San Juan International Airport instead of the smaller Isla Grande Airport located near Escobar Stadium.[4] Puerto Rico feels comfortable to stateside ballplayers because of the close ties it has maintained with the United States since 1898, when Spain ceded the Island to the United States.

The Island shares a common currency and postal system with the United States. Puerto Ricans serve in the U.S. military and have distinguished themselves in both World Wars, Korea, Vietnam and the Persian Gulf. United States citizenship was conferred on persons born in Puerto Rico by the 1917 Jones Act.[5] Under its provisions, the Island is self-governing but the federal government retains authority over defense, customs, the postal system and other governmental areas.

Because of these ties, stateside ballplayers do not have to worry about exchange rates or that mailing and receiving packages from relatives will cost an arm and a leg while they are playing in Puerto Rico. Nor is there any need for visas or passports when they travel between the States and the Island. Since Puerto Rico's health standards are good, ballplayers needn't get ulcers worrying about the quality of the drinking water or the food. Puerto Rico has a modern highway system, state-of-the-art telecommunication options and all the necessary accommodations for ballplayers.

President Harry Truman appointed the first native governor of Puerto Rico of the post–1898 period, Jesús T. Piñero.[6] Puerto Rico's governors have been elected by registered voters every four years since 1948. Truman also signed Law 600 on July 4, 1950, allowing Puerto Ricans to draft their own constitution. The constitution was adopted on July 25, 1952.[7]

While Puerto Rico observes federal holidays, it also has its own special days, including Three King's Day, a second Christmas on January 6; Constitution Day; Discovery Day, on November 19; days honoring esteemed Puerto Ricans; and religious holidays. The Island's winter holiday season is more festive than in the United States, lasting from Thanksgiving into the second week of January and coinciding with winter baseball.

Betting

The betting that goes on around Puerto Rican baseball is a big part of the show. It can reach "epic" proportions. Don Liddle, who was the pitcher on the mound for the New York Giants in the 1954 World Series when Willie Mays made his dramatic catch of Vic Wertz's long fly ball, would walk the six or seven blocks to his Darlington apartment from Escobar Stadium after San Juan's home games. He remembers one particular evening in the 1952-53 season when he received money from a fan under interesting circumstances. Liddle had just defeated Rubén Gómez during an exciting San Juan–Santurce game. Because of the excitement generated by this rivalry, Liddle received a police escort to his apartment. "As I was leaving Escobar Stadium someone jerked my pants and the policeman hit the fellow with a billyclub," recalls Liddle. "When I got to the Darlington, there was $300 stuffed into the back pocket of my San Juan uniform."

This showed how serious baseball was to the fans. Liddle was the beneficiary of a "take" from gamblers who had probably bet a large sum of money on the game's outcome. Liddle's take may have been enhanced by the odds against Rubén Gómez losing to San Juan. Gómez usually defeated San Juan and the chant "Ese es tu papá" ("He is your daddy") heard from Santurce fans toward the end of San Juan–Santurce games was meant to ridicule the San Juan faithful.

Six winters later, Jackie Brandt's working vacation included a productive season for Santurce in which he finished second to teammate Orlando Cepeda in the batting chase. Brandt lived across from Escobar in the Carmen Apartments and remembers hiring a maid for $10 per week who shopped, cooked and watched over the baby. Brandt often went to the racetrack and had dinner with Pedrín Zorrilla.

Brandt couldn't get over the betting he saw in Puerto Rico in 1958-59 and in Cuba three seasons earlier. For him, it only added to the excitement of winter ball. "It was unbelievable," he says. "The fans, their attitude, enthusiasm and betting. They would bet on everything—strikes, balls, fouls. Like, 'fifty dollars this guy hits a fly.'"

Ponce

The Ponce team, one of six original league franchises in 1938-39, was first known as the Kofresí Pirates, since their president, Juan Luis Boscio, worked with the Kofresí Rum company.[8] They became the Lions several years later. Ponceños take pride in their culture and in the fact that three of Puerto Rico's six elected governors between 1948 and 1992 were either born or raised there. Founded in 1692, Ponce is named for the Island's first governor, Juan Ponce de León.[9]

Hurler Dennis Kinney and slugger Roger Freed were two imports who lived in Ponce in the late 1970s. Ponce fans liked the way Kinney got the job done as a starter or reliever and appreciated his willingness to partake of the local hospitality. "When you lived in Ponce, you got to know the real locals," says Kinney. "I think they liked that; I got to be one of them. In my four years with Ponce, I lived there for three seasons and in San Juan

Roger Freed, Ponce slugger, 1977-78 season. Ponce cap made by the manufacturer of Philadelphia Phillies caps (courtesy of Rai García).

one year. Between Thanksgiving and Three Kings Day it was a laid back atmosphere with lots of open houses and activities like block parties in the U.S. I also went on a cruise to the U.S. Virgin Islands with Sergio Negrón, one of our team officials."

Roger Freed, the most productive home run hitter in Ponce history, with 33 blasts in only 405 at-bats over the 1976-77 and 1977-78 seasons, was appreciated by Ponceños almost as much for living in the community as for his long-ball prowess.[10] Ponce broadcaster Rafy Sepúlveda gives Freed credit for living in Ponce and sharing his time with the fans at a time when many imports were doing their own thing, staying in the tourist sections of San Juan, playing golf and not being as involved in community endeavors. "Yuyo González was the [team's] owner and he had a Jeep dealership," remembers Freed. "I drove one of his Jeeps to get around. He found a nice house to rent for my wife and three children. I enjoyed myself and played hard on the field. People want to see you do the best you can, and that's why I produced and gave 100 percent."

When Ernie McAnally and Phil Garner were with Ponce in 1973-74, Yuyo González made sure they and the other Americans lived within the city limits. McAnally and Garner were housemates, rode together to the ballparks, went to the beach, rented boats and snorkeled together. The extra $10,000 McAnally earned that winter came in handy. He was aware of being a minority in somebody else's country when he did normal day-to-day tasks. "Outside of being a ballplayer, it was crowded at times, on the streets, in the grocery stores," McAnally remembers. "Competition was keen for a dryer in laundromats."

Jay Johnstone had fun in Puerto Rico. The 23-year-old outfielder was on Ponce's 1968-69 team that won the Lions' first title in 22 years. A three-year big leaguer at the time, Johnstone became a regular for the Angels after that winter. "It was a fun thing, because it was my first experience in Puerto Rico," says Johnstone. "We lived in the beautiful downtown Darlington Hotel and I remember going around with Pat Corrales and his wife and mine. Then I had a good year with the Angels the next year. We had to go over those mountain roads. We used to have to get out of those buses and push."

Johnstone seemed to thrive in Puerto Rico. "Learning to live there and live with Christmas at 85 degrees, you know, and our wives bonding together and getting together with the native players and doing things. I think I had a better experience, culture-wise, off the field than playing the game."

Skeeter Barnes was a Ponce import in 1986-87 who felt the people of Puerto Rico were as friendly as you could meet. He enjoyed the culture, and played hard. "If you work hard, they notice it," he affirms. "A lot of American players treat it as just a vacation."

San Juan

San Juan is an older city than St. Augustine, Florida. It became the capital of Puerto Rico in 1521.[11] Old San Juan, a World Heritage Site, is where American players from Wilmer Fields and Bob Turley to Ken Dayley and Shane Mack have gone sightseeing and shopping with their spouses.

The San Juan franchise, a charter member of the league since 1938-39, moved to Bayamón for the 1974-75 season. Just west of San Juan, Bayamón dates to 1772 and derives its Indian name from the river which traverses it.[12] From 1974-75 to 1982-83, the Bayamón Cowboys (Vaqueros) played their home games in Juan Ramón Loubriel Stadium, with a seating capacity of 16,000.[13] The team returned to Bithorn Stadium in 1983-84 and became the San Juan Senators. From 1984-85 to 1992-93, they were the Metros; they became the Senators again in 1993-94.

When Chicago White Sox prospects Marv Staehle and Jerry McNertney played with San Juan in 1963-64, they roomed in a one-bedroom apartment converted from a garage. Staehle made a big hit off the field when he and teammate Deacon Jones did a Spanish-language interview on a radio program. "We had twin beds and a nice eating bar and a little living room. It was fantastic, and we loved it," says Staehle. "I took four years of Spanish

Yuyo Carrasquillo, San Juan's owner; Don Zimmer, manager; catcher Johnny Bench, 1967-68 (courtesy of Rai García).

in high school, where our teacher taught us the practical use of it . . . took us to downtown Chicago, where he made us order off the menu. Nothing would be in English, so I knew what *arroz con pollo* [rice and chicken] was. It really helped."

Staehle had fun on the field. In the playoffs, San Juan was beating a team very badly when the whole San Juan side in the stands lit matches. Staehle looked over to Cocó Laboy, who was playing third, and asked him what was going on. Laboy replied, "A funeral. We're burying them and they're holding a funeral." In Staehle's words, "It was incredible."

Staehle also remembers the 70-mile-an-hour bus trips late at night, but not so fondly. He recalls the younger native players having a ball, with music blaring, banging on the luggage rack with their hangers. Then there were the older veterans, who didn't want to do anything but sleep.

Milt May was a San Juan Senator in 1971-72 and 1972-73. The baseball experience was both fun and important to May. He caught Bruce Kison—one of his best friends—Bob Johnson, Jon Matlack and Jim Bibby. Palillo Santiago and Julio Navarro were two experienced hurlers. May says the pitching staff was fun to catch, and adds, "What was unique was the fact I hadn't been off the mainland U.S. my whole life. It was a vacation spot where I stayed, and a lot of tourists go to the area."

Chris Chambliss had gotten married at the end of the 1973 season, so his stint in Puerto Rico served as his honeymoon. Chambliss knew San Juan teammates Rusty Torres, Tom Hilgendorf and Charlie Spikes from the Cleveland Indians. A three-year big league veteran at the time, Chambliss found the transition to Puerto Rico winter ball to be fairly smooth. He hammered the ball on the field and relaxed in the tourist section of San Juan during his free time.

One of the most colorful hurlers ever to pitch for San Juan and Bayamón was Tom Hilgendorf. The veteran lefty was already 31 when he pitched for Jim Gilliam's 1973-74 San Juan ball club. As a much younger pitcher, Hilgendorf had spent a winter in Nicaragua on the Cinco Estrellas club with Ed Roebuck, Mel Queen and Jim Campanis — where he contracted hepatitis and his wife got food poisoning. What's more, the team's trainer had gone out to get a ball near a portable fence and was shot in the leg by a fellow who wanted the ball. The Dominican Republic and Puerto Rico seemed tame by comparison.

While living in Puerto Rico, Hilgendorf golfed with Chi Chi Rodríguez at the Dorado Beach Hotel, swam a lot and played tennis. When Dodger broadcasters Vin Scully and Jerry Doggett were in Puerto Rico, Hilgendorf and Gilliam would golf with them as a foursome at El Conquistador, an exclusive resort. Puerto Rico, says Hilgendorf, was his most pleasant winter experience.

Hilgendorf spent 1974-75 with Bayamón, in its brand-new stadium, with Art Howe, Ken Griffey, and Dan Driessen. He became one of the few American players in league history to receive the key to the city. Team owner Jorge Bird and general manager Roberto Inclán rewarded Hilgendorf after several final-series wins coupled with a victory in the 1975 Caribbean Series.

Hilgendorf: "The fans never stopped cheering, and Inclán told me, 'You better get out of here, because a lot of women will be after you.' I then flew to Tucson, since we had spring training coming up."

Caguas

The predominantly urban city of Caguas is south of San Juan and just north of the Cayey mountain range. Founded in 1775, its name comes from the Indian chieftan Caguax.[14] Caguas was one of the six original league franchises, but did not field a team between 1942-43 and 1945-46.[15] Some of their native players, Luis Olmo for one, played with Santurce and San Juan during those seasons. Caguas was again represented in 1946-47 and the team distinguished itself with 12 league championships during the next four decades.

The Caguas franchise moved to Bayamón in 1991-92, but low attendance and other problems resulted in Caguas-Bayamón's demise. Native players on this roster were made available to the other five teams in a 1992-93 draft. Juan González went to Santurce, while Iván Rodríguez and Omar Olivares were selected by Mayagüez. Caguas rejoined the league in 1994-95, aiming to reclaim its glory years.

In the early 1960s, Las Vegas–style entertainment and gambling came to San Juan's hotels and casinos. Havana was no longer the entertainment and gambling mecca it had been before the Cuban revolution of the late 1950s. Ballplayers who lived in San Juan or Caguas could have a night out on the town. Caguas lefty Pete Richert appreciated the efforts by his Island teammates to show him a good time. "It was fun. José [Pagán] and Félix [Mantilla] found a way to take care of us," says Richert. "After a game, four or five of us would get in a car and drive 30 miles to San Juan for a show and something to eat." Richert remembers Puerto Rico as a great place to play. It was also a place where one could learn about someone else's culture and lifestyle. "They went out of their way to make sure that everything was good. You were told about the right places to eat."

Woody Huyke, Richert's Caguas teammate, who later coached in Puerto Rico, recalls that American ballplayers in the early 1960s did not rent cars. (This became more prevalent in the mid–1970s.) He notes Caguas management would find furnished homes for the imports, and their wives would select kitchen supplies at the Caguas ballpark and take them to their winter home by taxis. The way American ballplayers adapted to Puerto Rico's lifestyle was a plus, from Huyke's viewpoint.

Caguas won the 1967-68 title, largely thanks to journeyman pitcher Tom Timmerman. The bespectacled Timmerman had been pitching in the minors since 1960. Frustrated with his baseball career, he was considering taking a job outside the game. Timmerman had just graduated from Southern Illinois University with a business degree when a phone call from Caguas's owner, Dr. Emigdio Buonomo, changed his mind.

Timmerman: "My friends told me, you can always get a job. So I went to Puerto Rico, where it was nice and warm. I didn't have to fight the winter, so if it wasn't for Puerto Rico, I would have taken that job and quit baseball. I lived in a beautiful three-bedroom home. The neighbors were nice, we had a lot of barbecues. A doctor took me fishing with lobster traps to Fajardo."

Californian John Strohmayer was pleasantly surprised with the unique flavor of Puerto Rico's food. He thought it might be hot and spicy, like Mexican food, but it wasn't. Strohmayer would order Puerto Rican food at restaurants on the way to road games, unlike most of his American teammates who were on the prowl for stateside food. *Asopao*, a thick soup with a variety of flavors, containing chicken and seafood, was a favorite.

Strohmayer was the Caguas Player of the Week several times. His prizes included the standard dinner for two at the Caguas Highway Inn and a trip to St. Thomas, a new radio and a $100 gift certificate. He could communicate a little bit in Spanish and read the local newspapers. "Where else can you 'work' in a vacation paradise, meet great people and play against great ballplayers?" says Strohmayer. "I wouldn't trade those years for anything. They were just fantastic."

When Bob Apodaca joined the 1973-74 edition of the Caguas Criollos, he was "on the bubble," in terms of the New York Mets pitching staff. Apodaca's working vacation paid dividends, since he impressed Yogi Berra with 18 scoreless innings the following spring. Twenty years after pitching in Puerto Rico, Apodaca contends it was the turning point in his career. "It was up to the American players who went down there to make sure they took it serious and not just as a vacation," claims Apodaca. "You know, make some money, be in Puerto Rico where it was nice and warm. You had to go down there and reestablish yourself in Puerto Rico."

Apodaca lived in the same building as Caguas teammates Mike Schmidt, Jay Johnstone, Craig Swan and John Montague. This was in the Condado section of San Juan, where many imports have lived since the 1960s. The Isla Verde section of San Juan and Carolina is another tourist area where imports live. There ballplayers can find discos, casinos and beaches.

John Montague remembers 1973-74 as an exciting season. Caguas won the title, and everyone chipped in on and off the field. "It was a job, but a fun job," he exclaims. "Craig Swan, myself and Schmidt played tennis for an hour earlier in the day. I really liked the rice and beans." Montague pitched for Bayamón in 1974-75 and was on his second straight Caribbean Series winner. He enjoyed the party atmosphere during this series and the hospitality of owner Jorge Bird.

Arecibo

Arecibo, founded in 1616, is the league's smallest market. With its 127 square miles, however, Arecibo has the largest area of Puerto Rico's 78 municipalities.[16] Its rural environs contrast with urban centers such as San Juan, Bayamón and Caguas. The city takes its name from the Indian Chieftan Arasibo.

The Arecibo Wolves have struggled to make ends meet at various times in their history. They did not field a team in 1981-82, and their native players—Candy Maldonado, Edwin Nuñez and Ramón Avilés—were drafted by other teams. Arecibo returned to the fold in 1982-83 and, miraculously, won their only league title. Moe Drabowsky only played one year of winter ball and it was with the 1961-62 expansion Wolves. He had the good fortune of winning the first game in Arecibo's history and witnessing a big celebration in the town plaza. "I thought to myself, this is great," chuckles Drabowsky. "But what will they do if we ever lose a game? They'll probably have you hanging by a tree there."

Drabowsky lived near the ocean in a house beside the one where Arecibo teammate Bob Uecker resided. He remembers the Saturday night block parties, hitting the rum factory and pretty much seeing what Puerto Rico had to offer. Perhaps the strangest episode that winter was Drabowsky being enticed by Peace Corps workers in Arecibo to climb trees using stout ropes. Drabowsky: "That messed up my shoulder, but other than that, Puerto Rico was a great experience."

A decade after Moe Drabowsky pitched for Arecibo, Gene Tenace settled in as the team's starting catcher. Arecibo finished the 1971-72 season in last place, but by then Tenace wasn't on the playing field. He was hospitalized by a beaning shortly after New Year's Day. Tenace had problems with intravenous feeding, among other matters, and left the hospital only to have a wealthy Arecibo doctor take him into his own home for a couple of weeks. "If it weren't for the doctor, I don't know where I would have ended up," says Tenace. "I was just with McKeon a short time after he became our manager, and after leaving Puerto Rico I went to Chicago to see a brain surgeon."

Tenace still considers Puerto Rico his favorite place to play winter ball. He liked Venezuela, Mexico and the Dominican Republic, but one reason Tenace enjoyed Puerto Rico so much was his Arecibo and Oakland teammate Angel Mangual. Mangual would treat Tenace to seafood meals and show him around the Island. The 1972 World Series hero gives credit to all the countries where he played winter ball. "That's why you go there. I was converted to a catcher, so winter ball really helped me fine-tune my catching skills for the big leagues."

Dennis Leonard had just come out of Class-A ball in 1973 when Carlos Pieve, Arecibo's general manager, took a calculated risk by signing the youngster. To insert a 22-year-old Class-A pitcher into the starting rotation was pure folly to fans and league officials. But Pieve recalled that a Class-A player by the name of Hank Aaron had starred in the league two decades earlier and stuck to his guns. "Pieve had lived in Brooklyn at one time, and I was born there, so we had something in common already," Leonard states. "He was real supportive to get me down and I got off to a good start." Leonard left during the season to be in the States for the birth of his first child, but returned in time to help Arecibo make the playoffs.

Arecibo had on its roster a number of Kansas City prospects who roomed together. Leonard shared a house on the ocean with Mark Littell, Gary Lance and Tom Poquette. His working vacation was often disrupted at 6 A.M. by fighting roosters, known as *gallos*. Leonard can laugh now about the recuperating roosters. At the time, however, the American ballplayers threatened to kill these warriors. Cock-fighting, or *pelea de gallos*, is a big pastime throughout Puerto Rico, so it is just as well the Kansas City prospects were diplomatic about being woken up.

Lance: "We not only shared a house, but a car, too. It was a Volkswagen that was kind of broken down. In fact, the driver's back door wouldn't open; you would have to crawl in through the driver's side. Me and Littell used it most of the time. He got up before everyone else and took the car. We didn't see him until the early afternoon." Lance notes it was tougher then, before the *autopista*, taking the long bus trips to Ponce. He remembers staying in downtown Ponce at the Hotel Melia. When Lance pitched for Arecibo in 1982-83, he drove to the games in his rental car on better roads and there were no hotel stays.

Lance sees Puerto Rico as different from Venezuela or the Dominican Republic, where he also played winter ball. "It's unique for Americans because you have U.S. dollars, the U.S. postal system, and the telephone system. In Venezuela, you had to have a *solvencia* [document] to leave that country, showing you didn't owe the employer or government any money. Puerto Rico is just like being in another state with the eateries, franchises, hotels and all the people who speak English."

Ken Wright was another Kansas City pitcher getting his work in for the 1972-73 Arecibo team. Wright pitched three seasons with Arecibo and simply loved it. "You were on vacation doing what you enjoyed doing," he says. "The pressure of the big city and constantly having your job on the line wasn't there. I enjoyed it very much."

The 1977-78 Arecibo team was in first place most of the season, before finishing one game behind defending champion Caguas. One reason for the Wolves' resurgence was 26-year-old reliever Tommy Toms, who had pitched a few innings for the San Francisco Giants. "When I first got there, they laughed at me because Arecibo was the laughingstock of the league," says Toms. "It was really neat . . . playing so well, plus my wife and I loved the atmosphere because we only played four times a week. We had a good opportunity to go out to the beaches, and snorkel and go shelling. We all lived together in a little community and had time together . . . nice mix of socializing, adventure and baseball. It was the most fun in all my baseball career and my wife felt the same way. We felt really at home and at peace there."

The team chemistry was outstanding, according to Toms with Iván de Jesús, Benny Ayala and Pedro García, all of them nice guys with a really professional attitude. Dennis Lamp and Donnie Moore were two of the team's top pitchers. Toms emphasizes it was important to get off to a good start. He remembers an early-season conversation with the owner, who told Toms he had better be good because of the good pay. It was a positive conversation

Toms: "When you're playing well, there was no pressure about going home. We felt like the 'Bad News Bears'—the underdogs—and it was fun; we worked together."

Tommy Toms and his wife experienced the same joy Hank Aaron and his spouse had nearly 25 years earlier when their oldest daughter was born in Puerto Rico. Arecibo's fans and the team owner appreciated the Toms' decision to have the child there and showered the family with gifts and goodwill.

Kevin Hagen was one of Arecibo's starters during the 1982-83 season. He lived in the resort community of Dorado and played golf with fellow pitchers Rich Bordi, Keith Creel and Gary Lance. When Arecibo won the 1983 Caribbean Series in Caracas, Venezuela, the working vacation became a party. Arecibo officials rewarded their players with a cruise to San Juan instead of taking the 500-mile flight from Caracas. Stops were made at Aruba and the Dominican Republic. "Coming into the port of San Juan was incredible—everybody had streamers," Hagen recalls. "Everyone was so excited. It was like we won the World Series. We visited the governor's mansion and the roads from San Juan to Arecibo were lined two, three deep with people on our parade route." For Gary Lance, who had had a cup of coffee with the 1977 Royals, it was his biggest thrill in baseball. "I had a no-hitter in AA and was later called up to the big leagues. But [this] was a Disneyland-type thing."

Santurce

Ronnie Samford had gone through emotions similar to those of Hagen and Lance 28 years earlier, when his 1954-55 Santurce club won the 1955 Caribbean Series in Caracas. Samford, too, experienced a parade from the airport, a reception at Governor Muñoz Marín's mansion and a lot of parties.

Samford: "It was the only time I met the governor. Shoot, we loved it." Samford and his wife socialized with Rubén and Teresa Gómez, their best friends in Puerto Rico. The Texan recalls fishing a lot with Gómez. A special day was when he became the first white U.S. Santurce ballplayer to be given a day in his honor.

Samford: "Santurce fans called me the 'White Sea' and Jim Gilliam the 'Black Sea' because we covered so much ground. They put money in two five-gallon buckets during the game. After the game, I walked to my apartment across the street with two buckets full of nickels and dimes. Oh, God, I get to thinking about it ... those good times."

Samford enjoyed Puerto Rico so much that he later defied his Detroit general manager's edict not to go back to winter ball. Samford returned to Puerto Rico, and his contract was sold to Charleston, West Virginia. He simply loved the fried bananas, or *plátanos*, with rice and chicken served at a restaurant on stilts in Mayagüez. Playing cards with his teammates was another pastime.

Craig Anderson's working vacation for Santurce in 1961-62 included playing bridge with Bob Gibson and his wife. Anderson, Gibson's St. Louis teammate in 1961, went from the 1961-62 champion Santurce team to the 1962 Mets. He made $1,000 a month in Puerto Rico and returned to the States with Gibson, flying first class thanks to Hiram Cuevas, after Santurce's Interamerican Series triumph. "Bob went home to Nebraska, but I didn't have a winter home then," says Anderson. "I visited my family in D.C. and Benton, Illinois, where my wife is from." Anderson particularly enjoyed pitching in Sixto Escobar Stadium during its last season as host to professional baseball. Escobar was to his liking—an old stadium with the fans close to the field.

Santurce shared Escobar with San Juan for 23 straight seasons beginning in 1939-40, the season Santurce joined the league. From 1962-63 through 1973-74, the Crabbers and San Juan played their home games at Hiram Bithorn Stadium. Santurce had Bithorn to itself from 1974-75 through 1981-82, except for several seasons when Caguas used the facility while its own stadium was being remodeled. Santurce played its home games at Bayamón's Loubriel Stadium starting in 1982-83, before returning to Bithorn. The worst experience for Santurce's Jim Beauchamp, who played there in 1964-65, was getting sick as the team bus went over the mountains. So he and a few teammates would fly Prinair, a local airline, instead of taking the bus to Ponce. For Beauchamp, it was the way to go.

Jim Beauchamp played under Preston Gómez at Santurce. Four years later he was with Santurce's archrival San Juan, managed by Sparky Anderson. Beauchamp also played for Caguas, during 1966-67. He was replaced by Orlando Cepeda on Santurce's 1964-65 roster during that season, but played the whole 1968-69 season with San Juan. Winter ball in Puerto Rico and the Dominican Republic helped Beauchamp understand their culture and made him appreciate what Latin players had to go through when they first came to the States. "This helped me patience-wise when I started managing in the minors," says Beauchamp. "I also managed Estrellas and the Escogido team in the Dominican."

Ted Davidson, a lefty reliever, was asked by Tany Pérez late in the 1966 season if he wanted to go down to Puerto Rico and pitch. Hiram Cuevas was making his annual swing through the States in search of talent. "I told Tony, yeah, I'd love to play," said Davidson. "Hiram signed me the next day."

While in Puerto Rico Davidson ate a few meals at Orlando Cepeda's house and befriended many of the native players on Santurce's roster. He roomed with Terín Pizarro on road trips to Ponce and Mayagüez, and they became very good friends. Davidson would bide time on long bus trips by playing cards with Santurce manager Earl Weaver, second baseman Dave Johnson and pitcher Dick Hughes, but Cepeda would fly to these games, according to Davidson.

Dick Hughes claims that one of the highlights that winter was playing hearts with Weaver and the players on the bus trips. For him, Puerto Rico was a true vacation, compared to other winter ball. Hughes pitched for Licey, in the Dominican Republic, in 1961-62, the season after Dominican dictator Trujillo was assassinated. "We were in the Embajador Hotel," he recalls, and "Willie Davis of the Dodgers was there. We only played 18 games, there were strikes, fire bombings going on ... we just stayed in the hotel. I went down there a couple of years later [1963-64] and played the whole season."

There were other differences between Dominican and Puerto Rican winter ball. During his second stint in the Dominican Republic, Hughes would fly to Caracas and Maracaibo, Venezuela, for home-and-home series with Venezuelan clubs. This was a common practice during the mid–1960s, but didn't include games with Puerto Rican, Nicaraguan or Panamanian league teams. All regular-season Puerto Rico League games were held on the Island. The only exception took place on December 20, 1969, when Santurce and Arecibo played a league game in St. Thomas to pay tribute to Elrod Hendricks, the U.S. Virgin Islands star.[17] Hendricks was honored at Lionel Roberts Stadium in his hometown.

Tom Bruno was one American who was swapped during his working vacation. He began with Arecibo, and had the league's best ERA in 1975-76.[18] Early the next season he found himself with Santurce. Bruno went to various Christmas activities with Santurce trainer Nick Acosta and mingled with everyday people, hardworking people with a modest existence who were very nice to him. The laid-back atmosphere in Puerto Rico in the mid- and late–1970s appealed to Bruno, who told me he would have been a 15- to 20-game winner in the majors if he had thrown the same way there as he did in Puerto Rico. "Hiram Cuevas was the GM, and I'll tell you what: If you were doing OK, he was nice to you," said Bruno. "If not, bye-bye."

Ken Dayley and Rick Mahler sparkled for Santurce in 1982-83 and 1983-84, respectively. Dayley and his wife found spiritual peace during the winter season. They lived in several resort areas and had time to sightsee, sample the local food and rejoice in their faith. Mahler, the league's last ten-game winner, didn't think about the young hitters he faced, including Tony Gwynn and Don Mattingly. He spent most of his free time on the golf course in Dorado. This was his sixth year of winter ball; he had previously played in Venezuela and the Dominican Republic. Puerto Rico was easier to adapt to for Mahler, with the U.S. currency and stateside-style restaurants and shops.

Santurce's Chris Gwynn found Puerto Rico rewarding—working on his game, the living conditions, the fans and the food. He played in 1986-87 prior to a season with Licey in the Dominican Republic. Gwynn liked the atmosphere on both islands, but saw differences. In Puerto Rico, he lived in a condo and found fast-food places everywhere. The Dominican experience entailed staying in hotels and relying more on Spanish.

Gwynn: "Puerto Rico was loaded with good players and a lot of fun. You were learning as you were having fun, so it didn't seem like work."

Pitcher David Nied left Puerto Rico on orders from the Atlanta Braves when he approached the 50-inning limit. Nied liked the food and didn't mind the travel, commenting on how pretty the country was, with contrasts between the mountains and the flat areas. He had Thanksgiving dinner with friends in Puerto Rico. Nied and Santurce teammates Ryan Klesko and Turk Wendell rented a car for road trips. "Down where I lived in Isla Verde it was like a vacation for me," says Nied. "I enjoyed it and hated to leave when I did."

Eric Fox patrolled center field for the 1991-92 Crabbers. A substitute teacher for three winters before the 1991-92 season, Fox had played well for the 1991 Tacoma Pacific Coast League team when they faced Mako Oliveras's Edmonton squad. When Atlanta prospects Keith Mitchell and Brian Hunter plans to play in Puerto Rico changed, Fox got a long-distance call from Oliveras asking him if he would like to play for Santurce. Fox flew to Puerto Rico the next day. "Everything's pretty much Americanized," Fox reports. "It's a good situation all around. Winter ball really helped me get into the big leagues with Oakland in 1992. I've always heard that if you came down here and did well, that can prepare you for the next level. That's exactly what it did—it got me to the big leagues."

Fox received a second phone call that winter that enabled him to continue his working vacation. His Santurce club was eliminated from the playoffs, and he had been in California for over a week when the Mayagüez team asked him to join them for the 1992 Caribbean Series. "I said, 'Sure, my tan is fading a bit.' We played in Mexico and enjoyed it. It was something to join a team like Mayagüez, and win it all, a great experience. The series ended ten days before spring training and I was ready to go." When Santurce need a center fielder for the 1993 playoffs, they again called Fox, who played on his second straight Caribbean Series championship team when Santurce won the event.

Mayagüez

Founded in 1760, Mayagüez, a city steeped in tradition, takes its baseball seriously. The origin of its name is derived from the Indian word *yaguex*.[19] An original league franchise, the Mayagüez Indians are linked historically to the India Brewery and Alfonso Valdés, longtime team owner and chief executive of the brewery. The greater Mayagüez region in western Puerto Rico is tranquil and known for its fine beaches, hospitality and seafood.

Charlie Lau caught for Mayagüez during the early 1960s and was an avid diver. Bob Dustal, Gordon Seyfried and Bob Bruce are a trio of Mayagüez hurlers who remember Lau as a very good catcher and an excellent diver. Dustal had many light moments in Puerto Rico. When Lau was with Mayagüez, Dustal had lobster three times a day. Dustal and some other teammates dove with Lau and ended up with so much lobster they didn't know what to do with it all.

Another time, Dustal went on a diving expedition with teammate Boog Powell, and the young slugger got badly sunburned. They went into downtown Mayagüez for suntan lotion, dressed in shorts and no shirts, and almost got arrested for indecent exposure. "If it weren't for the general manager we would have gotten locked up," recalls Dustal. "They called me 'PraPra' in Mayagüez. They were the round straw hats with a brim, worn in the 1920s and '30s. That's what I wore. In fact, ten years after I was done, my hat was still hanging in a Mayagüez barber shop. After we won the championship, my teammates were drinking champagne out of it. Unbelievable!"

The rubber-armed Dustal received a $500 Ocean Star watch for being the league MVP. Dustal: "I tell you what I did, every time I had a good game, I'd go downtown with my wife, and the fans loved me. They'd give me a bottle of rum or scotch and when they knew my wife liked champagne, they gave her champagne. We'd go shopping and come back with a free case of rum. Rum was 99 cents a bottle and they'd just give me cases and cases of that stuff."

Gordon Seyfried, a native of Long Beach, California, was comfortable with his Mayagüez living arrangements in a rented home two blocks from the ocean. The ocean reminded him of home, except that his wife and little girl could walk on the beach and knock coconuts from the palm trees and he would open them with a machete. But he was not comfortable on the long bus trips. "It was kind of scary with those two-lane highways. We always got the same driver, he drove like a madman, he'd drink a little bit when we were at the games . . . knew where [water] spigots were on the road, stop the bus, go out there and put his head under them to sober up. We held our breath going around the corners, and he'd use the horn. Those mountain roads were so narrow."

Seyfried recalls the night in San Juan when a former high school classmate who worked with the FBI came to the ballpark and spoke with him. His friend was assigned to President Kennedy during a visit to Puerto Rico, but Kennedy wasn't at the game. When Kennedy was assassinated, in 1963, Seyfried was playing with the Ponce Lions and lived in the Darlington. He remembers the Island shutting down for a couple of days and the people taking the president's death very hard.

Bob Bruce found out his contract had been purchased from Detroit by the expansion Houston Colt 45s while on a bus trip from Mayagüez to San Juan. It was the 1961-62 season, Bruce's third in Puerto Rico. He loved Puerto Rico and went back.

Bruce kept busy between games by coaching a grade school basketball team in Mayagüez. He says he will never forget the mornings when he would get the milk and paper only to find a dozen kids from the basketball team eagerly waiting for him. Bruce lived in the Darlington Apartments, the tallest building in Mayagüez at the time. The kids would get a big kick going up and down the elevator. They enjoyed going swimming with Bruce as well as practicing basketball.

When Bruce was at the Polo Grounds, and later at Shea Stadium, pitching for Houston against the Mets, he would hear his name being shouted from the stands. He was in for a pleasant surprise. "Somebody was yelling, 'It's Bruce! It's Bruce!' Some of the kids I coached in Mayagüez had moved to New York City with their families. It got to where I'd look for them in the stands. I just loved the people and had a great time."

Rick Dempsey spent a lot of his free time in 1975-76 and 1976-77 catching and eating lobster off Puerto Rico's west coast when he was not putting on the catcher's "tools of ignorance" for Mayagüez. He lived in Rincón, a peaceful west-coast town which has hosted international surfing events. Dempsey's two winters in Puerto Rico followed five seasons of Venezuelan baseball. He needed the winter work to make up for his lack of big league playing time.

The Mayagüez organization went to great lengths in the 1980s, under owner Luis Gómez, to ensure that imports were well taken care of. Players including Brett Butler, Dan Gladden, Tom Candiotti, Andy Van Slyke, Sid Bream, Terry Pendleton, Wally Joyner, Tom Pagnozzi, Jeff Brantley and Harold Reynolds enjoyed the relaxed atmosphere in the Joyudas sector of Cabo Rojo, where many imports lived.

Iván Méndez, who has been Mayagüez's owner since 1989-90, arranged fishing trips for Gladden and Bream when he worked for Mayagüez in lesser capacities. One outing during the 1985-86 season involved Bobby Bonilla, Harold Reynolds, Wayne Rowdon and Wally Joyner. It was a fishing trip to El Combate, near the beautiful Boquerón beach off Puerto Rico's southwest coast. The ballplayers took turns diving from the vessel, swam, and drank soda pop.

Pat Zachry was pitching for Mayagüez in 1985-86 at age 33. The ten-year major leaguer had first pitched for Bayamón in 1977-78, the winter after he was involved in the Tom Seaver trade between the Mets and Cincinnati. That season had had a honeymoon atmosphere, since he had gotten married in the middle of the 1977 big league season. His winter with Mayagüez was a bit different, since family members stayed in the States to recover from an accident. "When we played San Juan I'd go to the mall [Plaza Las Américas] with Tim Belcher, Dave Sax and sometimes Wally Joyner and Harold Reynolds went with us," says Zachry. "We'd get up early and drive there and see a movie before the game."

Zachry found a fun and relaxed atmosphere in the league. He pitched well both seasons and played on a Mayagüez team that won the league title. Zachry appreciated the first winter with Bayamón after the frustration of being traded to the Mets the year after he won a World Series game. He finished his career on a good note with Mayagüez, knowing he could still pitch effectively.

Mayagüez pitcher Jeff Brantley and his wife Cindy appreciated the warmth and hospitality of team officials, teammates and Island residents. Tom Pagnozzi was one of Brantley's teammates and neighbors in the late 1980s, and they carpooled to the games. Brantley recalls the "Indian of the Week" ceremony at the Mayagüez Bowling Alley (Bolera de Mayagüez) and other pastimes. "Every Thursday they had the ceremony at the bowling alley," said Brantley. "We were there with our wives and had a great time. We stayed right on the beach in Cabo Rojo, could surf in Rincón and golf at Dorado. I liked the food at the Metropol in San Juan. The oranges we bought for ten cents a bag were something else!"

Ismael Trabal, Mayagüez's public relations director at the time, remembers Brantley earning several "Indian of the Week" awards in the 1988-89 season, and recalls interviewing him throughout that season. Brantley was extremely cordial and respectful with the press and fans. This positive attitude enhanced Brantley's working vacation.

Working vacations in Puerto Rico have served their purpose on and off the field. Ballplayers who come to the Island with an open mind and a good work ethic tend to focus on the positive aspects of winter ball. They become better human beings for it.

3. ROBERTO CLEMENTE, #21

> *Roberto Clemente has served as an inspiration to me since my days as an amateur baseball player in Nicaragua. He is the reason why I devote so much time and energy to charitable work for youth.*
> —Dennis Martínez, former Caguas and Santurce pitcher

Roberto Clemente Walker chose uniform number 21 since his full name had 21 letters.[1] By doing so, Clemente honored his parents and upheld Puerto Rico's tradition of using two surnames. "Number 21" also paid homage to all Puerto Rican families and baseball fans with this choice. A proud human being and intense competitor, Roberto wore #21 in the Puerto Rico Winter League for three different teams—the Santurce Crabbers, the Caguas Criollos and the San Juan Senators.

Clemente's 15-year Winter League career spanned three decades. He won one batting title in 1956-57 with the decade's highest batting average—.396—and hit .323 lifetime. As a player, he contributed to five Puerto Rican League championships including the one earned by the 1954-55 Santurce club, considered by many the best Winter League team of all time. In his two managing stints with San Juan, Clemente led the team to the playoffs both times.

In 1952 Pedrín Zorrilla, owner of the Santurce baseball club, received a tip from Roberto Marín, a salesman for Puerto Rico's Sello Rojo Rice Company. Marín was managing a youth softball team for Sello Rojo when he discovered the 14-year-old Clemente hitting empty tomato cans with sticks—hitting them a long distance.[2] Clemente progressed from Marín's softball team to Juncos in Puerto Rico's AA amateur league. When Juncos played an exhibition game in Manatí, Pedrín Zorrilla's hometown, Zorrilla was impressed with Clemente's skills and offered him a $40 weekly contract and a $400 signing bonus for the 1952-53 professional baseball season.[3]

Roberto Clemente at the plate for the 1964-65 San Juan Senators (courtesy of *The San Juan Star*).

Santurce Crabbers

Clemente joined a talented Santurce club destined to win Puerto Rican and Caribbean Series titles. The Crabbers featured a solid outfield with former Kansas City Monarchs star Willard Brown, Pacific Coast League standout Bob Thurman, who had played for the Homestead Grays, ex–Negro leaguer Johnny Davis and Milwaukee Braves prospect Billy Bruton. They were strong up the middle with Junior Gilliam at second and Billy Hunter at short. Player-manager Buster Clarkson covered the hot corner and was one of the league's most dangerous sluggers. Clarkson, a Negro league, Texas League, and Pacific Coast League star, played 14 games for the 1952 Boston Braves. Future major league backstop Valmy Thomas handled the aces of the pitching staff, soon-to-be New York Giant Rubén Gómez and the pride of St. Louis Browns' owner Bill Veeck, Bobo Holloman. Billy Hunter, the 1952 Texas League MVP, remembers the 18-year-old Clemente as a quiet, hard-working rookie. "Clemente was just a kid," recalls Hunter. "I don't think he got much playing time."

Buster Clarkson brought the rookie along slowly. He gave the youngster's confidence a boost by sending him in to pinch-hit for Bob Thurman against Caguas hurler Roberto Vargas, "the Joe Page of Puerto Rico." Clemente responded by doubling in the game-winning run, and later called this the highlight of his early professional career.[4]

Clemente, a .234 hitter in the 1952-53 season, was a spectator during most of postseason play. He cheered on Bob Thurman, a man twice his age, when the lefty slugger drove in seven runs as Santurce trounced San Juan, 15-5, in game five of the finals.[5] Jackie Robinson happened to be in town and watched his future Dodger teammate Junior Gilliam rap four hits and play flawlessly at second base. Santurce went on to win game six, and their momentum continued in Havana, Cuba, as they finished 6-0 in the fifth Caribbean Series against squads from Cuba, Panama and Venezuela.

Clemente was ready to crack Santurce's starting lineup by the time October 1953 rolled around. He played in 66 of the team's 80 games and hit .288, the sixth-best league average.[6] Santurce, however, finished in the basement of the five-team league. Bob Thurman and Willard Brown had subpar seasons; Jim Gilliam, who had been the 1953 National League Rookie of the Year with Brooklyn, opted not to return; and Bobo Holloman left the team with a sore arm and an 0-2 record. Pitcher Tom Lasorda picked up some of the slack with seven wins, but it wasn't enough. Santurce's woes were compounded by a four-week suspension and $75 fine to player-manager Clarkson for allegedly spitting in the face of a home plate umpire. Local scribes duly noted that this marked the first controversy in Clarkson's 11-year Puerto Rican career.[7]

Clemente could not help but notice the exploits of a 19-year-old Milwaukee Braves prospect named Henry Aaron, the right fielder for league and Caribbean Series champion Caguas. Mickey Owen, Caguas's manager, wanted Clemente in his outfield. Owen's left fielder, Tetelo Vargas, was 47 years old, with former big leaguer Luis Olmo in reserve. "Aaron and Clemente would have been something else," muses Owen now. "We had the veteran Olmo as trade bait for Clemente, but a deal couldn't be worked out."

By the time Clemente was signed by the Brooklyn Dodgers, on February 19, 1954, for a $10,000 bonus and $5,000 salary for 1954, Hank

Aaron had left Puerto Rico. The Caribbean Series was being played in San Juan's Sixto Escobar Stadium, the same ballpark where Clemente had participated in a Dodger tryout. Al Campanis witnessed Clemente run two 6.4-second 60-yard dashes and hit line drives all over the lot.[8]

After a lackluster season with Montreal, where he played sporadically, Clemente was itching to wear the Santurce flannels again. Jack Cassini, a teammate of Clemente's with Montreal in 1954, played winter ball for the San Juan club in 1953-54 and 1954-55. "Brooklyn tried to hide him. In the seventh or eighth innings he would replace me for defensive purposes," says Cassini. "But I had played against him in Puerto Rico and knew what he could do. Later on, he autographed a bat for my youngest daughter at the 1971 All-Star Game in Detroit. What a nice guy."

Clemente had earned the respect of his American, Puerto Rican, Dominican and U.S. Virgin Islands teammates, not to mention the Santurce batboy. He would soon show his worth to a new Santurce manager, Herman Franks. Santurce firmed up their working agreement with the New York Giants and Franks, Leo Durocher's third base coach for the world champion 1954 Giants, accepted the job. Franks was familiar with winter ball, having managed the Magallanes club in the Venezuelan league the previous season.

Herman Franks put in a good word for Clemente to Branch Rickey, Jr., of the Pittsburgh Pirates before the November 22, 1954, major league draft. Clemente was the first pick of the draft and one of 13 minor leaguers taken out of 3,640 eligible players.[9] The Pirates got a bargain because under the new rules Pittsburgh had to pay only a $4,000 bonus for Clemente instead of the AAA rate of $10,000.

There was plenty of other excitement for Clemente and the Puerto Rican fans that winter. Of special interest to Santurce followers was the presence of Willie Mays in the starting lineup. There are several possible reasons for why Mays went to Puerto Rico. For one, Giants owner Horace Stoneham wanted to repay Santurce executive Zorrilla for alerting him to Rubén Gómez in 1953.[10] There was also a comfort level in having Mays play winter ball under the likeable Franks. Another reason may have been the distractions in New York City over the winter months making demands on Mays's time. Mays and Clemente were two of Santurce's youngest regulars. As the season wore on, Clemente played some games in centerfield when Mays was off the Island on trips to the States. Clemente took this responsibility seriously and wanted to show the fans he could play on a par with the Giants' superstar.

Canenita Allen, Santurce's new batboy in 1954-55, had developed a close friendship with Clemente during Roberto's days as a teenager in Carolina, Puerto Rico. The friendship continued in spite of Allen's being the San Juan batboy for several seasons prior to taking the Santurce job.

Early in the 1954-55 season, Allen would observe Willie Mays working with Roberto on outfield play well before game time at Sixto Escobar Stadium. This stadium is located near the Atlantic Ocean and the swirling trade winds could make outfield play tricky. Willie Mays lived a hop, skip and jump from Escobar, as did other Santurce imports, and enjoyed spending time at this ballpark.

Clemente was busy off the field, too, and graduated with a high school diploma from the Rio Piedras Business Institute on December 14. During the first two months of the 1954-55 season he would take morning classes and then shift gears to play baseball. The media were also interested in the young outfielder. El Mundo's sports editor Elmo Torres Pérez, interviewed Clemente and reported that some of his baseball skills could be traced to his prowess in other sports. Clemente's swift and accurate throws from the outfield were due to his being a top-notch javelin thrower, and his time of 52 seconds in the 400-meter dash was very good for high school athletes in the 1950s.[11]

Through 50 games of the 72-game season, Mays was hitting .404, with Clemente following at .378. For good measure, Bob Thurman, third in the batting race at that point, was hitting .366![12] Santurce outdistanced their four rivals with a 47-25 record. They won the league playoffs and the Caribbean Series crown. The Crabbers' powerful lineup included five sluggers—Clemente, Mays, Thurman, Clarkson and George Crowe—nicknamed "Murderers Row." Mays ended the season at .395 and added the Puerto Rico League batting title and MVP award to his trophy case. Clemente finished third in hitting at .344. Bob Thurman, still going strong at 37, showed the 23-year-old Mays and the 20-year Clemente he could still hit for average (.323) and power (14 homers, 60 RBIs). Thurman also sported a 2-0 record as a pitcher. Clarkson led the team in homers (15) and RBIs (61). First sacker George Crowe drilled 12 homers and drove in 40. Middle infielders Don Zimmer and Ronnie Samford played inspired baseball. The catching was in good hands with Valmy Thomas and Harry Chiti. Veteran flychasers Luis Olmo and Virgin Islander Alfonso Gerard produced as role players. "Sad Sam" Jones (14-4), Rubén Gómez (13-4) and Bill Greason (8-2) formed the best pitching trio in the league.[13]

Pete Burnside was a 24-year-old Dartmouth graduate with a degree in sociology who experienced the camaraderie and team chemistry of the 1954-55 Crabbers. In Burnside's opinion, the older Negro leagues players Thurman, Clarkson and Crowe provided important emotional and psychological balance to the team.

Mays made a late-season trip to the States to receive the Sid Mercer Award in New York City as the 1954 Player of the Year. As had not been the case with Hank Aaron a year earlier, the Giants gave Mays the green light to play in the Caribbean Series should Santurce qualify.

Santurce was at full strength in its playoff series with defending league and Caribbean champion Caguas. Clemente had four hits in Santurce's 10–3 opening win. The Crabbers took the series, four games to one. Buster Clarkson (.563) paced all hitters, but it was the pesky Don Zimmer, called "El Soldadito" (The Little Soldier) by Santurce fans, who took slugging honors with three homers and ten RBIs.[14]

Zimmer continued his torrid hitting in the Caribbean Series, played in Caracas, Venezuela, as Santurce won its first five games before dropping a meaningless contest to finish 5-1. Mays broke out of an 0-for-12 slump in game three with a two-run homer off Venezuela's Ramón Monzant in the bottom of the eleventh inning with Clemente on base to give Santurce a 4–2 win.[15]

It had been the happiest three months of Roberto Clemente's life. He got his diploma and a new lease on life with the Pirates; his fielding skills improved; and the sportswriters were busy keeping tabs on his and Willie Mays's batting averages. The fans and writers took pride in the fact that Clemente was the first Puerto Rican to hit two homers in the league All-Star Game. Only Josh Gibson and Hank Aaron had previously accomplished this feat.[16]

Bob Thurman was happy to be a part of it all. Clemente, Mays and the other teammates were his "family." His brilliant play in 1954-55 also earned him a major league shot, albeit in the twilight of his career, with Cincinnati. Today, Thurman puts it in perspective: "I've often thought about that kind of setup we had. I often thought we could beat any [major league] club."

When the 1955-56 season got underway, Clemente was 21 years old. He gave Puerto Rico's fans and manager Herman Franks another solid season, hitting .306 with 7 homers and 30 RBIs.[17] There were new faces on the team—Bill White and Daryl Spencer, as well as promising native players, Orlando Cepeda, José Pagán and Julio Navarro under the Giants' wing. Hard-throwing southpaw Terín Pizarro from the Milwaukee organization made his debut that season.

A first-place finish was dampened by injuries, illness and player turnover during the latter portion of the season. Bob Thurman was challenging Vic Power for the batting title when his campaign was ended by a shoulder injury. Daryl Spencer was traded to Caguas for outfielder Allie Clark, and would come back to haunt Santurce in the playoffs. Don Zimmer bounced back from an early-season wrist injury after being hit by a pitch, only to have an appendectomy knock him out of the picture.

Bill Greason was sporting a 6-4 record when Santurce released him to pitch for Licey in the Dominican winter league. Greason, who started his Negro leagues career in 1948 with the Birmingham Black Barons along with 17-year-old Willie Mays, has fond memories of Clemente. "I called

Santurce's "Murderers Row," 1954-55 season. *Left to right:* **Willie Mays, Roberto Clemente, Buster Clarkson, Bob Thurman and George Crowe** (courtesy of Diana Zorrilla).

Roberto *'hermano'* [brother].... We were real close," says Greason. "He was a very fine young man, dedicated and determined. Wouldn't say too much, just come to the clubhouse and speak to some of the guys, get his uniform on, field infield grounders, then go to the outfield. He had a fine disposition."

Caguas avenged the pasting it had taken from the Crabbers' 1954-55 "Murderers Row" by taking four of the six final-series games from Santurce. Steve Ridzik outdueled Caguas's Tom Lasorda, 1-0, in the 11-inning second game.[18] Ridzik, the league's top pitcher with a 14-3 record, had this to say about the young Clemente: "When you saw Clemente, you knew there was a lot of talent. I didn't know how far it was going, but to me, he was the Hall of Fame-type guy — very, very capable. You could see that in Clemente."

An era came to an end at Christmastime 1956, when Pedrín Zorrilla was forced to raise $30,000 to erase team debts.[19] Zorrilla, who had owned the club since its inception in 1939, was an altruistic and kind soul who cared more about his players than about the bottom line. Pete Burnside called him a "prince of a man." Burnside was released shortly before the end of the 1954-55 season, but was allowed to travel with Santurce to the Caribbean Series and to pitch batting practice.

Zorrilla sold his beloved Crabbers to businessman Ramón Cuevas, who promptly recouped his investment. On December 30, 1956, Cuevas entered the visitors' clubhouse at Mayagüez prior to a twin bill and informed the Santurce players that Roberto Clemente, Terín Pizarro and Ronnie Samford were now Caguas property as the result of a $30,000 sale.[20] Rubén Gómez was so livid he took off his uniform, stormed out of the clubhouse and drove home. Ironically, Gómez was such a good athlete that he replaced Clemente in the Santurce outfield. Years later, Marcial Allen tearfully recalled Clemente's reaction. "Roberto told me to grab the stuff," said Allen. "'You're coming to Caguas with me.' He was a brother and a friend."

Caguas Criollos

Clemente joined Caguas in the midst of an 18-game hitting streak, with his batting average over .400. Two weeks before the sale was announced, Clemente had kept his hitting streak alive with Santurce's only two safeties off Caguas's Sandy Koufax in a 2–0 loss to the fireballer.[21] By a strange turn of events, this was Koufax's final game in Puerto Rico, thanks to a newly implemented league ruling restricting the number of major leaguers on Puerto Rico's rosters.

The hitting streak reached 23 games after game one of a January 5, 1957, doubleheader with San Juan.[22] This broke the standard of 22 set by Francisco "Pancho" Coímbre of Ponce during the 1943-44 season. An old friend, Tite Arroyo, put an end to the streak when he collared Roberto in game two of the twin bill. Tom Lasorda took the loss for Caguas. "I was his teammate with Santurce and Caguas," Lasorda recalls. "What a great competitor. With Caguas we had Power, Mantilla, Luke Easter, Wes Covington, Koufax—some tremendous ballplayers."

When the regular season ended, Caguas and San Juan were tied for third place with identical 39-33 records. A tie-breaker was played at Caguas to decide the final playoff qualifier. San Juan manager Ralph Houk gave the ball to Tite Arroyo on only one day of rest. Terín Pizarro took the mound for Caguas. Arroyo prevailed, 4-1, but all eyes were on Clemente, who entered the day hitting .398. He would need a two-for-four day to reach .400, but fell short with one hit in four trips as his average dipped to .396.[23]

Tite Arroyo knew Roberto quite well, as the result of a favor he had done for Pedrín Zorrilla in the spring of 1954. At Zorrilla's request, Arroyo had accompanied Clemente on the latter's first stateside spring training trip. According to Arroyo, he flew with Clemente to Miami, purchased two bus tickets for the trip to the Dodgers' camp and checked Roberto into a hotel before leaving the next morning for the St. Louis training camp in Daytona. Arroyo then sent the bill to Pedrín Zorrilla.

When postseason awards were announced for 1956-57, José "Ronquito" García of Mayagüez garnered the MVP.[24] He finished second to Clemente in hitting, at .333, but propelled Mickey Owen's ball club to the Puerto Rico title. García remembers Clemente getting three or four hits whenever he would have two or three in a game. "Give Roberto credit for the batting title," he says. "We won the championship, and that's why the writers voted me the MVP."

Marcial Allen earned a roster spot with Caguas in 1957-58 as Clemente rested his ailing back. The former batboy earned his spurs by being named the league's Rookie of the Year. Allen and Clemente were reunited on January 12, 1958, when Roberto put on the Caguas uniform for the first time that season. Clemente received a standing ovation from 4,387 fans in Ponce's Paquito Montaner Stadium.[25] Roberto Clemente was primed for the 1958 finals against Santurce. He hit .529 to lead Caguas past Santurce in four straight as the Criollos claimed the championship.[26] Terín Pizarro and Ronnie Samford, holdovers from the "sale," did their part.

Caguas fans were looking forward to Clemente's return in 1958-59, but learned of his six-month commitment with the U.S. Marine Corps at Parris Island, South Carolina. Clemente completed the service program in time to join the 1959 Pirates, but spent only two weeks on leave in Puerto Rico that winter. The Caguas management was concerned that Clemente had played in only nine regular-season games over the past two winter seasons.

Marcial Allen found himself in the middle of another twist in his idol's fortunes. During the winter of 1958-59 Clemente, Allen and lanky, right-handed hurler Palillo Santiago were dealt to the San Juan Senators for two minor league native players and a reported $30,000.[27] Herminio Cortés and Rafael Sálamo were the outfield duo received by Caguas. At the time, Cortés had completed a season with York and Sálamo with Sioux City in the low minors. Marcial Allen insisted he was "insurance policy" in case Clemente was unable to play.

San Juan Senators

San Juan kept Clemente under contract at intervals over the next 12 years. He had something to prove in 1959-60, after three straight subpar big league seasons. Clemente was fit and running more, as attested by his 12 stolen bases in 57 Puerto Rico League games.[28] By season's end his .330 average was good for third place, behind Vic Power (.347) and Guito Conde

(.336).[29] Despite his strong performance, Clemente fell short in the MVP balloting to Conde of the Mayagüez club. Conde had a 17-year minor league career, but only a cup of coffee with the 1962 White Sox.

Nino Escalera, San Juan's player-manager, was in his thirteenth year with San Juan and related well to his star player. "Caguas wanted a power hitter and we had Cortés [a 10-homer producer in 1958-59]," says Escalera. "They thought Clemente wasn't going to play, but he was there for us."

Several of Clemente's teammates with the 1954-55 Santurce club were back in Puerto Rico. Pete Burnside hurled for Mayagüez through their working agreement with the Detroit Tigers. He had the utmost respect for Clemente, and it deepened after Roberto hit a long homer off him for San Juan's only run in a Mayagüez victory. Bob Thurman, Clemente's role model during his first two years in the league, was released by Ponce along with three other imports in a move to save money. The 42-year-old Thurman bowed out with class.

The San Juan games were broadcast by radio in English and Spanish during the 1959-60 season, thanks to the efforts of businessman Bob Leith. Phil Rizzuto was hired to do the games in English, while Luis Olmo did the Spanish transmissions. It marked the first time in Puerto Rican history that radio broadcasts of baseball games were carried in both languages.[30] Clemente was an inspirational leader on the scrappy San Juan club, which won the regular-season title and advanced to the finals. Tite Arroyo won 11 games and Jack Fisher had 13 wins. Carlos Bernier, the league's all-time stolen base leader with 285, hustled on the bases and in the outfield.

San Juan lost the best-of-nine finals to Caguas in six games as Tommy Davis, José Pagan, Félix Mantilla, Earl Wilson and Roberto Vargas came through for player-manager Vic Power. Power, who played with and against Clemente, and had briefly managed him at Caguas, was an established big leaguer by February 1960, but Clemente was not. Power still remembers Clemente playing in Puerto Rico with a bad back. "Even though he played hurt, Roberto toiled with pride and was a winner," says Power. "Because of his bad back, I wasn't sure Roberto was going to be the superstar he became with Pittsburgh from 1960 on, but felt he would always give his best effort."

Bob Leith was the new San Juan owner in 1960-61. He recalls his mistake of not sending player contracts out by the June 1 deadline. As a result of the oversight all San Juan players were technically free agents, and the press and radio stations made an issue out of this. Clemente came through like a true professional, and Leith remembers their phone conversation. "Forget about it," said Clemente. "I'll sign for the same amount I made last year, $1,500 per month."

Clemente was everybody's hero in Puerto Rico by the time the 1960-61 season began. The Pirates were world champions and Clemente had hit safely in all seven of the Fall Classic games against the Yankees. He was a hero in his homeland, but a tired one. Roberto took a couple of months off.

The timing of the rest was good. In a new format, the five league teams would play a "split" season of 32 first-half games and an equal number of second-half contests. Winners would face off in a best-of-nine series. When Clemente joined San Juan, they had compiled a sluggish 16-16 mark in the first half. With Clemente on the roster San Juan was 23-9 and earned a playoff berth. In 29 games, he hit .284.[31] His buddy Marcial Allen played strong baseball and finished at .275. Tite Arroyo won 10 games and the MVP award.[32] Ronnie Samford joined Clemente once more on a championship team and was a crowd favorite. Jerry Adair at short and third baseman Germán Rivera provided solid defense on the left side. Mack Jones supplied some punch. Virgin Islander Horace Clarke played superbly as a utility infielder and remembers Clemente being very nice to all the young San Juan players.

Clemente and company avenged their loss to Caguas a year earlier by winning the best-of-nine series in eight games. It was time for the Interamerican Series in Caracas, Venezuela. Havana, Cuba, was slated to host the 1961 Caribbean Series, but the tense political situation in Cuba resulted in the cancellation of the event. A hastily arranged series pitted the winners of the Puerto Rican and Panamanian league titles against the top two Venezuelan clubs.

San Juan reinforced itself with Orlando Cepeda and Terín Pizarro from Santurce. They were the team to beat, but ran into 18 innings of smoke courtesy of St. Louis pitcher Bob Gibson of the Valencia, Venezuela, club, the Valencia Industrialists. He allowed two San Juan runs on eight hits over his two games. The second win was a 1–0 gem.[33] Bob Leith recalls Clemente's reaction to seeing Bob Gibson warming up prior to his first start against San Juan. "Clemente says to me, 'we're in trouble.' I say, 'why?'" "'You see that pitcher warming up? Well, he throws aspirins!'"

Bob Leith had a few headaches before this series. San Juan's American players wanted more money for playing in Venezuela. It was Clemente who came to the rescue. "Clemente told me, 'Bob, let me handle this,'" says Leith. "So he closed the door to our dressing room and Clemente reminded them [the American players] that their contract said they get the same salary for playing in the Interamerican Series as they got back in Puerto Rico. That anyone who refused to honor their contract, he would be the first one to pick up the phone and call [Commissioner] Ford Frick." Leith called this ten-minute episode the shortest strike in baseball history. None of the imports argued with Clemente.

The Arecibo Wolves joined the league as an expansion team in 1961-62. Luis Olmo, a native of Arecibo, came home to manage them. Arecibo had a working agreement with the Milwaukee Braves, who sent Bob Uecker, Phil Niekro, Lee Maye and Tommie Aaron to the Wolves. Moe Drabowsky, Ed Charles and Cookie Rojas played inspired ball for Arecibo. When San Juan was floundering in fifth place with a 23-33 record, their fans were clamoring for the 1961 National League batting champion to make his debut.

Clemente laced on his spikes and sprang into action. San Juan won 18 of their next 24 games to finish the 80-game schedule with a record identical to Arecibo's, 41-39.[34] It was time for the fourth-place teams to play a tie-breaker at Sixto Escobar Stadium. This was the final "regular season" game played at Escobar, since the new stadium, Hiram Bithorn, was going to be inaugurated in 1962-63. Over 8,000 fans were on hand January 23, 1962, as Arecibo battled San Juan.[35] Phil Niekro was knocked out early, and by the time Clemente stepped into the hitter's box in the bottom of the second inning, it was a 3-3 game and the bases were loaded. Claude Raymond was on the mound. Germán Rivera, the Arecibo shortstop, takes it from here: "Roberto bounced one up the middle on a 3-2 pitch. There was a close play at first base and umpire Mel Steiner called him out. Nino Escalera and Napoleón Reyes [San Juan's manager] came up to Steiner and there were punches thrown. I intervened and helped break up the fight." In the melée, Steiner suffered torn ligaments in his left arm and a shoulder sprain. Nino Escalera was beside himself, claiming Steiner had had his hand up with the "out" sign before the ball reached first base.

Escalera: "I was willing to go back on the field when Steiner sarcastically told Reyes, our Cuban manager, to go back to Cuba. I told Reyes he should not take this and then it happened." Reyes ran to the field and bumped Steiner with his huge belly. Several San Juan players were involved in the skirmish. When peace was restored, Escalera was sent to the showers for the only time in his 17-year league playing career.

Clemente's version was made public in *El Mundo* three days later. According to Clemente, Tommie Aaron did not tag him nor have his foot on the bag. "Steiner's angle was not a good one. I argued the call. But my teammate Chico Ruiz grabbed me to keep Steiner from giving me the heave. If I had said something vulgar or even hit Steiner, he would have thumbed me out of the game."[36]

A hearing was later held, attended by the game umpires—Doug Harvey, Paul Pryor and Steiner—and by Clemente, Escalera and Reyes. Escalera was fined $50 and suspended for the first ten games of the next season, Reyes got a stiffer penalty—a $100 fine and a three-week suspension at the beginning of the 1962-63 season and Clemente was exonerated.[37] With the exception of 1963-64 and 1964-65, Clemente played sporadically the rest of the decade. He skipped the 1962-63, 1966-67 and 1968-69 seasons and made two pinch-hitting appearances in 1965-66.

Jerry McNertney, a 27-year-old catcher from Boone, Iowa, saw a hitter driving bullets into the outfield of Hiram Bithorn Municipal Stadium on a warm November 1963 afternoon. The White Sox prospect asked one of his San Juan teammates who the hitter wearing #21 was. McNertney had replaced John Bateman on the San Juan roster. He used his .333 mark that winter to claim a spot with the 1964 White Sox.[38] This San Juan team had a Chisox flavor, with Deacon Jones, Don Buford, Joel Horlen and Marv Staehle on the roster. It was more than a "working agreement," in the opinion of staff ace Palillo Santiago. A chemistry had developed between the White Sox prospects and other players on the team. Santiago called it a "bond" which continued well into the 1960s each time he encountered Buford, McNertney and others when his Red Sox played the White Sox. "Clemente played every winter game hard—to win," recalls McNertney. "He played 150-plus big league games, plus spring training. It had to be tough for him even though it was in front of his home fans. To see him come there and work so hard was very impressive."

Marv Staehle, San Juan's shortstop, asserted that Clemente never forgot where he came from. Staehle: "His people were first, and he played because of that. He didn't need to play; he loved the people over there and that's why he played. I speak proudly that I was a teammate of his."

Arecibo's Tony Oliva won the 1963-64 batting title at .365 as Clemente claimed the runner-up spot with a .345 figure.[39] It would be the final time Clemente had enough plate appearances to qualify for the Puerto Rican hitting crown. He began to play a month into the season and was soon in mid-season form. There was one managerial change during the season, with Les Moss replacing Joe Buzas about the time Clemente was activated.

Clemente was on his final league championship team, as the Senators, who finished the season in third place, at just 35-35, peaked at the right time. San Juan got the pitching in playoff wins over Ponce and Mayagüez. Joel Horlen was superb in the finals, with two victories against the latter team. Tite Arroyo had enough left in his 36-year-old arm to save a few games. And Palillo Santiago still remembers the best catch made by Clemente that winter: "In the finals against Mayagüez, I had a one-run lead with two outs in the ninth. Boog Powell was at the plate. I threw him a fastball. It was some 420 feet to dead center in Mayagüez and quite dark. The lights weren't too bright in that part of the stadium. Powell got hold of it, but Clemente was playing in center. He turned around, slid into the fence. It must have been dead quiet for five minutes, when I realized he caught the ball with his back facing the infield. The game was over."

The San Juan team flew to Managua, Nicaragua, for the Interamerican Series. It was Clemente's first trip to this Central American republic— but not his last one. Two Nicaraguan teams, the Panama champions and

San Juan vied for the title. Venezuela's top two teams, Caracas and Valencia, played a series in Santo Domingo with the Licey and Aguilas clubs. The Senators bolstered their team with Orlando Cepeda, Guito Conde, José Pagán and Terín Pizarro. As far as the Nicaraguan fans, writers and players were concerned, the San Juan team was invincible. But Nicaragua's Cinco Estrellas club won five of their six games to claim the title.

Clemente had a tough series. He lost a fly ball in the sun. José "Cocó" Laboy was sent to pinch-hit for Roberto and cracked a double. To compound matters, a fan in the bleachers threw a huge iguana toward Clemente in right field and he bolted to the dugout. According to Palillo Santiago, there were Nicaraguan soldiers in the dugout bearing rifles. Santiago spoke for his teammates when he claimed they felt like prisoners during this series. He remembers Clemente being reluctant to leave the dugout after the iguana incident. In spite of all this, Clemente was a fan favorite and made a lot of friends in Nicaragua. "What an irony," Santiago notes. "This experience is transformed into a mission to help the people of Nicaragua and history tells us what Roberto Clemente did for that country."

The iguana incident did not affect Clemente's hitting. He returned to Puerto Rico for the winter of 1964-65 after a 1964 big league season capped by his second senior circuit batting crown. Clemente had a busy winter that included his marriage to Vera Cristina Zabala, a freak lawn mowing accident and his designation as San Juan's manager.

It was a sentimental winter for other reasons. Bob Thurman was named manager of the Estrellas club in the Dominican League shortly before Clemente took his spot on the San Juan roster.[40] When Cal Ermer was let go as San Juan's manager on December 21, 1964, Clemente received an early Christmas present with his appointment to manage the team.[41] Ten years earlier, Clemente and Thurman had made their points on the playing field. Now they were asked to bring their skills and leadership qualities to the forefront in other ways.

As player-manager Clemente kept San Juan in the playoff hunt. He played in 14 games and hit .385.[42] It must have felt strange to him, inserting #21 into the starting lineup in his managerial debut against the Mayagüez team and their pitching prospect from Detroit, Denny McLain. In that game, Roberto drilled two doubles while driving in a pair of runs. He twisted his left ankle on the second extra-base hit and took himself out of the lineup for a few games. San Juan was 0-4 under Clemente when they defeated Arecibo, 4–3, in game two of a December 27 twin bill.[43] They continued to play well, finished fourth, qualifying for the playoffs.

There was no question as to how much Clemente meant to the league as a player and manager. A night was held in his honor on December 30, 1964, when San Juan played Ponce. Clemente received a huge trophy from San Juan's board of directors. Ponce owner Yuyo González and team official Carlos Negrón presented him with a plaque. A trio of Santurce fans gave Clemente a trophy on behalf of the team's loyal following.

Cal Ermer, San Juan's deposed manager, recalls that the San Juan brass wanted Clemente to manage so he would play on an everyday basis. Ermer attended Clemente's wedding and liked him a lot. "Roberto had just started playing and we lost a tough doubleheader," says Ermer. "The owners asked me to resign. But I told them, 'I didn't come here to resign, so put it in the paper and fire me.' Clemente was always hustling and played hard just like in the States. The first game he managed, he got hurt."

Don Buford led the San Juan regulars in hitting and developed a fine rapport with Clemente. Suffering from a bad knee, Buford would accompany Clemente on visits to a chiropractor. Buford remembers the managing responsibilities caused a little added pressure on Roberto, but notes he was very loose, in a sense, and did not interfere with his players. "A typical Clemente pep talk was, 'You guys know how to play; stay fundamentally sound and we'll be OK,'" says Buford. "It wasn't like Clemente had the San Juan players do additional things."

In the playoffs Clemente's old Santurce team was simply too strong, with sluggers Orlando Cepeda and Tany Pérez, middle infielders Marv Staehle and Art Miranda and pitchers Terín Pizarro, Rubén Gómez, Fred Talbot and George Brunet. Santurce defeated San Juan in six games and went on to win the finals against Mayagüez.[44]

The lawn mowing accident at Clemente's Rio Piedras home that winter involved a sharp rock that got caught in the mower and hit him on the thigh. It happened when he was managing San Juan, so he felt comfortable inserting Marcial Allen's name into the lineup. Clemente felt better by the time the league All-Star Game was held, this year pitting North American players against Latin Americans, and told Luis Olmo, the skipper of the Latin American squad, he was available to pinch-hit. When Olmo summoned him, Clemente responded with a base hit, but felt his thigh ligament pop and "something like water draining inside my leg." The upper thigh ligament had been partially severed and was being held together by a thin strand. After treatment, Clemente told a reporter, "The doctor told me that it will take some time for the injury to heal. Rest for now and not run too much in spring training."[45]

Clemente's courage, leadership and skills impressed San Juan pitcher Tommie Sisk. Sisk's locker was next to Clemente's the six years they were together in Pittsburgh, and the right-hander pitched for Clemente in Puerto Rico in 1964-65. Sisk: "Bobby was very proud of being a Puerto Rican. He never did anything dishonorable to his country. Bobby and I were very good friends. He was the best ballplayer I ever saw. I was in Puerto Rico to work on certain things, and don't ever remember being as tired from playing the game on a year-round basis."

Clemente was a four-time National League batting champion when he made his first appearance for the 1967-68 San Juan team. It was a pinch-hit single against Arecibo on December 2, 1967.[46] In 23 games that season, Clemente hit .382 with 4 homers and 15 RBIs.[47] San Juan went through three managers including Don Zimmer, Roberto's teammate with Santurce in the mid-1950s. A young Cincinnati prospect, Johnny Bench, turned 20 that winter while doing most of the catching. Lee May led San Juan in homers with 11. Tony Taylor, the Senators' second baseman, was the league's top hitter.[48]

Clemente meant a lot to his American and Latin teammates. Lee May emphasizes that Clemente helped him in his baseball thinking. "I would try to apply some of Roberto's ideas to my game," he says. Clemente's hospitality during the holidays made an impact on May as well. "They showed us a good time and I'll always be thankful to Roberto and his wife."

Tony Taylor, a Cuban who played winter baseball during the 1950s and 1960s, spoke for all his countrymen when he called Roberto "the Great One." These sentiments were echoed by others who played for San Juan. Manny Mota, a Dominican teammate of Clemente's at Pittsburgh and a San Juan outfielder in 1962-63, called Roberto an inspiration to all Latin American ballplayers. Ted Savage, an import who played outfield with the Caguas club, remembers Clemente as the kind of guy who would take you home and feed you—a baseball player's baseball player.

A new decade was dawning as Clemente returned to San Juan for the 1969-70 season. Instead of Johnny Bench behind the plate, it was up-and-coming Yankee catcher Thurman Munson. Winter league veterans Lee May and José Cardenal joined Clemente in the outfield. Mike Cuéllar, fresh from pitching in the 1969 World Series, was the staff's ace. But it was a disappointing season, and San Juan finished fifth and missed the playoffs by one game. Clemente played in 38 games and hit .296, second on the team to Munson's .333.[49]

San Juan's manager, Ellis "Cot" Deal, cherishes this memory: "Roberto made a statement to a friend from Puerto Rico, stating, 'I've never played for a manager that I enjoyed playing for more.'" Deal had met Roberto in the 1952-53 season, when he pitched and played the outfield for San Juan. Known by Puerto Rican fans as Mr. Refuerzo—Mr. Reinforcement—for being such a valuable import, Deal joined the 1952-53 Santurce team in the Caribbean Series.

Nino Escalera was at home in Puerto Rico in the summer of 1970 when he received a long-distance call from Pittsburgh. Roberto Clemente had just been offered the San Juan managing job for 1970-71 and was asking his old friend to join the team as a coach. Clemente would be the manager for one season, with the understanding that Escalera could have the position for the 1971-72 season.

Roberto Clemente and Santurce's manager, Frank Robinson, took their lineup cards to home plate minutes before the season opener at Hiram Bithorn Stadium, October 22, 1970. Nearly 20,000 paying fans were in the stands when a sudden power failure delayed the start of the game for some two hours. By the time San Juan's Ken Brett threw the opening pitch, the crowd had swelled to over 26,000.[50] According to one version of the story, some stadium officials opened the gates and let the fans in. Others say the fans may have opened the gates themselves.

Ken Brett, who pitched for San Juan the whole season, got some insights into Clemente as a manager from an individual and team perspective. "We loved him," says Brett. "There were times he would get frustrated because we didn't play at the level he expected us to play. I'll never forget the time he decided to play to prove his points. He was a hero down there, the people went crazy and it helped attendance."

Brett (8-3) was Clemente's ace. Jim Colborn (8-8), Palillo Santiago (5-1) and former Cy Young winner Jim Lonborg, in Puerto Rico to continue his comeback, contributed to San Juan's 1970-71 second-place finish.[51] San Juan's lineup included Pirate youngsters Al Oliver, Dave Cash and Manny Sanguillén. Freddie Patek, who was traded to Kansas City that winter by Pittsburgh, began the season as San Juan's shortstop. Mike Jorgensen and Ken Singleton played for Clemente, as did native players José Morales, Cocó Laboy, and future San Juan and Santurce manager Mako Oliveras.

Clemente played only three regular season games, but did suit up for the semifinal playoff series against the Senators' arch-rival Santurce. It was an intense rivalry, dating back to the 1939-40 season. When the two teams faced off at Bithorn Stadium, the San Juan club had the first-base dugout while Santurce used the third-base one. Each team had a cheerleader positioned on its dugout to exhort the fans.

San Juan and Santurce were tied at two games apiece on January 25, 1971, when Clemente penciled his name into the game five lineup card. It was a normal late-January evening, with the temperature in the high seventies. Over 12,000 fans anxiously waited to see their heroes in action. Clemente, Sanguillén and Singleton were San Juan's most feared hitters. Frank Robinson's Santurce lineup featured Don Baylor, Reggie Jackson and Tany Pérez. Robinson sent Terín Pizarro to the hill while Clemente summoned Jim Colborn.

With Santurce leading 1-0 in the top of the fourth inning, Clemente and Sanguillén both singled and San Juan had runners at the corners. Singleton hit a fly to right field which Jackson snared. Jackson let loose with his best throw of the season to nail Clemente at home plate and keep San Juan from a big rally.[52] Santurce won the game, 2-1, and went on to win game six to take the series. They would win their final series over the Caguas club.

Prior to the epic San Juan–Santurce series, Clemente had managed the Puerto Rico squad to a 4–1 victory in the league All-Star game, which that year was a contest of natives against imports. His team scored all their runs in the second inning on a double by Torito Meléndez and singles off the bats of Félix Millán, Cheo Cruz and Angel Mangual.[53] This would be Roberto's final Puerto Rico All-Star Game appearance as a player or manager. The ceremonial first pitch was thrown by Marvin Miller, Executive Director of the Major League Players Association.

Palillo Santiago, the San Juan player who knew Clemente better than anyone else, felt the biggest challenge facing Roberto that winter was time constraints. Santiago: "Roberto's problem was that he had so many different commitments that at times he would get to the park 15 or 20 minutes prior to game time. But he was a leader, and knew how to handle the young players. Some of them, Polilla Ortíz for one, wanted to emulate Roberto and this was just not possible."

Ken Brett felt Clemente's managing inexperience showed in terms of running a game. "He was a wonderful man and a great player, but as far as running a game he didn't do a great job. He had a very short temper at times about the way we played, because let's face it, he took it very seriously. It was *his* team, and he was going to get the credit or the blame for how the team played. As a result of our lackluster play at times, he used to get very mad at us and the guys would put the towels over their faces and kind of laugh a little bit—not at him [but] as a reaction to what was happening." Frank Robinson watched Clemente's growth as a major league player from the mid–1950s to the early 1970s. "I really can't judge him as a manager," Robinson says. But he feels that "with some more experience [he] would have made an outstanding major league manager."

An Exceptional Human Being

Mario Mendoza got to know #21 during spring training of 1971, shortly after Clemente's managing stint with the 1970-71 Senators. Mendoza, a native of Mexico, and other young Spanish-speaking prospects with the Pittsburgh Pirates were treated to Clemente's inspirational stories about winter ball and overcoming adversity. Roberto Clemente's human qualities will never be forgotten. "He was such a down-to-earth human being," says Mendoza. "Those of us in the minors would come in for dinner at 5:30 P.M. and leave an hour later when the big leaguers would have their meal. Roberto would stay outside the dining hall chatting with us and sharing advice and crack a few jokes. Then we would tell Roberto the last call was made for the big leaguers to eat, but he would tell us: 'The heck with the meal. I'll eat somewhere else later in the evening. Let's keep talking.'"

Roberto Clemente finally received the nationwide recognition he so richly deserved during the 1971 World Series. U.S. fans saw a 37-year-old Clemente do it all. Puerto Rico's fans had seen his ability displayed in local stadiums over the years and welcomed Clemente with open arms when the jumbo jet carrying him arrived in San Juan on October 21, 1971. Clemente had already made it clear he was going to "rest" this winter.

Bill Virdon managed San Juan that season and took the team to the final series, which they lost to Ponce. Virdon had a good look at young Pirates on the San Juan club, including Bruce Kison, Bob Johnson, Milt May, Rennie Stennett and Richie Zisk. His respect for Clemente, a former teammate with Pittsburgh and someone whom he had managed in 1972, never wavered. "I saw him quite often in Puerto Rico," says Virdon. "Roberto would come to some of our games. He was an exceptional human being — very articulate, very sharp, very smart. I can't say enough about Roberto as a teammate, someone who I coached and managed."

Midway through the 1972-73 season, Clemente managed the Puerto Rican team in the Amateur World Series held in Nicaragua. A veteran Puerto Rican umpire, Waldemar Schmidt, returned to Puerto Rico with Roberto and Vera Clemente via Santo Domingo. Schmidt remembers an invitation from the Clementes to visit them a few weeks later at their farm.

The visit never took place. A prop-driven DC-7 piloted by Jerry Hill with four passengers aboard, including Clemente, crashed into the Atlantic Ocean at approximately 9:30 P.M. on December 31, 1972.[54] Only Jerry Hill's body was recovered from the crash site. The U.S. Coast Guard and volunteer divers who participated in the search found a briefcase Clemente had been carrying, but nothing else. Witnesses said several explosions took place prior to the crash.

Clemente had played and managed in Nicaragua. He wanted to make sure food, medicine and other supplies got into the right hands. His gesture in reaching out to the Nicaraguan people after their earthquake was not forgotten by Dennis Martínez, the first Nicaraguan to play in the big leagues. Martínez looked up to Clemente when he was a 17-year-old amateur pitcher. "Roberto Clemente has served as an inspiration to me since my days as an amateur baseball player in Nicaragua," Martínez affirms. "He is the reason why I devote so much time and energy to charitable work for youth."

Pregame ceremonies at the January 6, 1973, league All-Star game were conducted in Clemente's honor.[55] A minute of silence was followed by placing a memorial wreath at the base of the right-field wall at Hiram Bithorn Stadium. Players on the "Native" and "Import" teams wore black arm bands. The game was played, and Mike Schmidt was named its Most Valuable Player by virtue of his three RBIs in the 4–2 win for the imported players.[56]

Elrod Hendricks was already a league veteran with Santurce when

Clemente perished. Hendricks remembers the Santurce players voting not to play a scheduled game two days after the tragedy. "Our owner wanted us to go out and play and that's when I started thinking and doing some soul searching. 'Where is the heart?'" Hendricks asked himself. "Here is an island where the world of baseball has lost one of its best players. We lost a great human being, someone who meant a lot to baseball, Puerto Rico and the world."

Ken Wright, of the 1972-73 Arecibo Wolves, had pitched against Clemente's San Juan club two winters earlier. He was touched by the tragedy and the emotions of the moment. Clemente will never be forgotten by the younger generation of baseball players. Rubén Sierra, who was a rookie with Santurce at age 18, just like Clemente, wears #21 in the majors as a tribute to him. "I used to watch old films of Clemente in action," says Sierra. He has always been an inspiration to me ... *todo es el* [he is everything]."

The U.S. Postal Service issued a 20-cent commemorative stamp honoring Roberto Clemente, one of only four major leaguers to be so honored, on August 18, 1984.[57] The stamp has a picture of Clemente with the flag of Puerto Rico in the background. Jackie Robinson, Babe Ruth and Lou Gehrig are the only other professional baseball players on U.S. stamps.

When the first Puerto Rico Professional Baseball Hall of Fame induction ceremony took place, in Ponce, Puerto Rico, on October 20, 1991, Roberto Clemente was one of ten players to enter this select circle. Five of his Santurce teammates—Orlando Cepeda, Rubén Gómez, Terín Pizarro, Willard Brown and Bob Thurman—were also inducted, as was Vic Power, a former Caguas teammate. It was fitting that many of Roberto's contemporaries were so honored.

Roberto Clemente's widow, Vera, was at the morning ceremony to accept the Hall of Fame plaque. After the ceremony, she told me, "Roberto played just as hard in Puerto Rico as in the majors. He felt very strongly about pleasing the local fans and did not want to let them down."

I was fortunate to see Clemente play right field at Bithorn.

4. Pioneers

It gave me a chance to polish the skills I had ... that's why I welcomed it so much.
—Monte Irvin, former San Juan player

Players from Puerto Rico and abroad, as well as government officials and private sector citizens, were league pioneers. Once play began in 1938-39, appreciative fans idolized the talented Negro leaguers, who played hard and set a good example for the local players. Fans would lavish gifts, cash and hospitality on stellar performers, who, in turn, appreciated the Islanders' carefree nature and kindness. Island culture was distinct from that of the United States, and the Negro leaguers shared precious moments with teammates, fans and team owners at homes, restaurants and the town plazas.

Satchel Paige

Satchel Paige arrived in San Juan on a Pan Am Clipper nearly four weeks after the 1939-40 season got underway.[1] Paige joined a Guayama team that had defeated the best semi-pro team from the United States, the Duncan Cementers, in a September 1939 series. The defending league champion Guayama Witches featured an all-star cast headed by shortstop Perucho Cepeda and outfielder Tetelo Vargas. Cefo Conde and Rafaelito Ortíz provided pitching depth.

Paige's first start, on October 29 against Mayagüez, was washed out after one frame. He endeared himself to the Guayama faithful on November 5, 1939, when he shut out Santurce by a lopsided 23–0 score.[2] Even Santurce's player-manager, Josh Gibson, pitched a third of an inning, and handled chores at first and third base during the morning contest of a Sunday doubleheader. (This season had 28 Sunday doubleheaders scheduled from October 1, 1939, through April 7, 1940, but some were rained out and played on other dates.[3] The twin bill contests took place in the morning and afternoon.)

Luis Alvelo, Puerto Rico's foremost historian on the Negro leagues era, remembers Rafaelito Ortíz telling him that Paige would warm up before games by throwing a much longer distance than the norm. Paige hurled the ball over a matchbox placed in front of his catcher. Cefo Conde did some of this catching, on the field and in other surroundings. Conde could start or relieve, and was a free spirit, much like his new friend. "We used to run around together during the week. My English was pretty good," Conde recalls. "One day I asked Satchel to show me how he worked on his pitches and control. We went up on the roof of a building in Guayama. Satchel made a circular gadget shaped like an arc and put it in front of an imaginary home plate. Then he had me place five sponges in my glove before he began throwing hard. After a few of these practices, I was pitching better. I caught Satchel against Aguadilla when William Perkins was unable to play, and used the same five sponges. Those sponges came in handy."

An interesting pattern developed in January 1940, when Conde started several contests before Paige would be inserted. Some of this may have been hype. On January 7, 1940, Bertrum Hunter of Caguas opposed Conde. Paige came to the mound after a scoreless first inning and shut out Caguas the rest of the way. *El Mundo*'s summary of the game noted that "Paige went in to hold on to his claim as the best pitcher in Puerto Rico."[4]

Paige was the 1939-40 league MVP, based on his 19-3 record and 208 strikeouts in 205 innings.[5] The wins and strikeouts remain single-season league records. He struck out 17 Mayagüez batters on December 3, 1939, to set a nine-inning record which stood for 14 years, until Bob Turley of San Juan duplicated the whiff total.[6] Mayagüez catcher Marco Comas remembers the classic 1-0 duel, won by Paige over Bud Barbee. "Barbee struck out 15 for us," says Comas. "But Tetelo Vargas scored the only run. You could say Paige threw aspirin tablets that morning at our ballpark."

Sunday pitching duels were eagerly awaited by the fans. The season featured 28 complete games in 28 starts by Humacao's Henry McHenry, an unprecedented feat.[7] Paige, Billy Byrd, Roy Partlow and Leon Day gave fans their money's worth. These hurlers became icons to the fans, who followed everything from their mannerisms to their pitching effectiveness.

Josh Gibson

Josh Gibson joined Santurce in time to catch Billy Byrd and Luis Cabrera in an October 22, 1939, twin bill against San Juan. That season Gibson challenged Perucho Cepeda for the batting title, but fell short. He became a player-manager during the season, and was one of Santurce's first three imports, along with Byrd and Dick Seay.

Gibson was an imposing figure to opponents. Mayagüez infielder Nica Bayrón recalls rounding third, trying for an inside-the-park homer, and

4. PIONEERS

Santurce's first three imports, 1939-40 season. *Left to right:* **Billy Byrd, Josh Gibson and Dick Seay; batboy Pookie Muñiz is in front of Gibson** (courtesy of Alvelo Collection).

seeing Gibson set to crouch. "He looked like a monument to me. I sort of stopped, and got a close look at him. He was so impressive."

Ponce infielder Millito Navarro remembers playing third base one Sunday against Santurce. Navarro's best position was the second sack. He could also play the outfield, and preferred anything but the hot corner. "I was trembling when Josh Gibson came up," Navarro admits. "I hoped and prayed he wouldn't hit one toward me. Those shots of his were rockets. Luckily, none were hit in my direction."

One rocket Gibson hit during his stay in Puerto Rico cleared the inner fence and the outer wall at Escobar Stadium, landing in the ocean. A conservative estimate put it at 600 feet because there was no way to measure it. Gibson's crowning moment was earning the 1941-42 MVP award after hitting .480 with 13 homers for Santurce.[8] The .480 mark remains the single-season standard. Luis Alvelo remembers a four-week tear, from January 12 to February 9, 1942, when Gibson's batting average rose from .355 to .460. Willard Brown had the upper hand during the season's first half, but finished a distant second despite hitting .410.[9] The MVP award and batting title were Gibson's most treasured accomplishments in baseball.[10]

Raymond Brown

Raymond Brown went 7-0 for San Juan in both 1938-39 and 1939-40.[11] He also pitched for Santurce and Ponce, as well as playing the outfield. One of the most talked-about transactions of this period was Ponce giving Santurce $500 for Brown's services prior to the 1941-42 season.[12] This was a huge sum at a time when the top American players made $50 per week in Puerto Rico. Brown would be Ponce's ace in their first title.

The long-time Homestead Gray pitching star enjoyed Puerto Rico. When Brown returned for his second winter with San Juan, he lived in a furnished apartment with a refrigerator and all the trappings. It cost $400 just to furnish the apartment. Brown's salary was $50 a week plus $10.50 a week for lodging.[13] Round-trip fare for Brown and his wife on a steamship was part of the deal.

One controversy arising from the league's roster-change deadline centered on Brown. After missing three weeks of the 1939-40 season because of some ailments, Brown recommended that San Juan contact Roy Partlow in Cuba. This was done and Partlow came to Puerto Rico. Center fielder Gene Benson became a "temporary" coach for a week to make room for Partlow on the roster. Since Brown was unable to pitch, San Juan officials released him and Benson was reinserted. But the story didn't end here. Mayagüez attempted to sign Brown, but this was disallowed by the league. An emergency meeting was called by franchise officials to discuss the case. The Aguadilla and San Juan franchises voted against Brown joining Mayagüez, and that ended it. Had the vote been unanimous for giving Brown a chance to sign with Mayagüez, there might have been further hearings.

In the league's maiden season, however, Guayama was allowed to sign Ponce import Bertrum Hunter for the playoffs. Hunter—a member of the Pittsburgh Crawfords when they featured Cool Papa Bell, Oscar Charleston, Josh Gibson and other stars—replaced George Britt on the Guayama roster prior to the finals against San Juan. He was the winning pitcher in three of Guayama's four victories.[14]

Raymond Brown's final Puerto Rican mound appearance was with Ponce when he defeated the 1947 New York Yankees on February 24, 1947.[15] He had won three 1946-47 decisions for Santurce, prior to becoming a Ponce coach. Ponce manager George Scales opted to start Brown in this spring training exhibition game since the league finals were coming up.

George Scales

George Scales first traveled to Puerto Rico in 1926 as a member of the New York Lincoln Giants to play a series of games against Island teams including the San Juan and Ponce clubs.[16] The Ponce Lions had a 17-year-old youngster, Pancho Coímbre, who caught Scales's eye. Coímbre would be a member of all five Ponce championship teams managed by Scales during the 1940s. Coímbre and others throughout Puerto Rico respected Scales for his constant encouragement and knowledge of the game. Scales managed the Aguadilla Sharks in 1939-40 before taking the Ponce job on December 16, 1940. He held the fort until Piper Davis replaced him on November 9, 1948. The Lions hired Scales a second time for the 1949-50 season, and a third time in 1958-59.[17] When Santurce won its 1950-51 title, Scales was at the helm.

It was Scales who rallied his troops from a three-game deficit in the 1946-47 finals. No other team in league history has done that. After game three, Caguas fans began roasting *lechones* (suckling pigs) in anticipation of a big celebration on Sunday, March 9, 1947, when games four and five were scheduled. Angel Colón, a longtime coordinator of league All-Star Games, spent some time with Scales after the third loss and found him to be his usual confident self. Colón remembers Ponce second baseman Fernándo Díaz Pedroso making a trip to Cataño — the hometown of Perucho Cepeda — after the third defeat. Díaz Pedroso, hero of Ponce's recent win over the Yankees with a three-run homer off Joe Page, proclaimed the Lions would win four straight before a multitude in the plaza. The slugger-turned-prophet was on target. Ponce swept Caguas in doubleheaders on March 9 and 16 to claim an unprecedented fifth title.

Perucho Cepeda

In 1946-47 Perucho Cepeda was a 40-year-old first baseman for the Caguas Criollos in the twilight of his career. But what a career it was. Cepeda earned two league batting crowns and one MVP award.[18] Fans throughout the Caribbean said he was special — a star among stars. Perucho passed away before his son, Orlando, played his first game for Santurce in the 1955-56 season.

Millito Navarro, a contemporary of Cepeda, knew him well: "Perucho had tremendous athletic ability. He could play the infield and the outfield. He was such a good hitter, and a bad-ball hitter at that. So the pitchers were scared stiff of him. If they pitched him outside, he could hit it out. The same for high stuff and inside pitches. One of the most feared hitters of any generation—that was Perucho Cepeda, Orlando's father."

Millito Navarro

Millito Navarro began his baseball career in 1922 and by the time league play began in 1938-39 he was already 33 years old. Navarro played with the 1928 and 1929 Cuban Stars of the Negro National League, becoming Puerto Rico's first representative at this level.[19] Earlier in that decade he had competed against his close friend Pancho Coímbre in track and field events.

Navarro: "The real tough one was the 220 yard hurdles. Pancho beat me in a photo finish. With three hurdles left, I was floating, and then I see Coímbre passing me. What an athlete he was." Navarro was no slouch, either. He was one of the league's top players in the late 1930s and early 1940s. A knee injury forced George Scales to insert Navarro in the outfield to ease the strain. When Ponce won its first title in 1941-42, the 36-year-old Navarro was still an everyday player. He retired as a player the following winter, but helped Scales as his coach. Navarro briefly managed Ponce in 1938-39 after the resignation of Agustín Daviú.

Pancho Coímbre Atiles

Pancho Coímbre Atiles was a star in Puerto Rico, Cuba, Mexico, Venezuela, the Dominican Republic and the United States. He played for the New York Cubans of the Negro National League between 1940 and 1946 and earned plaudits from Satchel Paige. Coímbre won two Puerto Rican batting crowns and one MVP award. In Ponce's five championship seasons, he hit a combined .367.[20] When Ponce earned their first title, in 1941-42, it was the troika of Coímbre, Howard Easterling and Sammy Bankhead who provided the firepower, while Raymond Brown and Juan Guilbe took care of the pitching. Coímbre's artistry at the plate was exemplified by his never striking out in league play for three straight seasons, from 1939-40 to 1941-42.[21]

Coímbre lived a block from Ponce's Charles H. Terry ballpark. Rather than change after home games in the locker room below the grandstand, he would walk home with his uniform still on. Carlos Costas, a young Ponce fan at the time, remembers an entourage of kids following Coímbre home, reminiscent of the "Pied Piper" tales. Years later, Roberto Clemente stated that Coímbre was a better hitter than himself.[22] Clemente: "It's a shame he couldn't play in the majors due to the color barrier. I've always insisted Pancho would have been one of the best ever."

Ponce star Pancho Coímbre, 1939-40 season (courtesy of Alvelo Collection).

Tetelo Vargas

Tetelo Vargas liked to be called "El Gamo Dominicano" (the Dominican Deer), since it was in Santo Domingo de Guzmán where he first saw the light of day. Many consider Vargas the best Dominican ballplayer of the pre-1950 era. Vargas had a lot of experience before 1938-39. He started as a 17-year-old on the amateur Escogido club in his native land and later played in the States, Canada, Cuba, Colombia and Venezuela. His stateside experience included stints with a House of David team, the New York Cubans, and the Cuban Stars between 1927 and 1944.[23]

Millito Navarro played with and against Tetelo throughout Latin America, and marveled at Vargas's professional baseball career. Navarro: "Tetelo was reliable and produced in the clutch. I saw him score from first on a single. Another time, he made it home from second on a long fly ball to right field. He was one of my idols in baseball—a very complete ballplayer."

When the 1947 New York Yankees played their series against various Island teams, Tetelo hit .500 in his three games.[24] Charley Dressen was a coach with the Yankees at that time, and had been Cincinnati's manager when the Reds visited Puerto Rico in 1936. Vargas impressed him the first time, too: "He could fly. He's just a very good ballplayer."[25] Mickey Owen, Vargas's manager at Caguas in 1953-54, told me Tetelo "ran like a deer" and could outrun Jim Rivera and Hank Aaron.

Juan Guilbe

Juan Guilbe was a member of all five Ponce championship teams and one of three brothers who played for the Lions. As Ponce prepared to sell his contract to the Aguadilla Sharks, Guilbe said, "Only my mother can sell me; my wish has always been to play with my beloved Ponce, the city where I was born and raised."[26]

Puerto Rico was represented by Guilbe in the javelin competition during the 1938 Central American and Caribbean Games held in Panama. Guilbe played in the Negro leagues with the Cuban Stars, the Baltimore Elite Giants and the Indianapolis Clowns, as well as in the Dominican Republic, Colombia and Venezuela.

Griffin Tirado

Griffin Tirado was not a Josh Gibson, but his nickname was "Caballo de Hierro" (Iron Horse) because he caught every game from 1941-42 to 1944-45.[27] Because of Tirado's presence, Ponce never imported a catcher from the Negro leagues during the 1940s. He was Ponce's starting catcher for 12 straight seasons, earning his bread and butter behind the plate.

Tirado's deft handling of Ponce's four starters in 1946-47 helped them post winning records. Juan Guilbe (8-4), Planchardón Quiñónes (9-4), Johnny Wright (8-5) — a 10-year Negro leagues veteran — and Pantalones Santiago (8-2) posted the equivalent of 20-win seasons, considering that Ponce played only 60 games.[28]

Luis Cabrera

"Cabrerita" was Santurce's meal ticket throughout the 1940s and early 1950s. When Santurce needed a win, they went to their sidearm hurler. Cabrera could neither read nor write, but this did not stop him from earning the 1940-41 MVP award.[29] Rubén Gómez was one of his admirers and best friends. According to Gómez, after Cabrera delivered a pitch, the knuckles on his pitching hand would touch the dirt. Gómez also remembers Cabrera as the best-dressed ballplayer in Puerto Rico.

It was Cabrera, a native of Ponce, who defeated the Lions in the decisive game of the 1948-49 semifinals. A Ponce high school student, Jorge Franco, wrote this in a letter to the sports editor of *El Mundo* shortly after Cabrera shut out the Lions: "You can imagine how Ponceños feel ... all except one — Cabrera. Ponce has been defeated by a son from its own soil. We're proud of having such a valiant son, the virtuous, immortal, intrepid, the brave, and above all, Luis Cabrera, the Ponceño."[30]

Hiram Bithorn

He was known as "Hurricane Hi" Bithorn when he won 18 games for the 1943 Chicago Cubs, but to his family and friends in Puerto Rico, it was Hiram. Hiram Bithorn Sosa, a robust 6'1" athlete of Spanish-Danish extraction, made his major league debut for the Cubs on April 15, 1942, after completing his fourth winter season with San Juan.[31]

Bithorn first captured the hearts of Puerto Rico's sports fans when he brought home a silver medal in volleyball and a bronze for the Island's basketball squad after the 1935 Central American and Caribbean Games held in San Salvador. On March 1, 1936, he put his name on the baseball map by pitching seven-plus innings for the Brooklyn Eagles against the Cincinnati Reds. Bithorn took a 4–1 lead into the eighth inning, but left the game when the Reds rallied to tie the score. Brooklyn prevailed, 5–4, behind the fine play of Buck Leonard and Ray Dandridge.[32]

Bithorn benefited from playing with Negro leaguers who barnstormed in Puerto Rico. One such player was Frank Duncan, the talented backstop with the Kansas City Monarchs and other teams throughout a storied career. (Dizzy Dean called Duncan "almost as good a catcher as Gabby Hartnett and I can't say no more than that about a catcher."[33])

Puerto Rico's first major leaguer, Hiram Bithorn, wearing San Juan flannels, early 1940s (courtesy of Diana Zorrilla).

Bithorn became the youngest manager ever in Puerto Rico winter ball at 22, when he replaced Billo Torruellas as San Juan's skipper during the 1938-39 season. He would manage San Juan for parts of four seasons and one full season in the next decade. A two-year military stint put a damper on his baseball career.

Hiram Bithorn died in Mexico under mysterious circumstances while en route to visit his sister, María Angelica. He was allegedly shot by a policeman on New Year's Day, 1952. But some 40 years later his sister told me her brother's new Buick was stopped on December 29, 1951, not New Year's Day, 1952. The trigger was pulled, she said, during an argument after the policeman asked Bithorn for the car's registration papers, a tourist card and other documents. Ten years later, in 1962, the new stadium bearing his name was opened.

Jimmie Crutchfield

Jimmie Crutchfield, a former Pittsburgh Crawford who also played for the Birmingham Black Barons and other Negro leagues teams, was one of San Juan's first three imports in 1938-39. He told me Bithorn was a nice guy who spoke good English. Crutchfield noted that the other imports with San Juan, Clarence Palm and Raymond Brown, had cordial relationships with Bithorn. "I first came down to Puerto in 1936," says Crutchfield. "At that time, we played six weeks with Paige and Gibson. It was a success, and they [Puerto Rico] decided to start a league, and in 1938 I was the first center fielder to play for San Juan."

Crutchfield returned to Puerto Rico in 1979 for an old-timer's game. Forty years had gone by, but many Island fans remembered him as a pioneer. Crutchfield: "If you were nice to the nice people, the sun would shine in your face all the time. It was a fun time. Tetelo, Perucho and Coímbre were fine people and great players. Ray Brown and I were teammates with the Indianapolis ABCs, so I knew him real well by the time we played with San Juan. He was a winner."

Ted Norbert

Ted Norbert was a white pioneer who married a Puerto Rican and loved Puerto Rico so much that he made it his home. Norbert played on various baseball teams, seeing action on Island diamonds, including Newark and Azteca, in the mid–1930s.

Norbert won the first of his three Pacific Coast League home run crowns in 1938 while playing for the San Francisco Seals.[34] The following summer he played against Oakland's Hiram Bithorn. Toward the end of that 1939 season, a press release in *El Mundo* alerted readers that Norbert was a New York Yankee scout who wanted to reinforce one of the Puerto Rico League teams. Norbert was described as a good contact for Puerto Rican players who wished to play organized ball. Moreover, there was no need to pay for his transportation or housing costs. Directors of league teams were advised in the article to write to Theodore Norbert, c/o the San Francisco Baseball Club, or Hiram Bithorn, c/o the Oakland Baseball Club.[35]

Mayagüez signed Norbert to a 1939-40 contract; he later played for San Juan, in 1941-42. Norbert was helpful to a host of young athletes who had professional baseball aspirations. Coaching and managing in the league were among his contributions. He managed the 1957-58 Caguas club to the Island title.

Luis Olmo

Bithorn had the right complexion to play in the majors, as did Luis Olmo, a Brooklyn prospect who joined the 1943 Dodgers. Olmo is now quick to point out that it took some adjusting for him to get used to the segregation he saw while playing for Richmond, in the Dodger chain, from 1940-42. And that helped him understand why his Caguas teammates during the early years, such as Billy Byrd, Roy Campanella and Leonard Pearson, appreciated Puerto Rico.

Olmo: "Our league was good for the Negro leaguers. They loved it here, where there wasn't racism—they could eat and sleep anywhere." Olmo served notice he was for real when he hit .335 as a rookie for the 1938-39 Caguas club.[36] The Caguas player-manager, Pito Alvarez de la Vega, remembers the 19-year-old Olmo as the revelation of the first season. He felt Olmo had the talent to make it to the majors and took him under his wing. Later, a proud Alvarez de la Vega covered Olmo's Winter League exploits as the Puerto Rico correspondent for *The Sporting News*. By then Olmo, after jumping to Mexico with Mickey Owen, Max Lanier and other big leaguers in 1946, had returned to the majors and the Puerto Rico League. "I earned seven dollars a week that first winter of 1938-39," Olmo recalls. "My top salary in the league was $1,500 a month, in 1954-55."

When Caguas won its first title, in 1940-41, Olmo was one of the stars, along with Roy Campanella, Billy Byrd and Manolo García. They defeated Santurce in a memorable seven-game series highlighted by Campanella's slugging.

Roy Campanella

Caguas won 21 of its first 28 games in 1940-41 to win the first *vuelta* (half season). Santurce earned the right to face Caguas in the finals by

4. PIONEERS

Roy Campanella with Puerto Rican schoolchildren, October 1965 (courtesy of *The San Juan Star*).

prevailing in the second half.³⁷ In game six of the finals, Caguas's catcher, Roy Campanella, was at the plate with the bases loaded in the bottom of the fifth. It was April 6, 1941. Santurce had won three of the first five games and was leading 2–1 when Campanella proceeded to clout a long homer over the left-field fence off Luis Cabrera.³⁸ When the 19-year-old crossed home plate, his teammates rushed to him and hoisted the hero on their shoulders. Caguas's excited fans took advantage of the lull to put dollar bills into Campy's hand. The homer broke Santurce's back. Before the damage was done, Caguas had scored 14 runs; they went on to take the series.

Campanella returned to Caguas in 1941-42, then played for Santurce in 1944-45 and for San Juan two winters later. After his big league career ended, Campanella was invited to Puerto Rico a number of times to throw out the first pitch at inaugural games. He would take time to visit schools and chat with the children. Roy Campanella was the youngest "pioneer" from the Negro leagues to grace Puerto Rico's diamonds in the early 1940s. Island fans old enough to remember him in a Caguas uniform still talk about the homer which changed the momentum of the 1940-41 finals.

Manolo García

Manolo García, Caguas's 36-year-old center fielder and leadoff hitter, started that 14-run rally against Santurce with a triple. He asserted that Campanella gave his heart and soul to Caguas, in addition to having a cannon arm and hitting for power. García's amateur baseball career had begun in 1920—before Campanella was born—for the Mayagüez Cardinals. He was talented enough to play in the States, and was approached by a minor league team from Allentown, Pennsylvania, but his father did not give Manolo permission to sign. Ponce's Agustín Daviú did sign with Allentown and was the first Puerto Rican to play organized baseball in the States.[39]

García, a college graduate, taught physical education for many years. He played against the Negro leaguers who came to the Island in the 1930s and was already 34 years old by the time Semi-Pro League play began in 1938. But García took very good care of himself, usually going to bed before 8 P.M. He played professionally into his early forties. One of his most cherished memories is being selected to the Northeast All-Star team for the 1941-42 doubleheader against the Southeast Stars. The Northeast team included players from Caguas, Humacao, San Juan and Santurce. It featured Campanella and Josh Gibson behind the plate, Monte Irvin, Ray Dandridge, Willard Brown, Billy Byrd and others. García still remembers Gibson's two homers in the afternoon game off Leon Day and Barney Brown: "After Gibson hit the one off Day, he just laughed as he rounded the bases. Later in the game I got a hit off Barney Brown. Gibson hits another one, and keeps laughing."

Leon Day

Leon Day pitched superbly for the Aguadilla Sharks from 1939-40 to 1941-42, recording 503 strikeouts in this span. The only league pitcher who came close to these numbers was Terín Pizarro, with his 463 strikeouts from 1957-58 through 1959-60.[40]

Day's salary increased more than twofold, from $20 to $50 a week, between his first and third Puerto Rico winters. The writers and fans called him "El Caballero del Box" (the Gentleman of the Box.) Day ate tasty barbecued goat along with the traditional rice and beans, rice and chicken. He lived an idyllic life in a house by the beach, pitched and played the outfield. The level of play in Puerto Rico impressed him. "You're talking about Paige, Byrd, Partlow, Coímbre, Cepeda, Gibson," Day says. "Buzz [Buster] Clarkson hit a ball off me in Mayagüez. It went over the left field fence like a knuckleball ... the hardest ball I've seen hit."

Day could also hit the ball. He accounted for all three Aguadilla homers in 1939-40.[41] But Day was no newcomer to Puerto Rico's shores, having toured the Island with the 1935-36 Brooklyn Eagles. When Aguadilla beckoned, they paid Day's round-trip fare on the steamer *Borinquén*. "I'd get seasick," Day recalls, laughing. "When I was in the service over in France, I saw that same ship down by the dock one day, and I thought, 'I've been riding that thing down to Puerto Rico.' The food would fly from the tables, the ocean was rough."

Bill Wright

Bill Wright was an outfielder for San Juan in 1941-42, and became the team's player-manager for a spell. He happened to be standing in the outfield before a game with Caguas's Roy Campanella when they heard the news of the Pearl Harbor bombing. When it came time to depart Puerto Rico, Wright and Campanella found passage to the States on a ship. "For eight days we were on that boat, only had cold lunch food," Wright later recalled. "One day Campanella said we ought to put all our money in a bottle and throw it overboard—since we weren't going to make it anyway. But we did get to Newport News."[42]

Buck Leonard, Buster Clarkson and Ray Dandridge

Buck Leonard and Ray Dandridge made waves in Puerto Rico in 1936 when they played for the Brooklyn Eagles. The fans could hardly wait to see them play the Cincinnati Reds and the Almendares club from Cuba.

Leonard returned to the Island in 1940-41 to play first base for Mayagüez. That season he tied Roy Campanella for the home run crown.[43] One of these blasts has never been forgotten by Gabriel Castro or Ismael Trabal of Mayagüez. "Mayagüez is playing at Aguadilla's Parque Colón where it's some 400 feet to the right field wall," says Castro. "Buck gets hold of one that took off to right field and cleared everything in sight. Next week, some fans placed a sign behind the wall which said, 'Buck Leonard Was the Only One to Hit One Through Here.'" The ball Leonard hit may have landed in the adjacent municipality of Aguada, according to Trabal. A river behind the wall once divided portions of Aguadilla and Aguada.

That season, in a game against Guayama, The Indians loaded the bases with no outs, and Buster Clarkson came up. According to Leonard, Satchel Paige told the catcher, William Perkins, he was going to walk Clarkson intentionally. Perkins reminded Paige a run would score. Paige's response was, "Well, I'd rather walk one run home than have him hit three or four home." The walk scored Mayagüez's only run of the game.[44]

Buster Clarkson played for Mayagüez, Caguas, Ponce and Santurce. He was a dangerous hitter whose clutch hitting created problems for pitchers throughout the season and in the playoffs. Clarkson combined speed with power. In his early years with Mayagüez, he was a base-stealing threat. By the late 1940s some of the speed was gone, but he could always hit.

Ray Dandridge had two stints with Santurce—1941-42 and then 1953-54. Dandridge filled Clarkson's roster spot in 1953-54 after Clarkson was suspended for spitting at an umpire. Even when he was past his prime, the fans kept asking themselves how the bowlegged Dandridge could be such a smooth fielder.

Gene Benson, Clarence Palm and Roy Partlow

Gene Benson, an outfielder with the Philadelphia Stars and a Negro National League All-Star, was San Juan's center fielder throughout the 1939-40 season. Raymond Brown recommended Benson to San Juan's management, and he was signed after several officials saw him play with Philadelphia in 1939. Benson liked his Puerto Rican sobriquet "Bicicleta" (bicycle), for the way he ran the bases. A smile still lights Benson's face when the name Clarence Palm comes up. "Clarence Palm was one of the most comical men around," Benson grins. "He and I were great buddies. We would walk into the city together, check what was playing at the different movies. He would look up and see *Hoy*, so he said to me, 'Ben, you know, *Hoy* must be a heck of a picture. It's playing all over town.' But it was the coming attractions of today, it meant 'today.'" Palm could hit and catch. As San Juan's catcher in 1938-39 and 1939-40, he helped them make the playoffs. He then hit .409 for Santurce in 1940-41 as Josh Gibson's replacement.[45]

Roy Partlow arrived in Puerto Rico in mid–December 1939, in time to make his league debut against Satchel Paige. Team official Pedro Vázquez traveled to Havana to sign the lefty. Partlow, a superb pitcher and hitter, had pitched for the East team in the 1939 Negro Leagues' All-Star Game as one of three Homestead Grays, with Josh Gibson and Buck Leonard.[46]

Partlow barely had time to unpack when he drove to Ponce on December 17, 1939, to join San Juan. The Senators were playing Guayama on a neutral field because of problems with their home stadium. This Paige-Partlow matchup ended in a 5–5 draw when darkness set in.[47] The game was made up six days later at Escobar Stadium with the same mound rivals. San Juan prevailed, 5–1, as Partlow pitched a two-hitter. After the victory, it was bedlam, with fans carrying Palm and Partlow on their shoulders.[48] On days he was not pitching, Partlow would play right field. He was the league's best hitter in 1940-41, Monte Irvin's first winter in Puerto Rico.

San Juan fans congratulate catcher Clarence Palm after a win, circa 1939-40 (courtesy of Alvelo Collection).

Monte Irvin

Monte Irvin credits Quincy Trouppe with the recommendation to play for San Juan in 1940. Irvin recalls, "It was a great experience. I hadn't been playing that long, so by going to Puerto Rico it gave me opportunities to practice my fielding, hit curveballs, hit change-ups. It gave me a chance to polish the skills I had. That's why I welcomed it so much."

Irvin returned to San Juan in 1941-42, and after three years in the Army came back for a third tour of duty. A team player in every sense of the word, he played second base during most of the 1945-46 winter campaign, since San Juan had an established outfield of Felle Delgado, Luis Olmo and Freddie Thon (grandfather of Dickie Thon). Irvin also filled in at the other infield positions and saw limited duty in the outfield.

The versatile Irvin won the league MVP award, but narrowly lost his bid for the batting crown to Ponce's Fernando Díaz Pedroso, .3684 to .3677. Pedroso had only 95 official at-bats to Irvin's 155, and to this day some statisticians remain at odds over the criteria used in determining the 1945-46 batting championship.[49]

These individual accomplishments paled in comparison to Irvin's slugging in the finals to give San Juan their first championship. In a doubleheader on February 17, 1946, Irvin crushed two homers in the opener and another four-bagger in the nightcap as San Juan bested Mayagüez, 14–8 and 13–8. Not to be outdone, Luis Olmo also hit a home run in each contest, including a blast during the morning game which cleared the stadium's outer wall.[50] The teams split the remaining four contests to give San Juan the title.

Irvin: "All I know is we won, were very happy and made some money doing it. It's a wonderful feeling about being a champion, a terrific feeling. We needed a second baseman, and Olmo told me, 'You're fast, can hit and have a great arm, so why not?'"

After Irvin's Newark Eagles bested the Kansas City Monarchs in the 1946 Negro League World Series, he had another fine winter for San Juan. Irvin finished second to Willard Brown in the 1946-47 batting chase, .390 to .387. His San Juan teammate Barney Brown was the league MVP, with a 16-5 record. San Juan's other import, Larry Doby, had a splendid year, hitting .349.[51] Irvin left the Island full of contentment. "What I liked about Puerto Rico was the weather, and the fans were so enthusiastic," he observes. "If they liked you, they could really turn you on to do your utmost. I used to visit them at their homes and talk to them at the ballpark ... nothing but fond memories. I met Pepe Seda and Luis Olmo. Luis is still one of my best friends."

Roberto Clemente idolized Irvin. Clemente would make the trek from Carolina to Escobar Stadium by public transportation to see him play. After the game, Clemente would wait for Irvin to come out of the ballpark so he could have a close glimpse of his favorite ballplayer.[52]

José "Pepe" Seda

One of the most multifaceted individuals in league history was José "Pepe" Seda. He was a player-manager on Caguas's 1940-41 championship team, but did much more than that. He authored a baseball rule book, helped get the Baseball Players' Association off the ground and was a physical education instructor at the University of Puerto Rico. As a high school senior, he was co-winner of an Island-wide English speech contest and his athletic skills were evident in volleyball, basketball and track and field.[53]

Seda scouted for the New York Yankees, and this was helpful in the Bronx Bombers' decision to begin their 1947 spring training sessions in San Juan and play a series of games there. Seda managed an Island All-Star team which split two games against New York. The Yankees sent a number of their prospects to San Juan in the mid–1950s, including Elston Howard, Bob Cerv and Johnny Blanchard. Harry Craft and Ralph Houk, from the New York organization, managed San Juan thanks to Seda's input. Pepe Seda served as San Juan's manager in 1947-48 and 1948-49 and was the general manager for a period.

Felle Delgado

Humacao-Arecibo's player-manager in 1941-42 was Felle Delgado, an outfielder for the 1941 New York Cubans. Delgado recalls Humacao's financial difficulties and the team's move to Arecibo, which had no ballpark of its own. This franchise folded after 1941-42. Its financial problems stemmed from a subpar sugarcane harvest and its adverse effects on Humacao's owners. The Arecibo team practiced during the week at a makeshift field near the ocean and played Sunday doubleheaders on the road.

Willard Brown made his league debut as a second baseman after Delgado arranged to bring him to Puerto Rico. Delgado will never forget one of the season's funniest moments, which occurred during a practice in Arecibo. Brown went near a cave to retrieve a ball. When he reached for the ball at the base of the cave, he found a crab straddling the horsehide and ran away, showing more speed than he did on the basepaths. Brown's crab experience was one of many strange episodes for a team which, at 10-34, had the worst record in league history.[54] This may have been an omen, since Brown would eventually break all kinds of records for the Santurce Crabbers.

Felle Delgado had his own share of experiences in the league. In a close game, Billy Byrd hit him with a pitch. When Byrd tried to pick Delgado off first base, the ball ricocheted off his arm. Felle zoomed toward second, and continued to third when he was hit in the back by the throw from first. Delgado rounded third and went home—and slid headfirst into Josh Gibson. "Gibson tagged me in the chest as I flew over the plate," Delgado recalls. "When I came to my senses, it was 9 P.M. and I was in the hospital. I'll never forget that torture."

Delgado once got a game-winning hit off Raymond Brown in a league game and was yelled at by Brown for hitting his best knuckleball. On the flip side, Delgado was one of Satchel Paige's three consecutive strikeout victims when the hurler called in his outfield during a Ponce-Guayama game.

Jaime Almendro

Jaime Almendro took over the shortstop position for San Juan in 1943-44. Felle Delgado was the team's top hitter and Freddie Thon its most effective pitcher. What impressed these veterans was Almendro's defense. He would snag everything, despite playing a shallow shortstop to compensate for his below-average throwing arm.

Almendro played for two weeks before receiving his first salary check for $32, or $16 per week. His double-play partners in 1945-46 and 1946-47 were Monte Irvin and Larry Doby, respectively. He played with pioneers, against pioneers, and in his own way was a pioneer.

Almendro recalled Pancho Coímbre using some psychology on him in his league debut against Ponce. Coímbre approached Almendro and told him to watch out: "The ball is coming your way, rookie, I'm going in hard." And sure enough, Coímbre spiked Almendro on a base stealing attempt. "Is that the way you treat rookies?" asked Almendro. "Why don't you do it to the other players!"

By the time Almendro was a veteran, he earned $500 a month and was looked up to as the best-fielding shortstop in the league. He remembered it was difficult to play the infield at Escobar, since it rained so much and the sand dumped on the field made for erratic bounces. The Aguadilla field was even more difficult to play on.

Quincy Trouppe

Quincy Trouppe began playing in Puerto Rico with Guayama, in 1941-42, and continued with San Juan and Caguas. His skills behind the plate and and as a clutch hitter kept Guayama in the hunt throughout 1941-42. As Caguas's player-manager in 1947-48, his positive attitude and inspired play led the Criollos to their second championship.

Trouppe: "I could communicate with the ballplayers. I could speak Spanish, talk to them, 'cause other than that, if I couldn't speak the language, it would have been difficult.... [I] learned Spanish by playing in Mexico." One talented local player Trouppe took under his wing was Vic Power, a rookie with the 1947-48 Caguas club. Power remembers, "Trouppe was my manager, teammate and father. He brought me to the Provincial League in Canada, where I played with ballplayers who had jumped to the Mexican League — Max Lanier, Sal Maglie."

Trouppe juggled his 1947-48 Caguas lineup to get the most out of his players. Perucho Cepeda and Power took turns at first. Various players covered left and right field. The middle was left alone, with Piper Davis at second and Sammy Bankhead as the shortstop; and Tetelo Vargas still covered a lot of real estate in center field at age 41. Trouppe's best pitchers were Chet Brewer and Rafael Ortíz.

Caguas edged Mayagüez in a seven-game final series, winning the deciding game, 7–6, in 10 innings.[55] It was Trouppe's homer off Mayagüez southpaw Tite Figueroa that tied the game in the top of the ninth. Trouppe stepped up from the left side of the plate and delivered. Perucho drove in the game-winner with an infield hit. Trouppe was overwhelmed by the emotion shown by the Caguas fans. "You didn't know what to expect. When we got to Caguas, they mobbed us. Those were great feelings."

Rafaelito Ortíz

Rafaelito Ortíz was called "El Mago de las Magas" (the Magician of Magas), having been born in a Guayanilla barrio called Magas Abajo. After helping Caguas win the 1947-48 title, he pitched his only Negro leagues season, for the 1948 Chicago American Giants, but suffered an injury that curtailed his future pitching in Puerto Rico.[56]

Ortíz worked his 1938-39 rookie season for Guayama, and finished 11-3 as the Witches claimed the title. He pitched brilliantly in Guayama's 1939 Semi-Pro World Series victory over the Duncan Cementers with two shutouts, one a six-inning no-hitter called because of rain.[57] By the time Satchel Paige joined Guayama's 1939-40 pitching staff, the pioneer Ortíz was a hero.

"El Mago" did what was necessary to win titles. He pitched for two championship teams in Ponce and one in Santurce, in addition to the Guayama and Caguas winners. No pitcher in league history has gone 15-0, as Ortíz did for the 1943-44 Ponce Lions. When Ortíz finished 12-6 for the 1946-47 Criollos, he became the first and only pitcher in league history to win 10 or more games with three different teams.[58]

The "pioneers" made their presence felt in Puerto Rico. They inspired a younger generation of ballplayers to carry the torch. Puerto Rico's fans, players and league officials owe a special debt of gratitude to the Negro leaguers and the local heroes who gave so much to the Island, yet asked for so little.

5. Stars and Workhorses

> *We see baseball as more of a game on the Island. In the U.S., it's more like a system.*
> —Edgar Martínez, San Juan player

The Island has too many stars to include in one chapter. Mostly, they were born in Puerto Rico. But Dickie Thon and Edgar Martínez are considered Island stars despite their birth in the United States. Víctor Pellot, known as Vic Power to stateside fans, was an Island star before making his big league debut. The common denominator among Island stars is the work ethic that enabled them to achieve hitting, fielding or pitching excellence in the league.

Rubén Gómez

Rubén Gómez was a star and a workhorse in Puerto Rico. Thanks to his screwball, he won 174 regular-season games during 29 winter seasons, all but one with Santurce.[1] Gómez's sobriquet was "El Divino Loco" (the Divine Madman). But Gómez was a disciplined fitness buff with a master's degree in physical education who had enough on the ball to shut out San Juan at age 46. Gómez always had time to take his American teammates fishing or for a spin through the mountains. In the mid–1960s, he would stop by the school I attended to pick up his son, my fifth-grade classmate, and join us in pickup games, pitching for both teams.

There were a handful of ballplayers from Puerto Rico with a college education in the late 1940s and Gómez was one of them. He pitched for the University of Puerto Rico team, which played Island amateur teams as well as other colleges. Pedrín Zorrilla traveled to Guayama for a visit with Gómez's mother in an effort to sign the 20-year old collegian to a 1947-48 contract. "I told Pedrín I wanted to continue studying," says Gómez. "Pedrín said I was afraid, and then I told him, 'Give me the ball.' That's what made me sign—the challenge he issued that day."

Rubén Gómez, #22 with Santurce, was clever on the mound. When

Gómez was 42, Dave Campbell, the future ESPN baseball analyst, was Mayagüez's second baseman. Daryl Patterson, a pitcher with Mayagüez, roomed with Campbell prior to a 1969-70 weekend series against Santurce. "We checked into some little hotel near the Condado Beach," remembers Patterson. "Dave was going to have to face Rubén Gómez that night. He was laying there on the bed and all of a sudden said, 'I'm not going to take it, I'm going to charge the mound if he throws at me one more time.' If I remember right, Gómez didn't have large hands or size, but he was a magician with the ball. I've always told people you don't have to have large hands to make that ball do things, 'cause I've seen one of the best doing it."

Gómez was a tough competitor who hated losing. One reason for his success was outstanding athletic ability. Through his skills in track and field events such as the 300-meter run, the 4×100-meter relay, the high jump and the pole vault, he earned a University of Puerto Rico athletic scholarship. Santurce used Gómez as an outfielder, pinch runner and pinch hitter on many occasions.

Gómez: "I lifted weights at home on a daily basis, and at the university I would make 50 long throws of close to 400 feet from the outfield to home plate. That's why my arm never bothered me. Even at age 65 I didn't have arthritis."

Tom Greenwade of the Yankees scouted Gómez during the 1951-52 season and signed him to a minor league contract. Casey Stengel interrupted his vacation in the U.S. Virgin Islands to see Gómez pitch a final-series game against San Juan, the team #22 usually had in his pocket. Gómez did not disappoint "the Old Professor," shutting out the Senators, 1–0, on February 12, 1952.[2] But Gómez wasn't Yankee property very long: "I pitched a game for Kansas City and they didn't use me for a month. So I went to play ball in the Dominican Republic and the Yankees suspended me. At the end of that season, I bought out my own contract with Kansas City for $3,000 by giving the money to another person who gave the cash to them."

Pedrín Zorrilla came to Gómez's rescue the winter of 1952-53, recommending the Giants sign the pitcher. A reported $10,000 bonus was part of the deal. Gómez began his big league career in 1953 after an excellent spring training. His impressive showing for the 1953 Giants laid the foundation for a working agreement between Santurce and the Giants that lasted through the 1950s.

When Gómez began his eighth campaign with Santurce, in October 1954, he was a star by virtue of being the first Puerto Rican hurler to win a World Series game. He defeated Cleveland, 6–2, on October 1, 1954, in game three, in which Willie Mays and Dusty Rhodes each had two RBIs.[3] Mays then joined Gómez with the 1954-55 Crabbers.

Gómez received a hero's welcome upon arriving at Isla Grande Airport.

He encouraged Mays to play for Santurce, reminding him of the nearly two full seasons he had missed in the majors due to military commitments, the fact that Santurce would do well, and the friendship between Horace Stoneham and Pedrín Zorrilla. "Once Willie made the decision to play in Puerto Rico, he made the adjustment quickly," says Gómez. "I never saw Willie drink alcohol; he was always drinking cherry soda ... the best athlete I ever saw or played with. With the Giants, no one gave him any signs. He coached himself."

Gómez suffered his share of injuries, including a separated right clavicle caused by diving for a ball in his center-field position in January 1957. This was shortly after Roberto Clemente had been sold to Caguas and Gómez had become an everyday outfielder on days he was not pitching. Gómez was hitting around .370 at the time of his injury, which put him second to Clemente for the batting title.

Pitching was Gómez's forte and he adjusted to the swirling wind at Escobar Stadium and later to the wind conditions at Bithorn Stadium. Gómez made sure his pitches to right-handed hitters were low and away at Escobar, since the wind tended to blow toward left field. At Bithorn, Gómez would throw higher pitches, conducive to hitting fly balls, since the wind came in from the outfield.

Bob Gibson was another Santurce teammate. Gómez recalls the time, early in the 1961-62 season, he and Gibson bet on whether the young St. Louis hurler could lift a 1953 Pontiac off the ground. Gibson got a case of beer from Gómez by accomplishing this feat but Gibson took a good two to three months to finish the case. Gómez was more impressed with Gibson's pitching ability. Gibson had a fastball like a cyclone and the most wicked slider Gómez had ever seen.

Gómez did not have Gibson's stuff, but he showed Earl Weaver what he was made of. He pitched 111 innings in 15 starts for Weaver in Santurce's 1966-67 season.[4] Santurce used only eight pitchers—three imports and five natives—all winter. Gómez also came through for Weaver with two postseason shutouts. According to Gómez, Weaver told him he was too old and was considering bringing down one of Baltimore's young pitching prospects. So Gómez walked out, telling Weaver to call him at home if he was needed. After Santurce used up five pitchers in their first two final-series losses to Ponce, Weaver called. Gómez's screwball was so effective against Ponce in game three that Roy White, a switch-hitter, batted right-handed.

When Gómez last pitched for Santurce, in 1975-76, he had been on nine championship Santurce teams piloted by eight skippers, beginning with George Scales and ending with Frank Robinson. Buster Clarkson, Herman Franks, Ramón "Monchile" Concepción, Vern Benson, Preston Gómez and Earl Weaver were the others.[5]

Gómez temporarily assumed managerial duties for Santurce in 1971-72, when Frank Robinson was on a postseason tour of Japan with Baltimore. Don Baylor, Dusty Baker and Rogelio "Roger" Moret were players who produced for Gómez. Baylor would visit the Gómez household and go fishing with his manager.

Before being managed by Frank Robinson, Gómez had faced him in Puerto Rico during the 1954-55 season and later in the National League. Robinson's only home run in Puerto Rico came off Gómez during a Ponce-Santurce game. Robinson left the Island early in the season due to an injury. Gómez remembers hitting Robinson on the head with a pitch in a big league game, and hoped it was not taken personally.

Gómez: "When I pitched for him in Puerto Rico, he told me I didn't have the same stamina as before. But I won some games for Frank and he had to admit I could still pitch. We ended up being good friends."

Luis Olmo

Rubén Gómez was a good friend of Luis Olmo, the first Puerto Rican to hit a World Series homer. Olmo received his own hero's welcome on October 12, 1949, when his plane arrived at Isla Grande.[6] Five days earlier, his Ebbets Field shot off New York's Joe Page had created enough pandemonium to carry into the 1949-50 winter season. "From what I heard, my home run off Page set off a chain reaction throughout Puerto Rico, as if an atomic bomb was dropped on the Island," said Olmo. "Island fans were celebrating well after my blast, Campanella's one and the game's final out."

Puerto Rico's fans were ecstatic that Olmo would play, after a three-year ban for jumping to the Mexican League in 1946. He became Caguas's player-manager, leading them to the Puerto Rico League title. Santiago Llorens, Puerto Rico correspondent for *The Sporting News*, captured the feeling: "Luis Olmo, the Brooklyn Dodgers' Puerto Rican outfielder, arrived home October 12, just in time to take charge of the Caguas club for the opening of the Puerto Rican League's Winter season. Greeted by a crowd of 3,000 fans at Isla Grande Airport, Olmo was presented with a truckload of gifts by his rabid fans the next night when he played with his team in an exhibition game."[7]

Caguas won the title under Olmo. Homestead Grays hurler Cecil Kaiser pitched superbly for Caguas as did Dan Bankhead. Roberto Vargas, "the Joe Page of Puerto Rico," won two final-series games and saved another. Tetelo Vargas, Vic Power, Bankhead and Olmo provided timely hitting, as did infielders Gene Markland, Roy Hughes and Stan Breard.

Olmo returned to the Caguas helm in 1950-51 and was rewarded with a 57-20 record, the most regular-season wins in league history.[8] Caguas's hitting stars included batting champion George Crowe, catcher Luis St. Clair, "Jungle Jim" Rivera, Power and Olmo. Olmo's Criollos usually got the better of Rogers Hornsby's Ponce club. Olmo recalls a win over Ponce in game one of a morning-and-afternoon twin bill, after which Hornsby put his troops through a workout instead of letting them go out to lunch. Ponce pitcher-outfielder Rudy Hernández remembers that Hornsby sent for sandwiches.

The season ended on a disappointing note for Olmo, as Santurce bested his team in a thrilling seven-game final series. Olmo's agony soon turned to ecstasy when he reinforced Santurce for the 1951 Caribbean Series held in Caracas. His three homers and nine RBIs led Santurce to the title. Olmo received the series MVP award, while Rubén Gómez and Pantalones Santiago received consideration for winning two games apiece.[9]

Luis Olmo was now an even bigger hero than before. Puerto Rico had just won their first Caribbean Series. Island fans temporarily forgot about local rivalries when the champions returned from Venezuela. Olmo, Gómez and Ponce's Pantalones Santiago all played for different league teams, but it did not matter. They were proud Puerto Ricans who had represented their Island with dignity against Cuba, Panama and Venezuela.

By the time Olmo signed a contract with the 1954-55 Santurce club, he was 35 years old and in the twilight of his career. When he flew to Caracas for the 1955 Caribbean Series, there was no MVP repeat performance. Olmo watched Don Zimmer, Clemente and Mays star for the Crabbers. Olmo's playing career ended with the 1956-57 San Juan club, a team he had first managed in 1944-45. After retiring as a player, Olmo managed San Juan, Santurce, Arecibo and Caguas.

Juan "Terín" Pizarro

Juan "Terín" Pizarro was signed by Olmo to a Milwaukee Braves contract at the age of 18. Pedrín Zorrilla had already secured Pizarro's services for Santurce in 1955-56 when Olmo made sure the young lefty got a hefty amount of cash ($36,000) to join Milwaukee.[10]

Pizarro won more regular-season games (157) in 22 Puerto Rico campaigns than big league games (131) over an 18-year career.[11] He was the dominant pitcher in Puerto Rico between the late 1950s and the early 1960s and led the league in strikeouts five straight seasons. His 183 strikeouts in 1957-58 are the most ever by a Puerto Rican and the fourth best of all time, behind Satchel Paige, Impo Barnhill and Leon Day.[12]

Paige and Bob Turley were supplanted in league record books on November 20, 1957, when Pizarro struck out 19 while pitching Caguas to a 1-0 win over Ponce at Caguas's Sola Morales Stadium.[13] Carlos Bernier fanned four times. Canena Márquez went down twice. Rafael Costas wrote, "No se salvó nadie" (no one was spared).[14]

5. STARS AND WORKHORSES

Rubén Gómez encourages Juan "Terín" Pizarro (in jacket) in the Santurce dugout (courtesy of Rai García).

A quiet and humble person, Pizarro said the lighting "wasn't so good" in Puerto Rico's ballparks. But in those days before radar guns, Pizarro could throw in the 90s. To prove the 19 strikeouts were no fluke, Pizarro pitched the league's sixth no-hitter on November 30, 1957, a 7–0 win over Mayagüez.[15] He struck out 11 and walked 4. When the 1957-58 season concluded, Pizarro was the MVP. He had the league's most wins, the best winning percentage and the lowest ERA.[16] Terín Pizarro then etched his name in Caribbean Series lore with 17 strikeouts in his 8–0 win over Carta Vieja of Panama on February 8, 1958.[17] The only hits off him were a double by future Pittsburgh trainer Tony Bartirome and a single by Héctor López.

Pizarro felt so strongly about playing winter ball that he refused an offer by Chicago White Sox general manager Bob Short in October 1964 to refrain from playing. This was after he had won 19 games to break Hiram Bithorn's single-season standard for big league wins by a Puerto Rican. The White Sox were willing to give Pizarro $5,000 not to play that winter, but Pizarro opted to play the three-month 1964-65 season for $1,300 a month.[18] He pitched Santurce to a pennant and the championship series title. Hiram Cuevas did not forget this. He made sure Pizarro was rewarded with a 20-year coaching contract when the lefty retired after the 1976-77 season.

José G. "Pantalones" Santiago

Pantalones could throw smoke in the low 90s. He burst onto the scene in 1946-47 as the Puerto Rico League Rookie of the Year after George Scales gave the 18-year-old an opportunity to showcase his repertoire. Scales had seen Santiago pitch on Randalls Island, in New York City, and was impressed with the youngster's velocity.[19]

Pantalones Santiago relieved Raymond Brown in the eighth inning of Ponce's 1947 contest against the New York Yankees, holding the New Yorkers at bay to save the game. But there was more. "That was a special year," says Santiago. "I remember pitching my first league game. It came against Caguas, when I relieved Planchardón Quiñónes and preserved the win. My first win came against San Juan and Jaime Almendro hit one out for them."

Santiago told me he was disappointed in his performance against Caguas during the 1947 finals, when he lost two games, but complimented Juan Guilbe and Planchardón Quiñónes for their clutch pitching. Pantalones Santiago continued his fine Puerto Rico career, becoming one of five league pitchers to win over 100 career games. A no-hitter was among the wins. He pitched with the New York Cubans in the Negro leagues and with several major league teams.

In one of Santiago's best games, a 1948 contest between the Birmingham Black Barons and the New York Cubans, he struck out Willie Mays five times.[20] A Cleveland Indians scout was there with Abe Sapperstein, owner of the Harlem Globetrotters and a friend of Cleveland owner Bill Veeck. Subsequently, Santiago and teammate Orestes "Minnie" Miñoso were purchased by Cleveland.

Tomás "Planchardón" Quiñónes

Planchardón Quiñónes fired bullets in the final World War II season for Ponce, going 16-3. 1944-45 was the winter that Planchardón pitched the league's first no-hitter, on December 3, 1944. His achievements gave him back-to-back MVP awards in 1943-44 and 1944-45.[21]

All of Ponce roared when Quiñónes threw his fastball past Caguas's William Perkins to give the Lions their fourth straight win over the Criollos in the 1946-47 finals. Ponce was king of the hill, thanks to this remarkable hurler.

Quiñónes's two years in the Negro leagues were spent with the 1946 and 1947 Indianapolis Clowns.[22] He returned to Puerto Rico and pitched for the Lions through the 1952-53 season. Quiñónes helped Ponce qualify for the 1949-50 playoffs, but the Lions' glory years were behind them and the title went to Caguas.

Luis "Tite" Arroyo

Tite Arroyo was a bullpen ace for the Yankees in the early 1960s and remembers Whitey Ford inviting him to finish his 1961 Cy Young Award acceptance speech. Bilingual Arroyo chipped in with two minutes of Spanish and English after Ford's seven minutes. "Whitey was the one who helped me out that winter," Arroyo testifies. "I must have made six trips [to the States] to do commercials with Whitey and I made around $30,000."

One reason Arroyo had time on his hands was the Yankees' decision to discourage him from pitching for San Juan. Yankee general manager Roy Hamey gave Arroyo $10,000 not to play winter ball after Arroyo indicated he could earn some $5,000 for pitching the whole winter. Hamey felt Arroyo could pitch a few more years with New York if he rested during the off-season. Arroyo also received around $10,000 as his winning share for the 1961 World Series so it was a lucrative winter.

Arroyo: "I'm almost 35 at the time, had a few drinks, ate a little too much ... [though I did] do some throwing, running. Before you know it, I'm overweight, and I know I made a mistake by not playing that winter. I asked them [New York] to let me pitch 40 innings. I tell you, that decision—I have to blame myself, too—cost me my ten years in the big leagues. I only got six years and two months. But I can't say that Hamey was trying to hurt me, maybe protect me. I followed a routine for 14 years and never had a sore arm."

Arroyo was on the same wavelength with Luis Tiant and others who claimed it was important to pitch year-round. During the 14 winters between 1947-48 and 1960-61, Arroyo pitched over 1,500 regular-season innings plus many more playoff frames.[23]

The southpaw was a rookie with the 1946-47 Lions. By 1950-51 Arroyo and Pantalones Santiago were the aces of Rogers Hornsby's pitching staff. Arroyo won 13 games for Hornsby that season, and 11 for Ralph Houk in 1956-57 while pitching for the San Juan club. Arroyo pitched to Yankee catching prospects Clint Courtney in 1950-51 and Johnny Blanchard six winters later. As far as Arroyo was concerned, Hornsby and Houk were night and day. "The way Hornsby was running the ballclub, I could tell he wasn't going to be a success managing again in the big leagues. He sent nobody to the mound . . . just walked in front of the dugout and said, 'You're in and you're out.'"

Arroyo endeared himself to Houk by pitching and winning a third-place tie-breaker against Caguas on only one day's rest. After the 1961 big league season, Houk said, "That man [Arroyo] showed me five years ago he could pitch and I'm not taking credit for Arroyo being with this [Yankee] ballclub, but this man shows me he wants to pitch and that's why he's having some success in the big leagues."[24] Give the screwball some credit. Arroyo began throwing this pitch in 1959-60 and it helped account for his 11-4 season with San Juan.[25] He then won five games for the 1960 Yankees before earning Puerto Rico MVP laurels in 1960-61 for San Juan, based on a 10-2 record and a 1.64 ERA.

Arroyo: "It really helped me to get the screwball to the point where I could throw it [with the count] three-and-two and use it when I was behind the hitters. With San Juan, I was able to do this. Winter ball really helps a lot of players, and I believe it's hurting a lot of players now not playing winter ball. Before, there was no money and you had to do it over here [in Puerto Rico] and there [in the States]."

Vic Power

Vic Power's name is synonymous with Caguas, the only Puerto Rican team he played for. Power was fortunate to be around quality player-managers, starting with Quincy Trouppe and continuing with Luis Olmo and Mickey Owen. Caguas won a championship under each of these leaders. From 1947-48 to 1959-60, Caguas won six Puerto Rico titles and one Caribbean Series, thanks in part to Power's glove work and hitting ability. In Puerto Rico he went by Víctor Pellot

Puerto Rico's fans sensed they were watching something special at first base and third base when Power displayed his fielding skills. Power won two Island batting and home run titles along with the 1955-56 league MVP award.[26] As Caguas's player-manager in 1959-60, he won his second batting crown and led his team to a berth in the Caribbean Series. Power became the second Puerto Rican player to win two league batting crowns, following Coímbre. "When I first joined Caguas, it was something to be around Tetelo Vargas, Perucho Cepeda and Piper Davis," says Power. "They were veterans who I looked up to. Trouppe did a lot for me, too."

Piper Davis was helpful to young players in Puerto Rico and the Negro leagues. He provided encouragement and support to Power in 1947-48, as he did with Willie Mays the following summer when they were teammates with the Birmingham Black Barons. This support came in handy for Power, a talented player who was ready for the big leagues before making his 1954 debut for the A's. "Puerto Rico ball was better than AAA in the 1950s," Power said. "Gómez and Pizarro were the best native pitchers in the league's history. Don't forget Burdette, Buhl, Turley, and Koufax."

Willie Montañez

Vic Power was Guillermito "Willie" Montañez's role model. In Montañez's first season as a regular (1966-67), Power played 17 games for the Criollos.[27] Their paths had nearly been linked in the States: Montañez played in eight games for the 1966 California Angels after Power's big league career ended with the 1965 Angels.

Montañez learned well, and played 18 winters, all but four with Caguas. He led the league in homers after clouting 30 homers for the 1971 Phillies.[28] A talented fielder, Montañez emulated Power's flair in catching pop ups and scooping up throws. "Whatever I learned about playing first base came from Vic Power," Montañez asserts. "He is the person I am in debt to for all he did—fielding tips, hitting left-handers, confidence factor."

Orlando Cepeda

Orlando Cepeda broke in with Santurce's 1955-56 team, but got little playing time, since Bill White was the Crabber first baseman. In a distinguished Puerto Rico career, Cepeda played a lot of first base and some outfield. His .323 lifetime league batting average is identical to Clemente's.[29] A two-time league MVP, Cepeda won one batting award, two RBIs and two home run titles. The Cepeda father-and-son duo, Perucho and Orlando, earned three batting crowns, five RBI titles and three MVP laurels between them. Cepeda's 19 homers in 1961-62 are the most ever by a Puerto Rican.[30] Cepeda says of Bill White, "He helped me a lot on how to play the position. The league prepared me for the majors."

Cepeda played on four championship Santurce squads: the 1958-59, 1961-62, 1964-65 and 1966-67 teams. His slugging propelled Santurce to the 1958-59 title. Tany Pérez and Cepeda were a strong one-two punch for the 1964-65 and 1966-67 teams. When they were Santurce teammates, it was not hard to guess that they would finish their big league careers with 379 homers apiece.[31]

Willie Mays and Bob Gibson were stateside teammates who played on Santurce winners. Cepeda practiced with the 1954-55 team featuring Mays and Roberto Clemente and was the star on the 1961-62 squad which included Gibson. "Willie spoke highly of Puerto Rico, its people, and our ballplayers," Cepeda recalls. "Bob and I are like brothers, and when I stop to think, it was a great honor to play with them. Bob really liked the rice and beans in Puerto Rico."

Orlando had chronic foot problems from childhood, and needed an operation to walk properly. In the mid- and late–1960s I would see Cepeda jogging on San Juan's beaches as part of his training regimen. Cepeda later told me that he jogged on a daily basis during the Winter League season to strengthen his knee. He remains grateful to Pedrín Zorrilla for believing in his playing ability and arranging for his signing with the Giants in 1955.

Félix Millán

Félix Millán found himself in the position of playing winter ball in Venezuela during the 1963-64 season. Caguas had Nate Oliver at second and plenty of infield depth. Felle Delgado, the scout who signed Millán, made contacts which enabled the young second baseman to play for the Pastora Milkers in Venezuela's Occidental League. It was a good league. Phil Niekro was one of Millán's teammates and Luis Tiant kept busy with the Lara club.[32]

Millán played for Caguas from 1964-65 until 1979-80. His U.S. teammates covered the gamut from Ferguson Jenkins to Mike Schmidt to Eddie Murray. He was player-manager of the 1978-79 champions replacing Jim Davenport. Eight years later, Millán was serving in Caguas's front office when they won the Caribbean Series.

A two-time National League Gold Glove recipient, Millán won Puerto Rican batting titles in 1968-69 and 1969-70,[33] his proudest achievements. Millán's most challenging role was as player-manager, when he had to keep a balance between game strategy and playing.

Jerry Morales

Nicknamed "El Teenager de Yabucoa," Jerry Morales went from the Puerto Rican national baseball team in the 1966 Central American and Caribbean games to Caguas. Morales—a native of Yabucoa, in the southeastern part of the Island, as is Félix Millán—was given his nickname upon joining the Caguas club at age 17. He became a regular at 19 and patrolled center field for Caguas during 11 of the next 13 seasons, taking 1977-78 and 1978-79 off. Morales continued Caguas's tradition of having the league's finest native talent. Millán came on board in 1964-65; Montañez was a league Rookie of the Year for Caguas in 1965-66; and Ed Figueroa, a pitcher on the 1966 Puerto Rican national team, joined Caguas with Morales in 1966-67.

Jerry Morales was Mr. Consistency in his 18-year Puerto Rican career. He covered a lot of ground, got clutch hits, provided some punch and ran the bases well. "Hey, don't forget I hit 14 homers for the 1973-74 club as a leadoff hitter," adds Morales. "That was tops on the team and I don't think any leadoff hitter in league history has hit so many."

Horace Clarke

Horace Clarke played shortstop and second base for Ponce from 1962 to 1968 after being acquired from San Juan in a trade which sent Eddie Olivares to the Senators. Clarke, born and raised in St. Croix, played in the league for nine years.

Clarke: "Most of the players from the Virgin Islands who got to the big leagues in those earlier years were fortunate to have been allowed to play in the Puerto Rico League as natives. That wasn't a league to really develop players; they played most of the veteran players, with the hope to win."

Clarke felt hitting against pitchers such as Bob Gibson, Earl Wilson and Dennis McLain really sharpened his skills on the way to the big leagues. He remembers being a second baseman in Puerto Rico and playing 49 straight errorless games for Ponce before bobbling a grounder hit by Mayagüez's Gates Brown.

Hitting and fielding weren't Clarke's only interests. He spent more time around Puerto Ricans than many other imports, in order to become fluent in Spanish. Clarke heard a lot of Spanish spoken on St. Croix—an island where a sizable portion of the population has Puerto Rican roots—but never had much interest in learning it. He later married a Puerto Rican and had plenty of time to practice his Spanish. When Clarke played with Ponce, he lived within easy access of Paquito Montaner Stadium, since he preferred to use public transportation or walk.

José "Cheo" Cruz

José "Cheo" Cruz watched Horace Clarke, Roy White, Roger Repoz, Dick Simpson, Nelson Briles and Steve Carlton lead Ponce to the 1966-67 pennant. The rookie saw some regular-season action and played in ten playoff contests.[34]

Cruz: "I felt so small in front of all those big imports—Repoz, Carlton, Briles and Simpson. I was 19, a few months out of high school and making $400 a month. [Elmo] Plaskett and Clarke were on that team. The Americans lived in a condominium near Catholic University. The players would drive to Montaner from where a bus would take us to the away games."

José "Cheo" Cruz as a Ponce veteran, mid–1980s (courtesy of *El Nuevo Día*).

By the time Cheo Cruz finished his Puerto Rican career, for the 1986-87 Ponce Lions, he was a 39-year-old big league star who had been the Puerto Rico League's highest-paid player. His 119 league homers were the most career blasts by anyone except Bob Thurman's 120. Cruz hit 49 of his homers for Ponce and 70 with Caguas.[35] He still remembers one homer that didn't count in the 1985-86 season. "It was a New Year's Day game in Mayagüez and I hit one over the right-field fence. It rained, but then the sun came out. The game was postponed, but if they had waited, they could have continued play."

There were many highlights in Cruz's 21-season winter career. His brothers Cirilo ("Tommy") and Héctor played with him on the Ponce championship team in 1971-72. Cheo Cruz was injured early in the 1972 Caribbean Series hosted by Santo Domingo, and returned to Puerto Rico. Seven years later, the three Cruz brothers played for Caguas in the Caribbean Series.

Superstars don't get traded often, but Cheo Cruz went from Ponce to Caguas with José Morales for Otto Vélez and others prior to the 1975-76 season. Cruz earned 1976-77 MVP laurels and led the league in hitting and stolen bases two seasons later.[36] He teamed with his brother Héctor and Cal Ripken in 1981-82 to give Caguas a trio of players who hit over .300 with 40-plus RBIs.[37] His final season for Caguas was 1983-84, when Don Mattingly was the hot prospect.

The veteran outfielder was back with the Ponce Lions during his final three seasons. Cruz bowed out with class, hitting .400 in Ponce's final series loss to Caguas.[38] During that series a raw, 17-year-old Juan González was biding his time on the Ponce bench, knowing that someday he would be a league star.

Iván de Jesús and Eduardo Figueroa

Iván de Jesús started his league career under manager Roberto Clemente with the 1970-71 Senators. But he had to wait 20 years before playing on a league champion, the 1990-91 Crabbers. His final season, as a player-coach on the 1991-92 Santurce edition, capped a 21-year career in which de Jesús only took the winter of 1979-80 off. "My heroes were Clemente and Cepeda, but I also looked up to Timba Alvarado [Luis Alvarado, another league shortstop]," says de Jesús. "When I started, the imports came to Puerto Rico knowing they would be or could be big league regulars the following season. Now it's the other way around. They come to improve their skills with the hope of making a major league team." San Juan traded de Jesús to Caguas after the 1970-71 season in an eight-player deal. Caguas then peddled de Jesús to Arecibo before the 1973-74 season for pitchers Ed Figueroa and Manuel Muñiz. Santurce later purchased de Jesús from Arecibo.

The de Jesús–Figueroa deal paid dividends for both teams. The 20-year-old de Jesús became a first-time league regular with the Wolves. Figueroa went on to have back-to-back 10-3 seasons for Caguas as the league's top pitcher in 1973-74 and 1974-75, after winning only 14 games the previous five winter seasons.[39] "The league helped me become a major league pitcher," says Figueroa. "It gave me seasoning and confidence." Ed Figueroa was on the comeback trail when he led the Puerto Rico League in ERA while pitching for the 1982-83 Crabbers and earned Comeback Player of the Year honors.[40] He retired the following winter.

Dickie Thon

Dickie Thon showed a lot of class and determination in his Puerto Rico career. Thon was born in South Bend, Indiana, where his father was completing a degree program at Notre Dame. He took his first swings for Bayamón in his late teens and his final at-bats for Santurce as a 36-year-old veteran. Thon won back-to-back league batting titles in 1980-81 and 1981-82.[41] After hitting .347 for Bayamón in 1982-83, he had an outstanding big league season with Houston—a .286 batting average and 20 homers—and was a National League All-Star.[42]

Thon's unfortunate beaning by the Mets' Mike Torrez on April 8, 1984, followed a winter season when he hit .313 for San Juan.[43] His comeback attempt included a total of 18 games for San Juan and Arecibo over the next three winter seasons. Thon had the heart of a champion and again became a big league starting shortstop.

Ken Duzich, a vision specialist who served as a hitting coach for several Puerto Rico League teams, worked with Thon at the Island's Albergue Olímpico (Olympic Village) prior to the 1989 big league season. Duzich focuses on baseball as a visual game and the importance of the eyes working together as a team. "Dickie was left-eye dominant, but because he was hit on that side, the dominance was shifting to the right," says Duzich. "But he had the same head position he had when he was left-eye dominant. I recommended he open up his head a little bit more so that the right eye had better vision. That's what happened to Dickie. He had a very good year with Philadelphia."

Thon's return to winter ball toward the end of the 1992-93 season was a pleasant surprise to many fans who remembered his grandfather, the San Juan pitcher-outfielder. Thon helped Santurce defeat San Juan in the finals. The presence of Thon and Juan González in the lineup, coupled with the San Juan–Santurce rivalry, brought out 90,369 fans over the six games, with an all-time league record attendance of 23,701 for game six.[44]

Thon: "The Puerto Rico League prepared me for the majors when I was young and helped me get ready for the 1993 big league season. It was great to see Juan González, Iván Rodríguez, Sandy Alomar, Jr., Omar Olivares return to the league."

Thon says his grandfather served as an inspiration to his baseball career. "From the time I was little, I saw how important baseball was to the people of Puerto Rico. My grandfather told me stories about his days with San Juan in the 1940s and early 1950s. He talked about Monte Irvin, Joshua Gibson and others who came down here."

Dickie Thon, Bayamón star shortstop, 1982-83 season (courtesy of Rai García).

Rubén Sierra

Dickie Thon was spraying line drives over Puerto Rican diamonds when 17-year-old Rubén Sierra was signed by Orlando Gómez for the Texas Rangers on November 21, 1982. Sierra twice ran the 60-yard dash in 6.4 seconds to repeat what his idol, Roberto Clemente, had done for Al Campanis 29 years earlier.[45] Gómez saw Sierra throw several bullets from the outfield. He had seen enough. A $30,000 signing bonus was in the works.[46]

Santurce drafted the Puerto Rico Winter League rights to Sierra the following year, but not until the 1984-85 season did he begin playing for the Crabbers. Sierra became the league's Rookie of the Year after helping Santurce qualify for the playoffs. "If I hadn't produced, I wouldn't have played," said Sierra. "I made the best of my opportunity. My goal was to be a baseball player. In high school, I ran the 100 and 400 meters."

Sierra lets his actions speak louder than words. He honed his baseball skills at the Roberto Clemente Sports Complex in Carolina. Sierra's off-the-front-foot swing is patterned after Clemente's.

Sandy Alomar, Jr.

Sandy Alomar, Jr., joined Sierra on the 1984-85 Crabbers. He did not hesitate to thank Frank Verdi and some of his teammates. "It was a special experience, because big league players like Beníquez and Iván de Jesús helped me a lot," said Alomar. "Frank Verdi was of great assistance that first season."

While Sierra made it to the big leagues in 1986, it took Sandy Alomar, Jr., a little longer. The strapping catcher became the 1990 American League Rookie of the Year after an 1989-90 winter season with Ponce. He played for his father that winter and made the league All-Star team. "That was a key winter season for me," recalls Alomar. "I had just been traded to Cleveland and had to come to spring training with all my weapons in place. And thanks to my father's support, I played well for Ponce and was ready to go."

Alomar feels it is important for young Puerto Rican players, namely those in the minors, to play year around. The Puerto Rico League helped develop his skills and he acknowledges that he wouldn't be where he is without winter ball. He returned to winter baseball in 1992-93 and 1993-94.

Danny Tartabull

Danny Tartabull completed his five-year Puerto Rican career just when Sandy Alomar, Jr., and Rubén Sierra were beginning their run. He played for Sandy Alomar, Sr., in 1980-81 with Ponce as an 18-year-old infielder, far from the slugger he became later in the decade. He remembers Rickey Henderson as the star of that Ponce team. Tartabull played as a native, having been born in Puerto Rico. His father, Cuban-born José Tartabull, was an outfielder for the 1962-63 Crabbers when Danny was born.

Tartabull: "My last year [1984-85] in the league helped me stay in the majors once I got there. I faced experienced big leaguers. Candy Maldonado and Carlos Lezcano with Arecibo taught me a lot. Chili Davis is a close friend from the days in Ponce."

Roberto Alomar

Roberto Alomar was drafted by Arecibo while in high school. He did not have a car and asked to be traded to a team closer to his home in Salinas. The 17-year-old Alomar was traded to Caguas prior to the 1985-86 season and began the season as a backup to Al Newman at second base.

Newman: "I tell you, when I first got down there, I was the second baseman and he [Alomar] was young. Later in the season I moved over to shortstop so he could play second." Alomar played in 22 games for Felipe Alou's Criollos.[47] He observes that Alou's style was similar to that of Toronto manager Cito Gaston. "Alou asks you to play hard, and if you're hurt, let him know," Alomar says. "I liked Alou. He's a straightforward guy."

Before Alomar made it to the majors, he played in the 1987 Caribbean Series, held in Hermosillo, Mexico. Caguas reinforced itself with Arecibo's Candy Maldonado, Mayagüez's Bobby Bonilla and Mambo de León, Ponce's David Cone and San Juan's Juan Nieves. The all-native starting lineup featured Carmelo Martínez, Edgar Díaz, Germán Rivera, Henry Cotto, Orlando Mercado and Hedi Vargas joining Alomar, Bonilla and Maldonado.

Caguas won this series despite losing a 14–13 game to the Dominicans, a game which featured eight Caguas homers as well as eight errors. Caguas executive Félix Millán replaced manager Tim Foli with Ramón Avilés after the loss, and Caguas won four straight games to earn the title.

Alomar: "Tim Foli was an aggressive type who taught me quite a bit. I like to play under pressure. After that loss, we came back." Caguas finished out of the playoff picture in 1987-88, but Alomar hit .302 and stole 14 bases.[48] He felt the team was stronger on paper than the 1986-87 team, with Roberto Kelly's speed and the relief pitching of Rob Dibble.

Alomar returned to Caguas in 1988-89 and led the team with a .314 average.[49] Caguas then traded him to Ponce for Juan González prior to the 1989-90 season. Roberto Alomar played for his father in both 1989-90 and 1993-94. In 1989-90 he played 17 games, but opted to take some time off because of nagging injuries. When he returned in 1993-94, it was to contribute to the league's success. "I hope fans realize this league is as good as any and probably better than most," Alomar said at the time. "We just need their support to make this season a great one."

Alomar was traded to San Juan for Javier López prior to the 1994-95 season, and once again played on a Caribbean Series champion. Alomar's stellar 1995 Caribbean Series play at Hiram Bithorn Stadium earned him the MVP award. He hit .560 with 10 RBIs to claim hitting honors while his two stolen bases and .633 on-base percentage put him at the top in these categories. Alomar also cracked two series homers and had an .840 slugging percentage.[50]

Roberto Alomar trying to steal a base, 1989-90 season (courtesy of *El Nuevo Día*).

Juan González

Moises Gómez, director of player personnel for Caguas in the late 1980s and early 1990s, recommended that Santurce draft Rubén Sierra during his stint with the Crabbers. Gómez had worked with Ponce before accepting the Caguas position. The Ponce club was interested in obtaining Roberto Alomar, since his father would be their manager in 1989-90. Gómez had been told by Sandy Johnson, the Texas Rangers' director of player personnel and scouting, that Juan González was ready to play every day.[51]

At the time of the trade, González had only one homer and a .132 batting average in 38 Winter League career at-bats.[52] González played the whole 1989-90 season with Caguas, finishing second in both homers (9) and RBIs (34).[53] He welcomed the trade. "Ramón Avilés [Caguas's manager] gave me a chance to showcase my skills," says González. "It was with Caguas that I proved to everyone that Juan González could play on an everyday basis." González reinforced San Juan for the 1990 Caribbean Series, held in Miami. He slugged two homers in the six-game set, which was won by the Dominican entry, the Escogido Lions.[54]

González returned to winter ball in 1992-93 and 1993-94 after winning consecutive American League home run titles. He saved the Puerto Rico League at the gate. Gonzalez did not play winter ball in 1990-91 or 1991-92, because of back and knee injuries. In 21 1992-93 games, he hit .333 with 7 homers and 14 RBIs, to become the MVP.[55] There was talk about a "deadened ball" before González went on his tear. The league used balls made in China rather than Haiti and some thought this was giving pitchers an edge. By season's end, eight pitchers who threw 40 or more innings in the 48-game schedule had ERAs below 2.00.[56]

González, called Igor since the age of 10 because of his interest in "Mighty Igor," a professional wrestler,[57] was selected by Santurce through a draft after the Caguas franchise folded. He felt the league had been more competitive three years earlier with six teams, but was happy to see the fans return to the ballparks. González rejoined Caguas in 1994-95 when the Criollos came back to the fold.

González: "My first championship was with Santurce and I celebrated to the hilt. The fans enjoyed it, and for a young player like myself, it was an emotional moment. I want to see the league continue because it would be a shame to see it fold after it has helped so many major league superstars. It meant a lot to win the Puerto Rico home run title after the first American League one."

His role as a savior was best expressed by Santurce manager Mako Oliveras: "Juan not only turned our team around, he turned the league around. This team had a different attitude with Juan in the lineup."

Juan González hits one out for Santurce, 1993-94 (courtesy of Angel Colón).

Roberto Hernández

Roberto "Bobby" Hernández joined the 1987-88 Mayagüez pitching staff. Hernández, a product of the New York City public school system, played Legion ball there but made Puerto Rico his home once he became involved in winter ball. He pitched to Mayagüez catchers who were or became big leaguers, including Tom Pagnozzi, Chris Hoiles, Kirt Manwaring, Chad Kreuter and Iván Rodríguez. Like Bobby Bonilla, Hernández played as a native in the league by virtue of Puerto Rican heritage. "I got to know Bobby [Bonilla] that year [1987-88] because as soon as I got on the Island, everybody started calling me "Bobby Junior"—we both look alike," Hernández says. "The example he set was always having fun and taking charge. We had a lot of major leaguers here with good work habits, and Bobby was one of them. We had guys like José Guzmán, Juan Agosto, Jeff Brantley, Jeff Gray pitching, and you see their work habits and their mannerisms and how they go about it."

Hernández was one of Mayagüez's heroes in their 1992 Caribbean Series championship, pitching an 8-0 win over Venezuela in the tiebreaker game.[58] He was moved by the chanting of the fans and the music and sounds which filtered to the field all through the round-robin, final series and Caribbean Series games.

Winter ball was vital to Hernández's becoming the Chicago White Sox's closer midway through the 1992 big league season. Hernández: "It's been very helpful; I'm in a situation where winter ball was a key spot in my life. I had blood clot surgery in 1992 and they [the White Sox] were a little tentative about the 1992-93 season. I told them there were only going to be five teams, and they let me pitch the whole season."

Iván Rodríguez and Wil Cordero

Rodríguez put on the Mayagüez uniform in 1992-93 after being selected by the Indians in the draft that saw Juan González go to Santurce. He played for Caguas in 1990-91 and Bayamón in 1991-92. "I played in 1992-93 and 1993-94 for the fans," says Rodríguez. "It's good for them to see a Juan González, an Iván Rodríguez in action. But I also want to keep in shape."

Wil Cordero, Mayagüez's shortstop, echoes Rodríguez's sentiments. Cordero opened some eyes when he was the 1990-91 league Rookie of the Year. He then became the 1991-92 MVP and went on to win the 1992-93 batting crown.

Cordero: "When the [native] big leaguers play, it gives a boost to the league, fans' morale and baseball in general. It's really helped me in my development as a ballplayer. I was able to get a lot of playing time at a young age and then compete at the AAA and big league level."

Carlos Baerga and Edgar Martínez

San Juan teammates Carlos Baerga and Edgar Martínez came into their own during the 1989-90 winter season by virtue of being co–MVPs. When the results were tallied from 37 participating sportswriters and radio announcers, Baerga and Martínez each finished with 11 first-place votes.[59] Baerga hit .341 with 4 homers and 35 RBIs during the 50-game season, while Martínez became the first player in 41 years to hit over .400 with enough plate appearances to qualify for the batting crown. Martínez hit .424 with 56 hits in 132 official at-bats. But he also drew 37 walks, to easily exceed the required 150 plate appearances.[60]

Not since Luke Easter hit .402 for Mayagüez's fabled 1948-49 team had a player led the league with such an astronomical mark. Martínez's banner season put him in select company with Josh Gibson, Perucho Cepeda, Roy Partlow, Willard Brown, Bob Thurman and the great Coímbre. Other .400 hitters in Puerto Rico include Artie Wilson, Ted Young, Orlando Cepeda, José Morales, Clarence Palm and Tetelo Vargas.[61]

Martínez became Seattle's regular third baseman in 1990, and won the 1992 American League batting crown, after hitting .354 in 23 games for San Juan during the 1991-92 season.[62]

Martínez: "Puerto Rico winter ball has helped me get untracked in spring training. There is less pressure and a more relaxed atmosphere in

Puerto Rico than in the majors. We see baseball as more of a game on the Island. In the U.S., it's more like a system."

There are few big league ballplayers as diligent or consistent as Carlos Baerga. He thinks of his former Cleveland hitting coach, José Morales, as being like a father and gives him much of the credit for his major league success. The San Juan Metros signed Baerga for the 1986-87 season, and he played for this team before and after he became a superstar.

Baerga: "It was with San Juan that I learned how to hit breaking balls. After the 1991 big league season I started playing in December to get ready for spring training. It's also important to help the league. When I play in Puerto Rico, I always play hard. Back when I was a kid, the fans used to 'die' in the ballparks."

Switch-hitting Baerga gives credit to Edgar Martínez for inspiring him to keep working hard. In the 1989-90 season, Baerga usually hit fifth in the San Juan lineup, behind Martínez and Héctor Villanueva. Baerga was the first player in over a decade to hit home runs from both sides of the plate during a league game. After becoming the first American League second baseman to hit 20 or more homers, drive in 100 runs, get 200 hits and have a .300 or better batting average, Baerga put on the San Juan uniform in December 1992. He repeated the same pattern a year later.

Javier López

Javier López was voted the league's All-Star catcher following the 1992-93 season. López became the toast of San Juan and Puerto Rico when he launched a rocket over the left-field fence at Bithorn Stadium to give his Senators a come-from-behind 4-3 win over the Cuban national team on December 1, 1993.

López, a league rookie in 1988-89, had to wait his turn. It was not until his fourth season, 1991-92, that he got significant playing time. The apprenticeship was worth it. "It can be tough for a Latin player to break in with a big league organization," López acknowledges. "That's why this league and other winter leagues are so important. They prepare us to be ready for the challenges ahead of us."

Island stars and workhorses met the challenges facing them, whether it was Rubén Gómez showing Earl Weaver he could still pitch at age 39, or Dickie Thon showing his old League form at 34. The stars performed double duty on big league and Island diamonds. Their noteworthy efforts made Puerto Rico proud. Island fans appreciated their willingness to shine in front of them.

6. They Played On

> *I took all my Puerto Rico at-bats as seriously as the big league pinch hitting trips.*
> —José Manuel Morales, former Arecibo, Caguas, Mayagüez, Ponce and San Juan player

The players in this chapter are known more for their Winter League play than for their careers in the big leagues; even those who did go on to the majors remained more identified with Puerto Rican baseball. Florentino Rivera never made it to the big leagues and finished his summers in Mexico. Guito Conde and Héctor Valle had more Winter League seasons under their belts than major league at-bats. Palillo Santiago, Elrod Hendricks, Sandy Alomar, Sr., José Morales and Candy Maldonado experienced big league success and played on in Puerto Rico.

Carlos Manuel Santiago

Carlos Manuel Santiago found himself on the 1944-45 Mayagüez baseball club with another league rookie, Canena Márquez. Tetelo Vargas and Perucho Cepeda were on this team. Santiago, a scrappy second baseman who played shortstop early in his career, would team with Mayagüez shortstops ranging from Artie Wilson to Maury Wills. Santiago first played organized baseball with Stamford in the Colonial League around 1947.[1] Several years later, he caught the eye of Bill Veeck and Lou Boudreau at the Cleveland Indians' training camp. But fate intervened. "The Korean War came," says Santiago. "I spent 25 months and 5 days in the Army and was honorably discharged as a sergeant."

While Santiago never got another shot at the majors, he played a steady brand of baseball before retiring after the 1959-60 season with Ponce. Santiago fondly remembers deceased teammates from Puerto Rico and the States, including Carlos Bernier, Canena Márquez, Luke Easter and Steve Bilko.

Santiago: "We all got along well. Bilko had played in Cuba and spoke some Spanish. He would practice it with us and really liked Foca Valentín. Easter was just a great guy. Canena and Bernier played with us and they played hard-nosed baseball."

Foca Valentín and Luis Villodas

"Foca" Valentín's real name was Gilberto. He was the fifth starter on Ponce's legendary 1946-47 team, but suffered from asthma. This condition worsened, and after a 4-7 record for Rogers Hornsby in 1950-51, Valentín rechanneled his energies into playing shortstop.[2] According to Ponce broadcaster Rafy Sepúlveda, Valentín would tire after five or six innings. But as a shortstop, he had a quick release to go with his strong arm. Valentín retired after the 1965-66 season, his twentieth with Ponce.

Luis "King Kong" Villodas was a Ponce native who spent most of his 13-year league career as a catcher with Mayagüez. Villodas's amateur team was the Ponce Cubans, and he caught the attention of onlookers with his defensive skills. When Roy Campanella left the Baltimore Elite Giants to play in the Dodger system, it was Villodas who got a call from George Scales, the Elite Giants' manager, to replace the future big league star.

Villodas: "I played for the Elite Giants and the New York Cubans, who had Pedro Formental and Pat Scantlebury. Scales knew me, since he managed Ponce, and gave me a chance." Villodas recalled that Jim Gilliam was the Baltimore batboy.

Villodas, at 6'2" and 210 pounds, one of the biggest Puerto Rican players of his era, did more than play in Puerto Rico. Mayagüez owner Alfonso Valdés had him contact Negro leaguers to play for the Indians in the late 1940s. "King Kong" traveled to Birmingham to touch base with Artie Wilson and Alonzo Perry, and met with Wilmer Fields of the Homestead Grays on the East Coast. He got his nickname the day Valdés traveled to the Villodas home in Ponce to sign the catcher. When Villodas was summoned by his mom from a nap, a startled Valdés stated, "That's King Kong."[3]

Canena Márquez

There was only one Canena Márquez. He burst on the scene in 1944-45 and hit .361, the highest batting average for a league rookie with 100 or more at-bats.[4] Márquez played many of his 20 seasons with Mayagüez, but also starred for his hometown team, Aguadilla, as well as San Juan and Ponce, on his way to connecting the most hits in league history. An adept third baseman in his youth, Márquez impressed onlookers with his hot corner play at the 1944 Amateur World Series, held in Venezuela. Carlos

6. THEY PLAYED ON

Manuel Santiago was also on this Puerto Rican squad. The affable Marquez played some third base in the Winter League, but was primarily an outfielder. It was the final weekend of the 1946-47 season when Canena Márquez broke Josh Gibson's league record of 13 homers.[5] Márquez, San Juan's Larry Doby, Caguas's Buster Clarkson and Ponce's Fernando Díaz Pedroso were in the running for the home run title.

Víctor Navarro, an Aguadilla native, took me on a tour of Aguadilla's Parque Colón 46 years after Canena Márquez clinched the home run title by hitting three over the fence in a three-game series against San Juan. This gave Márquez 14 homers, but he had to sweat out five homers by Larry Doby that weekend.

"Canena was something else," said Navarro. "He put up great numbers in the league, but was a warm, caring human being. I'll never forget that series in the middle of February 1947. It got to the point where the crowd cheered Doby and Canena, but this was the first time a Puerto Rican won an undisputed league home run title when the best Negro leaguers were playing. Before Canena won it, Gibson, Campanella, Leonard ... were the home run kings."

By 1947, Márquez was a star with the Homestead Grays, playing for the East in the 1947 and 1948 Negro League All-Star games.[6] When Márquez won his 1953-54 Puerto Rican MVP and batting titles, he was a 28-year-old veteran who had played with the Boston Braves in 1951. Márquez and Hank Aaron had Island fans buzzing with excitement in 1953-54, much as he and Doby had in 1946-47. At the All-Star break, December 24–26, 1953, Aaron and Márquez each had 57 hits in 166 at-bats, for .343 marks.[7] With less than a week left in the regular season, Aaron held a slight edge, .339 to .337. In a January 31 doubleheader against Mayagüez, Aaron went one for seven and dropped to .333.[8] Márquez brought his average up to .342 with a four-for-eight day. Aaron's three-for-eighteen finish gave him a .322 mark, while Márquez claimed the title at .333. Chuck Harmon finished at .325, good for second.[9]

Márquez was a complete ballplayer who could hit, run, throw, play good defense and provide power when needed. A three-time league stolen-base champ, Márquez and speedster Carlos Bernier had a friendly rivalry throughout the 1950s. They would race each other before league All-Star games.

Cal Ermer, the Mayagüez manager in 1962-63, recalls Canena's blazing speed at age 37 in a semifinal series against Arecibo. Ermer: "There was a ball hit to Bernier behind second and I had the 'stop' sign for Canena. But Luis continued as Bernier dropped his arm and threw wild. We went on to win the championship."

Carlos Bernier

Carlos Bernier would have played in the league for 20 straight years, but a salary dispute resulted in his sitting out 1961-62. Cefo Conde brought Bernier to Mayagüez from their Juana Díaz hometown in 1946. Bernier stole 285 bases in his league career to easily surpass all comers.[10] He garnered five base-stealing crowns, second only to Sandy Alomar, Sr.'s six stolen-base titles.

Puerto Rico's fans liked Bernier's aggressive style of play, but some compared him to Ty Cobb in terms of temperament. Carlos Bernier received several suspensions in his minor league career. Ronnie Samford, Bernier's teammate with San Juan in 1960-61 and in Hawaii in 1963, thinks Bernier's temper affected his career. "Bernier had the ability to have a ten- to fifteen-year major league career," Stamford says. "His temper got the best of him."

According to Ozzie Virgil, Sr., Bernier's Mayagüez teammate from 1952-53 to 1954-55, Bernier had a good "inside-out" stroke to right field. Jackie Brandt played against Bernier in 1958-59 when Santurce and San Juan locked horns. Brandt called Bernier an Aparicio-type player, a thorn in your side.

Perhaps the best compliment paid to Bernier was Rogers Hornsby's attempt in 1950-51 to acquire the stolen-base champ for Ponce via the trade route. Hornsby met with Mayagüez skipper Wayne Blackburn to discuss trade possibilities, but nothing came of these meetings, held at Blackburn's Mayagüez residence. By the time Bernier played his final season, in 1965-66, the 36-year-old outfielder was a reserve for Arecibo. It was humorous but sad to hear the fans in Bithorn Stadium fans yell *"vieja, vieja"* (old woman) at Bernier when he made a play in the outfield or came to the plate.

Natalio "Pachy" Irizarry

Natalio "Pachy" Irizarry did everything from winning Rookie of the Year laurels and pitching in All-Star games to owning the Mayagüez baseball club. Irizarry was at the University of Dayton in the late 1940s when Rogers Hornsby and Benny Huffman, a scout, came looking for baseball talent on the campus. Hornsby suggested that Irizarry attend his baseball school in Hot Springs, Arkansas. Irizarry recalls, "Hornsby liked my stuff and arrangements were made to join the Abbeville, Louisiana, team — my first professional team. I later played with Baton Rouge and St. Petersburg in the Florida League."

Santiago Llorens, the Mayagüez sportswriter and *Sporting News* correspondent, was instrumental in Irizarry's being drafted by Mayagüez for 1949-50. Irizarry came through with an 8-7 record and a 2.94 ERA and was voted the league's top rookie.[11]

Four years later he set a league record for Puerto Rican pitchers, with 29 consecutive scoreless innings. But he will never forget the long homer Hank Aaron hit off him on December 23, 1953, in the league All-Star Game. It was a tape-measure blast of over 450 feet which cleared a stone wall at Caguas's Sola Morales Stadium. "That was quite a shot," remembers Irizarry. "What I really liked about the All-Star activities was the reception hosted at La Fortaleza [the governor's mansion] by Governor Muñoz Marín. It was a nice atmosphere and all of us had a good time."

Rudy Hernández

Rudy Hernández began his Puerto Rican career as an outfielder and ended it on the mound 15 years later. Rogers Hornsby gave the Ponce rookie a lot of playing time in 1950-51, but noted Hernández had a hitch in his swing and suggested he focus on pitching.

Hernández recalls the time Hornsby was so annoyed with the team's lack of production that he called them in for a 3:30 P.M. batting practice session before an 8 P.M. game. Hornsby had player-coach Coímbre pitch to him and proceeded to hit 20 rockets. Then Foca Valentín pitched to Coímbre, who also impressed onlookers with his drives.

As a league rookie Hernández lived in the same Ponce building as Clint Courtney and Bill Skowron. Hernández had come to Puerto Rico via the Dominican Republic and New York City. His father was the son of Trujillo's top general in the Dominican military. His mom came from Puerto Rico, qualifying Hernández to play as a league native.

Hernández became the first Dominican-born pitcher to pitch in the majors when he made his debut for the 1960 Washington Senators.[12] Juan Marichal appeared in his first game 16 days later. In the late 1950s Hernández and Marichal both pitched for the Escogido Lions, the Dominican team featuring the Alou brothers, Manny Mota, Ozzie Virgil, Sr., and U.S. prospect Willie McCovey.

Ozzie Virgil, Sr.

Ozzie Virgil, Sr., the first Dominican-born athlete to play in the majors, played as a native in Puerto Rico by virtue of having a Puerto Rican father. He began his winter baseball career with Mayagüez, playing there from 1952-53 to 1954-55, and returned to the Dominican Republic for the next three seasons. But he returned to the Indians after witnessing an unpleasant event in a Dominican playoff game.

Virgil's Escogido team was playing Licey in the 1958-59 championship series when Escogido's Andre Rodgers was knocked down by a pitch. Rodgers charged the mound and a scuffle ensued. One of General Trujillo's brothers came out of the stands with armed guards to stop the fighting, and slapped Rodgers in the face. Virgil opted to play for Mayagüez in the 1960s, after major league baseball commissioner Ford Frick gave him permission.

When Virgil returned to Mayagüez for the 1959-60 season, Carlos Bernier and Carlos Manuel Santiago were no longer with the club. Florentino Rivera still played. Instead of using imports from the Dodgers—Tom Lasorda, Dixie Howell and Don Zimmer—Mayagüez now had a Tiger connection. Virgil fit in well, with his willingness to pitch and versatility in the infield. He would usually relieve four or five times each winter and could be pressed into starting duty if needed. "I helped Mayagüez in whatever way I could," says Virgil. "It was a good league with many great players. I'll never forget those Mayagüez-Santurce games when Lasorda pitched to Mays, or the time we won the championship in 1965-66."

Florentino Rivera

Florentino Rivera's summer baseball career began in Dublin, Georgia, during 1951 and over a 17-year period included St. Jean (Canada), Omaha, and Puebla/Jalisco, Mexico. The Ponce native pitched 16 winter seasons with Mayagüez, from 1952-53 to 1967-68. Rivera usually gave Mayagüez 80-plus regular-season innings, plus a couple of postseason starts and relief appearances.

Rivera: "Santurce was the best team when I started. They had Willard Brown, Bob Thurman, Buster Clarkson, Valmy Thomas. We traveled in *publicos* [jitneys], but by 1958-59 a team bus took us to the road games."

Rivera pitched in three international events—the 1957 Caribbean Series, held in Havana, and two Interamerican Series: San Juan's in 1962 and Panama's in 1963. His most important start came against Ponce and Steve Carlton in game six of the 1965-66 finals. Mayagüez won, 3–2, but Rivera was not involved in the decision.[13] "I won game two of that series at home, which gave us a 2–0 lead," Rivera recalls. "They came back to tie the series, but we took games five and six. John Hiller pitched well in relief for us."

Florentino Rivera was one of many Puerto Rican ballplayers in organized baseball to finish his career in Mexico. He played nine summers in Mexico and only eight in the United States. "Baseball in Mexico is good for us," he insists. "The game is based on prospects who can make it and have a long big league career. Once we're 28 to 30 years old, we're no longer prospects. We may still have the ability, but probably won't spend much time in the majors. Our contracts were sold to teams in Mexico, and we could produce there in a AA to AAA environment. The St. Louis Cardinals did buy my contract after a good showing with Nuevo Laredo, but I got injured pitching for Tulsa and they sent me back to Mexico."

Jim Rivera

Manuel Joseph "Jungle Jim" Rivera found himself in Mexico during the winter of 1955-56. A Caribbean Confederation ruling had stipulated that big leaguers with two or more years' experience, who were not natives of Cuba, Puerto Rico, Panama or Venezuela, could not play in those leagues. So Rivera signed with the Mexico City Reds, owned by Bobby Avila, in the Veracruz League. (Mexico's other winter league was the Pacific Coast League.) Rivera was limited to 45 games under the majors' barnstorming rules then in effect. But he made these games count, hitting over .400. In December the *Sporting News* correspondent for the Veracruz League called Rivera the hottest "article" in Mexico since the introduction of the hot tamale.[14]

Jim Rivera played as a native for Caguas from the early to mid–1950s. But by 1955 there were doubts about his Puerto Rican roots. Skeptics joked that a search was going on for one of Rivera's grandmothers on the Island. Luis Olmo used the term *chivo* (out of the blue) when asked whether Rivera could be considered a Puerto Rican for league purposes.

Rivera returned to the Island in 1961-62 as a native player once again. His big league playing career was over, but he and Frank Howard comprised a powerful one-two punch for Caguas. The Caguas brass made Rivera their player-manager that winter and the following two seasons.

There have been few league players with Rivera's intensity. In a November 25, 1953, game against San Juan, with Rivera on second base and Vic Power at the plate, Caguas manager Mickey Owen called for the hit and run. Power grounded out to second, but Rivera ran through Owen's "stop" sign and scored Caguas's only run in their 3–1 loss.[15] Owen attempted to discuss the matter in the clubhouse once the game had ended. Rivera got into a fight with his manager, but neither man suffered any injuries. Forty years later, Mickey Owen laughs about the incident: "Jim Rivera was something else. He hated losing, and we got along fine after that scrap. Rivera came to play."

When Rivera and Hank Aaron finished in a tie for most league home runs in 1954, Rivera ended up with the booty—cash and cartons of cigarettes. Aaron returned to the States and opted not to claim his share of the prizes.[16] Rivera then hit .450 to pace all hitters in the 1954 Caribbean Series and earn the MVP award.[17]

Bill Veeck decided Jim Rivera had been playing baseball too long without a rest—22 months—when he made an appointment with the outfielder shortly before Christmas 1951, at Rogers Hornsby's request. Rivera promised Veeck he could cover a lot of ground. Veeck then asked him how he was going to do against the American League pitchers in 1952. "Don't let that worry you," said Rivera. "I'll hit those guys. One thing in my favor is the good control American League pitchers are supposed to have."

A pensive Jim Rivera, Caguas's player-manager, early 1960s (courtesy of *The San Juan Star*).

He mentioned his experience playing all three outfield positions in Puerto Rico. And he made it clear to Veeck that Hornsby was the main reason for his success. Rivera related this conversation to me four decades later, stating he showed Hornsby he could hit, run and play defense, convincing Hornsby to take him north to play for the Seattle club. Prior to a Ponce-Caguas game, Hornsby spoke to Rivera in the dugout to arrange the meeting at a Ponce hotel where the outfielder signed a AAA contract with the 1951 Seattle Pacific Coast League team.

Nino Escalera

Nino Escalera wore a Caguas uniform in 1963-64 after 16 seasons with San Juan. He recalls Jim Rivera playing aggressive baseball at age 41—diving headfirst into the bases, providing real entertainment for the fans. But Escalera was no slouch either, finishing third on the all-time league hit list.

Escalera hit .337 for the 1947-48 Senators in his league debut.[18] He joined the San Juan club after a stellar performance in the November 1947 World Amateur Baseball Tournament hosted by Cartagena, Colombia. "I was chosen to play first base for Puerto Rico. Víctor Pellot [Vic Power] signed with Caguas and other first basemen became professionals as well," said Escalera. "Rubén Gómez signed a Santurce contract and I did likewise with San Juan, but there was a rule then that you could play amateur ball for two weeks after signing. So I was able to sign with San Juan just before the tournament and began my professional career upon returning."

When Luis Olmo did not return to manage San Juan in 1959-60, it was Escalera who got the nod. He came through in fine style as San Juan won the pennant with a 41-23 mark, their best regular season record in 20 years.[19] Escalera's other league managing stint was a charm. He replaced Vic Power as Caguas's 1967-68 manager and led the Criollos to an Island title.

Julio Navarro and José Pagán

Julio Navarro and José Pagán were on the Bithorn Stadium turf the night in 1968 when Caguas bested Santurce to put Nino Escalera in the books as the manager of a championship team. These two gentlemen had taken little time off since their rookie 1955-56 season. Their Puerto Rico careers were mirror images of each other. They were traded from Santurce to Caguas for Terín Pizarro just before the 1959-60 season.[20] Twelve years later, the duo was shipped to San Juan for Cocó Laboy, Luis Alvarado, Iván de Jesús and Sam Parrilla.[21] Pagán's 19-year playing career ended with the 1973-74 season, and he became the manager of the Bayamón Cowboys, taking Navarro with him as a pitcher and coach. Navarro's final three seasons were spent with Bayamón, capping a career that spanned 22 years.

Navarro: "When Pagán was appointed to manage Bayamón, he wanted me to continue pitching, but also had me coach the younger hurlers. John Candelaria was one of my major projects." Pagán was with the Pittsburgh organization at the time, and asked his buddy Navarro to pay special attention to Candelaria. Navarro worked closely with the tall lefty from New York, a native for league purposes, based on his Puerto Rican heritage. Candelaria had played amateur basketball in Puerto Rico and was a member of the Island's national team. Navarro told Candelaria he had a golden left arm and warned him not to waste his opportunity for big league stardom. And Navarro recalls the tears of gratitude which flowed from Candelaria's eyes after listening to one of his pep talks.

Navarro was born in Vieques, one of only two offshore Island municipalities, but his right arm was molded in St. Croix. He played ball as a youngster with Joe Christopher, Elmo Plaskett and Horace Clarke. During

February a team from Puerto Rico would usually play a series of games against a combined St. Thomas–St. Croix squad. Playing in one of these games, Navarro impressed Virgin Islander Alfonso Gerard, a veteran with Santurce.

Navarro: "Gerard spoke with me about coming to a tryout in Puerto Rico. In March [1955] I found myself with Orlando Cepeda and José Pagán working out under the watchful eyes of Pedrín Zorrilla. Right after our practice, Pedrín gave me a $300 bonus to sign with the New York Giants. Pagán and Cepeda got $500 each."

Navarro learned a lot from Bill Greason and Rubén Gómez, two of Santurce's veteran hurlers. Santurce's juggernaut had the best young talent in Puerto Rico, with Clemente, Cepeda, Pagán, Pizarro and others. By 1958-59 Navarro was one of the league's top pitchers.

The Caguas Criollos hoped sending Pizarro and $10,000 to Santurce in 1959 for the rights to Navarro and Pagán would pay off. This transaction was made subject to approval by the Braves and Giants. Much to the relief of Caguas and Santurce, neither big league organization objected to the deal. Caguas president Juan Vázquez was happy, because Navarro had been a nemesis of the Criollos.

Navarro's stuff baffled league hitters for another decade and a half. His 10-1 mark for the 1967-68 Criollos kept the team in contention for the pennant, but they finished second to Santurce.[22] Caguas upset the favored Crabbers in the finals in six games, as Navarro won the last contest by a lopsided 17–2 score.

Navarro cherishes the back-to-back championships won by the 1974-75 and 1975-76 Bayamón Cowboys. A stabilizing force on the 1974-75 squad, Navarro compiled a 5-2 record with a team-leading 1.41 ERA.[23] In 1975-76, he had a 2.35 ERA and won a game in the finals against the favored Caguas team, who thought Navarro was too old to pitch well.[24] Julio Navarro, the father of pitcher Jaime Navarro, retired on his own terms after the 1976-77 season.

José Pagán got off to a good start when he became Santurce's regular third baseman as a league rookie in 1955-56. By 1958-59, Pagán had emerged as one of the league's best hitters. Pagán was a team leader for Caguas and San Juan after his trades to those teams. He inspired his teammates, including Félix Millán, Willie Montañez and Jerry Morales with Caguas, and Milt May, Rennie Stennett and Richard Zisk on the San Juan club.

John Strohmayer was an import who became good friends with Pagán on the 1970-71 Caguas club. The following summer, Strohmayer was pitching against Pagán when Montreal played Pittsburgh. "I threw José a 1-2 fastball inside—he was looking for a slider outside—and the pitch came in and broke his wrist," Strohmayer recalls. "In fact, when I hit José, and heard that sickening thud and crack, I said, 'Oh, no, geez, here's a guy who's my friend.' I found out he had a broken wrist from a clubhouse report. A couple of innings later, Roberto Clemente, a good friend of José, hit a comebacker to me—wanted to hit the ball out of the park and show me I couldn't hit his friend and get away with it.... [After the putout he] made a big loop, and said a few things in Spanish which weren't so pleasant."

Strohmayer again played against Pagán during the 1971-72 Winter League season. "José was with San Juan and I returned to Caguas," Strohmayer says, recalling a conversation they had before a game. "He's still wearing his brace and tells me, 'I'm going to take it off. I went to the doctor and it's completely healed; the chance of it being broken again are a thousand to one.' The first time up in that game, someone threw a curveball and hit him in the wrist in that same exact spot, a re-break of the one a few months earlier." Pagán returned to action with San Juan and played through the 1973-74 season. He was San Juan's designated hitter in 1973-74, the first league season the DH rule went into effect.

Guito Conde

Ramón Luis "Guito" Conde, the pride of his dad, Cefo, played for 20 years and could have played a few more if the DH rule had been in effect. Conde began and finished his career with Ponce, but played for Mayagüez from 1959-60 to 1966-67 and briefly with Caguas in 1958-59. It was with Mayagüez that he earned league MVP laurels, in 1959-60, after winning the RBI title.[25] The clutch hitter played on three Ponce and two Mayagüez winners.

Conde played through many injuries, including a bum shoulder in the mid–1960s which limited his play to first base. He remembers a young Denny McLain in the 1964-65 season as someone who enjoyed doing things his way. "I remember we used to change in Mayagüez before the Arecibo away games," says Conde. "McLain insisted on playing shortstop during a practice session before leaving for Arecibo and a grounder took a bad hop and hit him near the eyes and stitches were taken."

Conde's 17 minor league seasons began in 1954, when he was Bill White's roommate at Sioux City in the Giants' chain. Toward the end of his minor league career, Conde helped make the contacts which resulted in two Indianapolis teammates, Bernie Carbo and Wayne Simpson, coming to Puerto Rico.

Conde: "Ponce owner Yuyo González told me Caguas was after Carbo and Simpson. I was on the 1969 Indianapolis roster at the time and talked with Bernie and Wayne about playing for Ponce. They decided to join Ponce after the minor league season."

The 1969-70 season was Conde's finest in terms of batting average (.386) as Jim Fregosi's pinch-hitter deluxe.[26] Simpson and Carbo were named to the league's All-Star team. Ponce fans still talk about Conde's base hit off Santurce's Fred Beene to give them a dramatic win in game six of the finals and the championship. Conde's heroics catapulted Ponce into the first Caribbean Series of the modern era, the 1970 event in Caracas.

Héctor Valle

Héctor Valle only had 13 big league at-bats, with the 1965 Dodgers, and hit .308.[27] His biggest thrill in the majors was catching Sandy Koufax in a game at Philadelphia. "They rested Roseboro after Los Angeles had a 7–1 lead," Valle remembers. "Koufax told me his experience with Caguas was a pleasant one and good for his career. He is a very nice person."

Valle was a five-year league veteran by that time, having begun his Puerto Rico career for the 1959-60 Caguas club. As a reserve catcher that season, Valle hit .333 for Vic Power in 39 at-bats.[28] He still gets chills remembering the 1960 Caribbean Series: "Just being in Panama was something. It was a joy being on the same team with players like Félix Mantilla and Roberto Vargas." There was a Caguas-Dodgers connection, according to Valle. Los Angeles scout Monchile Concepción coached and briefly managed Caguas during the early 1960s, a time when Frank Howard, Ron Perranoski and Pete Richert played for the Criollos.

A trade sent Valle and pitcher Carmelo Aquino from Caguas to Mayagüez for Joe Christopher before the 1965-66 season. Valle liked the Detroit-Mayagüez hookup, since the young Tigers knew each other and played well together. It was clear to Valle that they were trying to impress Mayagüez manager Wayne Blackburn, who was in the Detroit organization. They went out and played hard.

Mayagüez traded Valle to San Juan for catcher Willie Meléndez after the 1972-73 season. But he didn't mind, since his San Juan manager was Jim Gilliam, a former Dodger teammate in 1965. Valle responded by hitting .315 in 127 at-bats as a catcher and DH.[29]

Valle's league playing career ended in 1979-80 with Ponce. He was a rookie when Tommy Davis patrolled left field for Caguas and on his way out during Rickey Henderson's first winter as Ponce's left fielder. Valle particularly enjoyed assisting Ponce manager José Pagán with bullpen chores and hitting grounders and fly balls to infielders and outfielders at this stage in his career.

When Pagán accepted the Arecibo managing job for 1980-81, Valle went with him as a coach. Valle passed on his wisdom to Arecibo players, among them Jeff Reardon, Mookie Wilson, Candy Maldonado and Jesús "Samarito" Vega.

Woody Huyke

Elwood "Woody" Huyke broke in with Caguas along with Valle and became the 1959-60 Rookie of the Year, with a .302 average.[30] Huyke played third base and catcher in a career lasting into the early 1970s. His break as a rookie was when Félix Mantilla reported late. Huyke recalls going hitless in his first ten trips to the plate. But getting a single, a double and a homer off Luis Arroyo in a game at Escobar Stadium started a nine-for-ten year and Huyke stayed in Vic Power's lineup throughout the season. Power gave Huyke the final day of the season off to keep his batting average above .300. Huyke continued hitting throughout the league playoffs and in the 1960 Caribbean Series hit .350, to rank among the top ten hitters.[31]

Huyke liked having Jim Rivera as a manager and teammate in the early 1960s. "Jim had a rough background, but is a tremendous human being and someone you respect. I get a Christmas card from him every year." Huyke played on two more winners, the 1967-68 Criollos and 1971-72 Lions. He later coached four Caguas champions—in 1973-74, 1976-77, 1978-79 and 1980-81—plus the 1982-83 Arecibo winners.

About that Arecibo team, Huyke says, "God had divine hands over us that season. We were received by the governor and Senate after returning as Caribbean Series champions. The whole thing was apocalyptical."

Elrod Hendricks

Elrod Hendricks had a remarkable career in Puerto Rico with the Santurce Crabbers. The 1968-69 MVP was one of the top home run hitters in league history. Five of his Santurce teams won league championships in a career lasting from 1961-62 to 1977-78. And, like Woody Huyke, Hendricks played on a winner his rookie season. "I began catching Pizarro and Gibson," said Hendricks. "It was a thrill to catch Pizarro. As a matter of fact, I was his catcher in my first game. He made my whole stay a lot easier."

As a league rookie Hendricks served as backup to Valmy Thomas. He roomed for a couple of winters with Horace Clarke at the San Juan YMCA, until Clarke was traded to Ponce by the San Juan club. His closest friend on the Santurce team was veteran pitcher William de Jesús.

Hendricks: "When I was out of [summer] baseball, de Jesús was in Mexico. Their team needed a player and he recommended me to 'Jungle Jim' Rivera, Jalisco's manager. Jim Rivera still played for Caguas while I was in Puerto Rico and he gave me the opportunity to play again. That's when my career turned around."

Hendricks made it to the major leagues with Baltimore in 1968, and played winter ball for another decade. He relished the opportunity to play alongside Pizarro, Cepeda, Tany Pérez and Rubén Gómez. "We're talking about professionals—they knew how to win, how to play the game," Hendricks asserts. "These guys played their hearts out for the fans. They loved to play and wanted to come home and do well. I think fans expected them to hit homers or pitch shutouts all the time. I take my hat off to these guys—with all their adversity, they went out and played."

José Manuel Morales

José Manuel Morales set a major league record with 25 pinch hits for the 1976 Montreal Expos on his way to amassing 123 in his career.[32] But Island fans learned he could really hit during Elrod Hendricks's MVP season, when Morales finished with a .402 average, 4 homers and 18 RBIs in 112 at-bats for the 1968-69 San Juan club.[33] Morales continued his heavy hitting for San Juan, Ponce and Mayagüez.

Until the advent of the DH rule, Morales was primarily a catcher. With San Juan, he backed up Johnny Bench and Thurman Munson. Morales hit as many homers (5) as Bench did, but did it in only 70 at-bats, compared with Bench's 229.[34] Two winters later, Munson hit 3 homers for the 1969-70 Senators in 228 at-bats, while Morales clouted 4 in only 96 official trips.[35]

Morales: "I took all my Puerto Rico at-bats as seriously as the big league pinch-hitting trips. The Puerto Rico League did a lot for my big league career. It kept me in the majors for over ten years. At the time I played, there was pride in winning. Yet it was a relaxed atmosphere."

Morales was a league hitting machine throughout the 1970s, hitting .350 for the 1972-73 Lions as a role player and .329 two winters later as a full-time DH.[36] As a member of the 1976-77 Caguas team, he was one of seven regulars who hit over .300.

Morales's most enjoyable moments came in 1977-78 with Caribbean Series Champion Mayagüez, when he led all Caribbean Series hitters with a .421 average.[37] "I felt good representing Puerto Rico in Caribbean Series play with Caguas in 1977 and Mayagüez in 1978," he says. "The fact I wasn't named the 1978 Caribbean Series MVP didn't bother me that much—we won."

Sandy Alomar, Sr.

Santos "Sandy" Alomar, Sr., began his big league career in 1964, after honing his skills at shortstop for the Arecibo Wolves. Alomar was a big league All-Star with nine years of winter ball experience by 1970, and was the Puerto Rico League MVP and batting champion in 1970-71 with Ponce. "Luis Olmo signed me for Arecibo and Milwaukee," Alomar recalls. "He saw me play Little League and Pony baseball. I spent a lot of time practicing with my brothers. Tony played with Caguas, San Juan, Santurce; Demetrio with Santurce and Arecibo; Rafael with Ponce."

Sandy's first six league seasons were spent with Arecibo before he was traded to Ponce. After seven winters with Ponce, Alomar was again traded — to Santurce. Alomar played with Santurce from 1974-75 to 1977-78, and briefly for Ponce, in 1980-81, where he was a player-manager. He finished his Island career in fourth place on the all-time hit list, behind Márquez, Bernier and Nino Escalera.[38] Alomar retired as a player after the 1980-81 season, leaving a legacy for his sons and others to follow.

José "Palillo" Santiago

José "Palillo" Santiago was another in a series of league stars from Juana Díaz, including Cefo Conde, Carlos Bernier and Guito Conde. He won his first game for San Juan in their 1960-61 championship season. By 1962-63 he was San Juan's workhorse and best pitcher, with a 10-2 record and a 2.44 ERA in 136 innings of work.[39] Santiago's league career ended following his 1977-78 season with Ponce.

Santiago became the first pitcher from Puerto Rico to start game one of a World Series, when he opposed Bob Gibson to open the 1967 Fall Classic between Boston and St. Louis. His home run off Gibson set off celebrations in all of Puerto Rico. Santiago had played a key role in assisting his 1966-67 San Juan club to secure some Red Sox players. "I suggested that San Juan hire Dick Williams as their manager and some Red Sox prospects," says Santiago. "Williams was a dynamic manager for our Toronto AAA club, who was a candidate for the 1967 Red Sox managing job and unfortunately couldn't come to Puerto Rico because of his commitments that winter."

Boston sent Reggie Smith, pitcher Gary Waslewski and catcher Russ Gibson to San Juan as a result of Santiago's legwork. Smith cracked 11 homers to lead the team, while Gibson provided steady glovework. Waslewski had the team's best ERA (1.94). Santiago had a 6-5 record and a 2.67 ERA, but the team finished fifth, suffering from a lack of run production.[40]

Boston liked Santiago's idea of sending former Cy Young winner Jim Lonborg to Puerto Rico for the 1970-71 season. Santiago: "Lonborg thought this was a good idea and so did Boston. We shared some good times that winter season. He wasn't completely recovered from his injury, but began showing signs of improvement."

Santiago was beginning to take on the role of a mentor to some of the team's young pitchers like Julio Navarro did. Jon Matlack was one of San Juan's young 1971-72 pitchers who went on to have a good big league

José "Palillo" Santiago on the mound for San Juan in the early 1970s (courtesy of *The San Juan Star*).

career. Santiago found it ironic that Clemente got his three thousandth big league hit off Matlack less than a year after he worked with Matlack in Puerto Rico.

The highlight of Santiago's league career was winning the 1963-64 championship and going to Nicaragua for the Interamerican Series. He still can't get over the fact that San Juan lost the 1964 series with a team that included Clemente, Cepeda, Pizarro, McNertney, Pagán and Guito Conde.

Otto Vélez

Otto Vélez starred for Caguas and Ponce during the 1970s, tying Roger Freed for the 1977-78 home run title and battling Dan Driessen for the 1975-76 batting crown. He finished his career with Santurce in 1984-85. "I had been traded from Caguas to Ponce in the José Cruz–José

Morales transaction," Vélez recalls. "Cirilo Cruz, Juan López, myself and several others went to Ponce and there was cash involved. That season [1975-76] helped me stick with the Yankees the next spring. I was on a World Series team with Ed Figueroa and Sandy Alomar and we played the 'Big Red Machine.'"

Before Driessen's Reds faced off against Vélez's Yankees in the 1976 Fall Classic, they had gone down to the final day of the 1975-76 season in a dead heat for the Winter League batting crown. Driessen won the title, hitting .331 to Vélez's .328.[41] "On the last day of the season I went 0 for 3," says Vélez. "I had been hit by a pitch and was a bit tentative at the plate."

Vélez also saw action with the 1973-74 Caguas club. He calls it the best league team he ever played on. "There was no envy on that team, though there were many who could really play. Gary Carter wanted to become a better player, Schmidt had to overcome a season with a lot of strikeouts."

Vélez's 1982-83 Santurce club had some of his old Caguas mates, including Jerry Morales and Willie Montañez. Vélez felt the Crabbers were much better on paper than the Arecibo club which upset them. As a 32-year-old veteran, he enjoyed hearing the fans call his 42-year-old teammate Luis Tiant "older than Methusalah."

Gil Flores

Gil Flores was an exciting and fun player to watch, with his speed and ability to get the extra base. Flores finished his Ponce career second only to Pancho Coímbre in runs scored for the Lions.[42] He had a three-year stint in the majors with California and the New York Mets, but spent most of his summers in Tidewater and other minor league cities. He first played for Santurce in the early 1970s, but saw little playing time, with the likes of Don Baylor, Willie Crawford and Mickey Rivers playing for Frank Robinson. Santurce traded him to Ponce in 1974 in the Sandy Alomar deal.

Flores hit it off with Rickey Henderson, Chili Davis and other Ponce imports during his ten-plus seasons with the club. He played in the same outfield with Henderson, Davis, Roger Freed, Mel Hall, Ellis Valentine and Joe Carter. "Rickey and I would travel together to road games," says Flores. "Sometimes we'd go out to a disco, have a bite to eat. Rickey was well taken care of by the team owner."

Quique Rivera and Polilla Ortíz

Quique Rivera held down the hot corner for three Ponce title winners from the late 1960s through the early 1970s. He impressed managers Rocky Bridges, Jim Fregosi and Frank Verdi with his hitting and fielding. Although he played well in the league, Rivera never made it to the majors.

Rivera: "I would see players come down here for one season and then they would be in the majors within a year. I'd see lots of players move up. I left my AA or AAA team at various times."

José "Polilla" Ortíz made things happen from 1966-67 to 1976-77. His nickname means "termite," and Polilla dug in. He and Canenita Allen were reserve outfielders on San Juan's 1966-67 squad. In 1967-68 Ortíz was the starting right fielder until Clemente returned to action. Ortíz was Sparky Anderson's fourth outfielder with San Juan in 1968-69 and performed the same role for Cot Deal in 1969-70. Clemente made sure Ortíz got plenty of playing time during the 1970-71 season. "I led the team in hitting that year," Ortíz reminisces. "Clemente liked the way I hustled and produced."

Ortíz was dealt by San Juan to Mayagüez, who, in turn, shipped him to Ponce for the 1971-72 season. He vowed to get back at San Juan when Ponce qualified for the finals against his old team. True to his word, Ortíz hit .316 in the league finals to help Ponce win the title.[43]

Ortíz played for Frank Robinson with Santurce in 1974-75, when he and Sandy Alomar joined this team after Ponce traded them for Mangual and Flores.

Ortíz: "I liked playing for Frank Robinson, Frank Verdi and Sparky Anderson. They all knew how to handle the players and get the most out of them."

Juan Beníquez

Juan Beníquez was known as the "Clipper Cangrejero" for his fine play in center field with the Santurce Crabbers (Cangrejeros). Beníquez, along with Santurce legend Rubén Gómez, played in the league during four different decades. Beníquez first played as an 18-year-old for the 1968-69 Arecibo club. By the time he played on his second league champion, the 1990-91 Santurce team, Beníquez had turned 40. It was Beníquez's consistency and longevity which enabled him to finish his league career fifth on the all-time hit list.

A versatile player who could play both infield and outfield, Beníquez joined Santurce in 1972-73, the Crabbers' last winning team before the 1990-91 edition. By 1985-86, the 35-year-old Beníquez was Santurce's oldest player, sharing his wisdom and expertise with fellow outfielders Rubén Sierra and Devon White. Santurce players Mike Devereaux and Mike Sharperson appreciated Beníquez's counsel later in the decade.

Candy Maldonado

Candy Maldonado played with Arecibo from 1978-79 to 1988-89, with the exception of 1981-82, when Arecibo was out of the league and

Candy Maldonado was the hitting star of the 1981 Puerto Rico League's All-Star game, with two homers. He played for the "Isla" (Island) squad (courtesy of *El Nuevo Día*).

Bayamón selected him in a draft. Maldonado returned to Arecibo in 1993-94 as a gesture of solidarity with the league and the fans. He came into his own during the 1980-81 All-Star Game, clouting two homers in the "Island" team's 5–3 victory against the metro-area squad and becoming the fifth player in league history to accomplish this feat, after Josh Gibson, Hank Aaron, Roberto Clemente and Ismael Oquendo.[44]

Maldonado has lived in Arecibo since the early 1970s, when he played in Little League. When Arecibo went all the way in 1982-83, it was a dream come true.

Maldonado: "It was good for the town and Puerto Rico. To win it with the help of Dickie Thon, Jesús Hernaíz, Junior Ortíz, Mambo de León and Carmelo Martínez from other teams was great. I was named to that Caribbean Series All-Star team."

The "Candy Man" hit .348 in that series, the highlight of his league career along with two All-Star game homers.[45] He was durable, playing in over 300 consecutive league games from 1980-81 to 1984-85.[46] Maldonado reinforced Caguas's 1987 Caribbean Series winners and played in several more All-Star games. As a league veteran, he helped the younger players learn the ropes. "When I was young, I observed what the older players did," Maldonado says. "There were many players I talked with. The chance to face a Dennis Martínez, a Figueroa, a Tiant, helped a lot. Later it was my turn to set an example and help out."

Henry Cotto

Henry Cotto was to Caguas what Maldonado meant to Arecibo—an outfielder who gave over 100 percent each season. The Bronx-born Cotto played from 1980-81 to 1990-91 and 1994-95. In Cotto's rookie season, Cal Ripken played third base. A decade later, it was Dave Hollins at the hot corner. But Henry Cotto was a staple for Caguas fans. He was the team's and the league's MVP in 1984-85.

When Caguas won its 1986-87 title, Cotto had been a regular for five seasons. He thrived on winter ball, deriving a lot of benefit from the extra playing time. "The league has helped a lot of Puerto Ricans and Americans fine-tune their skills," insists Cotto. "Many Puerto Ricans who are in the majors would not be there without this league. My former Caguas teammates Ron Gant and Don Mattingly went on to become stars after playing in Puerto Rico."

Francisco Javier Oliveras

Francisco Javier Oliveras was a rookie with Cotto on the 1980-81 Criollos. He steadfastly pitched for the Caguas franchise, even when it moved to Bayamón in 1991-92. After Caguas folded, Oliveras was selected by Santurce. Oliveras once again joined Caguas in 1994-95.

Oliveras was the league's top pitcher in 1984-85 by virtue of an 8-0 record plus another win in the semifinal series.[47] He also won a game for Mako Oliveras's Senators in the Caribbean Series. "When I started, the league had a lot of big league players," says Oliveras. "Around 1984-85 things began to change, with fewer big leaguers, but Dennis Martínez still pitched some and there were others. I played for Vic Power that season and it was fun."

Carmelo Martínez

Carmelo Martínez and Henry Cotto were two of the final players signed to stateside contracts by Pedrín Zorrilla. Herman Franks was the manager of the Chicago Cubs from 1977 to 1979, and Zorrilla was pleased to serve the Cubs in a scouting capacity. Martínez recalls being scouted by Zorrilla in youth leagues: "When we reached an agreement, Pedrín was very proud, since he felt I would make it to the majors. When I first went to the States, Pedrín accompanied me and kept me from getting homesick. I owe a lot to Pedrín Zorrilla."

Before Carmelo Martínez—a cousin of Edgar Martínez—made his big league debut for the Cubs in the fall of 1983, he was voted MVP for the 1982-83 season, narrowly edging Bayamón teammate Brian Harper.[48] Martínez: "That was great and something I'll always be proud of. I hit 17 homers and people started comparing me with Orlando Cepeda."

Carmelo Martínez showed his stuff in 1993-94 to earn a second league MVP award with San Juan.[49] He finished among the league leaders in batting average, homers and RBIs.

Juan Agosto

Juan Agosto played youth baseball with Dickie Thon and Luis Aguayo during the early 1970s. They later all became Bayamón players. Agosto never forgot some advice from Rubén Gómez: "Keep the legs in shape." He learned a lot from Julio Navarro in Bayamón, and from Mike Cuéllar when he was Mayagüez's pitching coach. "Cuéllar was really my teacher in the mid–1980s," says Agosto. "He taught me the screwball and how to study game situations. I was fortunate in having good pitching coaches in the league."

Agosto's best seasons were with Mayagüez from 1983-84 to 1987-88, when the Indians had the best native pitching talent with himself, Jesús Hernaíz, José Guzmán, Luis Aquino and Mambo de León.

Luis Quiñónes

The Mayagüez teams of the 1980s counted on Luis Quiñónes who played second, short, third and left and right field, along with filling the DH role at times. He gave the team a lift when it needed one. His three homers against San Juan spelled the difference in the 1985-86 final series. Quiñónes also provided clutch hitting for the 1988-89 Mayagüez champions.

Quiñónes sat on the Mayagüez bench his first two seasons, 1980-81 and 1981-82, but he learned quite a bit watching Wade Boggs and Cal Ripken play third base.

Quiñónes: "What I saw was that they hustled, and if something didn't go their way, they worked on improving the situation. They gave 110 percent and loved to play."

Those who played on did so for the love of the game. It did not matter whether they were on a big league roster, in the minors, finishing up in Mexico, or even on their way to Japan. Like Boggs and Ripken, they gave their 110 percent.

7. Imports

If you didn't produce, your butt was coming across that creek and somebody else was on the way.
  —Wilmer Fields, former San Juan and Mayagüez player

There were imports who produced and those who were sent packing. Others left early for a variety of reasons. Most of the imports have come from the United States, but some were from Cuba, Panama or Nicaragua, among other countries. "Quality imports" came through for their teams, whether they played one, two or multiple seasons. The imports in this chapter came through between the latter 1940s and the early 1990s.

Wilmer Fields

Monte Irvin recommended that San Juan sign Wilmer Fields of the Homestead Grays for the 1947-48 season. Irvin played in Cuba that winter, and tipped off San Juan executives about the versatile Fields, who could pitch, play third and cover the outfield.

Fields looked forward to supplementing his income during the winter by doing what he loved most. By this time, a player with Fields's ability could earn $700 a month, with the opportunity to earn more. When Wilmer and his wife, Audrey, took a two-engine plane from New York City to San Juan, little did they know it would be a 15-hour ordeal including stops and delays. The hazards of reaching San Juan would be compensated by the enthusiasm and friendliness encountered by Fields in Puerto Rico for three full seasons and part of a fourth.

Satchel Paige, a few months away from getting his first big league shot at age 42, was on the mound for Santurce in a late-season game when Fields stepped into the batter's box at Sixto Escobar Stadium. Fields, who had homered earlier in the game, grabbed the lightest bat he could find, knowing Paige could still throw hard. After Fields swung and missed a fast one, Paige jokingly told him he couldn't hit. Paige threw another hummer, which Fields hit over the wall. The fans went wild.[1] Fields told me $125 was handed to him by the San Juan faithful through the wire mesh.

"If you done good in the States, you had a winter job," says Fields. "San Juan's owner met me in Trenton, New Jersey, for a game against the Newark Eagles. Puerto Rico was very good for black ballplayers. If you got the opportunity to go to a Latin American country, you would go. If you didn't produce, your butt was coming across that creek and somebody else was on the way."

Fields performed so capably with San Juan and Mayagüez that his services were soon in demand elsewhere—first Venezuela and Colombia and later the Dominican Republic and Mexico. Fields hit the first home run in Caribbean Series history during the 1949 event hosted by Havana.[2] He received $50 in cash and an electric shaver for this feat. Fields told me he got an extra $50 for each of his 1947-48 San Juan wins. In one weekend series against Mayagüez, he pitched an 11-inning shutout and won another game in relief. No wonder Mayagüez signed Fields for the 1948-49 season!

Fields: "[Mayagüez owner Alfonso] Valdés told me, 'I need a pitcher who can play third.' When we made the playoffs in 1949 and 1950, there were incentives."

Artie Wilson

Artie Wilson became Mayagüez's player-manager in 1948-49 after a spectacular 1947-48 season when he hit .405 for the Indians.[3] The 1948-49 "Tribe" won the franchise's first championship behind the slugging of Luke Easter, Wilmer Fields, Johnny Davis and Alonzo Perry. When Mayagüez claimed the title after besting Santurce in the decisive game at Escobar, over 10,000 of the Mayagüez faithful were in front of the *Alcaldía* (city hall) to greet their heroes. The Mayagüez caravan arrived around 4 A.M. on February 18, 1949, to a rousing welcome. Wilson was named honorary mayor for two days. Perry became honorary president of the Municipal Assembly, and other players were designated as city board members.[4]

"We came back in town up a one-way street," Wilson recalls. "For two days we celebrated. What a time!" It was the culmination of Wilson's most exciting winter. Tom Greenwade of the Yankees scouted Wilson in Puerto Rico and recommended he be signed. Lee MacPhail, Jr., farm director of the Yankees, opened negotiations with Tom Hayes, Jr., president of the Birmingham Black Barons, to purchase Wilson's contract. Wilson was pleased with this interest but not too happy about the $500-per-month offer to play for a Yankee farm team, the Newark Bears.[5] He had earned $725 a month with the 1948 Black Barons and a comparable amount with Mayagüez. So Wilson sent a telegram to MacPhail refusing the New York

7. IMPORTS

Wilmer Fields (left), with Jaime Almendro and Sam Hairston (right), in the San Juan dugout, 1947-48 season. Note the wire mesh at the Sixto Escobar Stadium (courtesy of Jaime Almendro).

offer. Then Bill Veeck came into the picture. He flew to Puerto Rico with Cleveland's traveling secretary, Bud Goldstein. An optimistic Veeck stated, "I trust Wilson will sign with us. After all, he's with the [Mayagüez] Indians and so are we."

Veeck booked a flight to Mayagüez on Caribbean Air Lines, hoping to track Wilson down. After the plane's departure, *Sporting News* correspondent Salvador Pabón called San Juan and notified Rafael Pont Flores that Wilson, Johnny Davis and Alonzo Perry were traveling by car to San Juan. Veeck arrived in Mayagüez and asked the pilot to fly as low as possible on the way back to San Juan, with the hope of overtaking Wilson. Veeck also left word with the Mayagüez officials to alert the Island's sports commentators to announce a meeting with Wilson and himself at the San Geronimo Hotel. Wilson picked up the announcement on the car radio and made it to the hotel.[6]

Artie Wilson signed a contract with Veeck, but Happy Chandler, the baseball commissioner, later ruled Wilson was property of the Yankees. The shortstop's contract was sold from San Diego, Cleveland's affiliate in the Pacific Coast League, to Oakland.

Wilson: "I came back to the States after Bill Veeck had signed me up. The commissioner ruled that I was first property of the Yankees so I had to leave Cleveland."

Wilson made it to the big leagues with the 1951 New York Giants, but his roster spot was taken by Willie Mays after he had played 19 games. In 1951-52 the left-handed-hitting shortstop returned to Mayagüez and hit .356.[7] He was Mays's teammate for a few weeks on the 1954-55 Santurce team.

Willard Brown

Rafael Pont Flores gave Brown the label "Ese Hombre" (that man). Brown wore Santurce flannels from 1946-47 to 1956-57 with the exception of 1954-55, and 1955-56. He spearheaded the first "Escuadrón del Pánico" (panic squadron) in the late 1940s, which featured Bob Thurman, Earl Taborn and John Ford Smith.

A two-time league Triple Crown winner, and three-time batting champ Brown brought fans to the ballpark with his torrid hitting. One of only three players to hit over .400 twice—Coímbre and Perucho Cepeda are the other two—Brown slugged 27 homers and drove home 86 runs with a .432 average his first Triple Crown season, 1947-48.[8] He earned his second Triple Crown two winters later, netting $200 in prizes.[9] Willard Brown hit well in his three Caribbean Series events, finishing at .343 with 5 homers and 19 RBIs. In the 1953 Caribbean Series, he clouted 4 home runs and drove in 13 to help Santurce win it.[10]

Cot Deal played against Brown in the 1950s, and was with him when Santurce won the 1953 Caribbean Series. When Deal coached the Houston Astros, from 1983 to 1985, he would see Brown during the course of the season, since the former slugger lived in Houston. "Willard Brown was one of the best hitters I ever saw, and that includes Williams and DiMaggio," says Deal. "As a player, he gave the appearance of loafing, but he was not. He would shuffle from the outfield to the dugout and dugout to the outfield. In Puerto Rico, he was loved by everybody—visited hospitals, able to do things the locals appreciated, unlike the situation in the U.S."

Some of the most touching comments made by Brown are in a letter to sportswriter Peter Anderson, published by *The San Juan Star* on October 28, 1961: "I received the article you wrote about me. God bless you ... also the Puerto Rican people. I will never forget them as long as I live. They helped me when I could not help myself. So God go with all of them. Mr. Anderson, you can thank all Puerto Rico for me." Anderson replied: "There is nothing I can do for this man who is unknown in his land, yet famous on the Island."

The person who did the most for Willard Brown, from getting him dental care to making sure he got proper rest, was Pedrín Zorrilla. When Zorrilla found Brown mingling with fans at bars in the Miramar section of Santurce, he would escort him to the house on Refugio Street where

Santurce's Willard Brown, with team trainer Pepo Talavera and owner Pedrín Zorrilla, 1947-48 season (courtesy of Diana Zorrilla).

the Santurce imports lived. Zorrilla's father-in-law provided dental treatment.

Charles Ferrer, son of the Santurce team doctor and cousin of actor José Ferrer, remembers when Brown came to the Ferrer household at 1 A.M. with a high fever. After receiving three penicillin shots over the next 14 hours, Brown responded with three homers. Ferrer: "Brown told my father,

'Doc, you should have given me another shot. I would have hit a fourth one.'"

Bob Thurman

Bob Thurman's Puerto Rico legacy included 12 winters and 120 homers.[11] The 120 homers are a safe bet to remain the all-time standard, and the combination of his hitting and pitching ability made him a fan favorite. He won 39 games in Puerto Rico, mostly during his earlier seasons.[12] Thurman's Puerto Rican nickname, "El Mucaro" (the owl), was given to him after sterling pitching performances in night contests in 1947-48.

The interest generated by the Thurman-Willard Brown duo in 1947-48 helped set a new league attendance record of 710,164.[13] In 1948-49, Thurman and Brown were the most devastating one-two punch in Puerto Rico League history, with 18 homers apiece.[14] This was the first of Thurman's seven double-digit home run seasons with Santurce.

The slugger-pitcher was 37 during the 1954-55 season when Gabe Paul and Birdie Tebbets were down in Puerto Rico and saw him hit a long homer against a top stateside pitching prospect. Thurman showed his talent and desire. "They gave me $10,000 to play with Cincinnati," says Thurman. "I knew I could play in the majors. They could sign me for nothing and I would play. When I told the old skipper [Tebbets] 'I'll play for Cincinnati,' they wrote me a check for $10,000."

Bob Thurman and Sandy Koufax were National League rookies in 1955 and Puerto Rico opponents in 1956-57. Thurman mixed his pitches up, and would tease Koufax about his velocity.

Thurman: "Koufax could throw that ball. I felt he might have elbow problems by the way his follow-through went and the elbow staying up—pushing that elbow out would cause a terrible strain. I had a loosey-goosey delivery; otherwise, I'd have arm problems."

Thurman's professional baseball career began after he came back from World War II, having seen plenty of action with the U.S. Cavalry in New Guinea. He played for the Homestead Grays, Kansas City Monarchs, Santurce, Cincinnati and minor league teams. He prided himself on staying in shape, and still weighed 210 pounds at age 75, his big league playing weight.

Bob Thurman and I were invited to take part in a radio sports talk and call-in show, "Foro Deportivo," in Ponce two days before his induction into the Puerto Rico Professional Baseball Hall of Fame in 1991. One of the callers asked Thurman about his throwing arm, noting that Clemente played left field in 1954-55. Thurman, who usually played right field, responded "strong and accurate." The people in the radio station roared in appreciation.

Cot Deal

Cot Deal was San Juan's Bob Thurman during the early 1950s. He earned MVP laurels in 1952-53, based on his 11 wins and timely slugging. The Oklahoman gave San Juan's fans their money's worth, and defended the colors of Puerto Rico in two Caribbean Series. San Juan officials and fans responded by honoring Deal on January 2, 1953. They gave him a new De Soto sedan and the flag of Puerto Rico. Deal's #8 was retired in the emotional event.

"They knew I gave it my best effort all the time. If I hit it back to the pitcher, I'd run it out," says Deal. "They knew I wanted to be part of their system, and appreciated my attitude. People would invite us into their homes for Thanksgiving and Christmas dinner. My apartment after a game was like Grand Central Station. Fans would bring beverages, call and have food sent in. Cot's apartment got to be a social club." All of Puerto Rico cheered Deal in the 1953 Caribbean Series. He was one of the heroes as a reinforcement for champion Santurce with some key hits and a couple of wins.

Lou Limmer

Lou Limmer was an import who fled Puerto Rico, but who later returned to continue producing on Island diamonds. Limmer played for Aguadilla in 1949-50 and the following winter. He earned a lifetime supply of single-edged razor blades by hitting for the cycle early in the 1950-51 season. But his main concern was getting some back pay from 1949-50, and he finally received it by mid–December 1950. Then he conceived a plan to leave Aguadilla.

At 3:30 A.M. on December 18, Limmer quietly took a *publico* from the Aguadilla town plaza to San Juan. Limmer chuckles as he remembers making it to the airport. "Aguadilla officials somehow got word I was leaving, but I was able to make it," he recalls. "The police came after me [but] I got to the airport for the flight to New York."

Many Americans have jumped ship in the league, but very few have returned, as Limmer did five years later to help Caguas win the 1955-56 title. Limmer was suspended from winter ball for two years as a result of the 1950 episode. He made amends and proved that fugitives can have second lives.

Willie Mays

Willie Mays left Puerto Rico in mid–January 1955, but vowed to return in two weeks for the final series. He was taking time off to rest and receive

Ellis "Cot" Deal after receiving the flag of Puerto Rico, January 1953. His wife and children share the moment (courtesy of Luis Moux).

awards for his 1954 big league performance. George Crowe, Buster Clarkson, Bob Thurman and others accompanied Mays to the airport as the "Say Hey" kid prepared for his departure to New York's Idlewild Airport. The same trio helped Mays with packing and jokingly called him the "Sey Juey" kid.[15] *Juey* is Spanish for crab, and Santurce fans couldn't get enough of their "Sey Juey" kid in 1954-55.

Mays will go down in history as the most talented import to play a league season in Puerto Rico. Only 23 at the time, he earned his second MVP trophy in three months by adding the Puerto Rico award to his 1954 senior circuit trophy.

Before Mays's arrival in Puerto Rico to a hero's welcome, on October 16, 1954, at 6:40 A.M., Island sportswriter Francisco Soto Respeto noted local fans had enjoyed watching Monte Irvin, Luke Easter, Larry Doby, Roy Campanella, Josh Gibson and Satchel Paige. Soon, he promised, they would see a new star named Willie Mays.

Would Mays give it his all in Puerto Rico, and with the same enthusiasm he displayed in the 1954 major league season? asked Soto Respeto. "The one person who has complete faith in Willie Mays' performance in Puerto Rico is Pedrín Zorrilla. To Pedrín, Mays is a ballplayer, a sincere human being, and a gentleman."[16]

Mays settled into his apartment near Escobar Stadium and began pounding the ball. Within a month, it became clear that Santurce was in high gear. One turning point took place on November 23, 1954. A two-run homer by Mays with Clemente on base in the bottom of the ninth gave Santurce a 7–6 win over Caguas, and the Crabbers went on to record 30 wins in their next 42 games.[17]

Willie Mays gave it his all every time he put on #24, from his first league homer, off Tom Lasorda, to a crucial blast off Venezuela's Ramón Monzant in the 1955 Caribbean Series. Mays will always be remembered by Island fans for his storybook season. "We had a good club, and everybody wanted to win," Mays recalled in his autobiography. "When you've got people like Gómez and Clemente on your side in the Puerto Rican League, you've got a chance to win, and we did win."[18]

Steve Bilko and Danny Kravitz

Danny Kravitz was one of the pallbearers at Steve Bilko's funeral in northeastern Pennsylvania more than twenty years after they played against Mays in the 1954-55 season. Bilko played first base for Ponce and Kravitz was a catcher with San Juan when they lived with their families in the Darlington Apartments.

Kravitz has recollections of the morning rainfall in San Juan making the field soft, followed by hot sun, the sunshine and Escobar's drainage system drying the field in time for night games. One of his most pleasant memories is of neighbors volunteering to babysit for him and his wife. "Many of the guys down there were in the big leagues at the time," says Kravitz. "I was just coming up myself, and learned a lot from them. It was a good experience." Kravitz led the Puerto Rico League in triples the season after Mays did so. Each hit seven three-baggers.

Steve Bilko played winter ball in Panama and Cuba prior to Puerto Rico, and then briefly in the Dominican Republic. Bilko played on the same Havana ballclub as Hoyt Wilhelm, but did not take part in the 1951 Caribbean Series since his wife, Mary, was pregnant and he wanted some time off before spring training. "We were the first American family to live in Ponce's Darlington Apartments," says Mary Bilko. "When the players had days off on Mondays, the wives would take a *publico* and go shopping. We would eat at a small corner restaurant after the home games."

The traditional three-hour afternoon siesta was still the norm in Puerto Rico in the mid–1950s, as it was in Cuba when the Bilkos wintered there in 1950-51. Thus, the stores were closed from noon to 3 P.M. Steve Bilko, however, woke some people up with his long home runs at Ponce's Montaner Stadium. Old-timers remember Bilko's tape-measure blasts and recall him practicing Spanish with native players and partaking of team owner Martiniano García's Three Kings Day parties.

Steve Bilko, Jr., told me the television program *Sergeant Bilko* was named after his father. A Pacific Coast League star from 1955 to 1957, Bilko Sr. befriended the comedian Phil Silvers, who starred in the show.

Frank Malzone and Hobie Landrith

Frank Malzone, Steve Bilko and two U.S. pitchers were kept by the Ponce club through the end of the 1954-55 season, but five imports, including Hobie Landrith, were released. Attendance was low and Ponce had no chance of making the playoffs. Malzone roomed with Landrith and recalls that, fortunately, his roommate was a good cook.

Hobie Landrith tried a different stroke in an attempt to gain confidence in his hitting. It worked—Landrith's batting average was .327 by the time he left Puerto Rico.[19] "My wife had given birth to our son on November 18 [1954], and at Christmas, with the owner's approval, I flew at my own expense to Detroit to see them," says Landrith. "After playing one game upon my return to Ponce, the owner released me and others."

Malzone played out the season and returned to the Island two years later to be Ralph Houk's shortstop with San Juan. The opportunity to play shortstop helped him become a better big league third baseman with the Red Sox.

Jim Landis and Luke Easter

Jim Landis began the 1956-57 season with Caguas and then went to San Juan. Landis showed the defensive skills which later earned him Gold Glove awards with the White Sox. He lived in the Normandie Apartments, as did teammates Ryne Duren and Sandy Koufax. The trio did some night fishing at the pier.

The young Landis was most appreciative of his Caguas teammate Luke Easter, whose suggestions and hints were helpful confidence builders. Easter had a league batting and home run title to his credit by the time the 1956-57 season began. He had opened Bill Veeck's eyes with his fabulous 1948-49 season with Mayagüez, tore up the Pacific Coast League with San Diego in 1949 and had some good seasons with Cleveland in the early 1950s.

Luke Easter, Canena Márquez and Wilmer Fields were three of the best Homestead Grays players in 1948. Easter, however, began the 1948-49 season in Venezuela. Alfonso Valdés sent Cefo Conde to Venezuela to bring back a pitcher, as Carlos Manuel Santiago later recalled. But Conde returned with Easter. The Mayagüez players would tease Conde throughout the season, but it proved to be a good move when Easter hit .402.[20]

Gary Blaylock and Ray Rippelmeyer

Two fan favorites were pitchers involved in strange trades. Gary Blaylock opened the 1955-56 season with Mayagüez and was traded to Ponce for Wally Moon before Moon landed in Puerto Rico. Ponce already had Luke Easter at first base, so the Lions beefed up their pitching staff with Blaylock and arranged to have Moon join Mayagüez when he arrived from the United States.

Two winters later, Blaylock was pitching for Licey in the Dominican Republic. Caguas contracted him for their stretch run, and he came through with some timely pitching as they won the title. Earlier that winter, Ray Rippelmeyer of the Estrellas Orientales in the Dominican was swapped to San Juan for Don McMahon in a rare interleague deal. It was more common for contracts to be purchased once a player was released. The Dominican League was not part of the Caribbean Confederation then, and it was easier for a team from Puerto Rico to make a trade with a Dominican club than with a Cuban, Panamanian or Venezuelan team.

Rippelmeyer gave San Juan quality innings in his three winters and particularly enjoyed pitching for Luis Olmo. Vic Power asked Rippelmeyer to reinforce the Caguas team in the 1960 Caribbean Series after the hurler won San Juan's only game in their final series with the Criollos.

Joe Hoerner and Joel Horlen

The 1963-64 San Juan team benefited from the presence of Joel Horlen, a veteran of winter ball, and newcomer Joe Hoerner. Hoerner was a 1963 teammate of Ed Olivares with San Antonio in the Texas League. Olivares played third base for San Juan with Cocó Laboy and knew San Juan could use bullpen help.

Joe Hoerner pitched for San Juan during three winters. Hoerner's stellar pitching in 1963-64 helped San Juan make it to Nicaragua for the fourth and final Interamerican Series. But it was no picnic, with the feisty fans and the excitement of Nicaragua's upset win. Hoerner continued performing well out of the San Juan bullpen in 1964-65 and 1965-66. "When you went down as an American, and did real well, the people really catered to you," says Hoerner. "It was a great experience and one I'll never forget. Puerto Rico helped some of my teammates on the 1967 Cardinals—Carlton, Hughes, Briles, Gibson. I felt honored to be part of that tradition."

Joel Horlen did not make it to Nicaragua in February 1964. He got dehydrated at season's end and was drinking six gallons of water per day. But he still won two games in the finals. When Horlen first came to Puerto Rico, for the 1961-62 season, he pitched for Mayagüez. "I must have pitched 180 innings that winter and won 16 games, including the playoffs and [Interamerican] Series," he says. "I pitched 230 innings in the States with 10 days off before coming to Puerto Rico. When I left Puerto Rico, there were only 10 days left until spring training."

Horlen's winter with San Juan solidified his position as a starting pitcher with the White Sox. He appreciated the extra income and the accommodations—Mayagüez arranged for him to live in a pre-fab house, and while in San Juan he lived across from the Caribe Hilton Hotel, where he had beach privileges. Horlen still likes the Puerto Rican food he sampled as a player—rice and beans, and chicken.

Ray Barker

Ray Barker played in all of Mayagüez's games in 1959-60 and returned to play for Arecibo in 1963-64. His first winter, he hit San Juan pitcher Jack Fisher as if he owned him. Barker, a West Virginia native, found it so hard to get a job in the winter months he opted to play winter ball in Puerto Rico, the Dominican Republic and Mexico. Some inconveniences in Puerto Rico, like shark-infested waters or apartments with cockroaches, were trivialities compared to the high level of competition, the good food and the rewards of a job well done. The fans called him "Buddy Baker."

John Herrnstein

John Herrnstein, a Philadelphia prospect, played with Arecibo and Caguas when both clubs secured Philadelphia players through the Luis Olmo connection. Herrnstein took advantage of the friendly confines of Luis Rodríguez Olmo Stadium in Arecibo to hit a league-leading 14 homers in 1962-63.[21] That's why the Arecibo faithful dubbed him "El Bambino." "The parent organization wanted me to go down and learn how to play first base," says Herrnstein. "I liked Luis [Olmo], we all did. Our coach Carlos Manuel Santiago was a down-to-earth guy."

The toughest pitchers for Herrnstein his first winter were southpaws Bob Veale, Sam McDowell and Terín Pizarro. Herrnstein, a lefty, noted that the poor lighting in various league stadiums made it difficult to pick up the hard stuff served up by this trio.

Claude Raymond and Phil Niekro

When Claude Raymond twirled for Arecibo his roommate was Phil Niekro. They would shower after home games in their Reparto Martell house, and as they walked home in their Arecibo uniforms, Raymond and Niekro would hear fans yelling "lobos del norte" (wolves of the north). Raymond picked up Spanish quickly because of his Quebec roots. It was easier for him to go from French to Spanish than from French to English to Spanish. He spent time with Arecibo teammates Roberto Vargas and "Jumpy" Jiménez.

Arecibo fans still remember Raymond as the winning pitcher in the tiebreaker win over San Juan to clinch a playoff spot for the 1961-62 Wolves. He also won the league All-Star Game that season. During the celebration after the win over San Juan, someone came up to him and thrust a $100 bill into his hand.

San Juan secured Raymond in a trade before the 1962-63 season. Carlos Bernier and William de Jesús were two San Juan players who went to Arecibo in the multi-player deal. Raymond roomed with Phil Linz, but did not pitch the whole season, since the Milwaukee Braves were concerned that he was pitching too much.

Phil Niekro hurled for Mayagüez as well as Arecibo. Both he and Raymond also pitched in the Dominican Republic. Niekro found he could experiment with his knuckler in Puerto Rico without any hesitation. This was helpful for Niekro's big league pitching aspirations. Looking back on the Puerto Rico experience, both Niekro and Raymond feel the confidence factor was important. "In winter ball you don't have as much to lose," Raymond points out. "When you retire a Clemente or Cepeda on a slider [you say,] 'I'm going to use that in the big leagues,' if you can get these hitters out."

Cookie Rojas, Mike de la Hoz and Tony Taylor

In October 1961 there seemed to be a pipeline from Cuba to other countries where winter ball was played. When the 1962 Interamerican Series began at Escobar Stadium, 16 Cuban players dotted the rosters of the four teams.[22] Santurce reinforced itself with Cookie Rojas from the

Arecibo club and with San Juan players Mike de la Hoz and Tony González. Another Cuban, Orlando Peña, was in the Crabbers' bullpen.

Cookie Rojas was Arecibo's most popular import in the 1960s. He had already represented Cuba in the 1960 Caribbean Series with the Cienfuegos Elephants. Tony González, Leo Cárdenas and pitchers Pedro Ramos and Camilo Pascual were on that team.

Rojas: "I was in New Jersey with the former Havana Cubans franchise, who had moved to Jersey City. I got word from Arecibo in 1961 that they were interested in my services. It was a joy from the beginning to play for Luis Olmo, a great player in his days and I'm proud of having played for, and learning a lot from him."

Rojas made Arecibo his home for seven years. The fans held a special day in his honor during the 1962-63 season when he was challenging for the league batting title. Arecibo's management thought so highly of Rojas that he was appointed to manage the 1965-66 team, a squad which made the playoffs. Tito Fuentes replaced Rojas as Arecibo's second baseman. "Winter ball meant a lot to the careers of many players," Rojas insists. "I played 21 years of winter baseball. If it hadn't been for the baseball in Cuba, Puerto Rico and Venezuela, I might not have had a big league career."

Mike de la Hoz represented Cuba in the 1959 Caribbean Series. He was a terror at the plate in four other leagues—Puerto Rico, Venezuela, the Dominican Republic and Mexico. His name was at or near the top of the list of batting leaders wherever he wintered. Matty Alou in the Dominican and Vic Davalillo in Venezuela narrowly surpassed him during several batting chases, but there was no better hitter than de la Hoz in Puerto Rico throughout 1961-62, when he won the batting crown.

His winters in Cuba were a good training ground for subsequent winter play, de la Hoz says. "Baseball in Cuba was really top-notch when I began. You played with four teams at the same stadium. The wind came in from center to home, and sometimes a batting champion there would hit less than .320. It all depends on how good the native players are. In the late 1950s, the Puerto Rico League was a notch below Cuba, but when I played in Puerto Rico during the 1960s, they had some quality native players in the big leagues."

When de la Hoz won his Puerto Rican batting title, over half his games were held at Escobar Stadium. He liked the visibility there and the way the ball traveled from left to left center. It was a better hitter's park than Bithorn Stadium.

San Juan's Tony Taylor played all his home games at Bithorn and earned the 1967-68 league batting crown in a down-to-the-wire race with José Pagán, ending with .344 to Pagán's .342.[23] In doing so, Taylor became the first Cuban to win batting titles in his native land and Puerto Rico. (Cookie Rojas and Tony González won Cuban hitting titles, but fell short

Arecibo's Cookie Rojas in the mid–1960s (courtesy of Rai García).

in their Puerto Rico quests.) Taylor won the batting crown the last weekend of the season as he went five for eight. Pagán sat out Caguas's final contest. Statisticians gave Taylor the nod, .3418 to .3417, when an extra at-bat was added to give him the required 217 appearances.[24] "Puerto Rico was a second home to me," says Taylor. "Our San Juan owner, Yuyo Carrasquillo, cared about his ballplayers. When we played Santurce, it was like Cuba's Havana-Almendares rivalry.

Larry Haney

Larry Haney played under Earl Weaver in Elmira, Rochester, Santurce and Baltimore. Both of Haney's seasons with Santurce were spent with Weaver at the helm. "This was Earl's first chance to manage good big league players," Haney mentions. "He wasn't intimidated, he managed his type of ballgame and gained the respect of Pizarro, Gómez and Pérez."

Haney was the league's All-Star catcher when the votes were tabulated at the end of 1966-67.[25] He returned the next season, but played a little less, as Elrod Hendricks got more work behind the plate. The two winters were special for Haney and his wife.

Haney: "People there are proud of their heritage, and they make you feel part of their culture. We did things with the people and they really made us feel at home. I still enjoy the black bean soup and rice and it has become a favorite of mine over the years."

Russ Gibson

Russ Gibson was behind the plate for San Juan in 1966-67. Dick Williams, Gibson's manager at Toronto, wanted his catcher to get more work after breaking his hand near the end of the 1966 AAA season. Gibson got his work in. "It was a tough league, better than AAA," says Gibson. "They got a lot of rain the first month or so, and later played a lot of doubleheaders. Catching can be really tough in 90 degrees."

Gibson first played for Arecibo in 1964-65 and remembers finding no hot water in the clubhouse nor fast food restaurants in the town. The Arecibo residents and fans were super, more than making up for the inconveniences, Gibson reports. With five of Arecibo's imports, he bought a used car for about $200 and drove it around town for errands.

Dave Leonhard

Dave Leonhard spent six summers with Baltimore and an equal number of winters with Santurce, but he pitched more innings and recorded more wins in winter ball.

Leonhard: "I enjoyed Puerto Rico, plus that was where the Orioles had the closest connection. I was right on the fringe, and went part of the year without pitching in the big leagues.... [I] had to play somewhere."

Leonhard experienced the thrill of being lifted on fans' shoulders when he defeated San Juan to nail down the 1970-71 semifinals. He also had the experience of being booed and threatened as he was introduced on the opening night of the 1971-72 season. But it turned out to be a misunderstanding.

The soft-spoken Leonhard had been asked to write a piece on his Puerto

Rican baseball experiences for the *Baltimore Sun*. Leonhard obliged with a positive report on his first four winters, interspersed with some humor. Excerpts appeared in a Puerto Rico newspaper the week before play began in 1971-72, with a headline stating Leonhard saw the Island as "a land of fleas, bed bugs and black magic." This was why the fans turned on Leonhard.

Positive points made by Leonhard in the article included the observation that a good sacrifice bunt is appreciated more in Puerto Rico than a base hit is in the States. Leonhard considered Puerto Rico a modern country that had come a long way, but his remarks were twisted to sound as if he thought the Island was backward.

One of Leonhard's amusing anecdotes involved a trip to a road game on a roach-infested team bus, when roaches took his sandwich off the luggage rack. And Leonhard did witness some voodoo at work during a Caguas-Santurce game: "Our second baseman came over and said, 'Those guys [several Caguas players] are witches,' and we said, 'No, no,' and made him go out. There was a cross made of chicken bone at his position and he wouldn't play, so the ump stopped the game. Elrod Hendricks picked up the cross and handed it to Frank Robinson, and about two pitches later, a guy smacks one and hits Elrod on the head—knocked him out and blood was everywhere. Frank got thrown out of the game. The cross had worked."

Leonhard cleared the air in the October 22, 1971, issue of *The San Juan Star*, two days after the catcalls from the stands. He asserted he loved to play baseball and loved Puerto Rico. As his World Series earnings were over $50,000 between 1969 and 1971, he pointed out, money wasn't a factor in his returning to the Island.[26]

Over twenty years later, Leonhard told me he had a chance to go with Baltimore on their tour of Japan after the 1971 World Series, but opted to go to Puerto Rico and straighten this out. He endured ten minutes of booing; bottles and oranges were thrown at him in the bullpen and he needed a police escort after the opening night game. The matter was put to rest in Arecibo, after a 40-foot long sign was unfurled which said "Cucaracha [cockroach] Leonhard Go Home." "Don Baylor and I bought the sign," Leonhard reports, "and after that we had no more problems."

Grant Jackson

Grant Jackson got his winter "baptism of fire" pitching for Nicaragua's Boer Indians in 1963-64 and 1964-65. He remembers "Sad Sam" Jones teaching him how to throw the curveball. Jackson then joined the 1965-66 Criollos as part of the Philadelphia connection. "Ferguson Jenkins and Johnny Briggs were down there. I did well, and it was a stepping stone," says Jackson. "Each year I played winter ball in Puerto Rico, I got better and better."

Marrying a Caguas native, Jackson got to know Puerto Rico better than any other American player in the past 30 years. "Back then we used to associate with the fans in the city," Jackson recalls. "We went over there to make money, learn to play ball and meet people. I learned how to speak Spanish, and after a lot of ballgames when I pitched, whether I won or lost, I would go down and sit at the corner bar around the corner and play dominoes. Some of my friends lived up in Cidra, the mountain people. I'd spent a lot of time with them; that's why I decided to live there when I married. That tells you how I feel about the place." Jackson's six Caguas seasons were productive. When the team wanted to trade him to Ponce he refused, knowing his father-in-law was a lifetime Caguas fan whose heart would have been crushed.

Fred Beene

No imported pitcher worked harder than Fred Beene. He pitched a no-hitter for Santurce against Arecibo his first winter, 1969-70, and remembers throwing the same number of pitches Don Larsen threw in his 1956 World Series perfect game—81. After Ponce won the final series against Santurce, Ponce's mayor came onto the Santurce team bus to give him the key to the city. "I pitched a shutout," says Beene. "The mayor asked me to go to the Caribbean Series. They picked up several pitchers, but I had a bad finger and appreciated being asked."

Beene, Santurce's opening night pitcher in 1970-71, blew his arm out in the third inning pitching to San Juan's Ken Singleton. "I tore a tendon and couldn't throw any more that winter, but stayed there about six weeks. [Rogelio] Moret came alive and Reggie [Jackson] hit 20 homers."

When Beene returned to Island play, it was with the 1972-73 Caguas team. Bob Boone was one of the best catchers Beene had ever pitched to, moving behind the plate the way he liked, helping a pitcher have better control. Beene responded with an 8-2 season.[27]

The Bayamón Cowboys signed Beene for 1978-79 and he continued pitching well. Ellie Rodríguez, his other all-time favorite catcher besides Bob Boone, called the signals that winter. Beene felt Rodríguez had mental telepathy and was very sharp in terms of working the hitters and reading the minds of the native players. But Beene began to see a lack of effort on the part of many imports. "They didn't seem to take it as seriously, going to play in another land ... take it more casually," says Beene. "I saw a lot of *gringos* [North Americans] do that—leave around Thanksgiving or Christmas and not play much while they were down there."

Wayne Simpson and Pat Corrales

Wayne Simpson and Pat Corrales formed the best battery of 1969-70. Simpson, the league MVP, completed 13 of 18 regular-season starts, won 11 games and hurled 7 shutouts.[28] Corrales set the tone with his aggressive brand of baseball, his laying out of what to expect and his fluency in Spanish.

After Ponce won the finals, to which he contributed with a shutout, Simpson saw more emotion displayed than anywhere he had ever been. "We had a celebration in the town plaza," he recalls. "Yuyo [González] was there, the media—like a team here in the States winning the World Series, but it was more intimate, more emotion."

Arm problems kept Simpson from having a long big league career. He returned to Ponce in 1972-73 and later pitched for Jim Bunning with Escogido in the Dominican Republic and with Caguas. The latter experience was in 1975-76 when Bunning managed the Criollos.

Bunning and Fregosi, Ponce's skipper, were top-notch managers in Simpson's book. Simpson felt Bunning should have been a big league manager. He liked the way Fregosi communicated, stating the rookie skipper gave you what he wanted you to do and let you do it.

What made Simpson popular, along with his wins, was a desire to pick up the Island slang. Simpson's aim was to converse in Spanish. "If you forced people to speak English or conform to your customs, things weren't going to go that well for you," says Simpson. "But if you really appreciate other cultures, they pick that up rapidly and appreciated you trying to learn Spanish."

Pat Corrales appreciated Ponce players who hustled and wanted to win. Once, when Bernie Carbo wasn't hustling, Corrales read him the riot act. Corrales first came to Puerto Rico in 1965-66 as a member of the Phillies and caught Ferguson Jenkins and Grant Jackson with Caguas. With Ponce he settled into a groove, playing for three Island champions and later earning Manager of the Year laurels.

Corrales was a second manager on the field for skippers Tite Arroyo, Rocky Bridges, Jim Fregosi and Frank Verdi. After Ponce won back-to-back titles with Corrales behind the plate, in 1968-69 and 1969-70, they struggled in 1970-71 without him. In 1972, with Corrales back, Ponce won the Caribbean Series. "That was the series everyone got the flu," Corrales recollects. "We got sick to our stomachs, but still won the first five games before playing more reserves in the last one."

Corrales appreciated playing an extra 70 or 80 games during those winters. He was a backup to Johnny Bench with Cincinnati from 1968 to 1971, and the winter work enabled him to stay sharp. He caught 67 of the team's 69 regular-season games in 1971-72, plus all 11 playoff games and five Caribbean Series contests.[29] Of all the pitchers Corrales caught in Puerto Rico, Venezuela and the Dominican Republic, Simpson, he told me was the best.

As a manager, Corrales led Ponce to the 1973-74 pennant and a final-series berth, and to a second-place finish in 1974-75. Corrales put himself behind the plate for 30 games in 1973-74, but did not play his second winter while managing Ponce.

Daryl Patterson

Daryl Patterson played on championship teams with Detroit and Ponce and in AAA ball. Detroit sent him to Mayagüez in 1969-70 and he responded with six wins and a 2.86 ERA.[30] By the time the 1971 big league season ended, Patterson had pitched for St. Louis and Oakland. Ponce got hold of Patterson at Yankee Stadium.

Patterson: "I pitched the last game of the season against the Yankees. Someone from Ponce had seen me pitch and I had to get permission from Charley Finley to pitch for them. Finley told me, 'Go down there and show me something.' Went down there and we won it all."

Patterson is upbeat about Pat Corrales: "Pat was the key. He made about as big an impression on pitching staffs as anybody I know of, with the possible exception of Johnny Sain. Pat could bring the concentration and focus to compete at that level and he was like another manager on the field for Frank Verdi, and showed us the way—a playing-manager type."

Because of arm problems, Patterson was on the Puerto Rico disabled list until mid–December 1971. He was teased—told all he did was go to the beach. Patterson worked his way back, and won two semifinal series games against Santurce. Then he threw seven scoreless innings against San Juan in the finals to win another.[31] For good measure, Patterson shut out Mexico's Guasave Cottoneers in the Caribbean Series.

Ken Singleton

Ken Singleton was one of the few 1970-71 San Juan imports to stay all winter; Mike Jorgensen, Al Oliver, Dave Cash and Freddie Patek were gone by season's end. It wasn't easy playing right field for San Juan in the shadow of Roberto Clemente's accomplishments, but Singleton put up good stats. When Clemente, now managing the team, activated himself for the semifinal series against Santurce and played in game five, Singleton stayed in the lineup at first base. "Puerto Rico was an easy adjustment, since I had taken Spanish in school," says Singleton. "The fans were particularly interested in the Puerto Rican players and those who had some big league experience. I can remember visiting Roberto Clemente's home, although most of the American players hung out together."

Ron Cey

Ron Cey proved he belonged in the big leagues after his winter with Santurce, 1972-73. He played all out for manager Frank Robinson. Cey, who preferred cold weather, was called "El Pinguino" (the penguin) by the Santurce faithful. He survived the over-80-degree heat and had a great time. Cey liked the competition and playing for Robinson. At season's end, he was the league's All-Star third baseman. It was Cey's .400 batting mark and seven RBIs which paced Santurce to the final-series win over Ponce.[32]

John Wockenfuss

John Wockenfuss was a throwback to the 1940s and 1950s. He played in all 60 regular-season games for the 1976-77 Criollos, a dozen playoff contests and six Caribbean Series encounters. Wockenfuss admits, "To be very honest with you, it turned my career around. I was wondering if I belonged in the majors.... [I] played for a good team and a good manager [Doc Edwards]. They called me the Iron Horse."

Wockenfuss returned to the Island some seven years later to play for Detroit in the annual Roberto Clemente Sports Complex benefit game. While he was warming up Aurelio López in the bullpen, a little kid spoke to the Mexican hurler.

Wockenfuss: "I asked López what the kid said. This boy may not have been born when I played for Caguas. López told me, 'When you were here, they called you "Caballo de Hierro" [iron horse].' I felt very good that maybe I left something for the people of Puerto Rico."

Dave Bergman and Denny Walling

Dave Bergman got a lot out of his three seasons with Bayamón. He lived in beautiful Dorado, enjoyed the hospitality of Luis Aguayo and Ellie Rodríguez and appreciated the team's front office, since Roberto Inclán, the general manager, was a father figure to him. Bergman had the proper philosophical approach: "Ballplayers have to understand they're guests when they go to another country and perceive it in that frame of mind and be very humble. I know when some Latin players come to the U.S., it's difficult for them."

Denny Walling won the league batting title in 1979-80.[33] He was Bergman's roommate for several seasons with the Astros, as well as his Bayamón teammate. Walling feels he was fortunate to play in Puerto Rico, where he was able to make up for the few big league at-bats he got with Houston while playing behind José "Cheo" Cruz, César Cedeño and Terry Puhl. "I enjoyed watching Cheo in Houston and Puerto Rico," says Walling. "I was pretty much a dead pull hitter, and watched a guy learn to go to left field and become a .300 hitter in front of my own eyes. I, too, began hitting the ball to left and center."

Dennis Martínez

Puerto Rico was a second home to Dennis Martínez, much as it was for the Cuban players of the 1960s. Martínez pitched four winters for Caguas before joining Santurce at the end of 1984-85. The quality of play appealed to Martínez, and he gave it his all, including the 1978-79 championship game when he bested Mayagüez's Jack Morris. "I felt comfortable and tranquil in Puerto Rico," Martínez says. "They received me with open arms and thanks to that, I gave it my best. There can't be better winter ball than Puerto Rico, with the quality of play, the *asaltos navideños* [Christmas carols at your door], Christmas with Tany Pérez and his wife."

Martínez was part of the Baltimore-Caguas axis between 1976-77 and 1980-81. During this period he was the Puerto Rico League's top pitcher, helping Caguas win three titles. He enjoyed spending time with native players, including Héctor and José Cruz, Félix Millán, Willie Montañez, Jerry Morales, Ed Rodríguez and Julio César González.

Chili Davis and Dennis Lewallyn

Jamaican-born Chili Davis propelled Ponce to their first title in ten years and the 1982 Caribbean Series. Davis's slugging nailed the league title. He returned to Ponce in 1983-84 to patrol the outfield with Joe Carter and Gil Flores.

Davis: "I had a lot of fun playing in Puerto Rico. I've been back during the holiday season to visit friends I made in Ponce."

Dennis Lewallyn enjoyed his six seasons in Venezuela, the Dominican Republic and Puerto Rico. He was a pitching star for Licey in the Caribbean Series before his stint with Ponce. As a reliever for the 1981-82 Lions, he earned eight regular-season saves and pitched well in the playoffs.[34] "When I was playing in the Dominican and Puerto Rico, there were major league teams every night, nine big league players at every position and it was major league ball," marvels Lewallyn. "When you go there and play, it gives you a much better understanding of their culture and has helped me work with youngsters as a minor league pitching coach with the Dodgers."

Dion James, Randy Ready and Dan Gladden

Mayagüez was fortunate in the 1980s to count on quality imports. Three stateside players helped the Indians to the 1983-84 league championship.

Dennis Martínez, the league's top pitcher in the late 1970s and early 1980s (courtesy of Rai García).

Dion James got the sense he could play in the big leagues when he played with "natives" Von Hayes and Ozzie Virgil, Jr., in 1983-84. (Hayes played as a native by virtue of his Puerto Rican mother from Moca.) James came through for the 1983-84 Indians. Two winters later he was traded by Mayagüez to San Juan for outfielder Paul O'Neill. Dion James later moved to the Dominican Republic and played there.

Randy Ready came within a hair of Don Mattingly in the 1983-84 batting chase. Ready returned to Mayagüez in 1985-86 and was the hitting star of the 1986 Caribbean Series when his .467 batting average topped the list.[35] Ready brought a positive attitude to Puerto Rico. "I liked Puerto Rico very much," says Ready. "It was a good atmosphere and helpful to my big league career."

Dan Gladden played in the 1982 Caribbean Series for Mexico and remembers earning All-Star honors along with teammate Fernando Valenzuela. Gladden and Valenzuela reinforced Hermosillo after playing for Mexicali and Navojoa, respectively. Gladden toiled superbly for the 1983-84 Indians, but opted to leave at the end of the regular season after a salary dispute. Gladden was a bit irritated when Mayagüez brought in two "hired guns" at the end of the season and offered them a good chunk of cash to pitch in the playoffs. When Gladden was told he would be paid his standard salary based on the number of days Mayagüez took part in the playoffs, he left the Island.

"I elected to go home," Gladden recalls. "But [Luis] Gómez and [Hiram] Cuevas liked to win, and that's what I liked about them. They would do anything they could to try and win games. It allowed me to see more pitches and put 60 more games on my résumé."

Tom Candiotti

Tom Candiotti pitched for Mayagüez in the 1983-84 playoffs and Caribbean Series. He came within two outs of pitching a no-hitter against Mexico's Los Mochis Sugarcane Growers.[36] It was Mayagüez's only Caribbean Series win. "I won't forget that," says Candiotti. "We were young players in Puerto Rico on the verge of making the big leagues, and we were real hungry, and I think that's what set us apart. I was throwing the knuckler and there were games I mostly threw knuckle balls."

Ponce beckoned two seasons later when the Lions' owner, Chiro Cangiano, called Candiotti while he was pitching in AAA ball. Cangiano remembered Candiotti's two starts against Ponce in the 1983-84 finals, resulting in Mayagüez wins. Candiotti accepted the offer, and proceeded to lead the league in strikeouts.

Candiotti: "I look back on it and think that it really helped me get to where I am today [1993]. Puerto Rico was between AAA and the big leagues. Transition players were there—a very good league."

Jerry Willard

Jerry Willard still has the 1983-84 Puerto Rico League MVP trophy in his room. During the past 25 years, only Reggie Jackson has hit more single-season homers (20) than Willard's 18 that season.[37] "The MVP is something they can never take from you," says Willard. "You accomplished something, something you worked on. The goal of mine was to be the best player I could be that winter."

Willard again led the league in homers when he returned to Santurce in 1984-85, and played with the Crabbers once more in 1987-88.

Roberto Kelly

Roberto Kelly went to Caguas in 1987-88 because of his close ties with Henry Cotto, a fellow outfielder with the 1987 Columbus Clippers and New York Yankees. He was another talented Panamanian League player, following Manny Sanguillén, and Rennie Stennett. "Henry thought I would enjoy playing and living in Puerto Rico," says Kelly. "I had a good time there, it was a good AAA League."

Tony Fossas and Rafael Palmeiro

Tony Fossas was on the mound when San Juan bested Santurce to win the 1984-85 finals. Six years later, Fossas's relief pitching helped Santurce win the title. A native of Cuba, Fossas made the transition from starter to reliever in Puerto Rico. Mako Oliveras believed in Fossas, and used him as a closer. "It gave me an opportunity to be on an island more or less like Cuba in terms of the weather and rabid fans," says Fossas. "I had a chance to prepare for my big league debut in Puerto Rico. Mako helped me as a manager and I wish him the very best."

Fellow Cuban Rafael Palmeiro feels the same way. He liked playing for Mako Oliveras as San Juan's 1986-87 first baseman. "It was a strong league which prepared me for the majors," Palmeiro attests. "The level was between AAA and the majors."

Chad Kreuter and Van Snider

Chad Kreuter was the hottest Mayagüez player toward the end of the 1992 Caribbean Series. His play was instrumental in Mayagüez's second Caribbean Series crown, and brought him the MVP award. "Anybody could have been the series MVP," he says modestly. "It was a nice capper." Kreuter made the 1992 Detroit team. His two seasons with Mayagüez — 1990-91 and 1991-92 — as the Indians' top receiver were fruitful. Kreuter caught on with Mayagüez for the 1994-95 stretch run.

Van Snider also played on the 1991-92 Mayagüez team, as well as on the 1986-87 Caguas champions. He was an import who played to win regardless of his status with the parent organization. Snider had just finished a season in AA when he first went down to Puerto Rico in 1986-87. He was a big leaguer — albeit for only 11 games with Cincinnati — when he returned to Caguas in 1988-89, and a AAA player before and after 1991-92. "The pressure in winter ball, even though it's a team game, is to put up numbers, because if you don't, they're going to release you and get someone else to take your place," Snider advises. "Everyone should be busting their butt to really do good — try hard for yourself — to make sure you still have a job."

Dennis "Oil Can" Boyd

Mississippian Dennis "Oil Can" Boyd spoke with me prior to a January 1993 round robin playoff game. He was in the midst of a comeback with San Juan. "The Puerto Rico Winter League has been outstanding," said Boyd. "I was surprised it was as good a league; I really was. You have players with big league time, AAA and a mixture of AA players. My agent talked to Félix Millán [San Juan's general manager at the time]. They know each other from way back. I'd like to say to everyone that wished me a lot of luck that it's been a great time in Puerto Rico."

Wilmer Fields and Van Snider said it best when they zeroed in on the "produce or pack" reality of winter ball. These and other imports have made the league a more interesting and competitive one over the years.

8. SKIPPERS

I wanted to find out if I could stay in the big leagues and manage.
— Jim Fregosi, former Ponce manager

A variety of skippers found the Puerto Rico League to be a step toward their big league managerial aspirations. Frank Robinson, Sparky Anderson, Jim Fregosi, Jack McKeon, Rene Lachemann, Art Howe, Ray Miller, Kevin Kennedy and Jim Riggleman went on to manage in the majors. Joe Buzas, Mickey Owen, Luis Olmo, Vic Power, Cal Ermer, Frank Verdi, Mako Oliveras, Ramón Avilés and Torito Meléndez made their presence felt in Puerto Rico. They won and were asked to return.

Frank Robinson

Frank Robinson was a 13-year big league veteran when Earl Weaver told reporters in Baltimore he would be unable to manage Santurce during the winter of 1968-69. Weaver had managed Santurce to the 1966-67 championship and a runner-up position in 1967-68.[1] Robinson asked Weaver to put in a good word, which he did.

Santurce owner Hiram Cuevas signed Robinson to his first managing job and provided the 33-year-old rookie skipper with a supporting cast including Elrod Hendricks, George Scott, Joe Foy, Leo Cárdenas, Julio Gotay, Paul Blair, Wally Bunker, Jim Palmer, Rubén Gómez and Terín Pizarro. Santurce won the most games in its history, but lost to San Juan in the semifinals. "I remember the season, 49 wins and a 15-game winning streak," says Robinson. "It was a tremendous ballclub, they played very well, and the thing I really liked was the effort they put in."

The Crabbers' 1969-70 edition advanced to the finals against Jim Fregosi's Ponce Lions, but would have to wait until the next season to give Robinson his first league title. And what a winter 1970-71 was, with Reggie Jackson, Roger Freed, Don Baylor and Tany Pérez supplying the necessary firepower.

Robinson: "That was a good season. We won it and Reggie hit more homers than anyone else since Willard [Brown] in 1947. Players came down from different organizations to play with the ballclub, and those having problems the year before in the States, like Reggie, were able to straighten them out."

Robinson returned to Santurce in 1972-73 after his summer with the Dodgers, and managed Ron Cey and Willie Crawford. Santurce won the league title, but the Caribbean Series was a disappointment as Tom Lasorda's Licey Tigers prevailed. The same Licey team had also taken the 1971 Caribbean Series crown.[2]

In the 1973-74 and 1974-75 seasons, Robinson managed the troika of Orlando Cepeda, Rubén Gómez and Terín Pizarro. He admired them, remembering their National League days, and found it was nice to be around them under different circumstances. "They treated me with respect and I treated them in the same manner," Robinson says. "The nice thing about managing in Puerto Rico was that you worked with the best native players, some of the best major league players and talented prospects coming out of other organizations. So it was a mixture and I enjoyed that experience and it certainly helped when I did become a manager in the major leagues."

Robinson again managed Santurce in 1978-79 and 1979-80. But he noticed some changes, with imports limited to players with four years' big league experience or less, or with a limited number of at-bats and innings pitched. "Fans down there love to see the Puerto Rican big leaguers. But they also want to see American players they only had the chance to see on television," Robinson explains. "And when they [the league] started eliminating those players, and the American players decided they didn't want to go play winter ball like they used to, you didn't see the same caliber of player."

Jim Fregosi

Jim Fregosi was only 28 when owner Yuyo González entrusted him with the Ponce managing job for 1969-70. Fregosi came through with flying colors, and led Ponce to the league crown and their first Caribbean Series berth. He counted on his 26-year-old double play partner with the California Angels, Sandy Alomar, Sr., and team leader Pat Corrales behind the plate. Winter ball veteran Jim Hicks, along with Bernie Carbo, and Luis "Torito" Meléndez, made a solid outfield. Jackie Hernández provided dependable glovework at shortstop, while Chago Rosario and Quique Rivera performed well at the corners. Wayne Simpson, Vern Geishert, Clyde Wright and Rob Gardner provided the pitching. "Pat Corrales helped me managing the ballclub," says Fregosi. "After being down there awhile, I could understand the language."

Fregosi laughs about the time his car broke down and Yuyo González bailed him out. "Yuyo said I was a smart manager as far as baseball was concerned, but to remember to put in the oil." Fregosi had a mission: "I wanted to find out if I could stay in the big leagues and manage. And I enjoyed the challenge of managing." After Ponce won the title, "To see people by the side of the road screaming as our bus went back to Ponce was a big thrill."

Sparky Anderson

George "Sparky" Anderson had never considered managing San Juan until newly named San Diego Padres manager Preston Gómez asked him to do so for the 1968-69 season. "I was to be one of Preston's coaches in San Diego," Anderson explains. "This was my second winter managing experience. I had managed Magallanes in Venezuela [in 1964-65], but it was a tough situation. Their native players were just young kids, and the other clubs had the star native players. Magallanes fired me 30 days into the season, and I have to say I was very happy to leave."

San Juan was a different story. Anderson led his charges to the playoffs, based on their fourth-place finish, and to an upset win over first-place Santurce in the semifinals. Anderson will never forget the stands going wild when José Cardenal hit two homers off Jim Palmer in the final game of the series, nor the two magnificent games hurled by Mike Cuéllar. He recalls Cuéllar was all business in the playoffs after a lackluster regular season.

Anderson: "Santurce was loaded. They had the best club, with Scott, Gotay, Cárdenas, Foy, Hendricks, Blair, Palmer, Pizarro, Gómez. Puerto Rico helped me to be around that many big league players at that time. All the clubs had at least six or seven big leaguers, and I think it was very helpful that I got to know them. We had Tony Taylor, Cardenal, Beauchamp, Kekich, Cuéllar, Orlando Peña. José Morales was a good hitter."

Anderson returned to Puerto Rico in November 1984 and donned the San Juan flannels in an old-timers' game at Bithorn. Anderson played second base against former Santurce players. I was a fan at this game and can attest to the warmth and appreciation felt by Puerto Rico's baseball fans toward Sparky Anderson.

Jack McKeon

Jack McKeon replaced Tony Castaño as Arecibo's manager near the end of the 1971-72 season, and managed the club the whole 1972-73 season, when they made their first playoff appearance in six seasons. McKeon led Arecibo to the playoffs several more times. His 1975-76 and 1976-77 Santurce teams also made the playoffs. "We started traveling in cars with

Sparky Anderson celebrates San Juan's win over Santurce in the 1968-69 semifinals (courtesy of Raí García).

Santurce because it got to where you only had six or seven guys on the bus," McKeon recalls. "So we got to the point where everyone went by car."

McKeon lived in Arecibo his first two winters—at a downtown hotel when he first arrived, and in a home he shared with coach Steve Boros near the Gran Café restaurant in 1972-73. McKeon made a lot of friends, who remembered him when he made scouting trips to Puerto Rico during the 1980s.

There were a number of reasons why McKeon endeared himself to the Puerto Rico League. For one, he continued managing in the league after his initial big league managerial stint with the 1973 Kansas City Royals. McKeon believed in being competitive and giving young native players a chance to prove themselves. His outgoing personality captivated the fans.

McKeon: "I had a lot of good rapport with the fans and the Puerto Rican players. They remember me as a manager who always gave the kids—Candy Maldonado, Carlos Lezcano, Mario Ramírez—a chance to play. I was trying to get these kids enough playing time so we could build up experience and not have to worry about imported players. It was time to begin infiltrating them, and build some tradition and depth of Arecibo's native players."

McKeon enjoyed the rice and chicken dishes, roasting pig on a spit, and the All-Star games on Three Kings Day. The most exciting and hectic times he found on the Island were during the 1972 and 1976 elections, with the parades, heavy traffic and noise. He appreciates the respect, camaraderie and hospitality shown by Island residents.

Doc Edwards

Doc Edwards learned Spanish well enough to let Latin players know that he cared about them. He played winter ball in Venezuela and Puerto Rico, and vowed to be able to communicate with Spanish-speaking players as he continued his baseball career. When Caguas general manager Ronquito García received favorable reports on Edwards, including his knowledge of Spanish and the fact he was liked by his minor league players, the Criollos' managing job was his.

Edwards's Spanish was improving when he managed the 1976-77 Caguas club, but pep talks were not a priority, as the team won 30 of their last 40 games to finish 40-20. Caguas hit .307 as a team, the highest figure in league history.[3] José Cruz, Eddie Murray, José Morales, Sixto Lezcano, Jerry Morales, Félix Millán, John Wockenfuss and Julio C. González did most of the hitting. Dennis Martínez, Scott McGregor, Mike Krukow, Ed Rodríguez and Mike Cuéllar formed a solid mound corps.

Baltimore's farm director, Clyde Kluttz, knew Edwards from the Yankee organization, and entrusted some of the organization's top players to him. Edwards later realized that managing top prospects Murray and McGregor, coupled with big leaguers in the mold of Cruz, Lezcano and Millán, gave him a head start managing the likes of Joe Carter with the Cleveland Indians in the late 1980s.

Edwards: "Winter leagues are still tremendous because they give the younger player a chance to play at a higher level of competition. When I managed, so many major leaguers were playing and I think the Caguas club then could beat some major league clubs now."

Rene Lachemann

Rene Lachemann managed in Venezuela the winter Edwards had the talented Criollos. Lachemann had major league managing aspirations and jumped at the chance to get more experience in winter ball managing Mayagüez the next season. "Puerto Rico was an outstanding experience for anyone who wanted to manage at the major league level," Lachemann affirms. "The reason for that was in the minors, the basic job was to develop players, but in winter ball, you had to win, or you were gone."

With several weeks left in the 1977-78 season it looked as though the Indians were done. But they somehow clawed their way to a fourth-place finish, then went on to capture the playoffs and the Caribbean Series crown.

Lachemann: "We felt we could beat anybody when the playoffs came around. LeFlore hit close to .400 and led the league in stolen bases. We had guys like Avilés who could move the runners over very well. Bombo Rivera and José Morales were there."

The Indians also counted on league MVP Kurt Bevaqua, Buck Martínez and Jim Dwyer, who hit six homers in the six-game final series. Danny Darwin and Nicaraguan Tony Chévez were two consistent pitchers. Mayagüez peaked in time and the momentum carried over to Mazatlán, Mexico, for the 1978 Caribbean Series. "That was one of the highlights of my managing career," Lachemann recalls. "The ownership wanted to bring other players, but I told them, 'These guys played for me all year and went through some tough times. They [reinforcements] aren't going to play for me unless my players don't want to go or can't make the trip.'" Lachemann's lineup remained intact with the exception of Rick Sweet replacing Buck Martínez behind the plate. But Mayagüez needed more pitchers and they were fortunate that Santurce's Tom Bruno and Ponce's Dennis Kinney answered the call.

Another motivator for Lachemann was the $250 bonus he would receive from team owner Luis Gómez for each win. Mayagüez did win, including all of the first five games of the series. But pride, says Lachmann, was more important: "We showed everyone throughout the territory of Puerto Rico that you never put anybody down. That you never say bad things about people—wait and see what the results are. Back in Mayagüez, I thought we just won the presidency of the U.S. People were driving all over the place. A celebration I'll never forget."

Rene Lachemann managed Arecibo after his Mayagüez success and later put in a good word for Ron Clark as manager. Clark replaced Steve Boros as Arecibo's manager in 1982-83 when the Wolves appeared to be out of the running.

Ron Clark

"When I went over, Arecibo was in last place, and we started putting everything together," says Ron Clark. "It was kind of a fantasy story. Everybody pitched in, we made it to the playoffs, won it, and in the first game of the Caribbean Series, we got beat 17–2 by the Dominican Republic team [Licey]. We won the next five games."

Clark recalls individual bonuses were offered to his players during the playoffs for homers, game winning RBIs and saves. He felt this made the team play a little better, as did the packed houses in Ponce and Arecibo during the finals. Having a coach of Woody Huyke's caliber didn't hurt. Huyke had been Doc Edwards's coach with Caguas and knew the league like the palm of his hand.

Clark: "Huyke and I have known each other for a long time and it was very comfortable knowing Woody would be there with me. He was a good luck charm. On the way to the game we would be talking strategy, and after the game, we had our coolers packed."

Ray Miller

Ray Miller knows a lot about pitching. He put his expertise to good use when he managed Caguas in 1980-81 and 1981-82, and Santurce in 1983-84. His 1980-81 Criollos were known more for their hitting, with José Cruz, Héctor Cruz, Willie Montañez and Cal Ripken. The pitching staff received a blow when Ed Figueroa was only able to pitch a few games. Dennis Martínez was the staff ace, but the local sportswriters questioned the team's pitching depth.

A key move was Miller's phone call to Mike Boddicker, asking the Iowan to pitch for Caguas. Boddicker won a couple of regular-season games and pitched a three-hit gem during the finals. "The league was a great tool for managers," says Miller. "I learned you had to take it on the chin every now and then. A lot of the U.S. managers were fired because they tried to win every game and burned out their pitching staff. The fans loved you as long as you attempted to learn the language and adapt."

Miller was able to win in 1980-81 by judicious use of his pitchers and timely hitting. The Caguas team, like Lachemann's 1977-78 Mayagüez squad and Clark's 1982-83 Arecibo team, peaked at the right moment, finishing fourth and then winning the playoffs. Caguas won the finals despite having seven players with the flu and stomach virus.

After securing Caguas's title, Miller had some kind words for team MVP Cal Ripken: "I've known Cal since he was 10 years old and I'm a good friend of his father's. I held off from saying anything to Cal all season long. But tonight when we won, I went over to him and said, 'You're a heck of a ballplayer.'"[4]

Art Howe

Art Howe was ineligible to play winter ball in 1979-80, since he had more than four big league seasons under his belt and over 250 big league at-bats in 1979. He knew Bayamón needed a manager, and the Cowboys' general manager, Roberto Inclán, got word that Howe wanted to get into managing. After four winters of playing for Bayamón, the 32-year-old Howe was ready to be a rookie manager. "If you can manage in Puerto Rico, you can manage in the big leagues. Down there, you have no minor league system to go to," says Howe. "During the holiday season and Christmas, one can get homesick.... [You] have to find ways to keep them

[U.S. players] around, to motivate them. It's important to keep the imports and native players in the right frame of mind."

Howe's Bayamón Cowboys finished second before claiming the league title by besting Santurce in five games. Howe was asked to manage Bayamón two more times before he managed Ponce in 1985-86. He makes no bones about the importance of this experience: "The success I had in winter ball helped me get the managing job in Houston. I owe Bayamón and the people in Puerto Rico an awful lot."

Houston players or prospects who played for Howe at Bayamón included Dave Bergman, Denny Walling, Vern Ruhle and Dave Smith. The Bayamón uniforms during this period were patterned after those of the Astros, with similar colors. An interesting aspect of Howe's managing experience was his friendship with Dickie Thon. "I got to play with Dickie and manage him at Bayamón," Howe recalls. "He was only 16 when be was working out with us [in 1974-75]. I helped get Dickie to Houston. Their front office asked me what I thought of Dickie for Ken Forsch. I knew the Thons and can see why he is such a fine man, a champion." José Cruz is another former Astro whom Howe managed in Puerto Rico. In 1985-86 Howe saw a 38-year-old Cruz hustle for Ponce and set a positive example for youngsters half his age.

Nick Leyva

Nick Leyva's Mayagüez team was upset by San Juan in the 1984-85 semifinals, but came back in 1985-86 to win the title. Leyva returned for a third season with Mayagüez in 1986-87, and managed Arecibo in 1992-93. He was the third-base coach for St. Louis when Mayagüez hired him, so it was no coincidence that Cardinals Terry Pendleton, Vince Coleman and Tom Pagnozzi played with the Indians.

Leyva saw Mayagüez as a first-rate organization, which made his job that much easier. "The players who went to Puerto Rico really enjoyed playing for [team owner] Luis Gómez," says Leyva. "He was first-class in everything that he did and always took care of his players. Cuevas [the general manager] knew how to put together a ballclub ... ran it very professionally and got me good players. Of course, there was Jorge Aranzamendi, Cuevas's assistant, who did an outstanding job."

Leyva managed Bobby Bonilla when the switch-hitter was just coming into his own and saw the slugger put in long hours to make himself a better player. He felt Wally Joyner's winning the Triple Crown in 1985-86 was due to Bonilla hitting behind the first baseman. The team's versatility was a plus, with Randy Ready and Luis Quiñónes able to play various positions.

The native pitchers helped Leyva. He could count on Juan Agosto, Luis Aquino, Mambo de León, José Guzmán and Jesús Hernaíz. It was not necessary to rely exclusively on imports Tim Belcher and Pat Zachry for the pitching, but having veteran pitchers in the mold of Zachry and Hernaíz was of great value.

Leyva: "Those guys had been around. They helped me as a manager in dealing with the younger players and I wasn't afraid to ask them for help in key situations. I really consider being able to manage there [Puerto Rico] as a big stepping stone, why I got a big league managing job."

Jim Riggleman

Jim Riggleman could not agree more with Leyva. Riggleman had managed in the St. Louis organization at the AA level for three years when he went to Mayagüez for the 1987-88 season. His prospects for managing at the AAA level were not too good at the time, but Riggleman took Mayagüez to the league championship. "To get to the next step [AAA], I needed winter ball to do it—to manage that quality of team, and play against that quality of competition," Riggleman observes. "Instead of managing players who I had in the minors in the 21- to 23-year-old group, I was managing players in the 23- to 33-year-old range, players who had anywhere from one to five years in the majors."

Riggleman was aware that Puerto Rico was a springboard for big league managers. He cites Howe and Fregosi as examples: "Howe played in the big leagues, and his last few years he managed in Puerto Rico, so what he was doing was getting his minor league managing experience down. Here is a guy who if somebody wanted to hire him as a major league manager, they could at least feel like he had managed; they wouldn't be bringing him in from the cold. I really admire him for the foresight to do that and to make the sacrifice, and Fregosi did pretty much the same years ago. His only previous managing experience [before 1979] was not in the States, but Puerto Rico."

Winter ball kept Riggleman busy. He managed 36 Mayagüez players and noticed attendance got better in the latter part of the season, when more veterans started to play. It was not until January 31, 1988, that Mayagüez won the league crown, and a number of their players opted to skip the Caribbean Series. This changed the chemistry of the ballclub. Yet the player turnover and roster changes helped Riggleman in the long term.

"It gives you confidence that what you're saying and telling players is not some rhetoric, but being well received," Riggleman asserts. "They're putting into play what you're talking about and doing it without mutiny, and it makes you feel that the style I'm using is being received in a positive way. In Puerto Rico, they're coming from different organizations, and they don't need to impress you."

Kevin Kennedy

Kevin Kennedy was in the Dodgers organization when Los Angeles set up a working agreement with Santurce. His three years managing Santurce followed summers at the helm in Great Falls, Bakersfield and San Antonio, and preceded a trio of seasons as Albuquerque's skipper.[5]

Kennedy feels that if one can manage in winter ball, one can manage anywhere. "You're faced with A, AA, AAA, big league players from different organizations," he says. "And when you play a season out, it's a great stepping stone. What the working agreement did was send Devereaux, Sharperson, Wetteland down to help their progress." Kennedy had played winter ball in Mexico and Venezuela, and he managed Licey in the Dominican Republic after three winters in Puerto Rico. This experience, plus his willingness to learn Spanish, was instrumental in getting the Texas managing job.

Kennedy: "I learned the language by going over there and mixing it up with everybody. It helps to understand the Latin player. Plus, it's good for the American player to go the Caribbean route, where they might have to cope with power failures and eat food they're not accustomed to. Managing-wise, I learned a lot," Kennedy says, citing other skippers whose styles he was able to observe. "Mako [Oliveras] will bunt early in the game. Felipe Alou in the Dominican used players well, and I couldn't take anything for granted."

For Kennedy, the transition from managing rookie ball in the States to taking over at Santurce was like going to the big leagues. In the 1988 finals against Riggleman's Indians, Kennedy's lineup included Rubén Sierra, Jay Bell, José Lind, Mike Devereaux and Juan Beníquez.

Luis Olmo and Víctor Pellot Power

Luis Olmo was the first league skipper to use pitching coaches and closers on a regular basis. While managing San Juan, he used Don McMahon as a closer in the 1957-58 season, and inserted Roberto Vargas as a middle and short reliever earlier in the decade.

Managing Arecibo in 1961-62 and 1962-63 meant a lot to Olmo, whose childhood home was a few miles from the ballpark. He takes pride that Arecibo made the playoffs in their first season. Olmo earned the respect of his teams' Puerto Rican, American, Cuban and Dominican players throughout the 1950s and 1960s through his baseball acumen, bilingual skills and will to win.

Vic Power, an Arecibo native like Olmo, managed Caguas at various intervals from 1959-60 through 1984-85. He was Arecibo's skipper for part of the 1968-69 season and was known to make unusual moves, such as the

8. SKIPPERS

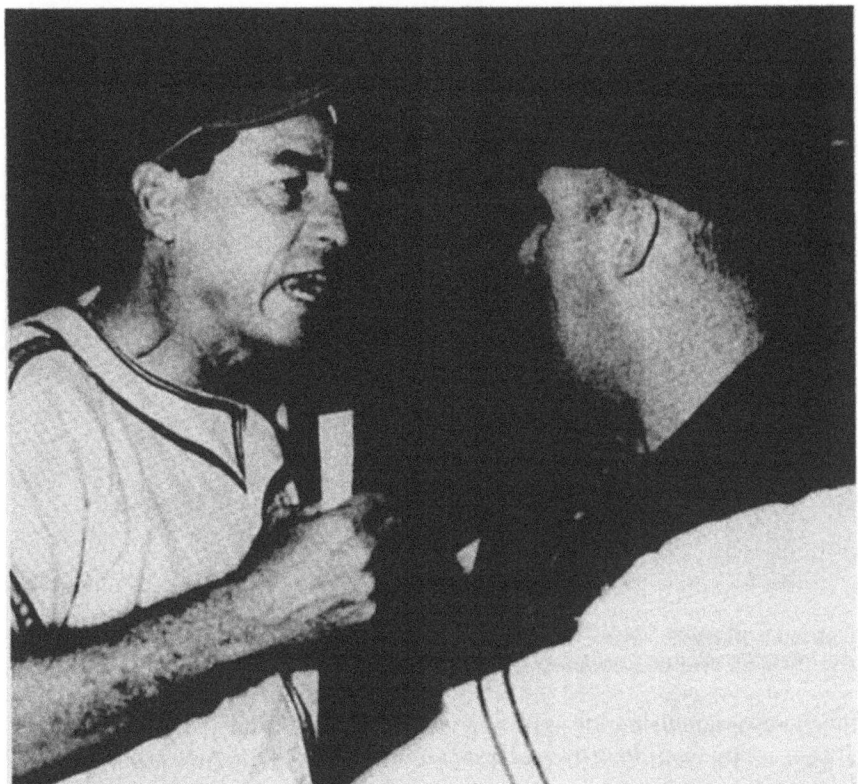

Arecibo Skipper Luis Olmo in a heated argument, early 1960s (courtesy of *The San Juan Star*).

use of Frank Howard as a relief pitcher. Power made history by benching himself for a pinch hitter when he sent up Herminio Cortés (the outfielder involved in the trade which sent Roberto Clemente to San Juan) to hit against Cuba's Camilo Pascual during one Caribbean Series contest.

Power: "With Caguas I managed everyone from Félix Mantilla and Tommy Davis to Montañez and Eliseo Rodríguez, to Don Mattingly and Henry Cotto. I truly liked working with the ballplayers who were on their way up to the majors, and did all I could to help them get there."

Herman Franks

Herman Franks counted on Luis Olmo as one of his two pinch hitters in 1954-55 when he first managed Santurce. Pedrín Zorrilla traveled to New York and sealed the deal which resulted in Franks, Willie Mays and several Giant prospects coming to Puerto Rico. "Pedrín would sit on the

Caguas's skipper Víctor Pellot Power (left) and coach Cocó Laboy during the 1984-85 season (courtesy of Rai García).

bench with me during the games in a cubby hole," Franks recalls. "He was always on the field. Pedrín got Rubén Gómez for the Giants and that's how it started."

Franks managed Santurce to 47-25 and 43-29 records in his two seasons.[6] His 1954-55 team dominated their opposition. The 1955-56 squad was also a talented group, but fell short after injuries to Don Zimmer and Bob Thurman.

Mickey Owen

Mickey Owen's main concern was for Caguas to win the pennant. On January 13, 1954, he activated himself for the stretch run when his Criollos trailed first-place San Juan by five games.[7] Caguas won 15 of their last 17 games to finish first. "Brooks Lawrence was the best pitcher on our staff; he could start or relieve," says Owen. "He was the reason I went back to catching. Lawrence moved the ball around the plate with a sliding curve and a big curveball and Guigui Lucas felt uncomfortable catching certain pitches. Guigui was a character—he carried his money and even a paycheck in his back pocket. He had played in lots of places where money was taken from locker rooms."

Caguas pitchers Bob Buhl and Ray Crone performed superbly with

Owen behind the plate. Crone, who joined the team in December and finished with a 6-1 record,[8] said there was a certain chemistry between them, that Owen brought out his best.

When Caguas clinched the Caribbean Series title in San Juan, Owen was given a Puerto Rican flag and asked to get on the team mascot, a *yeguita* (mule), for a victory lap at Escobar Stadium. Owen remembers this episode more vividly than Caguas's four wins. "I didn't have a big league managing career, but that Puerto Rico experience helped me get back to the big leagues with the Red Sox," Owen reports. They signed me as a player-coach, and I played for them in 1954 and coached full-time in 1955 and 1956. I qualified to get my major league pension. Joe Cronin and Tom Yawkey saw me catch and manage in Puerto Rico, and I was catching well there." Owen returned to Puerto Rico in 1955-56 as a player-manager with Ponce, following a player-manager stint in Venezuela in 1954-55. He managed Mayagüez during the 1956-57 and 1957-58 seasons, leading them to the 1957 Caribbean Series.

Owen appreciated the hospitality in Caguas, Ponce and Mayagüez, and he praises Mayagüez team owner Alfonso Valdés: "Anything Valdés said was as good as gold. I got over $1,000 a month, plus a car and living expenses and had the top floor of the Darlington. Ponce and Caguas were great places. I liked the food in Puerto Rico. In Caguas, I lived 200 yards from the ballpark."

Owen's greatest satisfaction in Puerto Rico was developing players such as Hank Aaron, Brooks Lawrence and Maury Wills. But he recognized that his first job was to win. That's why he kept going back to manage.

Wayne Blackburn

When Mayagüez first hired him, in 1950-51, Wayne Blackburn had just led the Carta Vieja Yankees of Panama's league to the 1950 Caribbean Series title. This upset win put Blackburn's name on Puerto Rico's managing map and Mayagüez came through with an offer.

Mayagüez's top pitcher in 1950-51 was Lew Burdette, then a Yankee prospect. Lee MacPhail, the Yankee farm director, tried to talk Blackburn out of bringing Burdette to Puerto Rico, but Blackburn prevailed. Blackburn wanted to bring Mickey Mantle to Mayagüez, but the slugger was in the low minors and Mayagüez preferred to go with the customary imports from AAA ball and the Negro leagues.

Blackburn outwitted Ponce manager Rogers Hornsby early in the 1950-51 season, stealing Ponce's signs with the help of Wilmer Fields and Alonzo Perry. When Fields left Puerto Rico to play in Venezuela, Mayagüez lost not only a leader but a good sign stealer.

By the mid–1960s, Mayagüez was in high gear, with young prospects from the Detroit organization, and Blackburn—now a manager in the Tigers' minor league chain—returned to manage the Indians in 1965-66. Blackburn had spent long hours working with Jim Northrup in the States, and the young outfielder repaid the encouragement by winning the league batting title. Tiger hopefuls Mickey Stanley and Ray Oyler also played well.

When the Mayagüez fans mobbed Blackburn and lifted him onto their shoulders after the Indians defeated Ponce at the Lions' den, "that was the icing on the cake." But Ponce fans were not celebrating. Blackburn recalls that Mayagüez official Babel Pérez "had the police out there. I waited two hours to get out of Ponce. After we beat Ponce in Ponce, and were on our way to Mayagüez, rocks were thrown at the bus from the little towns."

Benny Huffman

Benny Huffman, a scout with the White Sox, became Ponce's manager at the end of the 1950-51 season when Rogers Hornsby returned to the States. Huffman had first met Hornsby in February 1937 at the latter's baseball school in Hot Springs, Arkansas, after selling his 1930 Ford and leaving the Shenandoah Valley of Virginia to pursue the dream of becoming a professional baseball player. Hornsby brought Huffman north to St. Louis as the Browns' backup catcher.

When Hornsby signed a $10,000 contract to manage the 1950-51 Ponce Lions—the most lucrative agreement for any league player or manager at the time[9]—he asked Huffman to be his coach. Huffman and Hornsby lived in the Torres Apartments, from where they rode bicycles to and from Ponce's Montaner Stadium. Huffman took over from Hornsby with one week left in the 1950-51 season when his boss left Puerto Rico to attend the National League's seventy-fifth anniversary celebrations and to take care of his baseball school. Ponce made the playoffs and Huffman got a contract for 1951-52. Huffman: "At that time, Puerto Rico was better than AAA, the fans were excitable people, and something different happened every night."

Huffman suggested to Jack Harshman that he devote his energies to pitching, a good move for the future White Sox hurler. And Bob Boyd, another White Sox prospect, who had starred for the Memphis Red Sox in the Negro American League from 1947 to 1950, won the batting title for Ponce.[10] But Ponce missed out on the playoffs, and Joe Buzas was contracted for 1952-53.

Joe Buzas

One of the most colorful league managers was Joe Buzas, the second big league player from the States to manage in Puerto Rico. Joe Buzas took over the reins of the 1945-46 Mayagüez Indians after their manager, Bill

Steinecke, left the Island. Steinecke's four games with the 1931 Pittsburgh Pirates made him the first American big leaguer to manage a Puerto Rico Winter League team.[11] Buzas had played 30 games for the 1945 Yankees and knew Steinecke from the Yankee organization.

Buzas was popular with his players and the team's fans. There was the time in 1945-46 when Canena Márquez missed a team practice, but brought Buzas a big local pineapple, knowing that he loved fruit. Pitcher Cefo Conde, whom Buzas nicknamed "the Con Man," had a deal with Mayagüez team owner Alfonso Valdés whereby he would get a cow when he won a game. Buzas noticed that Conde was inclined to allow a run when he came in if Mayagüez was ahead by a run, in hopes of a game-winning rally, so he told Conde the cow would be his if he preserved the lead.

The Mayagüez fans gave Buzas a new car during the 1948 league finals. Fans in Aguadilla, San Juan and Ponce—other franchises where Buzas managed—could also relate to him. Buzas remembers, "The fans called me a real Puerto Rican. I had a temper like them; I used to argue with the umpires and get kicked out of a lot of games." Buzas recalls an argument on January 2, 1950, after the infield fly rule was not enforced. The wind at Escobar Stadium was blowing in, and his shortstop dropped a fly near the pitcher's mound, allowing a runner on third to score the tie-breaking run.

Buzas: "I told the umpires, 'You've done everything but take my shirt off my back,' so I took off my uniform shirt and gave it to them and went into the clubhouse. The players came in and I told them to get their asses back on the field. The team could be fined a great amount. Our new owner, Mr. Cobián, blamed this on me, but I didn't take them off the field."

As a result of this episode, Buzas was fined $100 by league president Jorge Luis Cordova Díaz and suspended for the rest of the season. When this decree became public, San Juan fans announced they were going on strike and would attend no more games until Buzas was reinstated.[12] Buzas went on San Juan radio to ask listeners to support the ballclub.

Buzas made more waves in Puerto Rico. He turned around the practice of fans reaching into their pockets and giving players cash after home runs were hit. He felt this was not professional and told his players to discourage this habit. Buzas used the "Ted Williams shift" against certain left-handed hitters. In bunt situations he might bring in an outfielder to play the infield. Island sportswriter Rafael Pont Flores wrote pieces on "The Craziness of Joe Buzas."

An important priority for Buzas was recruiting Negro leaguers. He knew they would go all out, hustle and want to make extra money during the winter. During the summers of 1946, 1947 and 1948 he went to the Polo Grounds and watched Negro leagues twin bills, then made his pitches to certain players.

Joe Buzas (center) arguing a call which went against Aguadilla, 1948-49 season. Canena Márquez in the background (courtesy of Luis Moux).

Vern Benson

Vern Benson managed Santurce in 1961-62 after his first year as a St. Louis coach. This accounted for Bob Gibson, Craig Anderson and Ed Bauta joining Santurce. It was not Benson's first trip to Puerto Rico. He had been the starting shortstop for Venezuela's Pastora Milkers in the 1954 Caribbean Series.[13] His backup had been Luis Aparicio, a 19-year-old talent from Maracaibo, who saw a lot of playing time in that event.

Benson's first excursion as a Winter League manager was successful, as Santurce toppled Mayagüez in the finals, then captured the second Interamerican Series over Venezuela's Caracas Lions, Panama-Nicaragua's Marlboro Smokers and the Mayagüez Indians.

Benson did more than manage the team. Injuries and player turnover had him scrambling for players. He made a trip to the Dominican Republic to secure the services of Julian Javier, St. Louis's second baseman, after play was suspended in the Dominican League on December 3, 1961, because of political unrest in the post–Trujillo era.[14] Javier joined Santurce and provided some spark, but opted to return to his homeland prior to the playoffs. Cliff Cook, Santurce's third baseman, left the team because of illness, and bullpen ace Ed Bauta was inactivated with a sore arm. "Orlando Cepeda and Bob Gibson contributed very well to our efforts," says Benson. "Nobody threw harder than Gibson and Pizarro. They were without question the two quickest in the league, and when they were on, they dominated the opposition. Orlando Peña came through at the end."

Benson found that winter's experience very helpful in handling and understanding Latin players. He went to the finals in three of his four years managing in Venezuela, and led Licey to the Dominican title, winning five straight in a nine-game series. Benson remembers a thank-you note he received from Bob Gibson after the pitcher's retirement from baseball. Benson: "I wouldn't want to take any credit for the success Gibson had after that [Puerto Rico], but that tells me something."

Cal Ermer

Cal Ermer managed Ponce in 1960-61 and 1961-62 before taking charge at Mayagüez. In his Ponce debut, Ermer realized how fickle winter ball could be, especially with pitching roster changes. "Pittsburgh moved me to [manage] Ponce after I had one year in the Dominican Republic," says Ermer. "Joe Gibbon and Tom Cheyney didn't want to stay in Puerto Rico. They were just off the [1960] World Series win."

Ermer appreciated pitcher Gary Peters. After Peters's release from Ponce, Mayagüez picked up the left-hander, who helped them win the pennant and playoffs. "I got Peters to use nothing but sinking fastballs. It took him to the White Sox, the 1963 American League Rookie of the Year—he won 19 games, and a good big league career," says Ermer.

Phil Niekro was another Ermer project. Niekro began the 1963-64 winter in the Dominican Republic, but was without a job when Mayagüez claimed him. Ermer encouraged Niekro to rely on the knuckle ball, his eventual big league meal ticket. "Ten years later, I had [Phil's brother] Joe Niekro at Mayagüez," Ermer recalls. "It's ironic, both Niekros made it after I suggested they use their stuff properly. Hey, Puerto Rico was a good league, better than AAA and just under the majors. I saw all the good ones down there and had a good rapport with all of them."

Johnny Lipon

Johnny Lipon was in the Cleveland organization when he managed Ponce in 1963-64 and 1964-65. Sonny Siebert, Steve Hargan, Bob Chance and Luis Tiant were Cleveland prospects who played for Lipon in Puerto Rico. Lipon agreed with Branch Rickey's philosophy that the more one played, the better one became. He felt the excitement of winter ball plus the confidence factor was good for players. "There was one extra-inning game when Siebert came on in relief and struck out Clemente with the bases loaded," says Lipon. "It was a turning point in his [Siebert's] career."

Lipon first picked up some Spanish when he played in Cuba during the 1954-55 season and later managed there at the AAA level. He was a skipper in Venezuela during four winters, as well as spending two seasons apiece in the Dominican Republic and Colombia.

Pancho Coímbre, now Ponce's hitting instructor, was a Lipon favorite. Lipon: "When I talked to Satchel Paige at one time in the minors, when he pitched for the Marlins, and this was before a [summer] game in Havana, Cuba, Paige said Coímbre was the best hitter he had ever faced. Another thing—Pancho would go to a bar or restaurant in Puerto Rico, and they wouldn't want to take his money. He was just a hero there."

Rocky Bridges

Rocky Bridges, a coach with the California Angels, preceded Jim Fregosi as Ponce's manager and led the 1968-69 team to their first title in 22 years. He was ably assisted, as was Fregosi, by coach Carlos Manuel Santiago. Bridges felt Santiago was an effective communicator who could relate well to the young players and the team veterans.

Some of the team's clutch performers came from the Angels. Jay Johnstone went down for extra work, and Ken Tatum worked on his relief pitching. "One of the fellows that we did play was Torito Meléndez," Bridges reports. "It was very unusual to play a younger player, and Yuyo was surprised when I played the rookie. He was one of the best players we had."

Frank Verdi

Frank Verdi was a successful minor league skipper who came within one game of leading three different Puerto Rico teams to a league title, a feat no one has yet accomplished (1994). Verdi's 1971-72 league champion Ponce Lions went on to win the franchise's first-ever Caribbean Series title.[15] Verdi then took the 1983-84 Mayagüez club to the league championship. But a dramatic Benito Santiago home run in game six of the 1985 finals, coupled with miscues, prevented Verdi's Santurce squad from winning this series. "You win in that league with young kids who are hungry," says Verdi. "The older guys play more for prestige than anything else." It was Verdi who penciled José Cruz's name into the Ponce lineup on an everyday basis in 1970-71. Cruz responded with 11 homers.[16] Verdi witnessed Cruz's transition from a cocky 23-year-old on his way up to a great player and a gentleman.

Rubén Sierra and Sandy Alomar, Jr., got their starts as Santurce rookies when they were both 18 years old. Verdi put them to the test and was satisfied with the results: "Sierra could run, hit, throw and hit with power. He had all the tools in the world. I wasn't trying to rush him in to play too soon, so he wouldn't get discouraged. Alomar had a good arm, catching ability, and was a big, hungry kid."

Verdi compiled an enviable league record, but, 24 days into the 1985-86 season, with Santurce at 7-14, he was fired.[17]

Sandy Alomar, Sr.

Santurce coach Sandy Alomar, Sr., took over from Verdi. From that point on, Santurce went 24-9 for the season, to claim a spot in the new round-robin playoff format.[18] "I liked managing in the league," Alomar observes. "My son caught for me in 1985-86 and 1989-90 when I managed Ponce. That season [1989-90], we finished first in the regular season and Sandy Junior, Iván Calderón, Joey Cora and Luis Aguayo came through." Roberto Alomar also played for his father during part of the 1989-90 season.

Alomar's first Winter League managing stint came in his final season as an active player, 1980-81, when Stan Williams resigned as Ponce's skipper. One of the major challenges for Alomar was handling Ponce's star left fielder, Rickey Henderson.

Alomar: "Henderson had tremendous talent, but he was difficult to manage. He might take a shower in the seventh inning. There were times he didn't feel like playing. Other times, he'd go all out." Alomar returned as Ponce's manager in 1993-94 and managed both sons a second time. Sandy Junior played some outfield and was a designated hitter that winter, while Roberto saw action for three weeks before being sidelined by a broken fibula. "I'm proud of what people say about my sons as human beings," says Alomar. "Everyone who knows them respects the way they handle themselves above and beyond what they do as ballplayers."

Orlando Gómez

Orlando Gómez knew the league as a result of his long playing career. He was a backup catcher for league champions with Ponce and Mayagüez, and made his league managing debut for Mayagüez in 1980-81. After leading the Indians to a regular-season second-place finish he was chosen Manager of the Year.[19]

Gómez managed Ponce to the regular-season title in 1986-87 and his Lions played an exciting final series with Caguas before bowing out in six games. He also managed Arecibo and Ponce in the 1990s. "The main differences between our league and AAA are the number of games played and the fact you have to start winning early on in Puerto Rico," Gómez points out. "You also have a broader range of talent here, from the kids in A ball to the big leaguers. Puerto Rico was a 'AAA-and-a-half' league when I played, but a lower level from the mid–1980s to early 1990s because many of the big leaguers stopped playing with the high salaries being paid in the majors."

Mako Oliveras

Mako Oliveras led San Juan and Santurce to two titles apiece in his first ten years as a league manager. As a player, he had had plenty of role models, beginning with Sparky Anderson in 1968-69, and continuing with Frank Verdi, José Pagán, Doc Edwards and Art Howe. Pagán was the manager he most patterned himself after. "About 90 percent of the things I do as a manager were learned from Pagán," Oliveras affirms. "Pagán had the ability to get the most out of the ballplayers. He found a way to get everyone involved, and that's what has made me successful—the rapport I've established with all my players, from the teenager in A ball to Juan González."

Oliveras received a Christmas surprise in late December 1984, when he was named San Juan's manager after the firing of Orlando Peña. San Juan qualified for the semifinals as fourth-place team and won the championship. It was during this postseason that the term "los pillos" [the rascals] was coined for Oliveras's bench players, those who rose to the occasion to help win games when given the opportunity to play.

Oliveras had been a scrappy utility infielder in winter ball who produced when called upon. One of his favorite phrases, "Si baila uno, baila todo el mundo o no se baila," translates as "If one gets to dance, everyone will or no one dances."

Mako Oliveras gave Benito Santiago, Edgar Martínez and Carlos Baerga a chance to play before they became household words in Puerto Rico. Yet he had the skill to work with top prospects like Rafael Palmeiro and Bryan Harvey as well as veterans such as Lonnie Smith and Juan Beníquez.

Ramón Avilés

Ramón Avilés's baptism of fire as a league manager took place in the 1987 Caribbean Series, when Caguas asked him to replace Tim Foli. Caguas had lost two of their first three games, and the team's management put Avilés, a coach, in charge. The Criollos won four straight games, including a tiebreaker with the Aguilas Cibaeñas of the Dominican Republic, to win the series. But Avilés wasn't overjoyed with the circumstances which put him in the limelight.

"I felt for Tim Foli because he has the ability to manage in the majors," Avilés says. "In Puerto Rico, he displayed a temper and I tried to help him. During the regular season, when I took the lineup card to the plate, there were times the umpires would ask me what inning would I like to manage the team because they planned to send him to the showers. I would defend Foli and tell the umps that this wasn't right, they shouldn't think this way."

Avilés managed the Caguas and Arecibo franchises for two seasons apiece, and Bayamón during the 1991-92 season. He gave Juan González a chance to play every day during the 1989-90 season. Caguas made it to the finals that season and Avilés was rewarded with Manager of the Year honors. But Avilés also weathered his share of storms. "When I managed Arecibo, the imports lived in Dorado," he recalls. "If a game scheduled in San Juan was postponed, there was no way we could practice in Arecibo. I'd call them up, but they would be playing golf or at the beach, so we couldn't even practice in our ballpark."

Pat Kelly

Pat Kelly managed a winner with the 1991-92 Mayagüez club. He led Mayagüez again in 1992-93, and Arecibo during the 1993-94 and 1994-95 seasons. When he first arrived in Puerto Rico, Kelly thought one of his major problems would be motivating the players not to treat the season as a vacation. But he inherited a blue-collar team. "Down there you really need some combination of players who are hungry," says Kelly. "We had a lot of AAA free agents, like Chad Kreuter, Van Snider and Bob Buchanan, who were looking for jobs and got into the mode of playing hard every night. Wil Cordero was on the verge of making it, and still hungry. The combination of playing hard and the team chemistry won it for us."

Kelly knew about potential pitfalls—holiday season parties for native players and family-related matters for imports. On the field, he might have an A-ball player at first base and a major league outfielder; a big league starter might be relieved by a minor leaguer or vice versa.

Kelly: "The basic thing here in the comparison to the stateside minor leagues is that you manage *every* game to win. It's a great experience for me. I play every game to win, and don't have to say, 'Well, I'll take this guy out because he's a prospect.'"

José "Cheo" Cruz and Luis "Torito" Meléndez

Two Puerto Rico League stars of the 1960s and 1970s debuted as managers in the 1992-93 season. Following a league playing career that spanned 20 years, José Cruz returned to the league for his first managerial stint, replacing Orlando Gómez as Ponce's manager. Cruz was pleased to see native big leaguers such as Juan González and his close friend Dickie Thon return to Island diamonds. A lot had changed in the six years since he had last swung a bat for Ponce. "It's been a good experience," says Cruz, "and I know that I can manage. The Ponce management gave me this opportunity and I thank God that I've been able to do this to the best of my abilities."

Torito Meléndez, a Ponce teammate of José Cruz from the late 1960s to mid–1970s, replaced Chris Chambliss as San Juan's 1992-93 manager and kept busy through the finals against Santurce. When Meléndez returned in 1993-94, he managed San Juan to the regular-season and playoff titles with the best winning percentage in the franchise's history. "I enjoy the challenge of managing," says Meléndez. "I'm glad our big league stars, Carlos Baerga, Edgar Martínez, Rubén Sierra and Juan González, played in 1993-94. Clemente, Cepeda and Pagán played in the league when I was starting."

Meléndez managed San Juan to the 1994-95 league and Caribbean Series titles thanks in large part to the presence of Baerga, Edgar Martínez, Sierra and Juan González, not to mention Roberto Alomar. Carlos Delgado, league batting champ Rey Sanchez, Bernie Williams and Carmelo Martínez rounded out an awesome Caribbean Series lineup. Sierra (Santurce), González (Caguas) and Bernie Williams (Arecibo) joined San Juan as series reinforcements. San Juan's pitching reinforcements from other teams—Chris Haney, Roberto Hernández and Doug Brocail of Mayaguez; Ponce's Ricky Bones and Eric Gunderson; and, Arecibo's José Meléndez and José Alberro—paid dividends, based on this "Dream Team's" unblemished record in their six Caribbean Series games.[20]

The skippers have made things happen over the past 50 years. They understood the nuances of winter baseball and were able to make the needed cultural and on-the-field adjustments to relate to their players and win ballgames. Puerto Rico is a stepping stone for future big league managers and a laboratory for other managers who can find the right formula for winning.

9. BEHIND THE SCENES

You never know what to expect in this league. It is something out of Alice in Wonderland.
— Rafael Pont Flores, Puerto Rican sportswriter

Behind-the-scenes talent includes umpires, owners and general managers, broadcasters and writers, trainers and team doctors, coaches and scouts.

Men in Blue

Puerto Rico is a stepping stone for U.S. umpires as well as for players and managers. Nestor Chylak, Doug Harvey, Stan Landes and Terry Tata got valuable umpiring experience in Puerto Rico during the 1950s and 1960s, as did Dale Ford, Tim McClelland, Durwood Merrill and Dan Morrison in the 1970s and early 1980s. Puerto Rican umpires earn extra money by umpiring in the league, but most do not umpire in the States during the summer months. They have other jobs and family responsibilities. Local umpires tend to work Puerto Rico's amateur tournaments. When league play began, a handful of Puerto Rican arbiters withstood the challenges of vocal fans and low pay. The attrition rate, however, was high. American imports were hired once attendance took off in the post–World War II period.

Doug Harvey echoed the sentiments of various American umpires when he told me his Puerto Rican experience taught him how to better handle tough situations. Harvey, who made his National League umpiring debut after the 1961-62 winter season, was one of three umpires in the final regular-season game played at Escobar Stadium. It featured the famous disputed call by Mel Steiner at first base, when Roberto Clemente was called out and a fistfight ensued. A decade later, Harvey was umpiring the big league game in which Clemente slapped his three thousandth hit, and handed Clemente the ball.

Two of Puerto Rico's top umpires for a generation were brothers Wally and Kermit Schmidt. The Schmidt brothers live in Ponce. They worked with Doug Harvey and other U.S. umpires between the mid–1950s and 1980s. Kermit umpired for 26 years, Wally for 28.

Wally Schmidt had a distinguished career as a world-class boxing referee, handling title fights throughout the globe. He hosts a sports talk show on a Ponce radio station and is an official with Ponce's Municipal Parks and Recreation Department. "Kermit and I started out as ballplayers and were the first brothers to form a battery in the Georgia state Class D league," says Wally. "I caught and Kermit pitched. But I never played in the Puerto Rico League, while Kermit did. In 1957 I graduated from umpire school, and umpired in Puerto Rico through 1984-85." Wally Schmidt had some stateside umpiring experience. In 1961 he worked in the Northwest League (Class D), comprising Eugene, Salem, Yakima and other cities. But it was in Puerto Rico and at international baseball tournaments where he made his mark.

Frank Robinson, Earl Weaver and Tim Foli were among the most hard-nosed managers, from Wally Schmidt's perspective. "Frank, one of the all-time greats, questioned a call I made in the very first game he ever managed," he recalls. "It was in Ponce and I was umpiring at first. He crossed the diamond to question my call and that hurt. I threw him out of the game."

Kermit Schmidt is now a pharmacist. He was a Ponce teammate of Pancho Coímbre in the late 1940s, called some of the games Sandy Koufax pitched as a league rookie umpire in 1956-57 and enjoyed working with Doug Harvey and other American umpires. "Doug and I were very good friends," says Kermit. "I touched base with Doug after he had umpired in Puerto Rico. He always sent me a Christmas card, and I'm sure if we meet again, we'll talk about those old times. I remember a doubleheader between Ponce and Mayagüez when it was my turn to call balls and strikes in the first game. Doug was to call the second game, but since it was the last weekend of the season, he told me, 'You call it.'"

Kermit recalls Denny McLain pitching to Roberto Clemente in one game. Clemente was in the hole with two strikes and no balls when Schmidt called a borderline pitch off the outside corner a ball. The count went full, then Clemente drilled a game-winning double. McLain had a few choice words for Kermit on his way to the dugout.

The Schmidt brothers earned as much as the American umpires did when their salary peaked at $1,500 per month, plus mileage and per diem expenses. But they might get home in the wee hours of the morning, then have to get up for their 9-to-5 jobs, while American umpires could lounge around during the day. Kermit: "Puerto Rico definitely was a *caldera* [cauldron] for developing the skills of U.S. umpires and many really liked umpiring here because it was a step toward the big leagues."

9. BEHIND THE SCENES

Tim McClelland made his American League umpiring debut in 1983 after two winters—1979-80 and 1980-81—in Puerto Rico. McClelland was one of the half dozen AAA umpire prospects selected by Dick Butler, the American League Supervisor of Umpires, to hone his skills during the Winter League season. "Butler would select the umpires from AAA to go down and get a better feel for what competition would be like in the major leagues," McClelland explains. "So he would select six prospects he thought were major league caliber, and come down and critique us."

The benefits of umpiring in Puerto Rico rang loud and clear for McClelland more than a decade after leaving the Island: "It was a tougher league, a tougher quality of competition than AAA. So I had to raise my umpiring to meet the level of play. The players were a little better and faster. The curveballs were curvier, fastballs faster and sliders slidier. All the hitters were more powerful."

Police escorts were a reality. McClelland remembers the game in which local umpire Manache Hernández made a call that went against Arecibo pitcher Jeff Reardon. Future American League umpire Rick Reed was working the game. After the contest ended, the police had on their riot gear. Tim McClelland takes it from there: "The police tell us they're going to form a tunnel so we can get to our cars. Then somebody with a handgun came over, and the riot guards pushed us back in the locker room and [we] got on a paddy wagon on the field. The lights blinked a couple of times, a couple of big doors swung open, and we two-wheeled around a couple of corners and got to the police station, where our driver met us."

At this point in league history, the six American umpires were picked up by drivers for the games. Local umpires tended to go on their own, but if they opted to go with the driver, they would meet the American umpires at their apartments or condominiums. The games were worked by four-man umpiring crews equally divided between Americans and Puerto Ricans—their camaraderie was a plus. "Manache and Charlie Román became our friends," says McClelland. "They would come over for dinner and parties and invite us to their houses. A driver named Mula had us over for parties with other umpires; that's where we got to learn the native customs. If we needed to get a ride during the day we'd get a ride with one of the native umpires or take a taxi cab." McClelland could lie out on the beach until 4 P.M., take a shower and have a bite to eat before being picked up by the driver. He got relaxation plus the experience.

Dan Morrison's three winters in Puerto Rico, from 1977-78 to 1979-80, were a great education prior to his 1982 American League umpiring debut. Morrison also appreciated the Puerto Rican umpires. "Manache and Charlie Román just took us in," says Morrison. "It wasn't like we were working with them; it was like we were just one of them—very unusual. Here we are in a different environment than what we're used to and these people took us under their wings. They felt free to introduce us to their friends and take us to places they would normally go."

Morrison, too, has a memory of police escorts: "My first year, we were in Mayagüez after a playoff game in Bayamón, won on a play at the plate. Joe West had a terrific argument after the play and got a police escort. The following night in Mayagüez, as we were walking on the field, somebody threw a rum bottle that fell beside Joe West and myself. In order to protect us, eight or nine policemen were on each foul line facing into the stands to keep such happenings from occurring again."

Morrison told me the "respect factor" came into play after he left Puerto Rico. Rene Lachemann, when managing Mayagüez and Arecibo, saw the kind of job Morrison did in Puerto Rico. "Lachemann would come back [to the American League] and tell some of the players, 'This guy [Morrison] worked his butt off in Puerto Rico and will be a good major league umpire when the time comes.' Things like that."

Not all the U.S. umpires had a field day in Puerto Rico. Durwood Merrill's experience, umpiring in the mid–1970s with fellow Americans (Steve Palermo, Ed Montague and Scott Harris) is a period he tries to blot out. "We went down there as tough, hardened young umpires looking to get into the big leagues, assaulted from every angle from a bunch of people who hated us," says Merrill. "No backing other than the police down there, who stayed with us. We were spat on, had guns pulled on us, we were bumped, we were hit, we were cursed, we had everything in the world you could do to a human being happen—they threw rocks, bottles, oranges. Sure, I came through them, but it was like a Marine—I lived to talk about it."

One Puerto Rican umpire Merrill liked was Charlie Román. Merrill remembers Román would carry a gun on the field. Merrill: "I was so tough, so hardened, so determined to make it. If they killed me, I would have went through it. Imagine an American umpire going against a Montañez, a Sandy Alomar, Orlando Cepeda—they [the fans] were going to take your side? You had a better chance of getting hit by a freighter."

Dale Ford's second year of umpiring in Puerto Rico, 1974-75, coincided with Merrill's first. Ford enjoyed all aspects—daily YMCA workouts, beach in the afternoon, and a day or two off per week. He really liked the atmosphere. "Those people are so hospitable down there, it's amazing. The holiday season was party," Ford says, referring to the Christmas season *parrandas*, when people revel until early morning with family and friends. They come to your apartment and you go with them to somebody else's house. If you get tired and go back home, they'll come back and get you. It's a beautiful thing." He liked the *carne frita* (fried beef) and the hospitality of umpires Manache Hernández and Charlie Román.

On the field, Ford benefited from the respect he earned from the

American and Puerto Rican big leaguers and those on their way up. "When they get to the big leagues, if they respect you, they'll keep the other guys off your case," says Ford. "'See what I mean, don't mess with that guy. I know him, he'll jack your ass out in a minute.' If they see you in the minors or Puerto Rico, they'll respect you and tell guys in the big leagues, 'Leave that guy alone or he'll nail you' and that's the way you get your reputation."

Ford's Puerto Rico salary was $1,200 per month plus meal money for road trips. Prior to his 1975 American League debut, Puerto Rico was an important part of Ford's umpiring career: "It's better baseball than you've worked before you get there. It's just a stepping stone to the big leagues, in my opinion—designed for experience, and you need all the experience you can get, especially in argument situations. You had guys like Frank Robinson, who managed Santurce. Those situations helped; he's a competitor, I'll tell you that."

Pete Celestino, an International League umpire, recalls his 1991-92 Puerto Rico season. There were only three American umpires that winter, and each was a crew chief. The league assigned four umpires per regular season game and six for the round-robin and the final series. Celestino: "The local umps didn't get the respect I got. They [the players] will argue with the local umps at every chance. I would step in and bring it to an end."

In one playoff game, a native umpire correctly ruled that a home run ball was foul, and the call went against the home team. The other umps wanted to take the umpire in question off the field, but Celestino would have none of that. Celestino, like Harvey, Ford, McClelland and Morrison, made friends with the Puerto Rican umpires. "They'd have us over for house parties—trying new dishes, learning new dances," he recalls. "I've kept in touch with them. Living there for three months was a great life experience. On the field, it was a AAA experience overall, a great learning tool."

Gerry Davis may have most clearly articulated the benefits of umpiring in Puerto Rico. The different environment and potential hazards on the playing field, he says, turned out to be long-term assets. "The experience is one I feel *all* umpires should see. It's like the service. You don't know what a good experience it is until you're done."

Owners

Pedrín Zorrilla was an executive with Shell Oil prior to owning Santurce. He later served two terms in the Puerto Rican House of Representatives. San Juan's Bob Leith is a longtime shipping executive active in community affairs. Ponce's Yuyo González had a successful Jeep dealership. Luis Gómez used his sharp business skills as an insurance industry executive to bring Mayagüez's franchise back to profitability. Reinaldo

"Poto" Paniagua, a lawyer and Santurce's present owner, was Puerto Rico's Secretary of State.

Zorrilla, Santurce's first owner, loved to win and remained loyal to all his players regardless of their nationality or socioeconomic background. The illiterate Luis Cabrera received financial help from Pedrín well after his retirement, according to Pedrín's widow, Diana. Pitcher Manolo Alvarez had his college tuition paid for by Zorrilla in the late 1940s. Pedrín was a father figure to all of Santurce's Negro League players, from Josh Gibson to Willard Brown. "Santurce's players adored Pedrín," says Diana Zorrilla. "When Orlando Cepeda visits Puerto Rico, he stops by to say hello. Rubén Gómez has stayed in touch over the years."

Bob Thurman, Bill Greason and Jackie Brandt appreciate Pedrín. Herman Franks's fondness for Pedrín has never wavered, even 40 years after Santurce's 1954-55 season. Poto Paniagua brought Pedrín back as his special assistant and advisor in 1979-80, before Zorrilla passed away in 1981. "Pedrín confronted many adversities, including getting Santurce into the league in 1939-40," Paniagua affirms. "He created a very favorable atmosphere for the Crabbers, and they became a team supported by the working class people, a team which eventually had the largest following throughout the Island."

Bob Leith has a way with people. Even before he took the San Juan helm before the 1960-61 season, he was active with the club, determined to find the right man for every job. It was Leith who brought Phil Rizzuto to Puerto Rico, where the "Scooter" first became a broadcaster. "My original plan was to bring Rizzuto to play [in 1959-60], even if it was for two to three weeks," Leith recalls. "It didn't take Phil long to realize this was a hotbed of baseball down here; consequently, he shifted to broadcasting. He came here and did radio transmissions of the San Juan games, and [Luis] Olmo was on board and did a great job as well with the Spanish version."

Bob Leith's friendship with Rizzuto brought him in contact with Lee MacPhail. When MacPhail moved in as president of the Baltimore Orioles, Leith sat down with him and secured the services of Jack Fisher, Wes Stock, and Luman Harris, the Orioles' third base coach. Leith recalls Brooks Robinson coming to the meeting and trying to pass as a rookie. Robinson had played in Colombia and Cuba during the 1950s.

Jack Fisher was nearly sent packing after some subpar performances. Leith remembers his manager, Luman Harris, phoning Lee MacPhail from the Normandie Hotel about this, and reports the subsequent running down Fisher received from MacPhail: "'If I have to bring you back from Puerto Rico, it's not going to look good on your record,' MacPhail said to Fisher. Jack did OK after that. He pitched a hell of a game against Gibson in the Interamerican Series."

Leith's challenges went beyond player slumps. San Juan was financially dependent on ticket sales and radio broadcasts, since they got nothing out of road games. The beer concessions went to one individual, but later Santurce and San Juan split concessions and billboard advertising. The rain-outs and relatively long drives from San Juan to Ponce and Mayagüez also posed headaches.

Hiram Cuevas, Santurce's owner throughout the 1960s and into the mid–1970s, had success at the box office and on the field, and negotiated fruitful working agreements with major league clubs. Cuevas's first year as Santurce's full owner was 1961-62, when the Crabbers won the Interamerican Series. Santurce would win four more league titles in the Cuevas era.

Cuevas and Earl Weaver saw eye to eye on the three-run homer approach. The signing of Weaver as Santurce's manager opened the door for the Crabbers' working agreement with the Orioles. "When I signed Weaver in 1966, I met Harry Dalton [Baltimore's director of player development] and we had a good chemistry," says Cuevas. "We developed a sincere friendship. Every Baltimore player under him had first refusal to play in Puerto Rico and my friendship with Harry never interfered with the business aspects."

The Baltimore-Santurce axis continued when Cuevas gave Frank Robinson his first managing opportunity in 1968-69. Cuevas: "Frank and I had lunch in the Baltimore Hilton, and agreed to everything except salary. Prior to that, I had Weaver tell Frank what he made as Santurce's manager. We cut a napkin in half and each of us was to put down a 'fair' dollar figure. I put $1,800, but Frank left it blank — he was willing to take whatever I offered. I gave him $2,000 [per month] and we became good friends."

After Robinson's summer with the 1972 Dodgers, Cuevas asked for Ron Cey when Los Angeles sent their other third baseman, Steve Garvey, to Licey in the Dominican Republic. Cuevas noted Licey had a preference for Dodger players, which had come about thanks to the efforts of Manny Mota in the early 1970s.

For Cuevas, the best promotion was having a winner on the field. But Cuevas also put together deals with corporate sponsors — banks, gas stations, airlines, rum distillers and soft drink companies. He found six sponsors per season to be a good number. Cuevas got $30,000 for the rights to the uniform logo and $12,000 for radio ads.

Yuyo González's tenure as Ponce's owner coincided with most of Cuevas's Santurce years. Ponce's fortunes had hit rock bottom in the early 1960s. González remembers, "I dealt with severe economic problems early on. I'll never forget a game on December 22, 1961, when we received $67 in ticket receipts, but paid $250 for the use of a bus to transport the team. By the mid–1960s, we had 200,000 fans coming to our home games."

González used a regional approach to generate fan interest. Players

Ponce owner Yuyo González at a press conference circa 1969-70 (courtesy of *The San Juan Star*).

would go on caravans to neighboring towns, where they lunched with the mayor, stopped at the local high school and town square, mingled with Lions and Rotary club members, and distributed free tickets to residents of various *barrios* (neighborhoods). González lowered ticket prices to $1 as a goodwill gesture during the second half of December each year.

González traveled to the United States in the summer to look at potential imports, becoming a close friend of Rollie Hemond, an executive with the California Angels. That helped bring Jay Johnstone and Clyde Wright to Ponce and led to the Jim Fregosi managing link. González kept a beach house for Hemond's use.

Once the imports arrived in Puerto Rico, González did all in his power to keep them in Ponce. He took the players and their wives to different parts of Ponce every Monday, normally an off day, to learn more about the local culture. He even hired private detectives to ensure their well-being.

González: "My policies were good for the local economy, as well as educational for the players. Plus, if the team was in a slump, it was easier to have them report for 10 A.M. batting practice from their Ponce apartments or homes than if they lived further away."

Like González in Ponce, Luis Gómez made the Mayagüez franchise competitive. The five league titles in his 15-year ownership speak for themselves. "I had been a Mayagüez fan for 20 years before purchasing the team's shares from the major stockholder in April 1974," says Gómez. "This was just before free agency in the majors, and I became aware of its implications for winter ball. Players would demand more money, but I was prepared to handle this."

Gómez surrounded himself with sharp front-office personnel, including Carlos Pieve, Hiram Cuevas and Jorge Aranzamendi. His managers, from Frank Verdi and Harvey Kuenn to Rene Lachemann and Jim Riggleman, did the job.

Gómez developed marketing strategies with India Beer and Puerto Rico Distillers. He used sponsorship contracts wisely, and fostered community involvement. Within four years of taking ownership of Mayagüez, Gómez had Isidoro García Stadium refurbished.

For Gómez, the highlight of his tenure was winning the 1978 Caribbean Series. He adds, "It was special when our principal corporate sponsor, the India Brewery, honored us in Mayagüez after returning home. There were over 25,000 persons in the plaza, including the mayor. As a Mayagüez native, it was an event I'll never forget."

Mayagüez established ties with St. Louis in 1982-83, thanks to Cardinal scout Jorge Aranzamendi, the team's assistant general manager. Aranzamendi helped secure Andy Van Slyke, Vince Coleman, Tom Pagnozzi and Ray Lankford, and provided Gómez with all major league scouting reports through the Scouting Bureau. "Our four titles in the 1980s were no accident," says Gómez. "We drafted well in Puerto Rico, made some good trades, and counted on imports who produced. I would put the defense in place, then the pitching, and lastly, add the offensive firepower."

One of the more interesting trades engineered by Gómez was for Bobby Bonilla. San Juan had drafted the rights to Bonilla before the 1983-84 season. Gómez and Hiram Cuevas felt Bonilla would develop into a fine player. They parted with shortstop Adalberto Peña and pitcher Orlando Lind for the young slugger in 1984-85.

Ernesto Díaz González had a long broadcasting career prior to becoming San Juan's owner in 1984-85. He gave the team a new name, the Metros, in an effort to attract a broader cross-section of fans from the greater San Juan metropolitan area. He released some veterans, made a few trades and a managerial change. The Bonilla trade was a key for San Juan's pennant aspirations. González: "We needed an everyday shortstop, in light of Dickie Thon's injury [the April 8, 1984, beaning by Mike Torrez] and Thon's status. I wanted my team to win that season and without Peña at shortstop we would not have won the championship."

San Juan did win, but Bonilla also came into his own, and went on to help Mayagüez claim two titles. González had become more concerned with the bottom line by this time. He saw the league's economic stability go sour in 1985-86 and proposed to reduce the number of imports from eight to five, with a $2,500 monthly salary cap. Native players, on the other hand, should have a $4,000 cap, he said. Nor did González like the rules which allowed teams to substitute imports for native major leaguers who sat out the winter season. González: "The situation was a mess. It was important to reduce the payroll and give more opportunities to home-grown talent. I felt strongly about reducing the number of imports."

Santurce owner Poto Paniagua, the elder statesman of league owners in the mid–1990s, did his part by encouraging Juan González, Rubén Sierra and Dickie Thon to return to the fold during the 1992-93 and 1993-94 seasons. This put the league on stronger economic footing.

Paniagua feels the Caribbean Baseball Confederation, comprising Puerto Rico, Mexico, Venezuela and the Dominican Republic, should be more respected by the big leagues and would like more cooperation between the majors and Caribbean baseball. The Los Angeles Dodgers certainly set a good tone. Los Angeles was one club that worked with Paniagua for a period. "When Kevin Kennedy came down in 1986-87 with some of the young Dodgers, it was basically a working agreement," says Paniagua. "The Dodgers provided us with some players and asked that we bring Kennedy down to manage. At the time, they were grooming Kennedy and moving him up in their minor league system."

Paniagua is a traditionalist who sees his Santurce club as a league "anchor." Paniagua: "Santurce brings the most fans to the ballparks. When they do well, it's good sign for the league. The Dodgers, Yankees and Red Sox are similar in that sense—they have more of a universal following. When they're in the hunt, they give baseball a boost."

Tuto Marchand, San Juan's co-owner as of 1993-94, did his part in revitalizing the league. Marchand and his staff decided the team should again be called the Senators, and the Metros nickname was scrapped. Marchand had enjoyed success as a basketball executive in Puerto Rico's summer hoop league. He convinced the Island's major bank, Banco Popular de Puerto Rico, to be a sponsor. In a move that would bring tears to the eyes of Brooklyn Dodger fans, Marchand formed a band of four musicians from San Juan's Trastalleres sector. They wear San Juan flannels and regale the fans with upbeat tunes.

Perhaps Marchand's boldest move has been arranging the December 1, 1993, game between San Juan and the Cuban national team. Marchand took the initial step of approaching Cuba. "I've been associated with basketball all my life and have friends in the Cuban sports movement," says Marchand. But the red tape was extensive. "It got to where I had to get six or seven special permits—the Amateur Baseball Federation, our Profes-

From left: **Peter O'Malley, Los Angeles Dodgers executive; Kevin Kennedy, Santurce manager; and Tom Lasorda, Los Angeles manager, 1986-87 season, when Santurce had a working agreement with the Dodgers (courtesy of Angel Colón).**

sional Baseball League. Then I had to make a special trip to Cuba to iron out some details. We finally got official permission from the Amateur Baseball group."

Marchand reports that 24,000 fans attended this game. Two days later, Arecibo set a home attendance record of 11,018 in a game with Santurce. Ponce hosted a game which brought 10,000 fans to the ballpark. I was fortunate to be in Puerto Rico the first two weeks of December 1993, and was able witness this excitement.

General Managers and Scouts

Tite Arroyo did it all in the league, from pitching, managing and coaching to serving as a general manager (GM). Arroyo was Yuyo González's GM for nearly eight seasons in the 1970s, and returned to Ponce in this capacity during the 1993-94 season. Players' agents were one of the more frustrating aspects of the job, he recalls: "Back in the 1970s we started dealing with agents for the young American players. You don't get players now unless you deal with agents. That's what made me stay away from that—too many headaches. They [players] want to go home; before you know it, you're out of ballplayers."

When Arroyo returned to the fray in 1993-94, after Pantalones Santiago became Ponce's principal owner, he had little time to secure imports before the start of the season. Ponce's problems were compounded when Toronto prospect Rob Butler, a Canadian, had visa problems and was unable to play. Joey Cora had off-season surgery after helping the White Sox win the American League Western Division title.[1] The Lions could not play at home during a four-week period prior to and during their 1993 Central American and Caribbean Games hosted by the city of Ponce.[2]

Jorge Aranzamendi did not face these challenges as Mayagüez's assistant GM or director of operations in the 1980s. His scouting for St. Louis enabled him to keep an eye out for team-oriented players. "It was like a game of chess," recalls Aranzamendi. "At the end of my Texas League career, I saw Dan Gladden play for Shreveport. He was a natural leadoff hitter, and we got him for Mayagüez. John Cangelosi had a good on-base percentage. Tom Pagnozzi also had the right stuff. To play in the Caribbean does not just require talent; the American player must have the will to leave his country and get used to a culture unlike his own." Aranzamendi liked the major league scouting reports on Bobby Bonilla, and seconded Luis Gómez and Hiram Cuevas's intention of obtaining him from San Juan. "In 1984-85, I prepared a five-year blueprint for Mayagüez," Aranzamendi says. "This was based on all major league scouting reports—I had access to them. It allowed us to know more about their future."

Another trade Aranzamendi helped orchestrate was obtaining Paul O'Neill from San Juan for Dion James in 1985-86. It was another piece in the Indians' championship puzzle. Aranzamendi facilitated off-the-field comforts for the players, such as planning beach volleyball events on off-days and making sure the Mayagüez imports were taken care of in the Joyudas section of Cabo Rojo, a ten-minute drive from the Indians' ballpark. "An apartment was waiting for the players and their families. The rental car was ready and we took them on an initial shopping trip to get things squared away. A bouquet of flowers in their apartment was a nice touch. If the spouses and kids were content, it could be an extra edge. This first-class treatment should be given to a player coming to another country and new surroundings," says Aranzamendi.

Luis Rodríguez Mayoral was GM with Arecibo in 1983-84 and with San Juan in 1984-85. As a league GM, Mayoral was not intimidated by players' agents. He loves baseball and thrives on competition. Mayoral completed his league career with the 1991-92 San Juan Metros, by which time working agreements were more like "gentlemen's agreements." "We had players, coaches and managers from the Cubs, Dodgers and Reds. But nothing was signed in black and white. Jerry Royster managed our club and

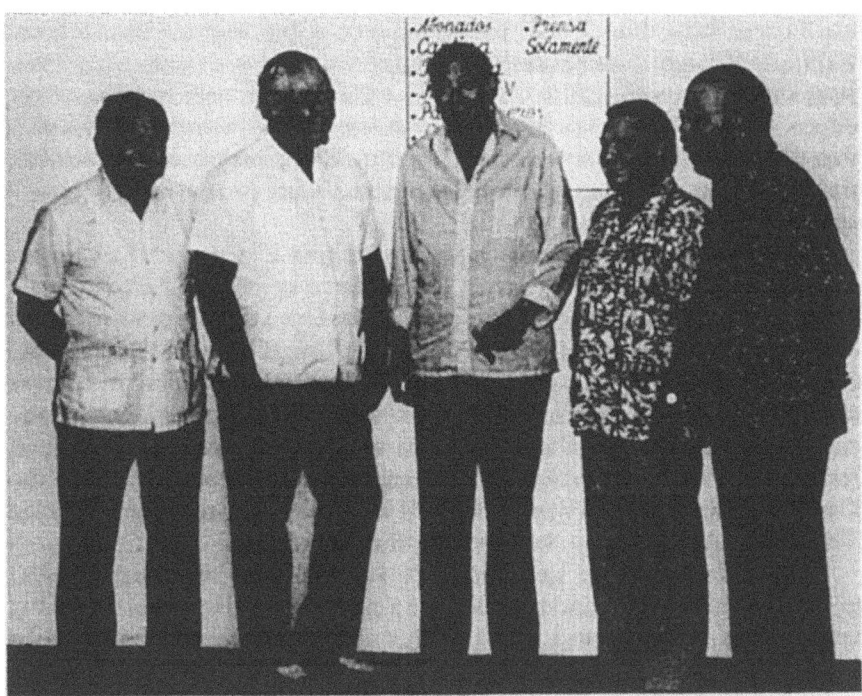

Broadcaster Howard Cosell enjoys a behind-the-scenes moment with league and team officials at Juan Ramon Loubriel Stadium, Bayamón, Puerto Rico, 1980-81 season. *From left*: Angel Colón, Luis Rodríguez Olmo, Roberto Inclán and Luis Rodríguez Mayoral (courtesy of Angel Colón).

was with the Dodgers at the time. Claude Osteen helped us as the pitching coach, and he worked with Cincinnati. Dwight Smith and Rick Wilkins from the Cubs came down." So did the Reds' Reggie Sanders.

Pachy Rodríguez started out as Arecibo's scorer in the early 1970s and has done it all—from the booth to public relations official to GM. He returned to Arecibo as the GM in 1992-93 and did the color commentary for 1993-94 radio broadcasts. He would rather do radio work. "There's so much pressure as a league GM," says Rodríguez. "I'm more at ease in the booth. I can go to bed without worrying how so-and-so has done. When I was a GM, I did work with Bob Gebhard of the Rockies, who was then with Minnesota, to bring players to Arecibo. I also set up links with the Mets and Giants."

Ronquito García, a big league scout with Montreal, Baltimore and San Diego, managed and coached the Puerto Rican amateur baseball team in various international tournaments. These experiences helped García as a GM for Caguas and Santurce. "I would scout the young talent throughout Puerto Rico. Plus, I had the confidence of big league organizations. Baltimore felt comfortable sending Dennis Martínez to Caguas when I was their GM. They sent Eddie Murray and Cal Ripken here because of my efforts. Ripken has always treated me the same way—with respect—and is thankful to our league for what it did for him. When I scouted for Montreal, the Expos sent Gary Carter, Steve Rogers and other prospects to Caguas," says García.

García developed a special rapport with Luis Tiant when they played together in Mexico. Tiant pitched for Santurce in 1982-83, when García first became the Crabbers' GM. García's Santurce contributions included drafting Rubén Sierra and Sandy Alomar, Jr. One reason for García's success has been the freedom given him by Dr. Emigdio Buonomo in Caguas and later by Poto Paniagua. Santurce was in the midst of their 1992-93 title run when García traded Carlos Delgado and another prospect to San Juan for Héctor Villanueva. Villanueva's slugging down the stretch and in the Caribbean Series helped Santurce win it all. García's acquisition of Dickie Thon from Arecibo gave Santurce another boost.

Cal Ermer took up Luis Gómez's $25,000 offer to become Mayagüez's GM in 1980-81, and returned for a second year. He called all the big league farm directors and rolled up his sleeves during the Puerto Rico League draft. Ermer: "I drafted Von Hayes number one—we found out his mom was from Puerto Rico, so he could play as a native. Then I got Iván Calderón for Gómez and made Luis Quiñónes the third pick."

One day during the 1980-81 playoffs, a friend called Ermer to tell him the game in Mayagüez was called off. There were storms all over the Island, but it hadn't rained in Mayagüez. "Luis [Gómez] wanted to give Eric Show another day's rest," Ermer recalls. "They got the fire department out to the ballpark and flooded the infield and I told Luis that only the umpires can call it off. So we ended up playing after all, and old Show struck out 12."

Carlos Pieve was Gómez's GM when Mayagüez won their 1977-78 title. Pieve loved the challenge of working with underdogs. He then engineered Arecibo's miracle in 1982-83, despite the obstacles. By mid–December 1982, it looked as if Arecibo's players might not get paid. So Pieve hoofed it to the Bacardi Rum Company in Cataño. The company had earmarked $25,000 for Arecibo later in the season, but Pieve had to request the funds right away. Pieve took six autographed balls to Bacardi executive Adolfo Comas as a goodwill gesture. Arecibo could go all the way, but would fall apart without immediate financial help, Pieve told Comas. Comas gave Pieve the good news that a $25,000 check would be ready that afternoon. Pieve later wrote, "The adrenaline flowed again through my veins. From then on I stopped drinking wine, and began drinking Bacardi."[3]

When Arecibo lost their first two semifinal series games to Santurce,

Pieve gave the Wolves a rousing pep talk and offered each player a $500 bonus if they came back to beat the Crabbers. Pieve said he would start fasting on a bed in the Arecibo plaza to raise the necessary cash.[4] There was yelling, screaming, and caps tossed in the air. Arecibo then won four straight games.

Gary Lance is Pieve's number-one fan. Pieve put in a good word for Lance after his playing career ended, which helped Lance land a minor league coaching job. "Carlos is controversial, like anyone else who speaks their mind," says Lance. "He helped me a lot. Some people call me his son. He's been real loyal to me; he's an honest person. It's not always a popular attribute to have in baseball; people want more yes men. Everywhere Carlos goes, there has been success."

Puerto Rico's busiest scout over the past two decades has been Luis Rosa. The players he signed before Puerto Rico was subject to the major league draft are an impressive bunch: "Oh, I signed Juan González, Iván Rodríguez, Benito Santiago, Roberto Alomar, Sandy Alomar, Jr., Carlos Baerga, Iván Calderón, Junior Ortíz, Luis Quiñónes, Mario Díaz ... there's quite a few. This was not only by participating with a team in the Puerto Rico League, but having personal contact with them."

Rosa began his league career as a Bayamón coach and instructor during the 1976-77 season. He worked with Arecibo and Santurce, and again with San Juan after their move from Bayamón. "I spent ten years with Winter League clubs, and they were great years, but you could see what was coming," Rosa adds. "When the agents started intervening with the contracts and everything, that really knocked down the quality of the player that was coming in here."

Jack McKeon and Rosa worked together with Arecibo in 1977-78. By 1979, Rosa was scouting for the San Diego Padres and had established a pipeline from Puerto Rico to that organization. Rosa: "I was able to look for the inborn reflexes which I could not teach. Somehow or other, those players with solid reflexes were able to show me something that a major leaguer was showing me at the time—if you get a flash of that, this guy is going to play."

When the Puerto Rico League draft was instituted around 1980, Rosa provided league teams with advice on whom to pick. According to Rosa, the team which had finished last the prior season had the first pick in the draft. Rosa remains grateful to the league: "It was a great, great teaching ground for me—I was able to judge and evaluate the veteran Latin player. I could watch my kids develop while seeing Tany Peréz, Iván de Jesús, Sixto Lezcano, the Cruz brothers. This was a good thing, to make the comparison, and go ahead and pick who I thought in my mind would emulate them or be better than what they were at the time."

Broadcasters and Sportswriters

League broadcasters Felo Ramírez, Buck Canel and Miguel Angel Torres went on to do big league games on a regular basis. But many others made things exciting for the Puerto Rican fans, from Pito Alvarez de la Vega, Juan Maldonado, Radamés Mayoral, Ernesto Díaz González, Héctor Rafael Vázquez, "el Paracorto" Andújar and Ismael Trabal to Palillo Santiago, Wito Morales and Rafy Sepúlveda.

Felo Ramírez, a Cuban, has spent almost 50 years in the broadcasting business. He got his start in 1945 during the Cuban winter league season. Leaving Cuba in 1961, he arrived in Venezuela. The Caracas Lions invited Ramírez to Puerto Rico for the 1962 Interamerican Series, where he made contact with San Juan team officials. When San Juan played the 1962-63 inaugural game at the new Hiram Bithorn Stadium, Ramírez was in the broadcast booth. "I still remember the first homer hit at Bithorn by Ponce's Don Leppert," says Ramírez. "After working with San Juan for a period, I spent several seasons broadcasting games in Nicaragua's winter league. Then I returned to San Juan. Santurce and Arecibo were other teams I worked with."

Ramírez became the Florida Marlins' broadcaster for Spanish transmissions in 1993. *Gracias a Dios* [Thank God] I enjoy good health and am as sharp as ever in the booth," he reports. "My reflexes and eyesight are fine. I've been very fortunate—[I] broadcast the last half of Don Larsen's perfect game, Hank Aaron's seven hundred fifteenth home run. But the highlight of my career was calling Roberto Clemente's three thousandth big league hit. It was a pleasure to work with Buck Canel on the 'Cabalgata Gillette' when we did the big league games."

Cooperstown Hall of Famer Buck Canel was born in Argentina. Canel broadcast big league games from 1936 to 1979 and was the only Spanish-speaking broadcaster to work the inaugural Hall of Fame ceremonies from Cooperstown, in June 1939.[5] Canel broadcast for the Caguas Criollos in the late 1940s. One of his favorite phrases, according to fan Charles Ferrer, was "El Pantano Iluminado" (the Lighted Swamp), as he called the Caguas playing field after another thunderstorm.

Canel's colleague, broadcaster Miguel Angel Torres, recalls, "During World War II, NBC did a series of Spanish-language radio programs for Latin America. Buck would do a ten-minute broadcast covering the highlights of one game. Canel was under contract with Don Q [a Puerto Rican rum] and local radio station WIAC transmitted these contests."

Canel was baseball's best broadcaster, according to Torres. Canel was at the mike for the first World Series televised live in Puerto Rico. Part of Canel's career was spent in Cuba, and his Spanish was flawless. Torres: "I asked Buck why he didn't invade the English language turf. He responded,

'Mas vale cabeza de ratón que rabo de león,' or 'It's better to reign in hell than to serve in Heaven.'"

Torres did live radio shows from the Escambrón Beach Club next to Sixto Escobar Stadium. In the 1950s, he was broadcasting San Juan's games. After relocating to the United States in 1960, Torres did boxing, baseball and space program broadcasts. He worked with Buck Canel on Madison Square Garden boxing matches. But his big baseball break came with the 1962 expansion New York Mets. "The Mets were looking for a broadcaster who could do their games in Spanish," Torres says. "I auditioned for the opening by doing a 1962 spring training game between the Mets and Detroit. Rheingold Beer, a sponsor of the Mets, offered me a contract and I did the Mets' games through 1974. My work also included covering the World Series for Voice of America."

Ismael Trabal Martell began his radio broadcasting career in 1947. A decade later he was a reporter for *El Imparcial* when Babel Pérez offered him the Mayagüez broadcasting job. Trabal's concise and clear style kept the "Tribe" fans glued to their radios. "That first [1956-57] team had the will to win and [Mickey] Owen was a good manager," says Trabal. "I broadcast games through the 1972-73 season except for 1971-72. Then I joined Luis Gómez in 1974 and continued my work with the team in different capacities."

Trabal was the director of media relations for Mayagüez from the mid–1980s to the early 1990s. He interviewed Bobby Bonilla, Harold Reynolds, Wally Joyner. Trabal: "I liked dealing with these and other future big league players. They were gentlemen and nice with the press. Of course I go back to the days we had Boog Powell, Dave McNally and Joel Horlen. Those are fond memories as well."

As a player, Luis "Wito" Morales debuted with George Scales's Ponce team in 1947-48, then sat out the 1948-49 season. He was traded from Ponce to Mayagüez for Roland Van Harrington under the orders of Rogers Hornsby. When Morales returned to Ponce, it was as a broadcaster. He got his radio break when Buck Canel left his job as Caguas's broadcaster. "Don Q [Rum] hired me as Canel's replacement," says Morales. "Then I went back to playing, but got injured in 1952. That's when my broadcasting career really took off.... From 1952 on I did the Ponce games. In 1972 I was elected mayor of Ponce, and devoted my energies to that job. After being elected to the Senate, I had more time for baseball."

Puerto Rico's sportswriters are second to none. Rafael Pont Flores was at the top of the list. After a zany game at Escobar one evening he wrote, "You never know what to expect in this league. It is like something out of *Alice in Wonderland.*"[6]

Pont Flores did not care to fly, but his choice columns and phrases were in the stratosphere when it came to brilliance. Toward the end of the

1953-54 season, he called Mickey Owen's catcher's mitt a "nest which Brooks Lawrence's pigeons and Bob Buhl's woodpeckers find to their liking."[7]

Miguel J. Frau's *Sporting News* summaries invariably had a "launching pad" twist to them. A case in point was a piece on two young Tigers during the 1965-66 season: "Although neither Jim Northrup nor Mickey Stanley set the world on fire with Detroit last season, the two may come out of winter ball with added confidence inspired by impressive batting performances."[8]

The younger generation of Puerto Rico's baseball writers includes *USA Today Baseball Weekly* correspondent Tony Menéndez. The Syracuse-educated Menéndez carries a torch. He told me, "It's tough to work full time as a sportswriter these days. So I've had a clothing business and am doing public relations work. But I love baseball, and the opportunity to do stories on our league. It's always great to see the Puerto Rican ballplayers do outstanding work in the big leagues, as well as the Americans who played here."

Medics

The team doctor I can best relate to is Dr. Dwight Santiago Pérez, San Juan's medic since 1987-88. Dwight studied in the same high school class as my brother Bill. When I played high school football at the same school, Dwight was an assistant coach. In 1977, after I had a judo injury which required surgery, it was Dwight who oversaw the rehabilitation process at his Sports Medicine Clinic.

Edgar Martínez was Dwight's major project during the 1993-94 season. Martínez had severe hamstring problems stemming from a tear just before the 1993 big league season. "Our sports medicine team had worked with Edgar after he had knee surgery," says Santiago. "But we disagreed with the emphasis placed on weights at the big league level to treat his hamstring problems. So this season [1993-94], Edgar underwent physical therapy and strengthening exercises under direct supervision."

Dwight is well aware of the pressures on him: "An important issue is the imported players. They might get hurt while playing here, and the parent organization will request the very best treatment. That's why we're extremely careful and provide a quality service."

When San Juan made it to the 1994 Caribbean Series in Venezuela, Dwight could not help but reflect on his father, Dwight Santiago Stevenson, San Juan's team doctor in the early 1950s: "My father accompanied the 1951-52 San Juan club to the Caribbean Series in Panama. Dad would bring me into the Escobar Stadium clubhouse. Those are very pleasant memories, and I like the fact I'm San Juan's team doctor, just like my father was."

Puerto Rico's trainers are a hard-working bunch. Nick Acosta is a former pugilist and boxing trainer who brings a lot of "smarts" to the table. Esteban "Steve" Meléndez came to Mayagüez in 1990-91 to pursue his dream of climbing the trainer ladder. Sometimes a U.S. parent team may send a trainer to Puerto Rico, as was the case with Richie Bancells in the early 1980s.

Nick Acosta is the dean of Puerto Rico's baseball trainers, with over 30 years of service to Santurce. He told me the players of earlier eras were more rugged than some of today's prima donnas. "Terín Pizarro was a starting pitcher in the majors who threw a lot here.... Rubén Gómez stayed in shape by pitching year round. There is no reason why pitchers today should throw so few winter innings." Acosta helps players on other teams. Rickey Henderson came to Acosta after pulling his right quadricep, and benefited from the treatment. Acosta got Félix Millán back in form after Millán suffered a fractured collarbone in 1977.

Steve Meléndez is a New Yorker of Puerto Rican heritage. He says, "Puerto Rico will always be a launching pad. It's a place for those who want to make the big leagues [or] stay on a big league roster, and where major league comebacks can take place. I've seen this happen in my years as Mayagüez's trainer."

José Angel "Gamby" González spent 17 league seasons with three different teams—Arecibo, Santurce and Ponce—as an assistant trainer and trainer. Gamby learned a lot from Nick Acosta. "David Cone was one player who liked to have his arm worked on and gave good tips," says Gamby. "The players called me 'Magic Fingers'—I'd make them as good as new. I was there to put them in optimum condition and helped them relax."

Richie Bancells was Rochester's trainer when Ray Miller asked him to work for Caguas. He was glad he went. When I spoke with him, Bancells was Baltimore's head trainer. "I'm half Spanish, so the food was no problem. It was my first baseball experience outside the U.S. The following winter I worked in Venezuela. The people of Puerto Rico were very hospitable. José and Héctor Cruz were a lot of fun," says Bancells.

Coaches

Carlos Manuel Santiago, Pochy Oliver and Germán Rivera were a trio of the savviest coaches in league history. Ken Duzich brought unique theories to the coaching profession. And Juan Nieves's youthful enthusiasm as a pitching coach was a plus.

Carlos Manuel Santiago learned a lesson or two from his Mayagüez skipper, Mickey Owen, in 1957-58. When Santiago coached Arecibo under Luis Olmo a few seasons later, he motivated Sandy Alomar, Sr., to become a switch-hitter, as Owen had done with Maury Wills. Santiago threw

Alomar 40 to 50 pitches a day. Alomar made the jump from AA to AAA and went on to a 15-year big league career.

Santiago kept track of the players during bus trips. On one occasion, Arecibo players had a late dinner in Caguas, and Santiago alerted them to be on the bus in 40 minutes. Two American pitchers stayed in the restaurant cracking jokes and missed the bus. "It was midnight and we were on a road called 'La Muda' on the way to Guaynabo," said Santiago. "All of a sudden there's a taxi speeding behind us with the horn blaring and the two pitchers waving their arms. I had our bus driver stop so they could get on, but told them the next time they would have to take the taxi all the way to Arecibo."

Reinaldo "Pochy" Oliver spent 16 years as a coach with Santurce following his playing career. Oliver, a physical education professor at the University of Puerto Rico, had represented the Island in the Olympic Games as a javelin thrower. Many Island sports fans consider Oliver the best Puerto Rican athlete of the 1950s.

Oliver and Germán Rivera would translate and interpret for Frank Robinson. Some Santurce players did not understand English well. Oliver and Rivera made sure nothing was left in doubt. "That's all part of a coach's job in our league," says Oliver. "If an American manager doesn't understand or can't communicate in Spanish, we're there to help."

Germán Rivera coached for Luis Olmo when Olmo managed Santurce in 1965-66. Then he worked with Earl Weaver and Frank Robinson before moving to Caguas to coach the Criollos. "Jim Palmer, Reggie Jackson, Don Baylor and Robin Yount all worked hard with Santurce when I coached there," Rivera says. "I was a Baltimore scout for 12 years, and worked closely with all the young Orioles. Don Baylor was a tremendous hitter, but all he lacked was a strong throwing arm. Reggie Jackson started practicing more when he recognized our league was a tough one."

Rivera pitched morning batting practice to Jackson when the slugger was in an early season slump in 1970. Jackson once got so disgusted that he threw his bat into the Bithorn Stadium stands. But, Rivera says, "Reggie told me he had to do his part. He realized the Puerto Rico fans expected a lot from him, and came out of his slump."

Robin Yount's work ethic impressed Rivera. Yount would come to Bithorn for a morning practice and return for an afternoon session—all this before a night game! "Practice does make perfect. Robin Yount constantly asked me, Pochy and Frank [Robinson] for advice. We worked with him," says Rivera.

After moving over to Caguas, Rivera worked with Dennis Martínez, Eddie Murray and other Baltimore prospects. Rivera had scouted Martínez when the Nicaraguan hurler was competing for his country's national team, and recommended that the Orioles sign him.

Ken Duzich became Mayagüez's hitting coach in 1987-88 and later coached with Ponce. Duzich worked with high baseball draft choices and college teams in the States after he and his Puerto Rican wife relocated to the Island. "Baseball is really a visual game and the main idea is that the eyes have to work together as a team," Duzich insists. "The individual gets full depth perception—eyes are telling you how far the object is from your body." Duzich used his visual training theories to help Bobby Bonilla, Dickie Thon and others, but did not force his theories on them.

Juan Nieves was Oneonta's 28-year-old pitching coach when I asked him if he was interested in coaching during the winter. "I'd like to return to Puerto Rico and share my knowledge with pitchers," he said. "It would be nice to be a pitching coach." Shortly thereafter, San Juan contracted Nieves to be their pitching coach. San Juan had a banner 1993-94 season, thanks to the league's best pitching staff. It was fun to see Nieves interacting with his pitchers prior to several San Juan contests.

10. Teams for the Ages

> *Without a doubt, it was probably the best winter league baseball club ever assembled.*
> —Don Zimmer, former Mayagüez and Santurce player, of the 1954-55 Santurce Crabbers

Pundits can discuss the merits of teams and never come to a consensus on the best one. Don Zimmer told me the 1954-55 Santurce Crabbers were "número uno." All the league franchises except of Aguadilla and Humacao have won a title. Mayagüez had an outstanding team in 1948-49, as did Caguas's in 1973-74. Ponce earned five titles in the 1940s and three more from 1968-69 to 1971-72. Arecibo's 1982-83 squad was special. San Juan had dynamite in 1994-95. And don't forget Guayama's two-time winners.

Guayama

Cefo Conde told me his 1939-40 Guayama team had the best battery in league history, with Satchel Paige and William Perkins. Conde stated Perkins was a better defensive catcher than Josh Gibson. Center fielder Tetelo Vargas and the double-play duo of Menchín Pesante and Perucho Cepeda were all voted into the Puerto Rico Professional Baseball Hall of Fame. Conde himself and Rafaelito Ortíz, Guayama's other starter, are Hall of Famers. The 1939-40 Witches became the league's first and only "world champions" with their win over the Duncan Cementers in the Semi-Pro World Series.

Luis Alvelo gives plaudits to the 1938-39 Guayama club as well as the 1939-40 edition. Both teams won the league championship. The 1938-39 team gave the league immediate credibility, according to Alvelo, with Cuban Alejandro Oms, American George Britt and Puerto Rican stars.

Caguas

Héctor Barea was the batboy for the 1940-41 Criollos. Three decades later he handled public relations and media work with the 1973-74 champions. "Let me tell you something about the 1940-41 team—our first champion," says Barea. "We had a teenager behind the plate named Campanella. Olmo was in left and Manolo García played a tremendous center field for us. Pepe Seda and Pito Alvarez de la Vega platooned at second. Leonard Pearson was a fine shortstop. Billy Byrd won 15 games for us."

But, Barea told me, the 1973-74 edition was Caguas's finest: "Gary Carter and Jim Essian caught; Guillermo Montañez played first; Félix Millán and Pedro García shared second; Mike Schmidt defended third and Rudy Meoli was at short. Jay Johnstone, Jerry Morales and Otto Vélez were a fine outfield. Craig Swan, Eduardo Figueroa, John Montague and Volanta Rodríguez came through on the mound. Bombo Rivera, Sixto Lezcano and Willie Hernández were on that team."

Félix Millán likewise ranks the 1973-74 Caguas team as the best one, position by position. Its chemistry was the icing on the cake. "That's why we won," says Millán. "We were a family who came together toward season's end."

Woody Huyke coached this team and later sang its praises, telling me it was a big league ballclub. Huyke complimented the team's Puerto Rican players who were in the majors—Millán, Montañez, Jerry Morales, Pedro García, Otto Vélez, Ed Rodríguez. They were true professionals and set a positive tone for the younger players.

The 1986-87 Caguas team also earned plaudits from Barea. But he made the point that Ellis Burks, Van Snider and other Caguas players did not participate in the Caribbean Series. Caguas's 1973-74 team was pretty much intact when they won their Caribbean Series.

Candy Maldonado, a reinforcement from Arecibo for the 1987 Caribbean Series, feels it would have done well at the big league level. Bobby Bonilla and Henry Cotto joined him in the outfield; Carmelo Martínez, Roberto Alomar, Deportivo Rivera and Edgar Díaz made for a solid infield; Orlando Mercado and Junior Ortíz caught; and Juan Nieves, David Cone and Mambo de Léon led the pitching staff.

Bernie Williams and Omar Olivares were rookies with the 1986-87 Criollos. Williams was a reserve outfielder who appeared in 27 games for the champions. Olivares pitched in relief. "The 1986-87 group was terrific," says Williams. "I was 18 at the time and looking forward to a career in baseball. I'll never forget the time Iván Calderón gave me one of his gloves during the 1985-86 season when I practiced with Caguas."

Olivares compliments Caguas's 1986-87 pitching coach, Ed Figueroa. He also has kind words for his father, Ed Olivares, a third baseman for various Puerto Rico League teams. "Eduardo Figueroa really helped me that winter and gave me confidence," says Olivares. "My father has always been supportive and was so proud of me when I made it to the big leagues."

There was one Caguas team which fell short, but won 57 regular-

season games. According to Vic Power, the 1950-51 Criollos measured up to any of the six championship clubs he played on, including the 1953-54 squad featuring Hank Aaron. "George Crowe, Jim Rivera, Olmo and myself were part of a powerful lineup," says Power. "In 1950-51 I drove in 63 runs—a league record for Puerto Rican players. Three years later we won it all with Aaron and Jim Rivera. But I still think that 1950-51 team was the strongest over the regular season."

José Cruz played on three Caguas champions—1976-77, 1978-79 and 1980-81. Cruz feels they were outstanding teams with a nice blend of imports coupled with the top Puerto Rican players. And he says the 1981-82 Caguas team compared favorably to the three champions. Cruz played that whole winter, unlike 1980-81, and Caguas did win the regular season title before bowing in the playoffs.

Mayagüez

The 1948-49 Mayagüez ballclub never looked back. Line drives screamed off their bats like the roars from the rabid fans. Four stars cracked 100 or more hits, a feat never duplicated.[1] Artie Wilson set the standard with 126, Wilmer Fields had 108 and Luke Easter and Alonzo Perry chipped in with 100 apiece. Easter, Fields, Perry and Johnny Davis knocked in over 50 runs in the 80-game season.[2] The team averaged 6.7 runs per game and five Indians scored 50-plus runs.[3]

Cefo Conde came up with the phrase "Lo importante es llegar a primera" (The key is to reach first), since it was a given the Mayagüez base runner would eventually score. Conde came through with ten wins for Mayagüez. Perry and Fields won eleven and nine games, respectively.[4] When pitching changes were made by player-manager Wilson, it often looked like musical chairs. Fields would go from the mound to third or vice versa. Perry would go to or from first base. Johnny Davis played the outfield when not pitching.

The 1965-66 Indians savored the franchise's fourth league title. They counted on John Hiller in the bullpen. Imports Jim Northrup, Mickey Stanley, Ray Oyler and Hiller brought a winning attitude to Puerto Rico which meshed well with the work ethic of natives Guito Conde, Julio Gotay, Héctor Valle, Ozzie Virgil, Sr., and Florentino Rivera. "Héctor Valle epitomized the character of that team," says Ismael Trabal. "He was like an octopus behind the plate. After some games, his body was covered with black-and-blue marks."

Opposite: **The 1939-40 Guayama Witches Puerto Rico and Semi-Pro World Champions. Standing is Satchel Paige; Tetelo Vargas is in the middle, above Perucho Cepeda,** *right,* **catcher William Perkins (courtesy of Alvelo Collection).**

Ramón Avilés was an integral part of the 1977-78 "Tribe." He reminisced about that winter: "We had seven players at .300 or better. Venezuela [Caguas] and the Dominican Republic [Aguilas Cibaeñas] were favored to win the Caribbean Series, but we won it."

Ron LeFlore, the league batting champ, paced an attack which featured the slugging of Jim Dwyer, Kurt Bevaqua, Bombo Rivera and José Manuel Morales. Danny Darwin was one hurler who came through. "That season did a lot for my career," Darwin testifies. "It was a great atmosphere and we were ready for the playoffs. We picked up some pitching help for the Caribbean Series [Tom Bruno and Dennis Kinney] and no one could beat us. I won a series game."

A most impressive Mayagüez squad won the 1985-86 league title. The middle of their lineup featured Wally Joyner, Bobby Bonilla, Paul O'Neill and Randy Ready. John Cangelosi and Harold Reynolds provided speed and solid defense. Luis Quiñónes gave them versatility. Bombo Rivera led a strong bench. "We had a good team, good players, and anytime you play with players like that, you improve," said O'Neill. "My trade to Mayagüez [for Dion James] worked out. You try to make yourself a better player to get in the big leagues."

Team pitching coach Mike Cuéllar still had fond memories of that season six years later. We had chatted for about an hour during a Kansas City–Boston spring training game when Cuéllar ambled over to where his former pupil Luis Aquino was warming up. "When are they going to put you in the game?" asked Cuéllar.

Cuéllar said it was a lot of fun working with that Mayagüez pitching staff, comprising Aquino, Juan Agosto, José Guzmán, Jesús Hernaíz, Mambo de León and imports Pat Zachry and Tim Belcher. Agosto, the screwball-throwing lefty, feels this was the best Mayagüez team of the 1980s. Luis Quiñónes, a regular on the four Mayagüez champions of this decade, agrees with Agosto's assessment.

John Cangelosi, considered a native in the league because of his Puerto Rican heritage (his mother is from Adjuntas), played on various Mayagüez title winners. Cangelosi thinks highly of all the Mayagüez winners he played on, particularly the 1984-85 regular-season champions with Pendleton, Bream, Coleman and others.

Mayagüez's only back-to-back league champions to date were the 1987-88 and 1988-89 Indians. Jeff Brantley hurled both winters. "We had great ballclubs and did a lot of things off the field together," says Brantley. "Ken Caminiti, Steve Finley and Ricky Jordan were there the second winter. Kirt Manwaring did a lot of the catching in the [1988-89] regular

Opposite: **The 1973-74 Caguas Criollos after winning the 1974 Caribbean Series (courtesy of** *The San Juan Star***).**

Mueblerías Minguela
Mayaguez, P. R.

MAYAGUEZ CAMPEONES – 1965-1966

J. CEPEDA, G. CONDE, O. VIRGIL, J. BLACKBURN, T. MARQUEZ, J. RODRIGUEZ JR., GUZMAN, R. OYLER
E. ROSENDO, F. FISHER, W. SANDERS, C. APPLETON, NORTHRUP, C. AQUINO, N. RODGERS
J.A. SILVA, H. VALLE, J. GOTAY, J. MILLER, L. HOLTGROVE, F. RIVERA
R. DELGADO, M. STANLEY, R. PUENTES, L. BUVE, C. LOZADA

season, and Pagnozzi played some first base. Chris Hoiles was the DH for a time. Puerto Rico was great for me," he attests. "It made all the difference to get to the big leagues as a reliever and get there more quickly."

Ponce

One has to tip one's cap to Ponce's streak of four straight titles from 1941-42 through 1944-45. But several Ponceños I spoke with also hold the 1946-47 champions in high esteem. For one thing, no team in league history has ever come back from a three-games-to-none deficit to capture a final series. This Ponce club defeated the New York Yankees before taking on Caguas in the finals. The 1946-47 squad won the title despite losing starting pitcher Johnny Wright in a salary dispute.

Ponce broadcaster Rafy Sepúlveda, who was a young lad at the time, recalls this era. "Several of those Ponce teams had Sammy Bankhead and Howard Easterling," he says. "When they needed a second baseman in the mid–1940s, team officials found out Cuban Fernándo Díaz Pedroso was one of two quality players Marianao had at this position. So an emissary went to Cuba and secured him. Easterling and Díaz Pedroso were the only imports who played against Caguas in that memorable 1947 series."

Sepúlveda informed me that Johnny Wright—Jackie Robinson's roommate with Montreal early in the 1946 season—wanted more money from team owner Martiniano García for postseason play. But García would have none of it. "Martiniano said, 'No way.' Wright had signed for a specified amount and that was it. Ponce depended on Juan Guilbe, Planchardón Quiñónes and Pantalones Santiago on the mound. Griffin Tirado was the league's best defensive catcher. Carlos Lanauze played first. José Burgos did a fine job at short. What else can you say about Pedroso at second and Easterling at third? Felo Guilbe was an artist in center. Marzo Cabrera and Coímbre were outstanding."

Rafael Costas noted Jackie Robinson was in Ponce's plans for the 1946-47 season, but Howard Easterling got the nod when Robinson became unavailable. Ponce survived a Three King's Day scare on January 6, 1947, when Coímbre "prematurely retired" because of an injured knee.[5] Coímbre, however, returned to action in time to help Ponce win the league title.

Ponce sports commentator Pedro Carlos Lugo provided insights to "Lion watchers" for several decades. Lugo still can not get over the team chemistry on Ponce's 1968-69, 1969-70 and 1971-72 winners. "It all started with Corrales behind the plate," Lugo recalls. "They all came together to

Opposite: **The Mayagüez Indians, 1965-66 league champions (courtesy of Ismael Trabal Martell).**

give us our first title in 22 years: Santos 'Sandy' Alomar, Jackie Hernández at short, first baseman Chago Rosario, Quique Rivera at third and Jay Johnstone, Joe Christopher and Torito Meléndez in the outfield. It was a team without superstars." Lugo also compliments Guito Conde, who retired during the 1971-72 season. "Guito came through for us in the twilight of his career. He was there when we needed him and set an example for everyone."

To both Lugo and Sepúlveda, Ponce's 1966-67 club, with a rotation of Carlton, Briles, Boozer and Pedro Ramos, was top-notch. This pitching staff recorded 16 shutouts, with Carlton and Briles accounting for five apiece.[6] Sandy Alomar and Quique Rivera were gamers. Roy White, Roger Repoz and Dick Simpson provided power.

Santurce

The 1954-55 Santurce Crabbers had power, speed, defense and pitching. Don Zimmer puts it best: "Without a doubt, it was probably the best winter league baseball club ever assembled. I mean, we had guys like Buzz Clarkson, myself, Ronnie Samford, George Crowe; Valmy Thomas and Harry Chiti catching. We had Mays, Thurman and Clemente in the outfield. I mean, you're talking about a big league ballclub. Not only that, but Herman Franks was an outstanding manager. We could have beaten National League clubs."

Puerto Rican television sportscaster Rafael Bracero was a kid when Mays and company were in action 40 seasons ago. "Mays simply electrified the crowds that winter. It was the type of electricity one sees when a champion boxer is in the ring," says Bracero. "That Santurce team had it all."

Rubén Gómez might be in the best position to assess Santurce's top ballclubs from 1947-48 to 1972-73. After all, he contributed to their nine champions in this 25-year period. "Those first couple of championship teams [1950-51 and 1952-53] were something else," says Gómez. "To see Bob Thurman and Willard Brown carry us. We had Junior Gilliam and many other greats. It was so special to play with them."

Gómez puts the 1954-55 team at the top because of the presence of Willie Mays, Roberto Clemente, Don Zimmer and the rest. The pitching punch of Gómez and Sam Jones, coupled with the team's lineup and reserves, was overwhelming.

Elrod Hendricks contributed to Santurce championships from 1961-62 through 1972-73. The first one was special because of the pitching duo of Terín Pizarro and Bob Gibson, the presence of Virgin Islander Valmy Thomas in his final league season, and the novelty for Hendricks of winning a championship as a rookie.

Frank Robinson's first Santurce squad (1968-69) remains his favorite one. He won the regular-season crown in dominant fashion. As Sparky Anderson put it, "They were loaded." Santurce's 1987-88 regular-season champions and 1990-91 league winners were tough, remembers lefty reliever John Burgos. For Burgos, the 1987-88 squad had the better hitting and fielding, with Rubén Sierra, Mike Devereaux, Juan Beníquez, José Lind and Jay Bell. The 1990-91 squad was stronger in the pitching department, with Jaime Navarro, Luis Aquino and David West.

The 1992-93 Santurce edition was another winner. Veterans Junior Ortíz, Deportivo Rivera and Héctor Villanueva, coupled with imports Eric Fox and Gerald Williams, got the job done in the playoffs. Infielder Luis López was a youngster who contributed. Juan González in the middle of the lineup gave Santurce a huge edge. Francisco Javier Oliveras and Billy Brewer pitched well.

Final series and Caribbean Series hero Dickie Thon feels this Santurce club had the right blend of veterans, big league stars, prospects and minor league kids. This was a *team*, not merely an aggregation of players with their own interests.

San Juan/Bayamón

The 1993-94 San Juan club had the league's best winning percentage in 43 years. One would have to go all the way back to the 1950-51 Criollos to find a better won-lost record. Santurce's 1968-69 squad was the last team to win over 70 percent of its regular-season games until San Juan won 73 percent of its 1993-94 contests.[7]

San Juan's 1994-95 club, however, went all the way in copping the 1995 Caribbean Series whereas the 1993-94 Senators fell short. The 1994-95 Senators featured Carlos Delgado behind the plate, two-time league MVP Carmelo Martínez at first, keystone ace Roberto Alomar, Carlos Baerga at third, 1994-95 league batting champ Rey Sánchez at shortstop and DH Edgar Martinez. They defeated Mayagüez in a hard-fought best-of-nine final series prior to posting an unblemished record in six Caribbean Series games. San Juan bolstered its Caribbean Series squad with an All-Star outfield of Juan González, Bernie Williams and Rubén Sierra plus seven hurlers from other league teams since Caribbean Confederation rules allowed a maximum of 10 reinforcement players per squad.[8]

Almost a decade earlier, when San Juan surprised Mayagüez and Santurce in the 1984-85 playoffs, they did it with a cast of *pillos*—role players who found ways to steal games from the opposition. Papo Rosado was one such player who became a team leader and the regular catcher. "Mako [Oliveras] gave me the chance to catch every day," says Rosado. "Our 1984-85 Metros were a 'no-name' team which never gave up. I was

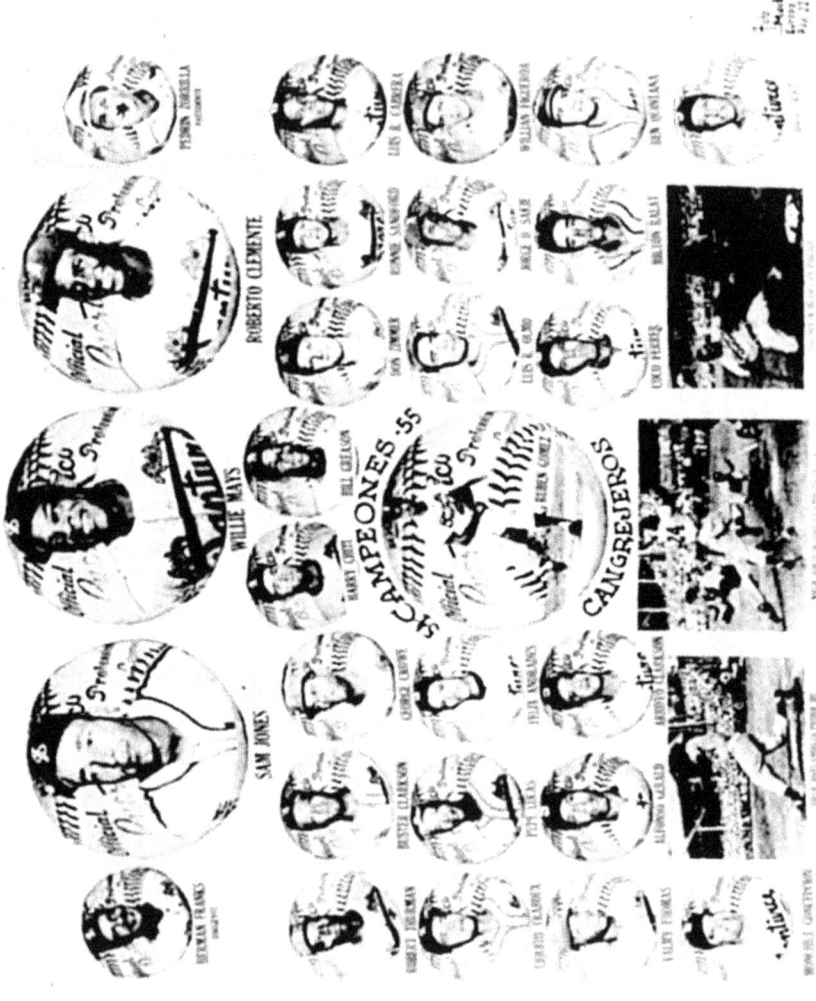

appreciated and helped the younger players, including my backup, Benito Santiago."

The Bayamón Cowboys of the mid–1970s were more talented, with Ken Griffey, Sr., Dan Driessen, Art Howe, Darrell Evans and Leon Roberts. Backstop Ellie Rodríguez was their leader. "When we won, we laughed and cried together," Rodríguez says. "I remember the guys coming to my house for a party after we won it all. Those seasons meant more to me than my big league experience. I caught one of Nolan Ryan's no-hitters with California, but those 1974-75 and 1975-76 Bayamón clubs were special."

Nino Escalera, meanwhile, still remembers San Juan's 1951-52 club with pride. He feels catcher Joe Montalvo and third baseman Canena Márquez were the glue. "Montalvo was big [6'4"] and a very good defensive catcher," says Escalera. "Canena did everything. Sam Jones could pitch. Jaime Almendro played tremendously at shortstop. Jack Dittmer was a fine second baseman."

Arecibo

For Arecibo fans, nothing can top the euphoria of the 1982-83 season. It was meant to be. Ramón Avilés gave his heart and soul to that Arecibo team, just as he did to Mayagüez's winning club in 1977-78 and to the 1981-82 Ponce champs. Avilés won as a league player, as a manager and as GM of the 1994-95 Senators. "Maybe I'm a good luck charm," marvels Avilés. "Arecibo gave me my first shot in Puerto Rico and it's where I ended my playing career. So that 1982-83 title was meant to be."

Rich Bordi, Keith Creel, Kevin Hagen, Gary Lance and René Quiñónes won on the mound. Onix Concepción teamed with Avilés to give Arecibo a steady double-play combination. Arecibo's "M&M" kids—Candy Maldonado and catcher Orlando Mercado—gave the team a strong middle defense and punch. Henry Cruz provided DH power. Jesús "Samarito" Vega had a banner year at first. Wayne Tolleson arrived at season's end to give Arecibo a boost at the hot corner. Orlando Alvarez, Carlos Lezcano and Glen Walker got the job done in the outfield. Dickie Thon, Carmelo Martínez and Mambo de León were "top gun" Arecibo reinforcements in the Caribbean Series.

These "teams for the Ages" delivered the goods. Most won the league playoffs in their banner seasons. They had the intangibles of team chemistry, unselfish players and a camaraderie which manifested itself on and off the field. Hall of Famers, big league regulars and role players, along with career minor leaguers, all made their contributions.

Opposite: **The 1954-55 Santurce Crabbers. Rubén Gómez, Sam Jones, Willie Mays and Roberto Clemente got top billing. Below, actions shots of Willie Mays (courtesy of Diana Zorilla).**

11. Games

> *We want to finish this up. The Lord put us here and I want to take advantage of it. We still have a chance.*
> —Orlando Gómez, Ponce manager,
> final series game 6, 1987

Records

Who would have thought an 18-inning game could be played in four hours? When Humacao visited San Juan on January 8, 1939, the stage was set for a 10 A.M. pitching duel between the visitors' Carmelito Fernández and the home team's Gerardo Rodríguez. As the sixteenth inning ended, on a pickoff play, one visibly moved fan yelled to home plate ump Rafael Brown, "Please hold up the game; I've got to have a shot because I can't stand it anymore."

Writer Muñoz Colón chronicled Humacao's eventual 2–1 win in *El Mundo*. "It was plain martyrdom, but a pleasant martyrdom ... like early Christians who saw their faith bearing fruit," wrote Colón.[1]

Caguas hurler Julio Navarro pitched the league's only regular-season no-hitter at Escobar Stadium. Caguas and Santurce played a twi-night doubleheader on January 14, 1962—two seven-inning games.[2] The opener was scoreless through seven innings. In the eighth, Al Schroll grounded to José Pagán, who threw wide to Frank Howard as the game's only run scored. "There were doubts about it being a hit," Navarro recalls. "The scorer first called it a hit, and changed his mind."

Pat Dobson was on form when his San Juan club visited Arecibo on December 10, 1967.[3] He made Johnny Bench's job easy, striking out 21 Arecibo hitters en route to a 6–3 win and a new nine-inning strikeout record. Dave Duncan was his nineteenth victim, as Dobson tied Pizarro's old record, then went on to break it by two. "Dobson had an incredible curve that day," affirms Palillo Santiago. "I sat on the bench the whole game and could not believe it ... 21 strikeouts! I don't think this one will be broken."

There were two perfect games in league history.[4] Arecibo's Luis de León and San Juan's Balor Moore pitched the games both in Bithorn Stadium. The de León gem, a seven-inning game, came in game two of a November 20, 1966, doubleheader.[5] José Manuel Morales caught this contest, and scored its only run on a base hit by Sandy Alomar, Sr. "Luis threw sidearm," Morales recalls. "He kept the ball low throughout the game."

The 1-hour, 36-minute game ended when Santurce's Paul Blair chopped one to third baseman Eddie Olivares. Kermit Schmidt had a perfect view from his third-base umpiring position. "No one really knew it was a perfect game until the very end," says Schmidt. "By the seventh inning, we were aware of it."

Balor Moore was not sharp before the November 25, 1973, game against Ponce. Papo Rosado warmed Moore up, and told catcher Ellie Rodríguez he was not throwing his usual hard stuff. So Rodríguez called many change-ups. Ponce's Phil Garner lined to Charlie Spikes in left to open the ninth inning. A diving Spikes caught the ball. Edwin Pacheco fanned and David Roselló skied to right. "The fans came on the field," Rodríguez remembers. "It was great."

Ponce's Rickey Henderson took his lead off first base in the January 2, 1981, home night game against Santurce. Bob Owchinko wound up and Henderson was off. It would be his record-breaking forty-second steal. Kermit Schmidt was the second-base umpire. "That was a close play," says Schmidt. "Santurce manager Cookie Rojas came out to argue. I told Rojas that Henderson just made it. A ceremony was held where Henderson received the base."

Santurce catcher Gary Allenson told me his throw nipped Henderson at second base. But then Henderson easily stole third. "I still remember throwing him out at second," says Allenson. "But he could have moon-walked going into third."

All-Star Games

Rickey Henderson received a trophy from Angel Colón, the secretary-treasurer of the Puerto Rico Professional Baseball Players Association, prior to the January 6, 1981, league All-Star Game, as Luis Rodríguez Mayoral looked on. Henderson was being honored for establishing the new single-season stolen base standard.

Puerto Rico League All-Star Games owe their success to long-time coordinator Angel Colón. He has given 50 years of his life to the league—working on the Bithorn and Loubriel stadium scoreboards, handling day-to-day duties of the Professional Baseball Players Association, coordinating the All-Star games.

From left: Angel Colón, Rickey Henderson and Luis Rodríguez Mayoral, as Henderson receives an award prior to the January 6, 1981, all-star game for breaking Carlos Bernier's single-season stolen base record (courtesy of Angel Colón).

Angel Colón makes sure everything is done, from soap and towels in the clubhouse to All-Star voting. Formerly, the fans and writers did the voting. Now four representatives from each club vote for players on other teams. Colón coordinates with corporate sponsors, finds a master of ceremonies, prepares statistics for the press and handles details for the All-Star party. "I suggested the January 6th date [Three Kings Day] so the proceeds could be used to buy gifts for children," Colón explains. "We now go with the date chosen by the network. Baseball has given me the chance to work with and get to know Frank Robinson, Sparky Anderson, Tany Pérez, Hank Aaron, Howard Cosell." Colón recalls the 1970 All-Star contest featuring ninth inning at-bats by Santurce manager Frank Robinson and Ponce skipper Jim Fregosi. Fregosi walked and Robinson got a hit.

Hank Aaron and Bob Feller were invited by Colón to partake of the January 6, 1976, festivities.[6] Feller threw out the first pitch as Aaron stepped in. Prior to the game, Félix Millán, Aaron's former Atlanta teammate, visited with the home run king. Leon Roberts of the Imports team earned

Félix Millán (in uniform) with his former Atlanta teammate Hank Aaron prior to the January 6, 1976, league all-star game (courtesy of *The San Juan Star*).

the game's MVP award when he drove in Ron LeFlore with the winning run. "I remember Ed Figueroa threw me an outside fastball after throwing me a couple of curveballs," says Roberts. "I lined one to right and got the trophy."

The 1987-88 All-Star Game, marking the fiftieth anniversary of the league, was dedicated to Colón. Kevin Kennedy's Metro stars bested Ramón Avilés's Island squad, 1-0, on a Henry Cotto homer.[7] All-Star games in Puerto Rico are preceded by old-timers' games, home run hitting contests and baserunning exhibitions. Cal Ripken won the home run hitting contest prior to the 1982 game.[8] Mookie Wilson was timed by Pochy Oliver at 13.2 seconds running around the bases, to claim top honors in 1980 pregame festivities.[9]

Special Games

The five-column heading in the sports section of the February 25, 1947, *New York Times* read "Yankees Are Vanquished by Puerto Rican Hitters." The 3 P.M. contest at Ponce's Charles H. Terry ballpark had the crowd in a tizzy. "President Larry MacPhail arrived by plane today to join his Yankees," wrote John Drebinger. "To the consternation of manager Bucky Harris and the frenzied delight of 5,000 onlookers, the bombers came down with a terrific crash as they blew their game with the Ponce Club of the Puerto Rican League by a score of 12–8." Ponce's hero was Fernándo Díaz Pedroso with a three-run homer off Joe Page in the sixth. He enriched himself by at least $70 and Ponce mayor Andrés Grillasca ran to home plate to shake his hand.

Raymond Brown pitched effectively until the eighth frame, when New York tallied four runs with the help of three errors. George Scales then summoned Pantalones Santiago, who fanned two Yankees to end the inning before retiring the side in the ninth for the save. The Yankees had defeated San Juan and Caguas prior to this game, and split their remaining two games against a Puerto Rico All-Star team. Canena Márquez got the game-winning hit in the other win.[10]

Joe DiMaggio sat out these games, suffering from an injured heel. DiMaggio visited a veterans hospital and performed other civic duties during the Puerto Rico visit. He returned to Baltimore from Puerto Rico to undergo skin grafting surgery at Johns Hopkins Medical Center.[11]

December 1, 1993, was a special day. The Cuban national baseball team stayed in Puerto Rico an extra day after competing in the Central American and Caribbean Games, hosted by Ponce, to play an exhibition game against San Juan. There was an eerie feeling in the press box at Bithorn at 10:45 P.M. Eduardo Valero stood to my left and regaled me with anecdotes on Cuban players of bygone eras — Díaz Pedroso, Cocaína García, Alejandro Oms.

With the visitors leading 3–2 in the bottom of the ninth, Cuba's ace reliever, southpaw Omar Ajete, began his second inning of work by retiring Carmelo Martínez. Ryan Thompson singled, to put the tying run on base. Then it was "launching pad" time, as Javier López smothered an Ajete slider which failed to break. It sailed over the left-field fence to give San Juan a 4–3 win. The ball was gone from the moment it left López's aluminum bat—the type agreed to. "That pitch just stayed over the middle of the plate," said López. "I was relaxed and waited for my pitch. But give credit to Cuba. They came to play and were aggressive. They played great."

San Juan skipper Torito Meléndez used five pitchers. With a full slate of games coming up, he treated it like an All-Star game. Carlos Reyes went three innings for San Juan. Reyes had pitched for the Waverley Reds in the 1992-93 Australian league while posting a 9-1 mark. Players in that league, except for the U.S. imports, use aluminum bats. "Australia was about AA level while Puerto Rico would be AAA or a little higher," according to Reyes. "The game with Cuba landed on my rotation. With aluminum bats, you've got to be a little cautious on what you're going to throw. They swing hard. I threw a lot of off-speed stuff—don't think they were used to off-speed stuff."

Playoffs

The "Pepelucazo" ended game seven of the 1950-51 finals before a record crowd of 16,713 at Escobar on February 16, 1951.[12] Santurce and Caguas were tied 2–2 when the Crabbers came to bat in the ninth. Caguas ace Mike Clark retired Willard Brown and Bob Thurman. Then José St. Clair, a.k.a. Pepe Lucas or Pepelucazo, stepped up. "Oh, boy—I had come in as a relief pitcher," Clark recalls. "He hit a homer off me and became a hero."

Luis Moux told me Clark threw his glove into the stands as pandemonium broke loose. Santurce fan Charles Ferrer remembers: "I was on the stadium roof. Cabrerita [Luis Cabrera]'s submarine ball was working. Buster Clarkson's homer tied the game. My uncle had recently died, and Clarkson hit it for him. [Then] Pepe Lucas hit it out. Olmo just looked up at it—he didn't move."

Caguas players were afraid Dennis Martínez would not make it to Mayagüez to face Jack Morris in game seven of the 1978-79 final series. Caguas coach Germán Rivera did some sweating. "Dennis decided to go by car instead of the bus," Rivera explains. "We told him to get to Mayagüez early for the 8 P.M. game. It was already 7:15 P.M. and no Dennis. It was the most important game of the season. When we saw him arrive, we were so happy, and he told us, 'Don't worry, I'll be ready!' Anyway, we won the game."

Cal Ermer recalls the disappointment. "We were ahead, 1–0. [Raúl] 'Boogie' Colón wasn't playing first. Jim Dwyer was there. A fluke play happened. Dwyer put the bouncer in his glove and waved Morris off, but dropped the ball. Morris broke stride and hustled to the bag, and it was a bang-bang play. Instead of the third out, they had a runner on. The guy takes off to second. Morris tells the ump time was called. Ump said no."

Mike Boddicker came through for Caguas in the 1980–81 league finals (courtesy of Rai García).

José Cruz drilled a single to tie the game, and his brother, Héctor, hit one out to give Caguas the momentum in their eventual 10–3 win. Lance Parrish's two-run shot for Mayagüez was not enough. Martínez was on the mound again when Mayagüez and Caguas faced off in the 1980-81 finals. Eric Show bested Martínez in game one, but Caguas bounced back to take the next four games. Mike Boddicker pitched a three-hit shutout in game four. "The writers were saying we [Caguas] only had Dennis Martínez as a quality pitcher," says Boddicker. "So that motivated me."

Caguas's Ellis Burks and Ponce's José Cruz were the cleanup hitters in game six of the 1986-87 finals, their final games in Puerto Rico. Fred Rehm of *The San Juan Star* covered Caguas's win. "The actual [9–3] victory itself was nothing less than anti-climatic," thirteenth he wrote, "but the bottom line is that the Caguas Criollos captured their baseball title early Friday morning [January 30] in one of the most unbelievable finishes ever in the 49-year history of the 'Old Winter League.'"[13]

With one out in the sixth frame, the game was delayed by rain for some 45 minutes. Then, when play resumed, the lights went out. Power was restored an hour later, but the drizzle persisted. Ponce skipper Orlando Gómez told Rehm, "We want to finish this up. The Lord put us here and I want to take advantage of it. We still have a chance." But league president Guigo Otero Suro declared the game official around 3 A.M.

The season and the playoffs taught Burks a lot. "It was fun. Everyone would compliment each other and have a positive attitude," he remarks. "Tim Foli was a very aggressive manager. Ramón Avilés and Jerry Morales were coaches who helped a lot. So did Félix Millán. I opted to go home and relax after the finals. The Caribbean Series would have been a good experience."

Caribbean Series

The 1987 Caribbean Series, in Hermosillo, Mexico, was a good experience for those who went. Juan Nieves, who pitched for San Juan in 1986-87, got last-minute permission from Ernesto Díaz González to join Caguas when the Criollos were desperate for pitching help. When Nieves arrived in Mexico, he joined a team that had split its first two games. Caguas played the undefeated Aguilas Cibaeñas of the Dominican Republic on February 5 at Héctor Espino Stadium. This was the 14–13 contest which Caguas lost after recording eight miscues but clubbing eight homers. Dominican starter José Rijo was knocked out of the box in the fourth. When the bloodbath ended, Caguas had 17 hits.[14]

By the time Nieves faced the Dominicans in game six, it was do or die. He pitched six scoreless innings while allowing one hit as David Cone saved the 4–0 win.[15] Caguas then won the one-game tiebreaker to claim the title.

Juan Nieves was voted to the Caribbean Series All-Star team, along with Javier Oliveras, Orlando Mercado, Carmelo Martínez, Candy Maldonado and Hedi Vargas.[16] Two months later, Nieves became the first Puerto Rican–born hurler to pitch a big league no-hitter. But the Caribbean Series title carried special meaning for him: "On the field, there is so much pride in terms of representing your country. Puerto Rico was in our heart. Off the field, we would share moments with opposing players and hear music at the night spots and discos, talk about our big league aspirations. But when we played, it was serious business."

A reflective Fernándo Valenzuela shared some thoughts on the 1993 Caribbean Series some six months after its conclusion: "Winter ball helped me return to the majors [in 1993]," said Valenzuela. "I think my 100-plus innings with Navojoa [Mexico] were important. When I was asked to reinforce our team in the Caribbean Series, I said yes. My arm felt good, and the series was in Mexico. It was a good chance to show my appreciation to all the fans. There's no guarantee I would impress the scouts, but I did pitch well."

Valenzuela pitched one gem against the Aguilas Cibaeñas, but his second scheduled start was canceled. "Puerto Rico and the Dominican Republic were playing for first place and didn't want to wait for us [Mexico and Venezuela] to play our game," he explains. "By the time we would have played, it would be midnight. We were ready to go, but Venezuela decided not to play."

Dickie Thon won this Caribbean Series for Santurce with his two-run homer in the tiebreaker game against the Aguilas Cibaeñas.[17] Tony Peña was behind the plate. "I didn't have to play in that series," recalls Peña. "But it was a patriotic duty. I've always prided myself on playing winter ball. Plus, more of our big league countrymen returned to winter ball [in 1992-93] and that helped attendance."

Manny Mota was Licey's player-manager in the 1971 Caribbean Series. Mota: "We had a moral obligation with the Dominican Republic to win and show that quality baseball was played in our country. Santurce had a *trabuco* [powerhouse], but we had momentum. Our fan support in Puerto Rico was strong. The players gave 100 percent after I told them we wouldn't win individually, but collectively. I emphasized we should represent our flag with pride and dignity."

Jim Beauchamp recalls that Licey went on a mission to win. Their 1971 series title started a trend that led Licey to seven titles through 1995.[18] The 1973 Licey champs had the Dodger connection, with Garvey, Yeager,

San Juan Manager Mako Oliveras with pitcher Juan Nieves (in jacket). Nieves reinforced Caguas in the 1987 Caribbean Series (courtesy of Angel Colón).

Lopes and others. Tom Lasorda was their manager. "That was a great ballclub and a good experience for me," says Lasorda. "I managed Licey some five seasons and enjoyed working with our owner, Monchín Pichardo."

When Licey won the 1977 Caribbean Series, their hero was Rico Carty, with a record-breaking five homers.[19] Licey won another series in 1980, thanks to the hurling of Dennis Lewallyn. "It was the highlight of my baseball career," says Lewallyn. "We were playing Bayamón—an excellent big league ballclub, and I beat them and Vern Ruhle, 1–0, in ten innings before 25,000 fans. In the bottom of the tenth, Del Crandall, our manager, says, 'Denny, I'm not going to let you go back. Your future is more important than one ballgame.' Damaso García scored the winning run."

Venezuela has fielded some powerhouses, beginning with their 1970 Caribbean Series champions, the Magallanes Navigators. The Navigators won their second title of the decade in 1979 behind the slugging of player-manager Willie Horton and Mitchell Page.[20] "That [1979 Caribbean Series] was well after my two seasons with Mayagüez," said Horton. "I enjoyed playing this series in Puerto Rico and winning it. Venezuela had a strong league."

The most memorable Caribbean Series hosted by Puerto Rico was held February 4–9, 1995, at Hiram Bithorn Stadium. A talented Dominican squad had big league hurlers José Rijo, Pedro Martínez, Pedro Astacio and Mel Rojas plus the Dodgers' trio of Raúl Mondesí, Henry Rodríguez and José Offerman. They trounced Venezuela, 10–1, and Mexico, 9–2, prior to taking on San Juan in game three.[21]

Puerto Rico's "Dream Team" brought the Dominicans down to earth, 16–0, thanks to Roberto Alomar's five hits and Edgar Martínez's five RBIs.[22] Three nights later, Dominican starter José Rijo exited in the fourth inning as Puerto Rico's bats once again came alive. Bernie Williams's two homers, a mammoth blast by Juan González, and Ricky Bones's steady pitching resulted in a 9–3 win.[23]

The Dominicans' pitching coach, Luis Tiant, told a reporter: "I was impressed with the [Puerto Rico] pitching staff. If we can put together a Dream Team like theirs for next year, I'm pretty sure that our pitchers will be the key."[24]

Series MVP Roberto Alomar was joined on the Series All-Star team by eight teammates—catcher Carlos Delgado, third baseman Baerga, shortstop Rey Sánchez, outfielders Williams and González, DH Edgar Martínez, and pitchers Doug Brocail and Eric Gunderson.[25]

Puerto Rico has dominated Caribbean Series events through 1995, winning 13 of the 37 events.[26] Following are the Dominican Republic (9), Cuba (7) and Venezuela (5). Mexico's two winners and Panama's lone champion round out the list. All active Puerto Rican franchises have won at least one Caribbean Series. Santurce leads the way with four crowns, Caguas is a three-time winner, Mayagüez has won twice, and Arecibo, Ponce, San Juan and Bayamon have earned one title apiece.[27]

Two of Mexico's best Caribbean Series ballclubs were the 1976 and 1986 champions. The 1976 Hermosillo club had Mexico's top all-time slugger, Héctor Espino, third baseman Celerino Sánchez, and catcher Sergio "Bazooka" Robles.[28] The 1986 Mexicali squad featured the clutch hitting of John Kruk. Kruk laughs about his Mexican experience. "Mexico was different and fun," he says. "We played some good ball in that [1986] series. I drove in some big runs."

Mario Mendoza played winter ball in his native Mexico for 20 seasons and participated in five Caribbean Series tournaments, those held in 1978, 1979, 1982, 1983 and 1987. No one played with more pride or determination in these events. "It was an honor representing Mexico and I played with a tremendous amount of emotion," says Mendoza. "I was one of the cogs on our 1978–79 Navojoa club, which played in the series hosted by Puerto Rico. The people of Puerto Rico are great. Please give them my best."

Mendoza's 1981–82 Hermosillo Orangegrowers made it to the series, with reinforcements Fernando Valenzuela and Dan Gladden. Mendoza recalls Valenzuela pitching superbly and beating the Dominican team, the Escogido Lions, which had Pedro Guerrero. Valenzuela and Guerrero—fresh from winning the 1981 World Series with Los Angeles—joked with each other throughout the game, according to Mendoza's memories.

By the time Mendoza played in the 1987 event, he was a utility infielder. He took over at third base when an injury felled the team's regular third sacker. And he still relishes playing against Tony Peña, Andrés Galarraga, Tony Armas and Candy Maldonado in that series.

Bill Howerton and Rance Pless drove home big runs when Caguas faced Cuba's tough Almendares squad in the 1954 Caribbean Series. The Cubans led 1–0 when Howerton—Hank Aaron's Caribbean Series replacement—stepped up in the bottom of the sixth. "I had been released by Cuba's Marianao team early that season [1953-54]," recalls Howerton. "But I could always hit."

Howerton drilled a fastball over the right-field fence at Escobar Stadium to knot the score. Rafael Pont Flores described it: "Angel Scull put on wings going after Howerton's blast. The fans put hands to their eyes like a sentry on the top of a post. Noise erupted from the stands which *never, never* stopped. When the import [Howerton] crossed the plate, he was received like a famous native who has been absent from the country a long time."[29]

The roar reached a crescendo when Rance Pless's two-run homer gave Caguas the lead and, eventually, the win. Pont Flores: "Hankies, coats, and ties were waved in the air by these happy lunatics. Pless took his time rounding the bases. A priest was waving his hankie—if that wasn't a blessing."[30]

Billy Howerton, Jr., aged eight at the time, attended this game with his mother. He told me he would never forget those moments: "The fans began to torch newspapers and anything they could lay their hands on. It was like a huge bonfire. After the game I remember my father being interviewed for several radio stations. He received gift certificates."

Rance Pless will never forget this experience, either: "The crowd went crazy. After we won the series, there were parades and we were serenaded all night long. I went up to the plaza and gave a speech.... [I was] given a portable television and other gifts. Winning that Caribbean Series meant a lot to us. Heck, the fans were passed out everywhere the next morning."

The Cuba–Puerto Rico rivalry was huge in the 1950s. Of the decade's ten Caribbean Series, Cuba won five and Puerto Rico four.[31] Minnie Miñoso and Camilo Pascual were two of many Cuban stars. Tommy Fine of Havana pitched a no-hitter in the 1952 event.[32] Jim Bunning came through for Marianao in 1957. "Winter ball was fun," says Bunning. "I thoroughly enjoyed playing in Cuba, and my later managing experience in Puerto Rico and the Dominican Republic. The Caribbean Series was exciting."

The 1957 Caribbean Series featured distractions off the field. Herb Plews, an infielder with the Washington Senators at the time, was one of Mickey Owen's top hitters with Mayagüez. "I don't remember that series, but I can still see the action in Havana," Plews says. "Castro was in the mountains at the time, and they told us to stay in our hotel as much as possible. There were soldiers around the stadium [El Cerro]."

Interamerican Series

When the Caribbean Series was discontinued in 1961, a short-lived Interamerican Series went into the books. Each of the participants—Nicaragua, Panama, Puerto Rico and Venezuela—won the event they hosted. There is something to be said about the home-field advantage and enthusiasm at these games. Just ask Cal Ermer. "I remember so many good memories about winter ball, but I think the one I'll never forget happened in Panama," says Ermer. "Panama thought they had it locked up—had conga lines on the right-field line and fireworks on top of their dugout."

It was Mayagüez's final game of the 1963 Interamerican Series. The Indians' victory in this game forced Chiriquí Bocas of Panama into a tiebreaker with the Boer Indians of Nicaragua. "Some son of a gun lighted a cigarette and lit the firecrackers," says Ermer. "All these damn things go fired away toward the infield. Pachy [Irizarry] got burned in the ear by one. The fireworks were over and the whole park was filled with black smoke and my first thought was, What am I going to tell Lee MacPhail? That Boog Powell is dead? All those things were shooting right down at him. The fireworks must have woke old Boog up, 'cause he hit two balls that are still going."

The only Interamerican Series no-hitter was recorded by Terín Pizarro against Valencia of Venezuela on the opening night of the 1963 event.[33] His gem was preserved by second baseman Guito Conde. On a hit-and-run play, Elio Chacón took off to second when Angel Scull hit a line drive toward the position vacated by Conde. But Conde reached back and made a one-handed stab to keep the no-hitter going.

Mike de la Hoz, Bob Gibson, Terín Pizarro and Orlando Peña were Santurce's heroes in the 1962 Interamerican Series, the final games played at old Sixto Escobar Stadium. Mayagüez, Caracas and the Panama-Nicaragua Marlboro Smokers joined Santurce in the series.

De la Hoz had two game-winning homers among his four clouts, including the final one ever hit at Escobar. That one, on February 14, came in the bottom of the eleventh inning off Mayagüez's Luis Tiant.[34] This

Valentine's Day homer ended the love affair between players and fans at Escobar.

Bob Gibson started this final contest after having won his two earlier starts, but did not figure in the decision. Gibson's first win came against the Marlboro Smokers, with relief help in the ninth from Orlando Peña. Gibson disposed of Caracas four days later, and helped his cause with a three-run homer in the 5–2 win. Craig Anderson put out a ninth inning Caracas fire to preserve the win.[35]

Semi-Pro World Series

Enrique Huyke contacted Raymond Dumont, president of the National Semi-Professional Baseball Congress, after reading a piece in *The Sporting News* in 1939. Dumont suggested a trip for the winner of the U.S. Semi-Pro League, and Huyke recommended a voyage to Puerto Rico.

Pancho Coímbre was asked by one sportswriter how he would fare against the visiting Semi-Pro champions from the United States, the Duncan Cementers. Coímbre replied, "If I can hit [Satchel] Paige and Raymond Brown, why would this be any different?"[36]

Guayama pulled away from the Cementers, four games to two, thanks to Rafaelito Ortíz's two shutouts. Ortíz's six-inning no-hitter became an official game when the rains came as he stepped to the plate in the bottom of the sixth.[37] Ortíz received two checks for his efforts. Guayama got a trophy and a $5,000 cash prize. Duncan received a check for $1,500, 15 percent of the gross proceeds. They were reimbursed $7,000 to cover travel, lodging and other trip-related expenses.[38]

The Enid Refiners, from Oklahoma, won the 1940 Semi-Pro World Series in seven games. Tetelo Vargas, the series' hitting star with 16 hits in 24 at-bats, including an inside-the-park homer,[39] flew to Puerto Rico for this series after playing in the Negro leagues that summer.

Regular-season, playoff and "World Series" games kept the fans wanting more baseball. Frequent rain didn't dampen their enthusiasm. They poured out their emotions like a tropical storm.

12. Fans

When something did happen on the field like a crisp, clean double play ... they would acknowledge it.... They were very baseball smart.
—Dan Morrison, former league umpire

Players, managers and umpires cannot help but notice the fans. Puerto Rico's baseball fans are just as quick to show their displeasure when a player isn't hustling as they are to cheer a fine play. There is no question Island baseball fans follow the sport more closely and religiously than their U.S. counterparts. "In the States, baseball is kind of laid back until something happens," says umpire Dan Morrison. "Down in Puerto Rico, in each community, they would start with—not necessarily chants—a certain song, and when something did happen on the field, like a real crisp, clean double play, something like that, they would acknowledge it, because they were very baseball smart."

Steve Lyons had been with Arecibo for only part of the 1984-85 season when he took note of the fans. "Down there, it's their major league season and they go nuts," Lyons says. "If the players take the time to communicate with the fans, then they love you down there. It was my first taste of what major league crowds could be like. They love their baseball."

Charley Manuel contrasted Puerto Rico's fans with those in Japan. Manuel played with Mayagüez in 1971-72, well before he was the top slugger in the Japanese league. "The Puerto Rico fans are more loud," says Manuel. "In Japan, they love it and keep up with it on the radio and TV. I think fans have more knowledge about the way the game is supposed to be played in Puerto Rico, and show more enthusiasm."

Tom Henke got a small taste of the fans when he joined Santurce shortly before the 1984-85 playoffs. But he saw what it was all about during the Santurce–San Juan finals. "I remember those fans more than anything else," he says. "They got in games, got on each other. I liked them."

Jamie Quirk got off to a slow start with Santurce in 1977-78 before getting back on track. The fans reminded him of this. "They were a little hard and weren't hesitant to boo you, whistle at you," he recalls. "The way I was playing, I deserved it. They truly like their baseball there."

George Culver pitched some fine games for Arecibo in the mid–1960s, including a one-hit shutout against Mayagüez's Denny McLain during the 1964-65 semifinals. Four days later, Culver again faced McLain, but lost because of Arecibo miscues. "After the loss, our fans were throwing rocks and bricks at their bus," says Culver. "It was quite an emotional time for the fans; we had a chance to win. After beating McLain earlier in the series, I remember coming to the plaza in Arecibo—they were celebrating and it was a great feeling."

Frank Thomas had been away from Puerto Rico some 40 years when he and his wife set foot in San Juan on a cruise stop. A new Radisson Hotel occupied the spot of the former Normandie. "What was really ironic was the cab driver who drove me and my wife back to the ship," says Thomas. "He remembered me from the [1951-52] season with San Juan."

Barry Jones's 1989-90 season with San Juan was noticed by the fans. Jones felt a bit uncomfortable when he first got to Puerto Rico, but the warmth of the fans helped quite a bit. "They're great fans. I was like a hero over there. The atmosphere and support really helped." When I spoke to them, Ken Caminiti and Al Newman complimented the 1988-89 Mayagüez fans. They felt those fans were "baseball smart" and fair.

Caguas's fans do more than watch the game. In a game during the 1970-71 season, John Strohmayer had pitched into the fourth inning against Santurce when the sky opened up. It rained all week, so the Caguas fans were in no mood for another postponement. "Within 20 minutes, the entire infield was covered with two inches of water," recalls Strohmayer. "So everyone went into the clubhouse and started getting undressed. I put my arm in a bucket of ice. Somebody came into the clubhouse ten minutes later saying it stopped raining, and maybe the game could be continued. No way, anytime it rained like that in the States, the game was finished."

What happened next is beyond comprehension. Fans who lived in neighboring houses went home and got their wheelbarrows. A big pile of loam was under the stands, and was put to use. The work was completed 40 minutes later and play resumed.

Strohmayer: "That epitomizes the word 'fan'; root coming from the word 'fanático.' They really loved their baseball and I felt a lot of satisfaction when I was able to perform well—so much appreciation on the part of the fans, more so than any other place I played."

When Mayagüez bested Santurce in the 1948-49 finals, fans from neighboring towns sent congratulatory messages to the front office. One fan took a 14-hour trek on his knees from home to the Catholic Church in the town plaza. Another went on a 12-hour walk from Aguadilla to Mayagüez in honor of the champions.[1] Classes were canceled and businesses closed the day after the final game.[2]

Ismael Trabal has followed his beloved Mayagüez Indians since the franchise's inception in 1938-39. Trabal, an eighth grader at the time, was asked to be Mayagüez's 1938-39 batboy by the franchise's first skipper, Enrique Huyke. Trabal recalls an incident that season at Mayagüez's Liga Paris when Guayama shortstop Perucho Cepeda became embroiled in a colorful dispute with the fans.

"Perucho came near the left-field bleachers from his shortstop position to snare a foul fly," Trabal says. "Our fans took aim with their *chupas de china* [orange rinds] — as a result, Perucho dropped the ball. He got so annoyed that he threw the ball into the bleachers. It hit a kid, and Pandemonium broke loose."

Twenty years later, Trabal was in the broadcast booth at Mayagüez's Isidoro García Stadium when Perucho's son, Orlando Cepeda, playing first base for Santurce, went through a similar experience. It came during the eighth inning of a Mayagüez-Santurce playoff game. Cepeda missed a foul fly near the right-field bleachers. He was met by a barrage of oranges, bottles and empty beer cans. Orlando picked up the ball, as his father had two decades earlier, and threw the sphere into the bleachers. Trabal notes that, oddly enough, that ball also hit a fan.

The Mayagüez fans were already steaming because Rubén Gómez had hit Joe Christopher on his batting helmet earlier in the game. Trabal will never forget Mayagüez partisans throwing stones at Santurce's team bus and Gómez's red corvette. The car suffered considerable damage, Trabal recalls.

The story had a happy ending when Santurce fans took up a collection a few days later to pay the $200 fine imposed on Orlando Cepeda for throwing the ball into the stands. Cepeda was ordered by league president Carlos García de la Noceda to pay the fine prior to a February 1, 1959, final-series playoff game against Caguas, or risk suspension for the remainder of the series. Crabber fans came through by raising the full amount.[3]

San Juan and Santurce fans have a rivalry which goes back to 1939. Bob Leith can recall attending wakes in which the deceased person is praised for many accomplishments, but with someone piping in, "Too bad he was a San Juan [or Santurce] fan."

Miguel Angel Torres has followed San Juan all his life, but one of his biggest thrills came as a 12-year old during the 1939-40 season, when Santurce's Josh Gibson played catch with him. Torres was in awe. "Do you know what it meant to have Gibson catch my throws and toss the ball back?" Torres marvels. "For us, the Negro leaguers were the greatest."

12. FANS

Juan Vené was an 11-year-old fan in Venezuela during the spring of 1940 who felt the same way about Josh Gibson, as well as Roy Partlow and Puerto Rican hero Perucho Cepeda. Vené, like future broadcaster Miguel Angel Torres, would later move to New York to continue his career. As a sportswriter Vené covered World Series, Caribbean Series and other baseball events. "As an 11-year-old, I saw Perucho Cepeda hit the longest home run I can recall over the center-field fence," Vené recalls. We got to see Cepeda and the U.S. Negro leaguers play in Venezuela."

Luis Alvelo still relives the moments when he shook the hands and patted the backs of the Negro leaguers who came to Puerto Rico. Alvelo affirms the 1940s were the league's "glory years." It is a period he keeps in his heart every day of the year.

Charles Ferrer was a diehard Santurce fan in his youth. Ferrer lives in the building that houses an office I worked in from 1980 to 1985. "From 1939 to the time Pedrín [Zorrilla] sold the team [in late 1956] I lived and died with Santurce," says Ferrer. "My uncle, Alvaro Calderón, was Santurce's treasurer, and dad was the team doctor." Ferrer remembers the fans at the games betting on who would score first. A big thrill would be another Willard Brown homer, after which fans would take a collection in a cap and bring the money to the slugger.

Ferrer recalls humorous nicknames given to players by the writers and broadcasters. Santurce catcher Earl Taborn was "Maricutana" because of his effeminate appearance. Southpaw Jim Lamarque's sobriquet, "Libertad Lamarque," paid homage to the singer of that name. Jim Gilliam became "the Black Sea," since nothing eluded him. Ronnie Samford was "the White Sea" for his defense.

Nothing could top the performances of the Negro leaguers, according to Ferrer's recollections. "What I admired most was their efforts to please the fans and win. They didn't make great salaries. I take my cap off to them."

Ernesto Camacho, my former neighbor, followed San Juan from its inception. Camacho remembers talking to San Juan and Santurce players at two area bars, Las Olas and El Picolino. His aunt owned the latter establishment. "The players would come in to celebrate," says Camacho. "I got to know Dick Seay, and he never drank water, just beer. Always wondered how such an athletic person could drink so much beer."

Camacho will always remember the fans who jumped the fence at Escobar to get in, and an older man from Old San Juan who used to sell little pieces of paper to fans with information on who might score first. This "pool" was known as "la leche del nene" (milk for the child) and cost 10 cents.

Some of San Juan's players came from the Puerta de Tierra sector of the city, where Camacho grew up. Camacho: "Millito Martínez, Leonardo Medina Chapman were from there. We followed them very closely. It cost 25 cents for bleachers, and 50 or 75 cents depending on whether you sat on the side or toward the middle. Remember, 50 cents was a lot of money in those days."

The most avid San Juan fan I came across was U.S. State Department official Luis Moux. Dr. Moux couldn't wait to hear daily reports from his Maryland home on how the 1994-95 Senators were doing in the 1995 Caribbean Series. "The first game I saw was from an apartment in the Normandie on a Sunday evening," remembers Moux. "I was only four and it looked like a fantasy world with the different uniforms and the lighting."

Moux attended his first game during the 1952-53 season. It was a San Juan–Santurce duel between Don Liddle and Rubén Gómez. Moux recalls San Juan jolted Gómez with four first-inning runs. Santurce then tied the game and Marota Salgado replaced Liddle. Cot Deal came in to hold Santurce at bay. The game ended with Deal striking Gómez out.

If Gómez or another Santurce pitcher shut San Juan out, Moux recalls, a San Juan fan would have to protect himself at work the next day from the pranks of gloating Santurce fans. When Moux attended away games, he found ways to protect himself from overzealous home fans. He tended to park his car several blocks from the ballpark, since he knew that home fans could recognize his license plate number as being from San Juan.

Moux also took no chances when buying tickets. He scurried to Bithorn Stadium on the morning of the 1970-71 season Opening Day to purchase his ticket. Upon arriving at the ballpark shortly after 8 P.M., he noticed the gates were open and a multitude had "crashed the party."

A delightful moment for Moux was watching José Cardenal's two homers off Santurce's Jim Palmer in game seven of the 1968-69 semifinals. He also remembers Cardenal's homer off Palmer in game three of that series prior to the two in game seven.

But Moux also delivers the "coup de grâce" to Balor Moore's perfect game on November 25, 1973: "I was sitting along the right-field line when Ponce's Jorge Roque lined one down the line which was called foul. But it was a home run! I was there and had a better view than the umpire. That wasn't really a perfect game."

The Ponce Lions of the 1940s were close to perfection to Carlos Costas. They still mean the world to him. Carlos Costas grew up on Torres Street in Ponce, two houses down from Millito Navarro's home. He began following the Lions in 1942, when they were the league's top club. Costas loved to imitate center fielder Felo Guilbe, whom he called "poetry in motion." Pancho Coímbre made several visits to Costas's household.

"Pancho would say hello whenever he saw me," says Costas. "Remember, professional baseball was *it* from the time I was eight. I'll never forget the way Griffin Tirado walked from the dugout to his position behind the plate—firmly and with a look on his face saying, 'Let's go, this is serious business!'"

Costas's heart remained in the Charles H. Terry (Liga del Castillo) ballpark after Paquito Montaner was inaugurated in 1949. Costas felt the intimacy of the smaller ballpark was lost, not to mention a sense of community, of family, where the same fans used to sit year after year. It was always fun to mosey around the concession stand and buy the best *platanutres* (plantain chips) imaginable. *Bacalaítos* (fried codfish), soft drinks, rum and fruit drinks were also sold. One could buy oranges and *piraguas* (crushed ice with syrup) outside the ballpark.

The locker rooms in the old stadium must have been primitive, since many Ponce players left the ballpark with their uniforms on. A high proportion of Ponce fans walked to the games. Inside the stadium, a patio led to the rest rooms. The grandstand along the first-base line had the largest seating area. Costas could see a few prisoners who watched games at a distance from the jailhouse behind left field.

An interesting feature of the park was the open area in right field. Costas saw Luke Easter hit one in the 1948-49 season that kept going some 50 feet above Pancho Coímbre's head. When Easter hit that one, Costas's father let out an expletive, "Ay, coño!" There was no *asopao* (a stew-like soup) in the Costas household that evening.

Not just Easter, but all the Negro leaguers created a most favorable impression on Costas: "Those gentlemen were imposing figures. They had the mystique of their accomplishments in the States, and were like giants to me. All seemed to be such good hitters; most hit with power, except for some, like Artie Wilson. Wilson just put them where he felt like, and always had a toothpick in his mouth."

Costas can still see the fans, including himself, giving Coímbre and Planchardón Quiñónes dollar bills through the wire net when their heroes hit a home run. If this was a game-winning blast, the batboy would assist the hero in collecting the cash. "Call it supernatural, innocence, or whatever. That was the magic which was evoked in those glory years," Costas says.

All good things have to end. Ponce folklore of the late 1940s tells of Ponce owner L. Martiniano García having some difficulties with the Guilbe brothers and of their mother casting a spell on García. Costas remembers it as a spell which worked, since Ponce never again won a title in the García era. It took 20 years before Ponce again came to the forefront under Yuyo González.

Puerto Rico's fans came out in droves during the 1994-95 regular season, playoffs and Caribbean Series. The 735,674 fans who went through the turnstiles in the 1994-95 regular season were the most since 756,815 did so 45 years earlier.[4] It was only the fourth time in league history that over 700,000 paid fans attended regular season games based on attendance figures of 710,164 for 1947-48 and 705,785 for 1951-52.[5] Fan support between the late 1940s and early 1950s was not influenced by television since it wasn't until 1955-56 that league games were first televised.[6]

The 1994-95 season was the best ever for Puerto Rico in terms of average attendance per game—4,541—since the six teams played 54 games apiece. By contrast, an average of 3,967 and 3,965 fans attended each game in 1947-48 and 1951-52, respectively. In 1949-50, some 3,207 paid fans on given day or night attended a game, based on the 80-game schedule prevalent that season.

Ismael Trabal Martell affirms the key reason for the league's resurgence through fan support in 1994-95 was the fact that most of Puerto Rico's major leaguers played the entire season. "In the seasons before the 1994 [major league] strike, our top players would usually start playing between mid–November and mid–December. But the uncertainty created by the major league strike definitely was a factor in our top big leaguers playing throughout the 1994-95 regular season, the playoffs and the Caribbean Series."[7]

Gabrielle Paese, a sportswriter with *The San Juan Star*, was fortunate to attend the last game of the 1995 Caribbean Series at Bithorn Stadium on February 9, 1995. She will always cherish the sight of 23,000 fans on their feet from beginning to end doing everything from clapping, singing and waving Puerto Rican flags. "It was the most amazing [baseball] game I've ever seen," says Paese. The fans were rooting non-stop for an entire big league lineup ... the spectacle had more drama than any World Series game."[8]

I, too, cherish many special moments in Puerto Rico's Liga de Béisbol Profesional. How can I forget Rubén Gómez shutting out San Juan at age 46? Or the time I went to my first game at Bithorn with my father, witnessing Tany Pérez's game-winning homer? What about Dickie Thon, my favorite league player, signing a baseball for my ten-year-old cousin Bryan, after a 1981-82 Bayamón-Santurce game? That's when I first thought of writing this book.

Appendices: Puerto Rico Winter League Statistics

1. TEAM STANDINGS: WINS-LOSSES, 1939–1995

1938-39
Guayama*	27-12
Humacao	23-19
San Juan	22-19
Ponce	20-20
Caguas	16-24
Mayagüez	12-26

1939-40
Guayama*	39-17
San Juan	38-18
Ponce	33-23
Santurce	26-29
Caguas	23-33
Humacao	22-33
Aguadilla	21-34
Mayagüez	20-35

1940-41
Caguas*	27-15
Guayama	24-18
San Juan	22-20
Santurce	21-21
Aguadilla	19-22
Humacao	19-22
Ponce	19-23
Mayagüez	16-26

1941-42
Ponce†	30-13
Guayama	29-15
San Juan	24-20
Aguadilla	21-22
Caguas	21-23
Santurce	21-23
Mayagüez	19-25
Humacao/Arecibo	10-34

1942-43
Ponce*	19-16
Santurce	18-17
San Juan	17-19
Mayagüez	17-19

1943-44
Ponce†	37-7
Santurce	22-22
Mayagüez	18-26
San Juan	11-33

1944-45
Ponce†	28-11
San Juan	22-20
Santurce	19-22
Mayagüez	11-27

1945-46
Mayagüez	24-16
San Juan*	23-18
Ponce	21-20
Santurce	13-27

1946-47
Ponce*	38-22
Caguas	35-25
San Juan	31-25
Santurce	25-30
Aguadilla	24-36
Mayagüez	22-37

1947-48
Mayagüez	39-21
Caguas*	33-26
Santurce	33-27
San Juan	26-34
Aguadilla	24-35
Ponce	24-36

1948-49
Mayagüez*	51-29
Ponce	47-33
Santurce	47-33
Caguas	41-39

*League playoff champion.   †Declared winners by winning both halves.

Aguadilla	32-48	**1955-56**		**1962-63**	
San Juan	22-58	Santurce	43-29	Mayagüez*	42-28
		Caguas*	38-34	Caguas	41-29
1949-50		San Juan	36-36	Santurce	36-34
Caguas*	47-31	Mayagüez	35-37	Arecibo	35-35
Ponce	45-35	Ponce	28-44	San Juan	30-40
Santurce	45-35			Ponce	26-44
Mayagüez	38-39	**1956-57**			
San Juan	35-44	Santurce	43-29	**1963-64**	
Aguadilla	26-52	Mayagüez*	41-31	Caguas	41-29
		San Juan	40-33	Ponce	36-34
1950-51		Caguas	39-34	San Juan*	35-35
Caguas	57-20	Ponce	18-54	Mayagüez	34-36
Santurce*	48-30			Santurce	33-37
Ponce	43-35	**1957-58**		Arecibo	31-39
San Juan	34-44	Santurce	36-28		
Aguadilla	25-51	Caguas*	33-31	**1964-65**	
Mayagüez	24-51	San Juan	33-31	Santurce*	41-28
		Ponce	30-34	Arecibo	38-32
1951-52		Mayagüez	28-36	Mayagüez	36-34
San Juan*	43-29			San Juan	34-36
Caguas	42-30	**1958-59**		Caguas	32-37
Santurce	41-31	San Juan	38-24	Ponce	28-42
Ponce	34-36	Santurce*	36-27		
Mayagüez	18-52	Caguas	30-33	**1965-66**	
		Mayagüez	28-36	Mayagüez*	42-28
1952-53		Ponce	26-38	Ponce	38-33
San Juan	45-27			Caguas	37-34
Santurce*	42-30	**1959-60**		Arecibo	34-36
Ponce	36-36	San Juan	41-23	San Juan	31-39
Mayagüez	31-41	Caguas*	39-24	Santurce	29-41
Caguas	26-46	Mayagüez	35-28		
		Santurce	25-37	**1966-67**	
1953-54		Ponce	17-45	Ponce	46-25
Caguas*	46-34	**1960-61**		Santurce*	45-26
San Juan	42-38	San Juan*	39-25	Arecibo	34-36
Mayagüez	41-39	Mayagüez	33-31	Caguas	33-37
Ponce	39-41	Caguas	30-34	San Juan	29-40
Santurce	32-48	Ponce	29-35	Mayagüez	23-46
		Santurce	29-35		
1954-55				**1967-68**	
		1961-62		Santurce	47-22
Santurce*	47-25	Mayagüez	45-35	Caguas*	43-27
Caguas	42-30	Caguas	43-37	San Juan	36-34
San Juan	38-34	Santurce*	42-38	Ponce	34-36
Mayagüez	27-45	Arecibo	42-39	Arecibo	28-41
Ponce	26-46	San Juan	41-40	Mayagüez	21-49
		Ponce	28-52		

APPENDIX 1

1968-69
Santurce	49-20
Ponce*	43-25
Caguas	37-33
San Juan	36-34
Mayagüez	23-45
Arecibo	19-50

1969-70
Ponce*	44-25
Mayagüez	42-28
Santurce	35-33
Caguas	34-35
San Juan	33-36
Arecibo	19-50

1970-71
Caguas	41-29
San Juan	37-30
Santurce*	37-32
Ponce	34-33
Arecibo	32-37
Mayagüez	25-45

1971-72
San Juan	39-30
Ponce*	37-32
Santurce	34-33
Caguas	34-35
Mayagüez	32-37
Arecibo	28-37

1972-73
Santurce*	45-25
Caguas	38-32
Ponce	38-33
Arecibo	37-34
San Juan	33-37
Mayagüez	20-50

1973-74
Ponce	42-28
Caguas*	39-31
San Juan	36-34
Arecibo	35-36
Santurce	34-37
Mayagüez	25-45

1974-75
Caguas	43-27
Ponce	40-30
Bayamón*	37-33
Arecibo	33-37
Santurce	30-40
Mayagüez	27-43

1975-76
Caguas	35-25
Bayamón*	34-26
Mayagüez	33-27
Santurce	28-32
Ponce	26-34
Arecibo	24-36

1976-77
Caguas*	40-20
Ponce	38-22
Bayamón	34-26
Santurce	32-27
Mayagüez	19-41
Arecibo	16-43

1977-78
Caguas	37-23
Arecibo	36-24
Bayamón	31-29
Mayagüez*	29-31
Santurce	27-33
Ponce	20-40

1978-79
Ponce	33-27
Mayagüez	32-28
Santurce	31-29
Caguas*	29-31
Bayamón	28-32
Arecibo	27-33

1979-80
Santurce	36-24
Bayamón*	33-26
Mayagüez	29-31
Arecibo	28-32
Ponce	27-33
Caguas	26-33

1980-81
Bayamón	39-21
Mayagüez	31-30
Arecibo	30-31
Caguas*	29-31
Santurce	28-32
Ponce	24-36

1981-82
Caguas	37-23
Santurce	33-27
Ponce*	28-32
Bayamón	27-34
Mayagüez	26-35

1982-83
Santurce	35-26
Ponce	34-27
Bayamón	32-28
Arecibo*	28-32
Caguas	26-34
Mayagüez	26-34

1983-84
Mayagüez*	38-22
Ponce	32-29
Santurce	31-30
Arecibo	30-30
San Juan	26-34
Caguas	24-36

1984-85
Mayagüez	38-22
Caguas	33-27
Santurce	32-28
San Juan*	30-29
Ponce	25-35
Arecibo	21-38

1985-86
Caguas	33-21
Mayagüez*	31-22
Santurce	31-23
San Juan	26-28
Ponce	24-29
Arecibo	16-38

1986-87
Ponce	34-19
Caguas*	31-23

Mayagüez	26-26
San Juan	25-28
Santurce	23-30
Arecibo	20-33

1987-88

Santurce	31-21
Mayagüez*	29-25
Ponce	27-27
San Juan	25-26
Caguas	24-30
Arecibo	23-30

1988-89

San Juan	35-25
Mayagüez*	33-26
Arecibo	31-27
Caguas	29-29
Ponce	25-34
Santurce	24-36

1989-90

Ponce	31-19
Caguas	28-22
San Juan*	27-23
Mayagüez	23-27
Santurce	22-28
Arecibo	19-31

1990-91

San Juan	33-25
Caguas	31-28
Santurce*	30-28
Mayagüez	31-29
Arecibo	29-30
Ponce	23-37

1991-92

San Juan	29-21
Mayagüez*	28-22
Ponce	27-23
Santurce	24-26
Arecibo	23-27
Bayamón	19-31

1992-93

Santurce*	29-18
Mayagüez	26-20
San Juan	20-22
Ponce	22-26
Arecibo	14-25

1993-94

San Juan*	35-13
Arecibo	25-23
Mayagüez	25-23
Santurce	21-27
Ponce	14-34

1994-95

Mayagüez	33-21
San Juan*	32-22
Arecibo	28-26
Ponce	26-28
Santurce	22-32
Caguas	21-33

2. ALL-STAR TEAMS, SELECTED SEASONS, 1939–1994

A=Arecibo **B**=Bayamón
C=Caguas **G**=Guayama
M=Mayagüez **P**=Ponce
S=Santurce **SJ**=San Juan

1939-40 to 1948-49*

C	Josh Gibson-S
1B	Luke Easter-M
2B	Fernando Díaz Pedroso-P
3B	Canena Márquez-M
SS	Perucho Cepeda-G
OF	Willard Brown-S
OF	Tetelo Vargas-G
OF	Pancho Coímbre-P
P	Roy Partlow-SJ

1949-50 to 1958-59*

C	Dixie Howell-M
1B	George Crowe-C
2B	Jack Dittmer-SJ
3B	Rance Pless-C
SS	Bill Harrell-S
OF	George Lerchen-M
OF	Willie Mays-S
OF	Roberto Clemente-S & C
P	Bob Thurman-S

*The All-Star selections for these decades are based on single-season batting averages compiled by Héctor Barea in 1981.

APPENDIX 2

1965-66

C	Héctor Valle-M
1B	Tany Pérez-S
2B	Horace Clarke-P
3B	Joe Foy-C
SS	José Pagán-C
LF	Dick Simpson-P
CF	Mickey Stanley-M
RF	Jim Northrup-M
RHP	John Boozer-P
LHP	Grant Jackson-C

1966-67

C	Larry Haney-S
1B	Deacon Jones-P
2B	Julio Gotay-M
3B	Tany Pérez-S
SS	Horace Clarke-P
LF	Walter Williams-A
CF	Roger Repoz-P
RF	Tony González-SJ
RHP	Nelson Briles-P
LHP	Terín Pizarro-S

1967-68

C	Johnny Bench-SJ
1B	Orlando Cepeda-S
2B	Tony Taylor-SJ
3B	José Pagán-C
SS	Sandy Alomar, Sr.-P
LF	Lee May-SJ
CF	Tony González-SJ
RF	Roberto Clemente-SJ
RHP	Darrell Osteen-S
LHP	Terín Pizarro-S

1968-69

C	Elrod Hendricks-S
1B	George Scott-S
2B	Félix Millán-C
3B	Quique Rivera-P
SS	Leo Cardenas-S
LF	Hank Allen-C
CF	Paul Blair-S
RF	Dave May-S
RHP	Rubén Gómez-S
LHP	Terín Pizarro-S

1970-71

C	Héctor Valle-M
1B	Mike Jorgensen-SJ
2B	Félix Millán-C
3B	Quique Rivera-P
SS	Milton Ramírez-S
LF	Bob Oliver-C
CF	Angel Mangual-A
RF	José Cruz-P
RHP	Mike Wegener-C
LHP	Ken Brett-SJ

1972-73

C	Elrod Hendricks-S
1B	Frank Ortenzio-A
2B	Sandy Alomar, Sr.-P
3B	Ron Cey-S
SS	Juan Beníquez-S
LF	Richard Zisk-SJ
CF	Rich Coggins-A
RF	José Cruz-P
RHP	Lynn McGlothen-A
LHP	Terín Pizarro-S

1977-78

C	Rick Sweet-A
1B	Otto Vélez-P
2B	Ramón Avilés-M
3B	Kurt Bevaqua-M
SS	Iván de Jesús-A
LF	Sixto Lezcano-C
CF	Ron LeFlore-M
RF	José Cruz-C
DH	José Morales-M
RHP	Dennis Lamp-A
LHP	Scott McGregor-C

1980-81

C	Junior Ortíz-C
1B	Willie Aikens-S
2B	Luis Aguayo-B
3B	Cal Ripken-C
SS	Dickie Thon-B
LF	Rickey Henderson-P
CF	Candy Maldonado-A
RF	Rusty Torres-M
DH	José Morales-M
P	Dave Smith-B

1984-85

C   Papo Rosado-SJ
1B   Sid Bream-M
2B   Mario Ramírez-C
3B   Skeeter Barnes-SJ
SS   Willie Lozado-M
LF   Vince Coleman-M
CF   Henry Cotto-C
RF   José Cruz-P
DH   Orlando Sánchez-S
RHP Javier Oliveras-C
LHP Zane Smith-S
Reliever-Juan Agosto-M

1985-86

C   Junior Ortíz-C
1B   Wally Joyner-M
2B   Juan Bonilla-SJ
3B   Germán Rivera-C
SS   Iván de Jesús-S
LF   Steve Hammond-C
CF   Henry Cotto-C
RF   Rubén Sierra-S
DH   Juan Beníquez-S
RHP José Guzmán-M
LHP Juan Agosto-M
Reliever-Brad Havens-M

1987-88

C   Orlando Mercado-C
1B   Randy Milligan-P
2B   Roberto Alomar-C
3B   Edwin Rodríguez-A
SS   Jay Bell-S
LF   Shawn Abner-P
LF   Tom Howard-M
CF   John Cangelosi-M
RF   Iván Calderón-P
DH   Bobby Bonilla-M
RHP Mike Pérez-S
LHP Tim Birtsas-P
Reliever-Bryan Harvey-SJ

1989-90

C   Sandy Alomar, Jr.-P
1B   Terry Francona-P
2B   Carlos Baerga-SJ
3B   Edgar Martínez-SJ
SS   Joey Cora-P
OF   Juan González-C
OF   Henry Cotto-C
OF   Greg Vaughn-P
DH   Roy Silver-M
RHP Ricky Bones-P
LHP David Rosario-SJ
Reliever-Dan Murphy-P

1992-93

C   Javier López-SJ
1B   Héctor Villanueva-S
2B   José Olmeda-M
3B   Germán Rivera-S
SS   Wil Cordero-M
OF   Alex Díaz-M
OF   Darrell Sherman-S
OF   Gerald Williams-S
DH   Juan González-S
Starter-José Lebrón-S
Reliever-Roberto Hernández-M

1993-94

C   Jorge Posada-P
1B   Carmelo Martínez-SJ
2B   José Muñoz-A
3B   Phil Hiatt-A
SS   Kevin Baez-A
LF   Ozzie Timmons-M
CF   Ryan Thompson-SJ
RF   Rubén Sierra-S
DH   Iván Calderón-S
RHP Rafael Montalvo-SJ
LHP Bob Gaddy-SJ
Reliever-Shawn Holman-SJ

3. SINGLE SEASON RECORDS: HITTING AND PITCHING

Category	Player	Team	Season	Record
Batting Average	Josh Gibson	Santurce	1941-42	.480
Slugging Percentage	Josh Gibson	Santurce	1941-42	.959
Home Runs	Willard Brown	Santurce	1947-48	27
RBI	Willard Brown	Santurce	1949-50	97
Runs	Luke Easter	Mayagüez	1948-49	81
Hits	Artie Wilson	Mayagüez	1948-49	126
Doubles	Luke Easter	Mayagüez	1948-49	27
	Canena Márquez	Aguadilla	1946-47	27
Triples	Luis Olmo	Caguas	1940-41	10
	Quincy Trouppe	Guayama	1941-42	10
	Canena Márquez	Mayagüez	1945-46	10
	Canena Márquez	Aguadilla	1949-50	10
	Nino Escalera	San Juan	1950-51	10
Stolen Bases	Rickey Henderson	Ponce	1980-81	44
Games	Bob Dustal	Mayagüez	1962-63	40
Games Started	Henry McHenry	Humacao	1939-40	28
Complete Games	Henry McHenry	Humacao	1939-40	28
Innings Pitched	Henry McHenry	Humacao	1939-40	248
Wins	Satchel Paige	Guayama	1939-40	19
Strikeouts	Satchel Paige	Guayama	1939-40	208
Earned Run Average	Fernando Figueroa	Mayagüez	1992-93	0.63
Shutouts	Terín Pizarro	Caguas	1957-58	9
Saves	Joe Boever	San Juan	1988-89	20

4. REGULAR SEASON .400+ HITTERS (100 OR MORE AT BATS)

Players	Team	Season	At-Bats	Hits	Average
Willard Brown	Humacao	1941-42	122	50	.410
Willard Brown	Santurce	1947-48	234	101	.432
Orlando Cepeda†	Santurce	1960-61	106	44	.415
Perucho Cepeda	Guayama	1938-39	170	79	.465
Perucho Cepeda	Guayama	1940-41	178	75	.421
Pancho Coímbre	Ponce	1940-41	167	67	.401
Pancho Coímbre	Ponce	1944-45	106	45	.425
Luke Easter	Mayagüez	1948-49	249	100	.402
Josh Gibson	Santurce	1941-42	123	59	.480*
Edgar Martínez	San Juan	1989-90	132	56	.424

*All-time record. †Orlando Cepeda and José M. Morales did not qualify for the batting title.

Players	Team	Season	At-Bats	Hits	Average
José M. Morales†	San Juan	1968-69	112	45	.402
Clarence Palm	Santurce	1940-41	159	65	.409
Roy Partlow	San Juan	1940-41	122	54	.443
Bob Thurman	Santurce	1947-48	248	102	.411
Tetelo Vargas	Guayama	1938-39	164	68	.415
Tetelo Vargas	Santurce	1943-44	134	55	.410
Artie Wilson	Mayagüez	1947-48	252	102	.405
Ted Young	Guayama	1940-41	148	63	.426

5. SELECTED PUERTO RICO CAREER RECORDS, 1939–1995

The numbers in parentheses after players' names indicate the number of regular league seasons played.

Batters

Hank Aaron (1)
BA .322
HR 9
RBI 42
SB 7

Roberto Alomar (8)
BA .287
HR 10
RBI 71

Carlos Baerga (9)
BA .294
HR 26
RBI 142

Ray Barker (4)
BA .258
HR 14
RBI 93

Skeeter Barnes (3)
BA .304
HR 15
RBI 88

Don Baylor (3)
BA .297
HR 22
RBI 84

Johnny Bench (1)
BA .323
HR 5
RBI 27

Juan Beníquez (22)
BA .274
HR 73
RBI 456

Dave Bergman (3)
BA .293
HR 17
RBI 80

Carlos Bernier (19)
BA .268
HR 48
RBI 416
SB 285*

Kurt Bevaqua (4)
BA .285
HR 25
RBI 161

Steve Bilko (2)
BA .269
HR 13
RBI 43

Paul Blair (3)
BA .303
HR 7
RBI 75

Wade Boggs (1)
BA .354
HR 3
RBI 22

Bobby Bonilla (5)
BA .297
HR 14
RBI 76

Bob Boone (1)
BA .272
HR 4
RBI 25

Bob Boyd (2)
BA .328
HR 8
RBI 87

Jackie Brandt (1)
BA .349
HR 3
RBI 30

*All-time record.

APPENDIX 5

Sid Bream (2)
BA .289
HR 9
RBI 70

Willard Brown (10)
BA .350*
HR 101
RBI 473

Don Buford (2)
BA .299
HR 2
RBI 31

Ellis Burks (1)
BA .291
HR 7
RBI 30

Brett Butler (1)
BA .327
HR 2
RBI 13
SB 14

Roy Campanella (4)
BA .276
HR 11
RBI 70

Dave Campbell (1)
BA .290
HR 9
RBI 46

Gary Carter (2)
BA .256
HR 6
RBI 35

Joe Carter (1)
BA .244
HR 10
RBI 35
SB 15

Orlando Cepeda (13)
BA .323
HR 89
RBI 340

Perucho Cepeda (11)
BA .325
HR 14
RBI 297

Ron Cey (1)
BA .298
HR 7
RBI 43

Chris Chambliss (1)
BA .362
HR 4
RBI 30

Horace Clarke (9)
BA .271
HR 12
RBI 140

Buster Clarkson (11)
BA .301
HR 98
RBI 460

Roberto Clemente (15)
BA .323
HR 35
RBI 269
SB 32

Pancho Coímbre (13)
BA .337
HR 24
RBI 322

Wil Cordero (6)
BA .266
HR 18
RBI 114

Henry Cotto (12)
BA .289
HR 32
RBI 184
SB 154

George Crowe (3)
BA .337
HR 32
RBI 179

José Cruz (21)
BA .296
HR 119
RBI 405
SB 152

Ray Dandridge (2)
BA .256
HR 2
RBI 32

Chili Davis (2)
BA .258
HR 10
RBI 42

Cot Deal (5)
BA .293
HR 25
RBI 140

Mike de la Hoz (3)
BA .318
HR 16
RBI 112

Dan Driessen (3)
BA .315
HR 22
RBI 99

Jim Dwyer (4)
BA .295
HR 34
RBI 140

Luke Easter (3)
BA .330
HR 38
RBI 145

Nino Escalera (17)
BA .275
HR 17
RBI 304

Wilmer Fields (4)
BA .325
HR 22
RBI 173

Gil Flores (13)
BA .278
HR 14
RBI 212

Eric Fox (1)
BA .291
HR 2
RBI 25

Roger Freed (5)
BA .277
HR 64
RBI 196

Josh Gibson (3)
BA .355

Gibson (cont.)
HR 19
RBI 85

Jim Gilliam (4)
BA .278
HR 3
RBI 110

Dan Gladden (1)
BA .321
HR 5
RBI 25

Juan González (7)
BA .267
HR 34
RBI 104

Ken Griffey, Sr. (3)
BA .342
HR 9
RBI 41

Tony Gwynn (2)
BA .346
HR 8
RBI 60

Brian Harper (2)
BA .336
HR 18
RBI 92

Von Hayes (2)
BA .314
HR 9
RBI 44

Rickey Henderson (2)
BA .298
HR 2
RBI 24
SB 63

Elrod Hendricks (15)
BA .275
HR 105
RBI 349

Willie Horton (2)
BA .300
HR 18
RBI 64

Elston Howard (1)
BA .369

HR 7
RBI 24

Frank Howard (2)
BA .300
HR 28
RBI 84

Art Howe (4)
BA .297
HR 16
RBI 147

Monte Irvin (4)
BA .322
HR 20
RBI 112

Reggie Jackson (1)
BA .272
HR 20
RBI 47
SB 9

Jay Johnstone (3)
BA .305
HR 24
RBI 118

Ron LeFlore (3)
BA .339
HR 10
RBI 55

Mark Lemke (1)
BA .347
HR 1
RBI 15

Buck Leonard (1)
BA .390
HR 8
RBI 40

Javier López (7)
BA .259
HR 11
RBI 60

Jerry McNertney (2)
BA .303
HR 4
RBI 32

Candy Maldonado (13)
BA .272
HR 88

RBI 342

Frank Malzone (2)
BA .277
HR 11
RBI 78

Canena Márquez (20)
BA .300
HR 97
RBI 498
SB 225

Carmelo Martínez (13)
BA .269
HR 63
RBI 250

Edgar Martínez (9)
BA .286
HR 8
RBI 91

Don Mattingly (1)
BA .368
HR 4
RBI 32

Lee May (2)
BA .285
HR 15
RBI 80

Willie Mays (1)
BA .395
HR 12
RBI 33
SB 10

Willie Montañez (18)
BA .266
HR 86
RBI 396

Jerry Morales (18)
BA .267
HR 63
RBI 318

José Morales (19)
BA .302
HR 84
RBI 467

Thurman Munson (1)
BA .333

APPENDIX 5

Munson (cont.)
HR 3
RBI 34

Eddie Murray (3)
BA .315
HR 18
RBI 76

Jim Northrup (2)
BA .341
HR 13
RBI 74

Tony Oliva (1)
BA .365
HR 6
RBI 25

Luis Olmo (16)
BA .290
HR 40
RBI 363

Lance Parrish (1)
BA .245
HR 10
RBI 35

Fernando D. Pedroso (5)
BA .323
HR 39
RBI 175

Tany Pérez (10)
BA .308
HR 59
RBI 292

Rance Pless (3)
BA .293
HR 9
RBI 82

Herb Plews (1)
BA .305
HR 2
RBI 18

Boog Powell (2)
BA .294
HR 15
RBI 66

Vic Power (16)
BA .296
HR 55
RBI 487
SB 80

Randy Ready (2)
BA .283
HR 9
RBI 49

Cal Ripken (2)
BA .299
HR 16
RBI 88

Jim Rivera (7)
BA .279
HR 43
RBI 179

Cookie Rojas (5)
BA .272
HR 7
RBI 94

Mike Schmidt (2)
BA .253
HR 21
RBI 52

George Scott (1)
BA .295
HR 13
RBI 46

Rubén Sierra (7)
BA .268
HR 27
RBI 146

Ken Singleton (1)
BA .300
HR 6
RBI 38

Bill Skowron (1)
BA .302
HR 3
RBI 29

Lonnie Smith (1)
BA .366

HR 7
RBI 42
SB 28

Marv Staehle (2)
BA .306
HR 1
RBI 25

Dickie Thon (13)
BA .292
HR 21
RBI 146
SB 97

Bob Thurman (12)
BA .313
HR 120*
RBI 565*

Tetelo Vargas (16)
BA .320
HR 20
RBI 247

Otto Vélez (14)
BA .258
HR 61
RBI 237

Denny Walling (2)
BA .335
HR 10
RBI 43

Jerry Willard (3)
BA .275
HR 28
RBI 90

Artie Wilson (5)
BA .345
HR 6
RBI 97

Robin Yount (1)
BA .306
HR 0
RBI 10

Richard Zisk (2)
BA .316
HR 24
RBI 85

Pitchers

Juan Agosto (16)
W-L	48-31
ERA	3.73
IP	606
K's	315

Tite Arroyo (19)
W-L	111-93
ERA	3.03
IP	1,720
K's	940

Fred Beene (5)
W-L	22-13
ERA	2.51
IP	294
K's	179

Vida Blue (1)
W-L	2-5
ERA	4.03
IP	58
K's	38

John Boozer (5)
W-L	51-34
ERA	2.36
IP	696
K's	516

"Oil Can" Boyd (1)
W-L	2-3
ERA	2.40
IP	56
K's	35

Jeff Brantley (2)
W-L	6-1
ERA	2.15
IP	50
K's	40

Ken Brett (2)
W-L	8-3
ERA	3.00
IP	90
K's	82

Nelson Briles (1)
W-L	12-3
ERA	2.00
IP	144
K's	88

Barney Brown (3)
W-L	34-15
ERA	2.23
IP	408

Raymond Brown (6)
W-L	40-20
ERA	2.16
IP	496

Bob Bruce (3)
W-L	26-25
ERA	2.59
IP	376
K's	252

Tom Bruno (4)
W-L	17-19
ERA	3.17
IP	258
K's	159

Tom Burgmeier (1)
W-L	9-3
ERA	2.96
IP	125
K's	53

Pete Burnside (2)
W-L	11-6
IP	195
K's	146

Billy Byrd (3)
W-L	40-24
ERA	2.17
IP	593
K's	377

Luis Cabrera (18)
W-L	105-99
ERA	3.37
IP	1,677
K's	863

Mike Caldwell (1)
W-L	4-3
ERA	3.24
IP	78
K's	56

Tom Candiotti (2)
W-L	9-5
ERA	2.70
IP	133
K's	93

Steve Carlton (2)
W-L	11-9
ERA	2.67
IP	165
K's	121

David Cone (2)
W-L	7-7
ERA	2.40
IP	127
K's	91

Danny Darwin (2)
W-L	8-3
ERA	4.03
IP	114
K's	83

Leon Day (4)
W-L	35-28
ERA	2.63
IP	571
K's	518

Ken Dayley (1)
W-L	9-1
ERA	4.05
IP	73
K's	67

Mambo de León (17)
W-L	41-36
ERA	3.19
IP	666
K's	427

Rob Dibble (3)
W-L	1-3
ERA	2.94
IP	49
K's	24

Moe Drabowsky (1)
W-L	7-6

Drabowsky (cont.)
ERA 3.70
IP 105
K's 63

Ed Figueroa (15)
W-L 46-40
ERA 3.61
IP 791
K's 447

Todd Frohwirth (1)
W-L 6-2
ERA 1.30
IP 55
K's 31

Bob Gibson (1)
W-L 6-8
ERA 2.12
IP 136
K's 142

Rubén Gómez (29)*
W-L 174-119*
ERA 2.96
IP 2,488*
K's 1,389

Rich Gossage (2)
W-L 8-7
ERA 3.34
IP 151
K's 85

Bill Greason (7)
W-L 46-31
ERA 2.99
IP 701
K's 372

José Guzmán (7)
W-L 20-12
ERA 2.80
IP 292
K's 139

Harvey Haddix (1)
W-L 6-2
ERA 1.09

IP 74
K's 62

Kevin Hagen (3)
W-L 12-10
ERA 3.06
IP 220
K's 87

Jack Harshman (2)
W-L 20-13
ERA 3.15
IP 291
K's 122

Bryan Harvey (1)
W-L 2-1
ERA 2.01
IP 31
K's 39

Roberto Hernández (7)
W-L 15-17
ERA 3.05
IP 289
K's 188

Tom Hilgendorf (2)
W-L 15-10
ERA 2.73
IP 208
K's 103

Joe Hoerner (3)
W-L 11-14
ERA 1.81
IP 184
K's 127

Joel Horlen (2)
W-L 20-10
ERA 2.82
IP 262
K's 196

Dick Hughes (1)
W-L 11-2
ERA 1.79
IP 126
K's 79

Grant Jackson (6)
W-L 39-31
ERA 3.06
IP 597
K's 455

Ferguson Jenkins (2)
W-L 18-12
ERA 1.70
IP 206
K's 156

Doug Jones (2)
W-L 5-4
ERA 1.48
IP 67
K's 57

Sam Jones (2)
W-L 27-9
ERA 2.22
IP 325
K's 311

Dennis Kinney (4)
W-L 21-16
ERA 3.10
IP 322
K's 158

Bruce Kison (1)
W-L 9-4
ERA 2.33
IP 93
K's 69

Sandy Koufax (1)
W-L 3-6
ERA 4.74
IP 65
K's 74

Dave Leonhard (6)
W-L 26-21
ERA 3.44
IP 406
K's 229

Paul Lindblad (2)
W-L 14-13
ERA 2.83

*All-time record.

Lindblad (cont.)
IP 248
K's 142

Ernie McAnally (2)
W-L 14-5
ERA 1.99
IP 149
K's 112

Denny McLain (1)
W-L 12-4
ERA 2.00
IP 134
K's 126

Greg McMichael (1)
W-L 4-2
ERA 1.35
IP 60
K's 40

Rick Mahler (1)
W-L 10-2
ERA 3.50
IP 113
K's 55

Dennis Martínez (5)
W-L 22-16
ERA 3.13
IP 328
K's 177

Jon Matlack (1)
W-L 7-2
ERA 3.12
IP 87
K's 46

Balor Moore (2)
W-L 10-12
ERA 2.81
IP 157
K's 114

Jack Morris (1)
W-L 7-3
ERA 4.84
IP 102
K's 58

Julio Navarro (22)
W-L 98-84

ERA 2.96
IP 1,623
K's 989

Denny Neagle (1)
W-L 4-3
ERA 2.96
IP 67
K's 64

David Nied (1)
W-L 4-2
ERA 1.46
IP 49
K's 36

Phil Niekro (2)
W-L 7-11
ERA 3.72
IP 156
K's 81

Juan Nieves (2)
W-L 6-5
ERA 2.42
IP 78
K's 60

Javier Oliveras (15)
W-L 58-47
ERA 3.53
IP 921
K's 462

Satchel Paige (3)
W-L 23-11
K's 304

Jim Palmer (1)
W-L 5-0
ERA 2.79
IP 29
K's 33

Roy Partlow (5)
W-L 34-22
ERA 2.86
IP 553
K's 450

Daryl Patterson (2)
W-L 9-9
ERA 2.65
IP 119
K's 69

Terín Pizarro (22)
W-L 157-110
ERA 2.48
IP 2,400
K's 1,798*

Tomás Quiñónes (13)
W-L 82-38
ERA 3.34
IP 1,028

Claude Raymond (2)
W-L 10-9
ERA 3.27
IP 107
K's 79

Jeff Reardon (2)
W-L 4-6
ERA 2.93
IP 77
K's 64

Carlos Reyes (2)
W-L 11-3
ERA 2.33
IP 120
K's 68

Pete Richert (1)
W-L 7-6
ERA 3.02
IP 110
K's 102

Steve Ridzik (4)
W-L 26-17
ERA 2.69
IP 308

Ray Rippelmeyer (3)
W-L 22-10
ERA 2.47
IP 302
K's 125

Ed Roebuck (1)
W-L 10-13
ERA 3.47
IP 132
K's 71

Joe Sambito (1)
W-L 4-1
ERA 2.27
IP 44
K's 22

José G. Santiago (16)		IP	41	**Tommy Toms** (2)	
W-L	107-96	K's	44	W-L	6-3
ERA	3.13			ERA	3.17
IP	1,682	**Robert G. Smith** (2)		IP	85
K's	975	W-L	15-5	K's	45
		ERA	2.25		
José R. Santiago (16)		IP	167	**Bob Turley** (2)	
W-L	60-52	K's	110	W-L	8-11
ERA	2.84			ERA	2.78
IP	1,070	**Zane Smith** (1)		IP	162
K's	612	W-L	6-2	K's	145
		ERA	2.01		
Gordon Seyfried (3)		IP	58	**Corky Valentine** (2)	
W-L	24-14	K's	28	W-L	14-8
ERA	2.81			ERA	2.10
IP	310	**John Strohmayer** (3)		IP	180
K's	145	W-L	13-10	K's	148
		ERA	3.02		
Sonny Siebert (2)		IP	250	**Turk Wendell** (1)	
W-L	12-8	K's	143	W-L	7-1
ERA	3.17			ERA	0.94
IP	176	**Fred Talbot** (2)		IP	67
K's	149	W-L	16-7	K's	45
		ERA	2.24		
Wayne Simpson (3)		IP	225	**Ken Wright** (4)	
W-L	20-10	K's	151	W-L	22-20
ERA	2.31			ERA	3.14
IP	297	**Luis Tiant** (3)		IP	287
K's	190	W-L	15-16	K's	310
		ERA	3.60		
Tommie Sisk (1)		IP	250	**Chris Zachary** (5)	
W-L	4-7	K's	191	W-L	27-14
ERA	3.09			ERA	2.63
IP	96	**Tom Timmerman** (3)		IP	418
K's	95	W-L	18-13	K's	287
		ERA	2.21		
Lee Smith (1)		IP	228	**Pat Zachry** (2)	
W-L	3-2	K's	179	W-L	9-5
ERA	2.85			ERA	3.33
				IP	100
				K's	52

6. MOST VALUABLE PLAYERS, 1939-1995

Season	Player	Team
1938-39	Perucho Cepeda	Guayama
1939-40	Satchel Paige	Guayama
1940-41	Luis Cabrera	Santurce
1941-42	Josh Gibson	Santurce
1942-43	Francisco Coímbre	Ponce
1943-44	Planchardón Quiñónes	Ponce

Season	Player	Team
1944-45	Planchardón Quiñónes	Ponce
1945-46	Monte Irvin	San Juan
1946-47	Barney Brown	San Juan
1947-48	Willard Brown	Santurce
1948-49	Luke Easter	Mayagüez
1949-50	Willard Brown	Santurce
1950-51	Bob Thurman	Santurce
1951-52	Rubén Gómez	Santurce
1952-53	Cot Deal	San Juan
1953-54	Canena Márquez	Mayagüez
1954-55	Willie Mays	Santurce
1955-56	Vic Power	Caguas
1956-57	Ronquito García	Mayagüez
1957-58	Terín Pizarro	Caguas
1958-59	Orlando Cepeda	Santurce
1959-60	Guito Conde	Mayagüez
1960-61	Tite Arroyo	San Juan
1961-62	Orlando Cepeda	Santurce
1962-63	Bob Dustal	Mayagüez
1963-64	Danny Cater	Ponce
1964-65	Mike Cuéllar	Arecibo
1965-66	John Boozer	Ponce
1966-67	Tany Pérez	Santurce
1967-68	José Pagán	Caguas
1968-69	Elrod Hendricks	Santurce
1969-70	Wayne Simpson	Ponce
1970-71	Sandy Alomar, Sr.	Ponce
1971-72	Rogelio Moret	Santurce
1972-73	Lynn McGlothen	Arecibo
1973-74	Benny Ayala	Arecibo
1974-75	Jay Johnstone	Caguas
1975-76	Héctor Cruz	Mayagüez
1976-77	José Cruz	Caguas
1977-78	Kurt Bevaqua	Mayagüez
1978-79	Jim Dwyer	Mayagüez
1979-80	Jesús Vega	Arecibo
1980-81	Rusty Torres	Mayagüez
1981-82	Edwin Nuñez	Ponce
1982-83	Carmelo Martínez	Bayamón
1983-84	Jerry Willard	Santurce
1984-85	Henry Cotto	Caguas
1985-86	Wally Joyner	Mayagüez
1986-87	Skeeter Barnes	Ponce
1987-88	Bryan Harvey	San Juan
1988-89	Lonnie Smith	San Juan
1989-90	Carlos Baerga, Edgar Martínez	San Juan
1990-91	Héctor Villanueva	San Juan
1991-92	Wil Cordero	Mayagüez

Season	Player	Team
1992-93	Juan González	Santurce
1993-94	Carmelo Martínez	San Juan
1994-95	Carlos Delgado	San Juan

7. MAJOR LEAGUE TITLES AND AWARDS, PUERTO RICO LEAGUE PLAYERS, 1950–1994

Batting Titles

American League
Wade Boggs (5)
Tony Oliva (3)
Alex Johnson
Edgar Martínez*
Don Mattingly
Paul O'Neill
Frank Robinson

National League
Tony Gwynn (5)
Roberto Clemente (4)
Hank Aaron (2)
Tommy Davis (2)
Keith Hernández
Willie Mays
Al Oliver
Terry Pendleton

Home Run Titles

American League
Reggie Jackson (4)
Larry Doby (2)
Juan González (2)*
Frank Howard (2)
Gorman Thomas (2)
Darrell Evans
Eddie Murray
Frank Robinson
George Scott

National League
Mike Schmidt (8)
Hank Aaron (4)
Willie Mays (4)
Johnny Bench (2)
Dave Kingman (2)
Orlando Cepeda

RBI Leaders

American League
Don Baylor
Albert Belle
Joe Carter
Larry Doby
Frank Howard
Reggie Jackson
Hal McCrae
Don Mattingly
Lee May
Eddie Murray
Frank Robinson
George Scott
Rubén Sierra*

National League
Hank Aaron (3)
Johnny Bench (3)
Orlando Cepeda (2)
Roy Campanella
Gary Carter
Tommy Davis
Monte Irvin
Deron Johnson
Al Oliver

Stolen Base Titles

American League
Rickey Henderson (10)
Bert Campaneris (6)
Ron LeFlore
Freddie Patek
Jim Rivera

National League
Vince Coleman (6)
Maury Wills (6)
Willie Mays (4)
Billy Bruton (3)
Sam Jethroe (2)
Ron LeFlore

MVP Awards

American League
Cal Ripken (2)
Robin Yount (2)
Don Baylor
Vida Blue
Rickey Henderson
Willie Hernández
Elston Howard
Reggie Jackson
Denny McLain
Don Mattingly
Thurman Munson
Boog Powell
Frank Robinson

National League
Roy Campanella (3)
Mike Schmidt (3)
Johnny Bench (2)
Willie Mays (2)
Hank Aaron
Orlando Cepeda

*Puerto Rico League players during the 1994-95 season.

Roberto Clemente
Bob Gibson
Keith Hernández
Sandy Koufax
Terry Pendleton
Frank Robinson
Maury Wills

Cy Young Winners

American League
Jim Palmer (3)
Denny McLain (2)
Vida Blue
David Cone
Mike Cuéllar
Willie Hernández
Lamar Hoyt
Jim Lonborg

Bob Turley†
Pete Vuckovich

National League
Steve Carlton (4)
Sandy Koufax (3)†
Bob Gibson (2)
Mark Davis
John Denny
Ferguson Jenkins
Mike Marshall

Rookies of the Year

American League
Tommie Agee
Sandy Alomar, Jr.*
Chris Chambliss
Joe Charboneau
Thurman Munson
Eddie Murray

Tony Oliva
Gary Peters
Cal Ripken

National League
Johnny Bench
Orlando Cepeda
Vince Coleman
Jim Gilliam
Frank Howard
Sam Jethroe
Jon Matlack
Willie Mays
Wally Moon
Frank Robinson
Jack Sanford
Benito Santiago
Earl Williams
Pat Zachry

8. PUERTO RICO PROFESSIONAL BASEBALL HALL OF FAME INDUCTEES

1991
Willard Brown
Orlando Cepeda
Perucho Cepeda
Roberto Clemente
Francisco Coímbre
Rubén Gómez
Canena Márquez
Terín Pizarro
Vic Power
Bob Thurman

1992
Tite Arroyo
Carlos Bernier
Pedro Caratini
Cefo Conde
Nino Escalera
José Figueroa
Juan Guilbe
Millito Navarro
Luis Olmo
Rafaelito Ortíz
Rafael Pont Flores
Griffin Tirado
Tetelo Vargas
Pedro Vázquez
Pedrín Zorrilla

1993
Pito Alvarez de la Vega
Leon Day
Manuel "Manolo" García
Menchín Pesante
Planchardón Quiñónes
Carlos Manuel Santiago
José "Pantalones" Santiago
Luis Villodas
Artie Wilson

*Puerto Rico League players during the 1994-95 season.   †Turley and Koufax won their awards when only one Cy Young award was given.

9. PUERTO RICO WINTER LEAGUE COOPERSTOWN INDUCTEES

Inductee	Team
Hank Aaron	Caguas
Johnny Bench	San Juan
Roy Campanella	Caguas, San Juan, Santurce
Buck Canel*	Caguas
Steve Carlton	Ponce
Roberto Clemente	Caguas, San Juan, Santurce
Ray Dandridge	Santurce
Leon Day	Aguadilla, Santurce
Bob Gibson	Santurce
Josh Gibson	Santurce
Rogers Hornsby†	Ponce
Monte Irvin	San Juan
Reggie Jackson	Santurce
Ferguson Jenkins	Caguas
Sandy Koufax	Caguas
Buck Leonard	Mayagüez
Willie Mays	Santurce
Satchel Paige	Guayama, Santurce
Jim Palmer	Santurce
Phil Rizzuto*	San Juan
Frank Robinson§	Ponce, Santurce
Mike Schmidt	Caguas

10. PUERTO RICO WINTER LEAGUE TEAMS AND STADIUMS

Teams	Stadiums
Aguadilla Tiburones (Sharks)	Parque Colón
Arecibo Lobos (Wolves)	Luis Rodríguez Olmo
Bayamón Vaqueros (Cowboys)	Juan Ramón Loubriel
Caguas Criollos	Ydelfonso Solá Morales, José Gautier Benítez, Hiram Bithorn
Guayama Brujos (Witches)	Parque Ina Calimano
Humacao Grises Orientales (Oriental Grays)	Jáyase Hernández
Mayagüez Indios (Indians)	Liga París, Isidoro García
Ponce Leones/Piratas Kofresí (Lions/Pirates)	Paquito Montaner, Parque Charles H. Terry (Liga del Castillo)
San Juan Senadores/Metros (Senators/Metros)	Sixto Escobar, Hiram Bithorn
Santurce Cangrejeros (Crabbers)	Sixto Escobar, Hiram Bithorn, Juan Ramón Loubriel

*Team broadcasters. †Rogers Hornsby managed Ponce in 1950-51. §Frank Robinson played for Ponce in 1954-55 and managed Santurce from 1968-69 to 1970-71, 1972-73 to 1974-75 and 1979-80.

Notes

1. The Launching Pad

1. Eduardo Valero, "Guayama ganó primera serie mundial semi-pro," *El Deportista*, June, 1989, p. 12.
2. Rafael Costas, *Enciclopedia béisbol Ponce Leones* (Santo Domingo, Dominican Republic: Editora Corripio, 1989), p. 57.
3. Ismael Trabal, "Adiós al padre del béisbol organizado de Puerto Rico," *El Vocero*, Sabado Deportivo, November 24, 1984, pp. 8–9.
4. *El Mundo*, April 4, 1940.
5. Costas, pp. 212, 215.
6. *El Mundo*, February 8, 1940.
7. Costas, pp. 204–250.
8. *Compilaciones oficiales, de la Liga de Béisbol Profesional de Puerto Rico*, with Howe Sportsdata International, Inc. (San Juan, Puerto Rico, and Boston: 1985-86 to 1993-94).
9. José Seda, and Jorge Fernández, *Béisbol semiprofesional* (Caguas, Puerto Rico: Imprenta Aguayo, 1941), pp. 42–43.
10. *The Sporting News* 1949-1973; and, *Compilaciones oficiales*, 1968-69 to 1993-94.
11. Héctor Barea, *Libro Oficial Béisbol Profesional de Puerto Rico* (Guaynabo, Puerto Rico: Art Printing, 1981), p. 54.
12. *Don Q Baseball Cues* (Ponce, Puerto Rico: Destilería Serrallés, Inc., 1951), no. 10, p. 101.
13. *The Sporting News*, December 28, 1949.
14. *Don Q Baseball Cues*, no. 10, p. 101.
15. *Don Q Baseball Cues*, no. 25, 1968-69, p. 116.
16. *Don Q Baseball Cues*, no. 10, p. 101.
17. *The Sporting News*, February 17, 1954.
18. Henry Aaron, with Lonnie Wheeler, *I Had a Hammer* (New York: HarperCollins, 1991), p. 79.
19. *USA Today*, December 22, 1988.
20. *The Sporting News*, January 13, 1954.
21. *The Sporting News*, December 26, 1956.
22. Costas working papers.
23. *The Sporting News*, February 15, 1961.
24. Barea, p. 62.
25. *Official Baseball Guide and Record Book* (St. Louis: Spink, 1965), p. 466.
26. Frank Otto interview with Luis Arroyo, January 29, 1993.
27. Ibid.
28. Costas, p. 323.
29. *The Sporting News*, January 2, 1971.
30. Costas, pp. 328–329.
31. *The Sporting News*, January 2, 1971.
32. *The San Juan Star*, October 25, 1988.
33. Ibid., January 24, 1971.
34. Víctor Navarro, *The Book of the 14 and Other 33 Ways to Enter It* (Aguadilla, Puerto Rico: Navarro's Publishing Services, 1993), p. 34.

35. Costas, pp. 334–335.
36. *Compilación oficial*, 1981-82.
37. Ibid.
38. Ibid.
39. *Compilación oficial*, 1982-83.
40. *Compilación oficial*, 1987-88.
41. Ibid.
42. *Compilación oficial*, 1988-89.

2. A Working Vacation

1. José A. Toro Sugrañes, *Almanaque Puertorriqueño* (Rio Piedras, Puerto Rico: Editorial Edil, 1990), p. 47.
2. *Qué Pasa*, (San Juan, Puerto Rico: Puerto Rico Tourism Company, January-March 1993), p. 56.
3. Toro Sugrañes, p. 130.
4. William H. Stead, *FOMENTO—The Economic Development of Puerto Rico* (Washington, D.C.: National Planning Association), p. 41.
5. Fernando Bayrón Toro, *Elecciones y Partidos Políticos de Puerto Rico* (Mayagüez, Puerto Rico: Editorial Isla, 1978), p. 148.
6. Toro Sugrañes, p. 257.
7. Roland Perusse, *The United States and Puerto Rico* (Malabar, FL: Robert E. Krieger Publishing Company, 1990), p. 35.
8. Costas, p. 53.
9. Toro Sugrañes, p. 109.
10. Costas, pp. 252–253.
11. *Qué Pasa*, (San Juan, Puerto Rico: Puerto Rico Tourism Company, October-December, 1993), p. 26.
12. Toro Sugrañes, p. 87.
13. *Guía de prensa, Vaqueros de Bayamón* (Bayamón, Puerto Rico: Bayamón Baseball Club, 1978), p. 7.
14. Toro Sugrañes, p. 88.
15. Costas, pp. 212, 215–217.
16. Toro Sugrañes, p. 86.
17. *The Sporting News*, January 3, 1970.
18. Costas, p. 341.
19. Toro Sugrañes, p. 105.

3. Roberto Clemente #21

1. Luis Rodríguez Mayoral, *Mas Allá de un sueño* (Hato Rey, Puerto Rico: Ramallo Brothers Printing, 1981), p. 19.
2. Hal Wagenheim, *Clemente!* (New York: Praeger Publishers, 1974), p. 23.
3. Luis Rodríguez Mayoral, *Roberto Clemente aún escucha las ovaciones* (Hato Rey: Ramallo Brothers Printing, 1987), p. 11.
4. *El Mundo*, December 17, 1954.
5. *The Sporting News*, February 25, 1953.
6. *The Sporting News*, February 17, 1954.
7. *The Sporting News*, December 9, 1953.
8. Rodríguez Mayoral, *Roberto Clemente*, p. 13.
9. *The Sporting News*, December 1, 1954.
10. Conversation with Diana Zorrilla, January 2, 1992.
11. *El Mundo*, December 17, 1954.
12. *The Sporting News*, January 5, 1955.
13. *The Sporting News*, February 9, 1955.
14. *The Sporting News*, February 16, 1955.
15. *The Sporting News*, February 23, 1955.
16. Víctor Navarro, *Los Juegos de estrellas* (Aguadilla, Puerto Rico: Navarro's Publishing Services, 1992), p. 11.
17. *The Sporting News*, February 8, 1956.
18. *The Sporting News*, February 15, 1956.
19. Conversation with Hiram Cuevas, January 4, 1993.
20. *The Sporting News*, January 9, 1957.

21. *The Sporting News*, December 26, 1956.
22. *The Sporting News*, January 6, 1957.
23. *El Mundo*, January 29, 1957.
24. Barea, p. 48.
25. *El Mundo*, January 13, 1958.
26. *The Sporting News*, February 12, 1958.
27. Conversation with Palillo Santiago, January 9, 1993.
28. Costas working papers.
29. *The Sporting News*, February 10, 1960.
30. *The Sporting News*, October 21, 1959.
31. Roberto Inclán, *Senadores de San Juan, 1938-39 a 1982-83* (San Juan, Puerto Rico: San Juan Baseball Club, 1983), p. 27.
32. Barea, p. 48.
33. *The Sporting News*, February 22, 1961.
34. *The Sporting News*, January 31, 1962.
35. Ibid.
36. *El Mundo*, January 26, 1962.
37. *San Juan Star*, February 4, 1962.
38. Inclán, p. 32.
39. *The Sporting News*, February 1, 1964.
40. *The Sporting News*, December 26, 1964.
41. Conversation with Cal Ermer, February 3, 1993.
42. Inclán, p. 33.
43. *The Sporting News*, January 9, 1965.
44. Costas, p. 238.
45. *The Sporting News*, February 13, 1965.
46. *The Sporting News*, December 16, 1967.
47. Inclán, p. 36.
48. Ibid.
49. Ibid., p. 38.
50. *The Sporting News*, November 7, 1970.
51. Inclán, p. 39.
52. *El Mundo*, January 26, 1971.
53. Navarro, *Juegos*, p. 34.
54. *The Sporting News*, February 3, 1973.
55. *The Sporting News*, January 20, 1973.
56. Ibid.
57. Rodríguez Mayoral, *Roberto Clemente*, p. 51.

4. Pioneers

1. *El Mundo*, October 28, 1939.
2. *El Mundo*, November 6, 1939.
3. *El Mundo*, September 24, 1939.
4. *El Mundo*, January 8, 1940.
5. Armada working papers.
6. *The Sporting News*, January 13, 1954.
7. Navarro working papers.
8. Costas, pp. 314, 328.
9. Luis Alvelo, "The Golden Age of Puerto Rican Ball," *The National Pastime*, 1991 edition, Society for American Baseball Research (SABR), p. 57.
10. Robert Peterson, *Only the Ball Was White*, 1970 (Reprint, New York: Oxford University Press, 1992), p. 167.
11. Inclán, pp. 3–4.
12. Costas, p. 58.
13. *El Mundo*, February 8, 1940.
14. Costas, p. 53.
15. *The New York Times*, February 25, 1947.
16. Costas, p. 89.
17. Ibid., pp. 200–201.
18. Navarro, *Book*, pp. 13–14.
19. Alvelo working papers.
20. *Primera Exaltación al Salón de la Fama del Béisbol Profesional de Puerto Rico* (Ponce, Puerto Rico: Salón de la Fama del Beisbol Profesional de Puerto Rico, Inc., October 20, 1991), p. 20.
21. Victor Navarro, *Sucedió en el béisbol profesional de Puerto Rico* (Aguadilla, Puerto Rico: Navarro's Publishing Services, 1991), p. 17.
22. Rodríguez Mayoral, *Roberto Clemente*, p. 48.

23. Pedro Carlos Lugo, "Juan Esteban 'Tetelo' Vargas" in *Segunda Exaltación al Salón de la Fama del Béisbol Profesional de Puerto Rico* (Ponce, Puerto Rico: Salón de la Fama del Béisbol Profesional de Puerto Rico, Inc., November 8, 1992), p. 24.
24. *Don Q Baseball Cues*, no. 4, 1947, p. 67.
25. *El Mundo*, March 9, 1947.
26. Jorge Tirado, Jr., "Juan Guilbe" in *Segunda Exaltación*, p. 18.
27. Costas, p. 55.
28. Ibid., p. 218.
29. Navarro, *Book*, p. 15.
30. *El Mundo*, February 16, 1949.
31. John Thorn, and Peter Palmer, with David Reuther, eds., *Total Baseball* (New York: Warner, 1991), p. 1436.
32. *El Mundo*, March 4, 1936.
33. Phil Dixon, and Patrick J. Hannigan, *The Negro Baseball Leagues* (Mattituck, New York: Amereon, 1992), p. 246.
34. Bill O'Neal, *The Pacific Coast League* (1903-1988), (Austin, Texas: Eakin Press, 1990), p. 332.
35. *El Mundo*, September 5, 1939.
36. Seda and Fernández, p. 9.
37. Costas, p. 209.
38. Víctor Navarro, *Crónicas de las series finales: Béisbol profesional de Puerto Rico, 1938-39 a 1947-48*, (Aguadilla, Puerto Rico: Navarro's Publishing Services, 1991), Serie 7, p. 8.
39. Costas, p. 35.
40. Navarro, *Book*, pp. 10, 21–22.
41. Navarro working papers.
42. Shelley Smith, "Remembering Their Game," *Sports Illustrated*, July 6, 1992, p. 86.
43. Costas, p. 328.
44. Peterson, p. 142.
45. Barea, p. 51.
46. Peterson, p. 295.
47. *El Mundo*, December 23, 1939.
48. *El Mundo*, December 26, 1939.
49. Navarro, *Sucedió* anexo 1.
50. Navarro, *Crónicas*, Serie 5, p. 3.
51. *Don Q Baseball Cues*, No. 6, 1948-49, p. 108.
52. Rodríguez Mayoral, *Roberto Clemente*, p. 64.
53. *El Mundo*, January 31, 1940.
54. Inclán, p. 6.
55. Navarro, *Crónicas*, Serie 7, p. 8.
56. Edgardo Cales Rivera, and Pedro Carlos Lugo, "Rafael Ortíz (Rafaelito)," in *Segunda Exaltación*, p. 20.
57. *El Mundo*, September 11, 1939.
58. Costas working papers.

5. Stars and Workhorses

1. *Primera Exaltación*, p. 28.
2. *The Sporting News*, February 27, 1952.
3. *The Sporting News*, October 13, 1954.
4. Panchicú Toste, *Paloviejo en los deportes* (Camuy, Puerto Rico: Barceló Marqués & Co., 1966-67 edition, October, 1967), p. 7.
5. Ibid.
6. *The Sporting News*, October 26, 1949.
7. Ibid.
8. Costas, p. 224.
9. *The Sporting News*, March 7, 1951.
10. Conversation with Luis Olmo, January 6, 1992.
11. *Primera Exaltación*, p. 29.
12. Costas working papers.
13. *The Sporting News*, November 27, 1957.
14. Costas, p. 64.
15. *The Sporting News*, December 11, 1957.
16. *The Sporting News*, January 29, 1958.
17. *The Sporting News*, February 19, 1958.
18. Conversation with Hiram Cuevas, January 4, 1993.
19. Fufi santori, *Con Pantalones* (Aguadilla, Puerto Rico: Quality Printers, 1987), p. 23.

20. Ibid., p. 39.
21. Pedro Carlos Lugo, "Tomás 'Planchardón,' Quiñónes," in *Tercera Exaltación al Salón de la Fama del Béisbol Profesional de Puerto Rico* (Mayagüez, Puerto Rico: Salón de la Fama del Béisbol Profesional de Puerto Rico, Inc., October 31, 1993), p. 18.
22. Alvelo working papers.
23. Costas working papers.
24. Conversation with Luis Arroyo, October 19, 1991.
25. Inclán, p. 26.
26. Barea, p. 48.
27. Toste, 1966-67, p. 15.
28. *Revista de los Criollos de Caguas* (team magazine, 1980-81).
29. Costas working papers.
30. Navarro working papers.
31. Thorn & Palmer, pp. 800, 1191.
32. *The Sporting News*, December 14, 1963.
33. Barea, p. 64.
34. Costas, p. 240.
35. *Compilaciones oficiales*.
36. *Revista Criollos*, 1980-81.
37. *Compilación oficial*, 1981-82.
38. Costas, p. 294.
39. *Revista Cangrejera* (Santurce team magazine), 1981-82.
40. *Compilación oficial*, 1982-83.
41. Costas, p. 315.
42. Thorn & Palmer, p. 1330.
43. *Compilación oficial*, 1983-84.
44. *The San Juan Star*, January 28, 1993.
45. Tony DeMarco, "High Sierra," *Fort Worth Star-Telegram*, April 12, 1992, p. 5.
46. Conversation with Orlando Gómez, October 19, 1991.
47. *Compilación oficial*, 1985-86.
48. *Compilación oficial*, 1987-88.
49. *Compilación oficial*, 1988-89.
50. Tony Menéndez update.
51. Tracy Ringolsby, "No Growing Pains—Rangers' González Hastens Maturing Process in Winter Ball," *Dallas Morning News*, January 21, 1990, "Baseball" section feature.
52. *Compilaciones oficiales*, 1986-87 to 1988-89.
53. *Compilación oficial*, 1989-90.
54. Ibid.
55. *The San Juan Star*, January 2, 1993.
56. Ibid.
57. Tom Verducci, "Puerto Rico's New Patro Saint—Like Clemente Before Him, Ranger Slugger Juan González Is a Hero and an Exemplar to His Countrymen," *Sports Illustrated*, April 5, 1993, p. 67.
58. *USA Today Baseball Weekly*, February 12-25, 1992.
59. *The San Juan Star*, January 3, 1990.
60. *Compilación oficial*, 1989-90.
61. Navarro, *Sucedió*, Anexo 4.
62. *Compilación oficial*, 1989-90.

6. They Played On

1. Conversation with Ismael Trabal, January 15, 1994.
2. Costas, p. 224.
3. Conversation with Luis Moux, January 22, 1994.
4. Víctor Navarro, "Luis Angel 'Canena' Márquez," in *Primera Exaltación*, p. 16.
5. *El Mundo*, February 17, 1947.
6. Peterson, pp. 306–307.
7. *The Sporting News*, January 9, 1954.
8. *El Mundo*, February 1, 1954.
9. Costas, p. 227.
10. Pedro Carlos Lugo, "Carlos Bernier," *Segunda Exaltación*, p. 13.
11. *Don Q Baseball Cues*, no. 8, 1949-50, pp. 31, 35.
12. Thorn & Palmer, p. 1593.
13. Panchicú Toste, *Paloviejo en los deportes* (Camuy, Puerto Rico: Barceló Marqués & Co., 1965-66 edition, October 1966), p. 42.
14. *The Sporting News*, December 28, 1955.
15. *The Sporting News*, December 9, 1953.
16. Aaron & Wheeler, p. 80.
17. Barea, p. 55.

18. Inclán, p. 13.
19. Ibid., p. 26.
20. *The Sporting News*, October 14, 1959.
21. *The Sporting News*, October 15, 1971.
22. *Don Q Baseball Cues*, no. 25, 1968-69, p. 98.
23. Inclán, p. 25.
24. Ibid., p. 46.
25. Barea, p. 48.
26. Costas, p. 244.
27. Thorn & Palmer, p. 1345.
28. *El Mundo*, January 30, 1960.
29. Inclán, p. 44.
30. *The Sporting News*, February 10, 1960.
31. *The Sporting News*, February 24, 1960.
32. Thorn & Palmer, p. 2358.
33. Inclán, p. 37.
34. Ibid., p. 36.
35. Ibid., p. 38.
36. Costas, pp. 248, 250.
37. *Compilación oficial*, 1977-78.
38. Barea, p. 80.
39. Inclán, p. 29.
40. Ibid., p. 35.
41. Costas, pp. 251, 311.
42. Ibid., pp. 306–307.
43. Ibid., p. 288.
44. Navarro, *Juegos*, p. 42.
45. *Compilación oficial*, 1982-83.
46. *Compilaciones oficiales*, 1980-81 to 1984-85.
47. *Compilación oficial*, 1984-85.
48. Navarro, *Book*, p. 80.
49. *USA Today Baseball Weekly*, January 12–25, 1994.

7. Imports

1. Wilmer Fields, *My Life in the Negro Leagues* (Westport, Conn.: Meckler Publishing, 1992), p. 32.
2. *The Sporting News*, March 2, 1949.
3. Barea, p. 80.
4. *The Sporting News*, March 2, 1949.
5. Office of the Commissioner, Decision no. 26, May 13, 1949.
6. *El Mundo*, February 11, 1949.
7. *The Sporting News*, February 13, 1952.
8. Dick Clark, and Larry Lester, eds., *The Negro Leagues Book* (Cleveland, Ohio: SABR, 1994), p. 270.
9. *Don Q Baseball Cues*, no. 8, 1949-50, p. 108.
10. Eduardo Valero, "Willard 'Ese' Hombre," *Primera Exaltación*, p. 25.
11. Ibid., p. 24.
12. Ibid.
13. Barea, p. 54.
14. Costas, p. 328.
15. *El Mundo*, January 16, 1955.
16. *El Imparcial*, October 10, 1954.
17. *The Sporting News*, December 8, 1954.
18. Willie Mays, as told to Charles Einstein, *My Life In and Out of Baseball* (New York: E.P. Dutton & Co., 1972), p. 171.
19. Costas, p. 228.
20. Ibid., p. 314.
21. Ibid., p. 328.
22. *El Mundo*, February 6, 1962.
23. *Don Q Baseball Cues*, no. 25, 1968-69, p. 96.
24. *El Mundo*, January 17, 1968.
25. Toste, 1966–67, p. 47.
26. *The San Juan Star*, October 22, 1971.
27. *Compilación oficial*, 1972-73.
28. *Compilación oficial*, 1969-70.
29. *Compilación oficial*, 1971-72.
30. *Compilación oficial*, 1969-70.
31. Costas, p. 288.
32. *Compilación oficial*, 1972-73.
33. Costas, p. 314.
34. *Compilación oficial*, 1981-82.
35. *Compilación oficial*, 1985-86.
36. *Revista Cangrejera*, 1984-85, p. 82.
37. *Compilaciones oficiales*, 1970-71 to 1993-94.

8. Skippers

1. Costas, pp. 240–241.
2. Peter Bjarkman, "Caribbean Series

Legends: Statistics, Heroic Deeds and Unmatched Diamond Thrills," *The Minneapolis Review of Baseball*, 1990, p. 59.
3. Barea, p. 17.
4. *The San Juan Star*, January 29, 1981.
5. Texas Rangers Media Guide, 1993, p. 9.
6. Costas, pp. 228–229.
7. *The Sporting News*, January 27, 1954.
8. *The Sporting News*, February 17, 1954.
9. Conversation with Rafy Sepúlveda, January 13, 1993.
10. Costas, p. 314.
11. Thorn & Palmer, p. 1302.
12. *The Sporting News*, January 18, 1950.
13. *El Mundo*, February 19, 1954.
14. *The Sporting News*, December 20, 1961.
15. Bjarkman, p. 59.
16. Costas, p. 245.
17. *Revista Cangrejera*, 1986-87, p. 37.
18. Costas, p. 261.
19. *The San Juan Star*, January 24, 1981.
20. Tony Menéndez update.

9. Behind the Scenes

1. *The San Juan Star*, October 28, 1993.
2. Ibid.
3. Carlos Pieve, *Los Genios de la insuficiencia* (Santo Domingo, Dominican Republic: Alfa y Omega, 1984), p. 246.
4. Ibid., p. 248.
5. Ibid., p. 272.
6. *The San Juan Star*, October 27, 1961.
7. *El Mundo*, February 25, 1954.
8. *The Sporting News*, January 15, 1966.

10. Teams for the Ages

1. *Don Q Baseball Cues*, no. 6, 1949, pp. 7–8.
2. Barea, p. 75.
3. *Don Q Baseball Cues*, no. 6, 1949, pp. 7–8.
4. Ibid., p. 18.
5. Costas, p. 60.
6. Ibid., p. 66.
7. Tony Menéndez update.
8. Ibid.

11. Games

1. *El Mundo*, January 9, 1939.
2. *El Mundo*, January 16, 1962.
3. *The Sporting News*, December 23, 1967.
4. Barea, p. 63.
5. Toste, 1966-67, p. 49.
6. *The San Juan Star*, January 7, 1976.
7. Navarro, *Juegos*, p. 47.
8. Ibid., p. 44.
9. Ibid., p. 42.
10. *El Mundo*, February 26, 1947.
11. *El Mundo*, February 27, 1947.
12. Barea, p. 16.
13. *The San Juan Star*, January 31, 1987.
14. *The San Juan Star*, February 6, 1987.
15. *The San Juan Star*, February 9, 1987.
16. Conversation with Héctor Barea, January 4, 1992.
17. Conversation with Dickie Thon, August 4, 1993.
18. *Compilaciones oficiales*, 1970-71 to 1993-94.
19. *The San Juan Star*, February 10, 1977.
20. *Compilaciones oficiales*, 1969-70 and 1978-79.
21. *The San Juan Star*, February 6, 1995.
22. *The San Juan Star*, February 7, 1995.
23. *The San Juan Star*, February 10, 1995.
24. Ibid.
25. Tony Menéndez update.
26. Various publications including *The Sporting News* from 1949 to

1970, and *Compilaciones oficiales* from 1969-70 to 1993-94.
27. Ibid.
28. Conversation with Mario Mendoza, May 22, 1994.
29. *El Mundo,* February 23, 1954.
30. Ibid.
31. *The Sporting News,* 1950-59.
32. *The Sporting News,* February 27, 1952.
33. *The Sporting News,* February 23, 1963.
34. *The Sporting News,* February 21, 1962.
35. Ibid.
36. *El Mundo,* September 6, 1939.
37. *El Mundo,* September 13, 1939.
38. Seda & Fernández, p. 43.
39. Ibid., p. 45.

12. Fans

1. *El Mundo,* February 24, 1949.
2. Ibid., February 20, 1949.
3. *The Sporting News,* February 11, 1959.
4. Tony Menéndez update, and Barea, p. 54.
5. Barea, pp. 54, 56.
6. *The Sporting News,* November 2, 1955.
7. Conversation with Ismael Trabal, February 12, 1995.
8. Conversation with Gabrielle Paese, February 11, 1995.

Selected Bibliography

Newspapers

Puerto Rico
El Imparcial, 1954–55.
El Mundo, 1936–87.
El Nuevo Día, 1970–94.
The San Juan Star, 1959–95.
El Vocero, 1974–94.

U.S.A.
Baseball America, 1994.
The New York Times, 1947.
The Sporting News, 1949–73.
USA Today, 1988.
USA Today Baseball Weekly, 1992–94.

Books

Aaron, Henry, with Lonnie Wheeler. *I Had a Hammer*. New York: HarperCollins, 1991.
Barea, Héctor. *Libro oficial béisbol profesional de Puerto Rico*. Guaynabo, Puerto Rico: Art Printing, 1981.
*Bayrón Toro, Fernando. *Elecciones y partidos políticos de Puerto Rico (1809–1976)*. Mayagüez, Puerto Rico: Editorial Isla, 1978.
Clark, Dick, and Larry Lester, eds. *The Negro Leagues Book*. Cleveland: Society for American Baseball Research, 1994.
Costas, Rafael. *Enciclopedia béisbol Ponce Leones*. Santo Domingo, Dominican Republic: Editora Corripio, 1989.
Dixon, Phil, and Patrick J. Hannigan. *The Negro Baseball Leagues*. Mattituck, N.Y.: Ameareon, 1992.
Fields, Wilmer. *My Life in the Negro Leagues*. Westport, Conn.: Meckler Publishing, 1992.
Inclán, Roberto. *Senadores de San Juan, 1938-39 al 1982-83*. San Juan, Puerto Rico: San Juan Baseball Club, 1983.
Mays, Willie, as told to Charles Einstein. *My Life In and Out of Baseball*. New York: E. P. Dutton & Co., 1972.
Navarro, Víctor. *Crónicas de las series finales: Béisbol profesional de Puerto Rico, 1938-39 al 1947-48*. Aguadilla, Puerto Rico: Navarro's Publishing Services, 1991.
———. *Los Juegos de estrellas*. Aguadilla, Puerto Rico: Navarro's Publishing Services, 1992.
———. *Sucedió en el béisbol profesional de Puerto Rico*. Aguadilla, Puerto Rico: Navarro's Publishing Services, 1991.

*=non-baseball books

―――. *The Book of the 14 and Other 33 Ways to Enter It.* Aguadilla, Puerto Rico: Navarro's Publishing Services, 1993.
O'Neal, Bill. *The Pacific Coast League (1903-1988).* Austin, Texas: Eakin Press, 1990.
*Perusse, Roland. *The United States and Puerto Rico.* Malabar, Fla.: Robert E. Krieger Publishing Company, 1990.
Peterson, Robert. *Only the Ball Was White.* 1970. Reprint, New York: Oxford University Press, 1992.
Pieve, Carlos. *Los Genios de la insuficiencia.* Santo Domingo, Dominican Republic: Alfa y Omega, 1984.
Rodríguez Mayoral, Luis. *Mas Allá de un sueño.* Hato Rey, Puerto Rico: Ramallo Brothers Printing, 1981.
―――. *Roberto Clemente aún escucha las ovaciones.* Hato Rey, Puerto Rico: Ramallo Brothers Printing, 1987.
Santori, Fufi. *Con pantalones.* Aguadilla, Puerto Rico: Quality Printers, 1987.
Seda, José, and Jorge Fernández. *Béisbol semiprofesional.* Caguas, Puerto Rico: Imprenta Aguayo, 1941.
Stead, William H. *FOMENTO—The Economic Development of Puerto Rico.* Washington, D.C.: National Planning Association, 1958.
Thorn, John, and Peter Palmer, with David Reuther, eds. *Total Baseball.* New York: Warner, 1991.
*Toro Sugrañes, José A. *Almanaque Puertorriqueño.* Rio Piedras, Puerto Rico: Editorial Edil, 1990.
Wagenheim, Hal. *Clemente!* New York: Praeger Publishers, 1974.

Articles

Alvelo, Luis. "The Golden Age of Puerto Rican Ball." *The National Pastime*, 1991 edition. Society for American Baseball Research.
Bjarkman, Peter. "Caribbean Series Legends: Statistics, Heroic Deeds and Unmatched Diamond Thrills." *The Minneapolis Review of Baseball*, 1990.
DeMarco, Tony. "High Sierra." *Fort Worth Star-Telegram*, April 12, 1992.
Ringolsby, Tracy. "No Growing Pains—Rangers' Gonzalez Hastens Maturing Process in Winter Ball." *Dallas Morning News*, January 21, 1990.
Smith, Shelley. "Remembering Their Game." *Sports Illustrated*, July 6, 1992.
Trabal, Ismael. "Adiós al padre del béisbol organizado de Puerto Rico." *El Vocero*, Sabado Deportivo, November 24, 1984.
Valero, Eduardo. "Guayama ganó primera serie mundial semi-pro." *El Deportista*, June 1989.
Verducci, Tom. "Puerto Rico's New Patron Saint—Like Clemente Before Him, Ranger Slugger Juan Gonzalez Is a Hero and an Exemplar to His Countrymen." *Sports Illustrated*, April 5, 1993.

Other Sources

Compilaciones oficiales de la liga de béisbol profesional de Puerto Rico. Puerto Rico Winter League final official statistics, 1968-69 through 1993-94.
Don Q Baseball Cues. Statistical booklets focusing on Puerto Rico Winter League seasons, 1948-49 through 1968-69.
Guía de prensa, Vaqueros de Bayamón. Media Guide for Bayamón Cowboys, 1978-79.

Primera Exaltación, October 20, 1991; *Segunda Exaltación*, November 8, 1992; *Tercera Exaltación*, October 31, 1993. Programs for Puerto Rico Professional Baseball Hall of Fame award ceremonies. When player profiles have a by-line, credit is given in the appropriate note.

Qué Pasa. Official tourist guides to Puerto Rico, Fall and Winter 1993.

Revista de los Criollos de Caguas, Revista Cangrejera. Magazines for the Caguas and Santurce Puerto Rico Winter League teams.

Toste, Panchicú, ed. *Paloviejo en los Deportes*, 1965–66, 1966–67 editions. Detailed Statistical Booklets on the 1965-66 and 1966-67 Puerto Rico Winter League seasons.

Unpublished Working Papers

Also helpful in preparing this book were works in progress by Luis Alvelo, Angel Armada, Rafael Costas, and Víctor Navarro. Their unpublished sources are referenced as working papers. Armada was particularly helpful in providing career hitting and pitching statistics. Tony Menéndez facilitated a steady flow of information from 1993 to 1995 cited as "Tony Menéndez updates."

INDEX

Aaron, Hank 7, 12–13, 44–46, 55–57, 80, 119, 121, 123, 135, 194, 177, 210, 222–223, 231, 248, 257, 259
Aaron, Tommie 64
Abbeville (minor league team) 120
ABCs *see* Indianapolis ABCs
Abner, Shawn 246
Acosta, Nick 22, 48, 205
Adair, Jerry 63
Agee, Tommie 258
Agosto, Juan 114, 137, 172, 213, 246, 252
Aguadilla Sharks 8–9, 11–12, 35, 74, 76–77, 80, 86–87, 118, 145, 179–180, 208, 241–242, 247, 259
Aguayo, Luis 28, 137, 159, 183, 245
Aguilas Cibaeñas (Dominican Winter League Team) 111, 185, 213, 227–228
Aikens, Willie 245
Ajete, Omar 224
Alacranes *see* Almendares Alacranes
Alberro, José 186
Allen, Hank 245
Allen, Marcial "Canenita" 56, 60, 61, 63, 134
Allenson, Gary 221
Allentown (minor league team) 86
Almendares (amateur team) 1
Almendares Alacranes (a.k.a. Almendares Blues) (Cuban Winter League team) 2, 17, 34, 87, 153, 231
Almendro, Jaime 91–92, 100, 141, 219, 258
Alomar, Antonio "Tony" 131
Alomar, Demetrio 131
Alomar, Rafael 131
Alomar, Roberto 4, 8, 111–113, 183, 186, 201, 209, 230, 246, 248
Alomar, Santos "Sandy", Jr. 8, 108, 110, 183, 200–201, 246, 258
Alomar, Santos "Sandy", Sr. 8, 25, 110, 117, 120, 130–131, 133–134, 166, 183, 190, 205–206, 216, 221, 245, 256
Alou, Felipe 111, 121, 174
Alou, Jesús "Jay" 121
Alou, Mateo "Matty" 121, 152
Alvarado, Luis "Timba" 107, 125
Alvarez, Manuel "Manolo" 192
Alvarez, Orlando 219
Alvarez de la Vega, Pito 84, 202, 209, 258
Alvelo, Luis 74, 76, 208, 237
American Giants *see* Chicago American Giants
Anderson, Craig 47, 180, 232
Anderson, George "Sparky" 5, 47, 134, 165, 167, 168, 184, 217, 222
Anderson, Peter 142
Andújar, "Paracorto" 202
Angels *see* California Angels; Midland Angels
Aparicio, Luis 180
Apodaca, Bob 43
Aquino, Carmelo 128
Aquino, Luis 137, 172, 213, 217
Aranzamendi, Jorge 172, 195, 198
Arecibo Wolves 3, 10, 11, 16, 26, 35, 43–46, 48, 63–64, 66, 68, 72, 98, 107–108, 110–111, 117, 119–120, 127–131, 133–136, 150–154, 156, 167, 170–172, 174–175, 184–186, 189–190, 197–201, 205–206, 208–209, 219–221, 230, 234–235, 241–246, 256, 259
Armas, Tony 231
Arroyo, Luis "Tite" 4, 8, 16, 19, 20, 60–63, 65, 101–102, 129, 157, 197–198, 252, 256, 258
Artificial turf 11

INDEX

Astacio, Pedro 230
Astros *see* Houston Astros
Athletics *see* Oakland Athetics; Ogden Athletics
Atlanta Braves 31–32, 49, 222, 223
Atlantic Ocean 11, 35, 57, 75
Autopistas 19, 45
Avila, Bobby 123
Avilés, Ramón 43, 111, 113, 165, 170, 185, 213, 219, 223, 245
Ayala, Benigno "Benny" 45, 256
Azteca (team from Mexico) 2, 83
Azucareros del Este (Dominican Winter League team) 230

Baerga, Carlos 4, 7, 8, 115–116, 184, 186, 201, 217, 230, 246, 248, 256
Baez, Kevin 246
Baker, John "Dusty" 7, 97
Bakersfield Dodgers (A team) 174
Baltimore Elite Giants 80, 118
Baltimore Orioles 16, 21–22, 27, 96–97, 129, 154–155, 160, 165, 169, 192–193, 199–200, 205–206
Bancells, Richie 205
Bankhead, Dan 97
Bankhead, Sammy 78, 92, 215
Barbee, Bud 74
Barea, Héctor 208–209, 244
Barker, Ray 150, 248
Barnes, Skeeter 39, 246, 248, 256
Barnhill, Impo 98
Bartirome, Tony 99
Bateman, John 65
Baton Rouge (minor league team) 120
Bauta, Ed 180
Bayamón Cowboys 27–28, 35, 39, 41, 43, 47, 51–52, 108–109, 115, 125–126, 135, 137, 156, 159, 171–172, 190, 201, 217, 219, 229–230, 240, 243–245, 256, 259
Baylor, Don 7, 22, 69, 97, 133, 155, 165, 206, 248, 257
Bayrón, Nica 74
Bears *see* Newark Bears
Beauchamp, Jim 47, 59, 167, 228
Beene, Fred 128, 156, 252
Belcher, Tim 52, 173, 213
Bell, James Thomas "Cool Papa" 76
Bell, Jay 31, 174, 217, 246
Belle, Albert 257
Beltrán, Martín 17–18
Bench, Johnny 3, 7, 20–21, 40, 68, 130, 157, 220, 245, 248, 257–259
Beníquez, Juan 5, 110, 134, 174, 184, 217, 245, 246, 248
Benson, Gene 76, 88
Benson, Vern 96, 180–181
Bergman, Dave 159, 172, 248
Bernier, Carlos 26, 62, 98, 117–120, 122, 131, 151, 222, 248, 258
Berra, Yogi 43
Bevaqua, Kurt 170, 213, 245, 248, 256
Bevington, Terry 31
Bibby, Jim 40
Bilko, Mary 148
Bilko, Steve 117–118, 147–148, 248
Bilko, Steve, Jr., 148
Bird, Jorge 41, 43
Birmingham Black Barons 58, 83, 100, 103, 118, 140
Birtsas, Tim 246
Bisons *see* Buffalo Bisons
Bithorn, Hiram 2, 4, 7, 81–84, 100
Bithorn, Dra. María Angelica 83
Black Barons *see* Birmingham Black Barons
Black Yankees *see* New York Black Yankees
Blackburn, Wayne 120, 128, 177–178
Blair, Paul 21, 165, 167, 221, 245, 248
Blanchard, Johnny 90, 101
Blaylock, Gary 149
Blue, Vida 252, 258
Blue Jays *see* Toronto Blue Jays
Blues *see* Almendares Blues; Kansas City Blues
Boddicker, Mike 171, 226, 227
Boer Indians (Nicaraguan Winter League team) 155, 232
Boever, Joe 247
Boggs, Wade 7, 27, 138, 248, 257
Bolin, Bob 16
Bones, Ricky 186, 230, 246
Bonilla, Bobby 29, 30, 51, 111, 114, 172, 195, 198, 203, 207, 209, 213, 246, 248
Bonilla, Juan 246
Boone, Bob 23, 156, 248
Boozer, John 216, 245, 252, 256
Bordi, Rich 46, 219
Borinquén (steamer) 87
Borinquén (Puerto Rican Amateur Team) 1
Boros, Steve 168, 170
Boscio, Juan Luis 37
Boston Braves 5, 11, 12, 55, 119

INDEX

Boston Red Sox 27, 65, 131, 177, 196, 213
Boudreau, Lou 117
Boyd, Bob 178, 248
Boyd, Dennis "Oil Can" 164, 252
Bracero, Rafael 216
Bragaña, Ramón 2
Brandt, Jackie 37, 120, 192, 248
Brantley, Cindy 52
Brantley, Jeff 51, 52, 114, 213, 215, 252
Braves *see* Atlanta Braves; Boston Braves; Milwaukee Braves; Richmond Braves
Bream, Sid 29, 51, 213, 246, 249
Breard, Stan 97
Brett, Ken 69-70, 245, 252
Brewer, Billy 217
Brewer, Chet 92
Brewers *see* Milwaukee Brewers
Bridges, Rocky 133, 157, 182
Briggs, Johnny 155
Briles, Nelson 7, 19, 20, 35, 105, 150, 216, 245, 252
Britt, George 76, 208
Brocail, Doug 186, 230
Brooklyn Dodgers 3, 11, 15, 34, 55-56, 61, 84, 118, 122, 196
Brooklyn Eagles 2, 81, 87
Brown, Barney 86, 90, 252, 256
Brown, Gates 105
Brown, Rafael 220
Brown, Raymond 2, 4, 7, 76, 78, 83, 88, 91, 100, 142, 224, 233, 252
Brown, Willard 12, 22, 54, 55, 72, 76, 86, 90-91, 115, 122, 142-143, 166, 192, 216, 225, 237, 244, 247, 249, 256, 258
Browns *see* St. Louis Browns
Bruce, Bob 50, 51, 252
Brunet, George 67
Bruno, Tom 48, 120, 213, 252
Bruton, Billy 54, 257
Buchanan, Bob 185
Buffalo Bisons (AAA team) 20
Buford, Don 65, 67, 249
Buhl, Bob 12, 14, 103, 176, 204
Bunker, Wally 21, 165
Bunning, Jim 157, 231-232
Buonomo, Dr. Emigdio 42, 200
Burdette, Lew 103, 177
Burgmeier, Tom 252
Burgos, John 217
Burgos, José 215
Burks, Ellis 209, 227, 249

Burnside, Pete 57, 59, 60, 62, 252
Butler, Brett 51, 249
Butler, Dick 189
Butler, Rob 198
Buzas, Joe 65, 165, 178-180
Byrd, Billy 74, 75, 84, 86, 91, 209, 252

Cabrera, Luis 74, 81, 85, 192, 225, 252, 255
Cabrera, Marzo 215
Cadore, Leon 1
Caguas Criollos 2, 5-6, 8, 10-13, 15-18, 23-24, 27-28, 31, 35, 41-43, 45, 47, 53, 55, 58-63, 68-69, 72, 74, 77, 80, 84-87, 90, 92-93, 96-98, 100-104, 106-107, 111, 113, 115, 117, 119, 123-133, 136, 145, 147-150, 153, 155-157, 159-161, 163, 169-171, 174-177, 185-186, 199-200, 202-203, 205-206, 208-209, 211-213, 220, 224-231, 235, 241-247, 256, 259
Calderón, Alvaro 237
Calderón, Iván 183, 200, 201, 209, 246
Caldwell, Mike 25, 252
California Angels 103, 133, 182, 194, 219
Camacho, Ernesto 237-238
Camden (minor league team) 2
Caminiti, Ken 213, 235
Campanella, Roy 4, 7, 84-87, 97, 118-119, 147, 209, 249, 257, 259
Campaneris, Bert 257
Campanis, Al 56, 109
Campanis, Jim 41
Campbell, Dave 95, 249
Canaries *see* Sioux City Canaries
Candelaria, John 125
Candiotti, Tom 51, 162, 252
Canel, Buck 5, 202-203, 259
Cangelosi, John 30, 198, 213, 246
Cangiano, José "Chiro" 162
Captains *see* Shreveport Captains
Caracas Lions (Venezuelan Winter League team) 66, 181, 202, 213, 230, 232-233
Caratini, Pedro Miguel 1, 258
Carbo, Bernie 127-128, 157, 166
Cardenal, José 68, 167, 238
Cárdenas, Leo 21, 152, 165, 167
Cardinals *see* Mayagüez Cardinals; St. Louis Cardinals

Caribbean Baseball Confederation 123, 196, 217
Caribbean Series 4, 10, 33, 41, 43, 46, 49, 54–55, 57–58, 60, 63, 68, 98–99, 102, 107, 111, 113–114, 122, 128–130, 136, 140, 145, 147–148, 152, 156, 158–163, 166, 169–170, 173, 177, 180, 182, 185–186, 209, 213, 217, 219, 227–233, 237–238, 240
Carlton, Steve 7, 20, 105, 122, 150, 216, 252, 258, 259
Carrasquillo, Yuyo 40, 153
Carta Vieja Yankees (Panama Winter League team) 99, 177
Carter, Gary 133, 200, 209, 249, 257
Carter, Joe 7, 133, 160, 169, 249, 257
Carty, Rico 229
Cash, Dave 69, 158
Cassini, Jack 56
Castaño, Tony 167
Castro, Fidel 232
Castro, Gabriel 9, 87,
Cater, Danny 256
Cedeño, César 159
Celestino, Pete 191
Cementers *see* Duncan Cementers
Central American and Caribbean Games 80–81, 104, 19
Cepeda, Orlando "Peruchín" 4, 8, 19, 25, 37, 47–48, 58, 63, 66–67, 72, 103–104, 107, 115, 126, 130, 132, 137, 151, 166, 181, 186, 190, 192, 236, 245, 247, 249, 256–258
Cepeda, Pedro "Perucho" 5, 74, 77–78, 83, 86, 92, 102–103, 115, 117, 142, 208, 210, 236, 244, 247, 249, 255, 258
El Cerro Stadium (Havana, Cuba) 232
Cerv, Bob 90
Cey, Ron 158, 159, 166, 193, 245, 249
Chambliss, Chris 40–41, 186 249, 258
Chance, Bob 182
Chandler, Happy 141
Chapman, Leonardo Medina 238
Charboneau, Joe 258
Charles, Ed 64
Charles H. Terry (Liga del Castillo) Ballpark 78, 224, 239, 259
Charleston, Oscar 76
Charleston Senators (AAA team) 46
Charlotte Orioles (AA team) 27
Chévez, Tony 170
Cheyney, Tom 181
Chicago American Giants 93

Chicago Cubs 81, 137, 198–199
Chicago White Sox 25, 39, 62, 65, 100, 114, 115, 150, 178, 181, 198
Chiriquí Bocas Farmers (Panama Winter League team) 232
Chiti, Harry 57, 216
Christopher, Joe 125, 128, 216, 236
Chylak, Nestor 187
Cienfuegos Elephants (Cuban Winter League team) 152
Cincinnati Reds 2–3, 12–13, 51, 58, 68, 80–81, 133, 144, 157, 163, 198–199
Cinco Estrellas (Nicaraguan Winter League team) 41, 66
Clark, Allie 58
Clark, Mike 225
Clark, Ron 170–171
Clarke, Horace 19, 63, 105, 125, 129, 245, 249
Clarkson, Buster 4, 54–55, 57–59, 86–88, 96, 118, 122, 146, 216, 225, 249
Clemente, Roberto 4, 7, 15, 21, 53–72, 78, 90, 96, 98, 103, 107, 109–110, 126–127, 132, 134–135, 144, 147, 151, 158, 175, 186–188, 202, 216, 218–219, 244–245, 249, 257–259
Clemente, Vera 66, 71–72
Cleveland Indians 17, 18 41, 95, 100, 110, 116–117, 141, 149, 169, 182
Clippers *see* Columbus Clippers
Clowns *see* Indianapolis Clowns
Cobb, Ty 120
Cobián, Rafael Ramos 179
Coggins, Rich 245
Coímbre, Francisco "Pancho" 2, 60, 77–79, 83, 86, 92, 102, 115, 121, 133, 142, 182, 188, 215, 233, 238–239, 244, 247, 249, 255, 258
Colborn, Jim 69
Coleman, Vince 29, 172, 195, 213, 246, 257–258
Colón, Angel 24, 77, 199, 221–223
Colón, Muñoz 220
Colón, Raúl "Boogie" 225
Colorado Rockies 199
Colt 45s *see* Houston Colt 45s
Colts *see* Richmond Colts
Columbus Clippers (AAA team) 163
Comas, Adolfo 200
Comas, Marco 74
Concepción, Onix 219

Concepción, Ramón "Monchile" 96, 128
Concordia (All-Star team assembled in Venezuela) 2
Conde, Ceferino "Cefo" 73, 74, 120, 127, 131, 132, 149, 179, 208, 211, 258
Conde, Ramón "Guito" 61, 62, 66, 117, 127, 128, 131, 132, 211, 216, 232, 256
Cone, David 111, 205, 209, 227, 252, 258
Cook, Cliff 181
Cora, Joey 183, 198, 246
Cordero, Wil 115, 185, 246, 249, 256
Córdova Díaz, Jorge Luis 179
Corrales, Pat 39, 157, 158, 166, 215
Cortés, Herminio 61, 62, 175
Cosell, Howard 199, 222
Costas, Carlos 78, 238, 239
Costas, Rafael 98, 215
Cotto, Henry 111, 136, 137, 163, 175, 209, 223, 246, 249, 256
Cottoneers *see* Guasave Cottoneers
Courtney, Clint 101, 121
Covington, Wes 60
Cowboys *see* Bayamón Cowboys; Jalisco Cowboys
Crabbers *see* Santurce Crabbers
Craft, Harry 90
Crandall, Del 229
Crawford, Willie 133, 166
Crawfords *see* Pittsburgh Crawfords
Creel, Keith 46, 219
Criollos *see* Caguas Criollos
Crone, Ray 176–177
Cronin, Joe 177
Crowe, George 57, 59, 97, 146, 211, 216, 244, 249
Crutchfield, Jimmie 7, 83
Cruz, Cirilo "Tommy" 107, 133, 201
Cruz, Héctor 27, 107, 160, 171, 205, 227, 256
Cruz, Henry 219
Cruz, José "Cheo" 4, 8, 19, 26–27, 70, 105–107, 132, 159, 160, 169, 171–172, 186, 201, 211, 227, 245–246, 249, 256
Cuban National (Amateur) Team 10, 116, 196, 224–225
Cuban Stars 78, 80
Cubans *see* Havana Cubans; New York Cubans; Ponce Cubans
Cubs *see* Chicago Cubs
Cuéllar, Mike 7, 16, 17, 68, 137, 167, 169, 213, 258

Cuevas, Hiram 21–22, 47–48, 100, 162, 165, 172, 193, 195, 198
Cuevas, Ramón 60
Culver, George 235

Dalton, Harry 21, 22, 193
Dandridge, Ray 2, 4, 81, 86–88, 249, 259
Dark, Alvin 11
Darwin, Danny 170, 213, 252
Davalillo, Vic 152
Davenport, Jim 104
Davidson, Ted 47
Davis, Chili 5, 110, 133, 160, 249
Davis, Gerry 191
Davis, Johnny 6, 54, 140–141, 211
Davis, Lorenzo "Piper" 77, 92, 102
Davis, Mark 258
Davis, Tommy 62, 128, 175, 257
Davis, Willie 48
Daviú, Agustín 78, 86
Day, Leon 2–4, 9, 74, 86–87, 98, 252, 258, 259
Dayley, Ken 39, 48, 252
Deal, Ellis "Cot" 5, 68, 134, 142, 145–146, 238, 249, 256
Dean, Dizzy 81
de Jesús, Iván 45, 107, 110, 125, 134, 201, 245–246
de Jesús, William 129, 151
de la Caridad Méndez, José 1
de la Hoz, Mike 151, 152, 232, 249
de León, Luis (father) 221
de León, Luis "Mambo" (son) 111, 136–137, 172, 209, 213, 219, 252–253
Delgado, Carlos 186, 200, 217, 230, 257
Delgado, Félix "Felle" 89, 91, 104
Dempsey, Rick 51
Denny, John 258
Designated Hitter Rule (first used in Puerto Rico) 127
Detroit Tigers 17, 26, 46, 50, 62, 66, 128, 158–159, 178, 203–204
Devereaux, Mike 134, 174, 217
Díaz, Alex 246
Díaz, Edgar 111, 209
Díaz, Mario 201
Díaz González, Ernesto 195, 202, 227
Dibble, Rob 32, 111, 252
Dihigo, Martín 2
DiMaggio, Joe 142, 224

Dittmer, Jack 219, 244
Dixon, Rap 2
Dobson, Pat 21, 220
Doby, Larry 90, 92, 118, 147, 257
Dodgers *see* Bakersfield Dodgers; Brooklyn Dodgers; Los Angeles Dodgers
Doggett, Jerry 41
Drabowsky, Moe 43–44, 64, 252–253
Drafts (Puerto Rico franchises) 42, 110–111, 113, 115, 135–136, 200–201
Drebinger, John 224
Dressen, Charley 80
Driessen, Dan 7, 41, 132–133, 219, 249
Dublin (minor league team) 122
Dumont, Raymond J. 2, 9, 233
Duncan, Dave 220
Duncan, Frank 81
Duncan Cementers (U.S. Semi-Pro team) 73, 93, 233
Duren, Ryne 148
Durocher, Leo 56
Dustal, Bob 50, 247, 256
Duzich, Ken 108, 205, 207
Dwyer, Jim 170, 213, 225, 249, 256

Eagles *see* Brooklyn Eagles; Mexicali Eagles; Newark Eagles
East (Negro Leagues) All-Star team 88, 119
Easter, Luke 6, 60, 115, 117–118, 133, 147–149, 211, 239, 244, 247, 249, 256
Easterling, Howard 78, 215
Ebbets Field 97
Edmonton Trappers (AAA team) 49
Edwards, Doc 159, 169–170, 184
Elephants *see* Cienfuegos Elephants
Elite Giants *see* Baltimore Elite Giants
Elmira Pioneers (class A team) 154
Emeralds *see* Eugene Emeralds
Enid Refiners (U.S. Semi-Pro team) 233
Ermer, Cal 66–67, 119, 165, 181, 200, 225, 232
Escalera, Saturnino "Nino" 16, 62, 64, 68, 124–125, 131, 219, 247, 249, 258
Escogido Lions (Dominican Winter League team) 15, 47, 80, 113, 121, 157, 231
Espino, Héctor 230
Essian, Jim 209
Estrellas Orientales (Dominican Winter League team) 47, 66, 149

Eugene Emeralds (minor league team) 188
Evans, Darrell 219, 257
Expos *see* Montreal Expos

Farmers *see* Chiriquí Bocas Farmers
Feller, Bob 222
Fenway Park 11
Fernández, Carmelito 220
Ferrer, Charles 143, 202, 225, 237
Ferrer, José 143
Fields, Wilmer 5, 6, 39, 118, 139–141, 149, 164, 177, 211, 249
Figueroa, Eduardo 4, 8, 27, 104, 107, 133, 136, 171, 209, 223, 253
Figueroa, Enrique "Tite" 92
Figueroa, Fernando 247
Figueroa, José 258
Fine, Tommy 231
Finley, Charley 22, 158
Finley, Steve 213
Fisher, Jack 15, 62, 150, 192
Flores, Gil 133–134, 160, 249
Florida Marlins 202
Foli, Tim 111, 185, 188, 227
Ford, Dale 5, 187, 190–191
Ford, Whitey 101
Formental, Pedro 118
Forsch, Ken 172
Fossas, Tony 163
Fowler, Art 17
Fox, Eric 49, 217, 249
Foy, Joe 21, 165, 167, 245
Franco, Jorge 81
Francona, Terry 246
Franks, Herman 56, 58, 96, 137, 175–176, 192, 216
Frau, Miguel J. 5, 204
Freed, Roger 22–23, 37–38, 132–133, 165, 249
Fregosi, Jim 5, 128, 133, 157, 165–167, 173, 182, 194, 222
Frick, Ford 63, 122
Frohwirth, Todd 253
Fuentes, Tito 152

Gaddy, Bob 246
Galarraga, Andrés 231
Gant, Ron 31, 136
García, Dámaso 229
García, José "Ronquito" 61, 169, 199–200, 256
García, L. Martiniano 148, 215, 239

García, Manuel "Cocaína" 2, 224
García, Manuel "Manolo" 84, 86, 209, 258
García, Pedro 45, 209
García de la Noceda, Carlos 236
Gardner, Rob 166
Garner, Phil 25, 38, 221
Garvey, Steve 193, 228
Gaston, Cito 111
Gebhard, Bob 199
Gehrig, Lou 72
Geishert, Vern 166
Gerard, Alfonso 57, 126
Giants *see* Jersey City Giants; New York Giants; San Francisco Giants
Gibbon, Joe 181
Gibson, Bob 7, 15–16, 32, 47, 63, 91, 103–105, 129, 131 181, 192, 216, 232–233, 253, 258, 259
Gibson, Josh 2, 4, 15, 58, 73–76, 83, 86, 88, 91, 108, 115, 118, 135, 147, 192, 208, 237, 244, 247, 249–250, 255, 259
Gibson, Russ 131, 154
Gilliam, Jim 7, 34, 41, 46, 54, 55, 118, 128, 216, 237, 250, 258
Gladden, Dan 51, 160, 162, 198, 231, 250
Globetrotters *see* Harlem Globetrotters
Goldberg, Bryan 240
Goldstein, Bud 141
Gómez, Luis A., Jr. 51, 162, 170, 172, 191, 195, 198, 200, 203
Gómez, Moisés 113
Gómez, Orlando 109, 183, 184, 186, 220, 227
Gómez, Preston 47, 96, 167
Gómez, Rubén 3–4, 14, 16, 19, 21, 34, 37, 46, 55–57, 60, 67, 72, 81, 94–99, 103, 116, 125–126, 130, 134, 137, 147, 154, 165–167, 176, 192, 205, 216, 218–219, 236, 238, 240, 245, 253, 256, 258
Gómez, Teresa 46
González, José Angel "Gamby" 205
González, Juan "Igor" 4, 7, 42, 107–108, 111, 113–115, 184–186, 196, 201, 217, 230, 246, 250, 256, 257
González, Juan "Yuyo" 8, 20, 38, 66, 127, 157, 166–167, 182, 191, 193–194, 196–197, 239
González, Julio César 160, 169
González, Tony 21, 152, 245
Gossage, Rich 25, 253

Gotay, Julio 19, 165, 167, 211, 245
Gray, Jeff 114
Grays *see* Homestead Grays
Greason, Bill 57–59, 126, 192, 253
Great Falls (minor league team) 174
Greenwade, Tom 95, 140
Griffey, Ken, Sr. 7, 41, 219, 250
Grillasca, Andrés 224
Guasave Cottoneers (Mexican Pacific Coast League team) 158
Guayama Rotary Club 9
Guayama Witches 2, 5, 8–10, 13, 35, 73–74, 76, 87–88, 91–93, 208, 210, 233, 236, 241, 244, 247–248, 255, 259
Guerra, Fellito 2
Guerrero, Pedro 231
Guilbe, Félix "Felo" 215, 238–239
Guilbe, Jesús 239
Guilbe, Juan 78, 80–81, 100, 215, 239, 258
Gunderson, Eric 186, 230
Guzmán, José "Chevel" 114, 137, 172, 213, 246, 253
Gwynn, Chris 48–49
Gwynn, Tony 7, 28, 48, 250, 257

Haddix, Harvey 7, 12, 253
Hagen, Kevin 46, 219, 253
Hairston, Sam 141
Hall, Mel 133
Hamey, Roy 101
Hammond, Steve 246
Haney, Chris 186
Haney, Larry 154, 245
Hargan, Steve 18, 182
Harlem Globetrotters 100
Harmon, Charles "Chuck" 7, 12–14, 119
Harper, Brian 28, 137, 250
Harrell, Bill 244
Harris, Bucky 224
Harris, Luman 192
Harris, Scott 190
Harshman, Jack 7, 13, 178, 253
Hartnett, Gabby 81
Harvey, Bryan 30, 184, 240, 253, 256
Harvey, Doug 64, 187–188, 191
Havana Cubans (minor league team) 152
Havana Reds (Cuban Winter League team) 148, 153
Havens, Brad 246

Hayes, Johnny 2
Hayes, Tom, Jr. 140
Hayes, Von 161, 200, 250
Hazleton (minor league team) 2
Héctor Espino Stadium 227
Hemond, Rollie 194
Henderson, Rickey 7, 26, 110, 128, 133, 183, 205, 221–222, 245, 250, 257
Hendricks, Elrod 5, 21, 25, 48, 71–72, 117, 129–130, 154–155, 165, 167, 216, 245, 250, 256
Henke, Tom 234
Hermosillo Orangegrowers (Mexican Pacific Coast League team) 162, 230
Hernaíz, Jesús 136–137, 172–173, 213
Hernández, Jackie 166, 216
Hernández, Keith 257–258
Hernández, Manache 189–190
Hernández, Roberto 114–115, 186, 246, 253
Hernández, Rudy 98, 121
Hernández, Willie 209, 257–258
Hernández Agosto, Miguel 8
Herrnstein, John 150–151
Hiatt, Phil 246
Hicks, Jim 166
Hilgendorf, Tom 41, 253
Hill, Jerry 71
Hiller, John 122, 211
Hiram Bithorn Municipal Stadium 3, 4, 39, 47, 64–65, 69–72, 96, 111, 120, 152, 167, 202, 206, 221, 224, 230, 238, 240, 259
Hockette, George 2
Hoerner, Joe 149–150, 253
Hoiles, Chris 114, 215
Hollins, Dave 136
Holloman, Alva "Bobo" 55
Holman, Shawn 246
Homestead Grays 54, 76, 88, 97, 118–119, 139, 144, 149
Horlen, Joel 65, 149–150, 203, 253
Horn, Sam 31
Hornsby, Rogers 98, 101–102, 118, 120–121, 123–124, 177–178, 203, 259
Horton, Willie 7, 17, 229, 250
Houk, Ralph 60, 90, 101–102, 148
House of David (Negro leagues team) 80
Houston Astros 108, 142, 159, 172
Houston Colt 45s 51
Howard, Elston 90, 250, 257
Howard, Frank 7, 15, 16, 123, 128, 175, 220, 250, 257–258
Howard, Tom 246
Howe, Art 41, 165, 171–173, 184, 219, 250
Howell, Dixie 122, 244
Howerton, Bill 231
Howerton, Bill, Jr. 231
Hoyt, Lamar 258
Hubbell, Carl 14
Huffman, Benny 120, 178
Hughes, Dick 48, 150, 253
Hughes, Roy 97
Humacao Oriental Grays 2, 8, 35, 74, 86, 91, 208, 220, 241, 259
Hunter, Bertrum 2, 74, 76
Hunter, Billy 34–35, 54–55
Hunter, Brian 49
Huyke, Elwood "Woody" 42, 129, 170–171, 209
Huyke, Enrique 9, 233, 236

"Import" All-Star Team 10, 70–71, 222
Ina Calimano Ballpark 88, 259
Inclán, Roberto 41, 159, 171, 199
Indianapolis ABCs 83
Indianapolis Clowns 80, 101
Indianapolis Indians (AAA team) 127
Indians see Boer Indians; Cleveland Indians; Indianapolis Indians; Mayagüez Indians
Industrialists see Valencia Industrialists
Interamerican Series 6, 10, 18, 63, 65–66, 122, 151, 180–181, 193, 202, 232–233
Irizarry, Natalio "Pachy" 17, 120–121, 232
Irvin, Monte 4, 7, 73, 86, 88–90, 92, 108, 139, 147, 250, 256–257, 259
Isidoro García Stadium 10, 190, 195, 225, 227, 236, 259
"Isla" (Puerto Rico Winter League) All-Star Team 10, 135, 223

Jackson, Grant 16, 155–157, 245, 253
Jackson, Reggie 7, 22–23, 69, 156, 162, 165–166, 206, 250, 257, 259
Jacksonville (minor league team) 16
Jalisco Cowboys (Mexican League team) 122, 129
James, Dion 160–161, 198, 213
Javier, Julian 181
Jáyase Hernández Ballpark 259

Jenkins, Ferguson 3, 7, 16, 104, 155, 157, 253, 258–259
Jersey City Giants (minor league team) 152
Jethroe, Sam 257–258
Jiménez, "Jumpy" 151
Johnson, Alex 257
Johnson, Bob 23, 40, 71
Johnson, Dave 48
Johnson, Deron 257
Johnson, Lou 17
Johnson, Sandy 113
Johnstone, Jay 23, 39, 43, 182, 194, 209, 216, 250, 256
Jones, Barry 235
Jones, Deacon 39, 65, 245
Jones, Doug 253
Jones, Mack 63
Jones, Sam 57, 155, 216, 218–219, 253
Jordan, Jimmy 2
Jordan, Ricky 213
Jorgensen, Mike 69, 158, 245
Joyner, Wally 51–52, 172, 203, 213, 246, 256
Juan Ramón Loubriel Stadium 5, 39, 41, 47, 221, 259
Juncos (Puerto Rico AA team) 53

Kaiser, Cecil 97
Kansas City Blues (AAA team) 95
Kansas City Monarchs 54, 81, 90, 144
Kansas City Royals 44–46, 168, 213
Kekich, Mike 167
Kelly, Pat 185
Kelly, Roberto 111, 163
Kennedy, John F. 50
Kennedy, Kevin 5, 165, 174, 196–197, 223
Kingman, Dave 257
Kinney, Dennis 37, 170, 213, 253
Kison, Bruce 23, 40, 71, 253
Klesko, Ryan 49
Kluttz, Clyde 169
Kofresí Pirates see Ponce
Koufax, Sandy 7, 15, 60, 103, 128, 144, 148, 188, 253, 258–259
Kravitz, Danny 34, 147
Kreuter, Chad 114, 163, 185
Kruk, John 230
Krukow, Mike 169
Kuenn, Harvey 195

Laboy, José "Cocó" 40, 66, 69, 125, 149, 176
Lachemann, Rene 5, 165, 169–171, 190, 195
Lamarque, Jim 237
Lamp, Dennis 45, 245
Lanauze, Carlos 215
Lance, Gary 44–46, 201, 219
Landes, Stan 187
Landis, Jim 148–149
Landrith, Hobie 148
Lanier, Max 84, 92
Lankford, Ray 195
Larsen, Don 156, 202
Lasorda, Tom 17, 55, 59–60, 122, 147, 166, 197, 229
Latin American (Puerto Rico Winter League) All-Star Team 10, 67
Lau, Charlie 50
Lawrence, Brooks 176, 177, 204
Lebrón, José 246
LeFlore, Ron 170, 213, 223, 246, 250, 257
Leith, Bob 62–63, 191–193, 236
Lemke, Mark 32, 250
Leonard, Buck 4, 81, 87–88, 119, 250, 259
Leonard, Dennis 44
Leonhard, Dave 21, 154–155, 253
Leppert, Don 202
Lerchen, George 244
Lewallyn, Dennis 160, 229
Leyva, Nick 29, 172–173
Lezcano, Carlos 110, 168, 219
Lezcano, Sixto 169, 201, 209, 245
Licey Tigers (Dominican Winter League team) 33, 49, 58, 66, 121, 149, 160, 166, 170, 174, 181, 193, 228–229
Liddle, Don 36–37, 238
Liga Paris Ballpark 74, 236, 259
Limmer, Lou 145
Lincoln Giants see New York Lincoln Giants
Lind, José "Chico" 31, 174, 217
Lind, Orlando 195
Lindblad, Paul 253–254
Linz, Phil 151
Lionel Roberts Stadium (St. Thomas, U.S. Virgin Islands) 48
Lions see Caracas Lions; Escogido Lions; Ponce Lions
Lipon, Johnny 18, 182
Littell, Mark 44–45

Llorens, Santiago 97, 120
Logan, Johnny 7, 11–12, 27
Lonborg, Jim 69, 131, 258
Lopes, Davey 229
López, Aurelio 159
López, Héctor 99
López, Javier 4, 8, 111, 116, 224–225, 246, 250
López, Juan 133
López, Luis 217
Los Angeles Dodgers 15, 41, 48, 128, 166, 174, 193, 196–199, 228, 230–231
Los Mochis Sugarcane Growers (Mexican Pacific Coast League team) 162
Lozado, Willie 246
Lucas, Guigui (Luis St. Clair) 97, 176
Lucas, Pepe (José St. Clair) 225
Lugo, Pedro Carlos 215–216
Luis Rodríguez Olmo Stadium 11, 150, 259
Luque, Adolfo 1
Lyons, Steve 234

McAnally, Ernie 38–39, 254
McClelland, Tim 5, 187, 189, 191
McCovey, Willie 25, 121
McCrae, Hal 257
McDowell, Sam 151
McGlothen, Lynn 245, 256
McGraw, John 1
McGregor, Scott 169, 245
McHenry, Henry 74, 247
Mack, Shane 39
McKeon, Jack 44, 165, 167–168, 201,
McLain, Denny 7, 16–17, 66, 105, 127, 188, 235, 254, 257–258
McLish, Cal 16
McMahon, Don 149, 174
McMichael, Greg 32, 254
McNally, Dave 203
McNertney, Jerry 39, 65, 132, 250
MacPhail, Larry 224
MacPhail, Lee 177, 192, 232
MacPhail, Lee, Jr. 140
McQuinn, George 2
McReynolds, Kevin 28
Magallanes Navigators (Venezuelan Winter League team) 56, 167, 229
Maglie, Sal 92
Mahler, Rick 48, 254
Maldonado, Candido "Candy" 5, 43, 110–111, 117, 128, 134–136, 168, 209, 219, 228, 231, 245, 250

Maldonado, Juan 202
Maldonado, Teofilo 9
Malzone, Frank 148, 250
Mangual, Angel 44, 70, 134, 245
Mantilla, Félix 12, 42, 60, 62, 128–129, 175
Mantle, Mickey 177
Manuel, Charley 234
Manwaring, Kirt 114, 213
Maple Leafs *see* Toronto Maple Leafs
Marchand, Jenaro "Tuto" 196–197
Marianao Tigers (Cuban Winter League team) 215, 231
Marichal, Juan 121
Marín, Roberto 53
Mariners *see* Seattle Mariners
Markland, Gene 97
Marlboro Smokers (Panama-Nicaraguan League team) 181, 232–233
Marlins *see* Florida Marlins; Miami Marlins
Márquez, Luis "Canena" 5, 12, 98, 117–119, 131, 149, 179–180, 219, 224, 244, 247, 250, 256, 258
Márquez, Rafael Delgado 9
Marshall, Mike 258
Martínez, Carmelo 28, 31, 111, 136–137, 186, 209, 217, 219, 224, 228, 246, 250, 256–257
Martínez, Dennis 5, 27, 53, 71, 137, 160–161, 169, 171, 200, 206, 225, 227, 254
Martínez, Edgar 4, 8, 94, 115–116, 137, 184, 186, 204, 217, 230, 236, 246–247, 250, 256–257
Martínez, Horacio 2
Martínez, John "Buck" 170
Martínez, Millito 238
Martínez, Pedro 230
Matlack, Jon 23, 40, 131–132, 254, 258
Mattingly, Don 7, 28–29, 48, 107, 136, 161, 175, 250, 257
May, Dave 21, 245
May, Lee 7, 21, 68, 245, 250, 257
May, Milt 23, 40, 71, 126
Mayagüez Cardinals (Puerto Rico Amateur team) 86
Mayagüez Indians 2, 5, 8–10, 13–14, 16–18, 22, 26, 28–29, 34–35, 42, 49–52, 60–62, 65–67, 73–74, 76, 84, 86–87, 89, 92, 95, 99, 106, 111, 114–115, 117–122, 127–128, 130, 134, 137, 139–142, 149–151, 158, 160–163,

169–174, 177–179, 180–186, 188, 190–191, 193, 195–196, 198, 200, 203, 205, 207–208, 211, 213–215, 225, 227, 230, 232, 234–236, 241–248, 256, 259
Maye, Lee 15, 64
Mayoral, Luis 198–199, 221–222
Mayoral, Radamés 202
Mayos *see* Navojoa Mayos
Mays, Willie 5, 7, 34, 36, 56–59, 95–96, 98, 100, 102–103, 142, 145–147, 175, 216, 218–219, 244, 250, 256–259
Meléndez, Esteban "Steve" 205
Meléndez, Luis "Torito" 70, 165–166, 182, 186, 216, 225
Meléndez, Willie 128
Memphis Red Sox 178
Méndez, Iván 51
Mendoza, Mario 70, 230–231
Menéndez, Tony 204
Meoli, Rudy 209
Mercado, Orlando 111, 209, 219, 228, 246
Merrill, Durwood 187, 190
"Metro" (Puerto Rico Winter League) All-Star Team 10, 135, 223
Metros *see* San Juan Metros
Mets *see* New York Mets
Mexicali Eagles (Mexican Pacific Coast League team) 162, 230
Mexico City Reds (former Veracruz League team) 123
Miami (class A team) 22
Miami Marlins (minor league team) 82
Midland Angels (class AA team) 30
Milkers *see* Pastora Milkers
Millán, Félix 8, 70, 104, 111, 126, 160, 164, 169, 205, 209, 222–223, 227, 245
Miller, Marvin 70
Miller, Ray 165, 171, 205
Milligan, Randy 246
Milwaukee Braves 5, 12, 54–55, 58, 64, 98, 126, 130
Milwaukee Brewers 24
Minnesota Twins 199
Miñoso, Orestes "Minnie" 100, 231
Miranda, Arturito 67
Mitchell, Keith 49
Monarchs *see* Kansas City Monarchs
Mondesí, Raúl 230
Montague, Ed 190

Montague, John 43, 209
Montalvo, Joe 219
Montalvo, Rafael 246
Montañez, Guillermo "Willie" 4, 8, 27, 103, 126, 133, 160, 171, 175, 190, 209, 251
Montreal Expos 126, 130, 199–200
Montreal Royals 56, 215
Monzant, Ramón 58, 147
Moon, Wally 149, 258
Moore, Balor 221, 238, 253
Moore, Donnie 45
Morales, Jerry 8, 23–24, 27, 104–105, 126, 133, 160, 169, 209, 227, 250
Morales, José Manuel 5, 69, 107, 115–117, 130, 133, 167, 169–170, 213, 221, 245, 248, 250
Morales, Luis "Wito" 202–203
Moret, Rogelio 97, 156, 256
Morris, Jack 7, 26, 160, 225, 254
Morrison, Dan 187, 189, 191, 234
Moss, Les 65
Mota, Manny 68, 121, 193, 228
Moux, Dr. Luis 225, 238
"Mula" 189
Muñiz, Manuel 107
Muñiz, Pookie 75
Muñoz, José 246
Muñoz Marín, Luis (Governor of Puerto Rico) 46, 121
Munson, Thurman 20, 68, 130, 250–251, 257–258
Murphy, Dan 246
Murray, Eddie 104, 169, 200, 206, 251, 257–258

National Semi-Professional Baseball Congress 9, 233
"Native" (Puerto Rico Winter League) All-Star Team 10, 70–71
Navarro, Emilio "Millito" 2, 75, 77–78, 80, 238, 258
Navarro, Jaime 126, 217
Navarro, Julio 40, 58, 125–126, 131, 137, 220, 254
Navarro, Víctor 119
Navigators *see* Magallanes Navigators
Navojoa Mayos (Mexican Pacific Coast League team) 162, 228, 230
Neagle, Denny 254
Neal, Charley 12
Negrón, Carlos 67

Negrón, Sergio 38
New York Black Yankees 2
New York Cubans 78, 80, 91, 100, 118
New York Giants 3, 5, 14, 36, 55–58, 95, 104, 126, 142, 175–176
New York Lincoln Giants 2, 77
New York Mets 23, 26, 43, 47, 51–52, 108, 133, 199, 203
New York Yankees 19, 63, 68, 76, 80, 84, 90, 95, 97, 100–102, 133, 140, 163, 196, 224
Newark (minor league team) 83
Newark Bears (class AAA team) 140
Newark Eagles 90, 140
Newman, Al 111, 235
Newport News (class B team) 12
Nied, David 32, 49, 254
Niekro, Joe 181
Niekro, Phil 64, 104, 151, 181, 254
Nieves, Juan 111, 205, 207, 209, 227–229, 254
Norbert, Ted 83–84
Norfolk Tars (class B team) 2, 12
North American (Puerto Rico Winter League) All-Star Team 10, 67
Northeast (Puerto Rico Winter League) All-Star Team 86
Northrup, Jim 7, 17, 178, 204, 211, 245, 251
Nuevo Laredo Owls (Mexican League team) 122
Nuñez, Edwin 43, 256

Oakland Athletics 22, 26, 44, 49, 158
Oakland Oaks (minor league team) 83, 84, 141
Ogden A's (class AAA team) 26
Oilers see Tulsa Oilers
Oliva, Tony 65, 251, 257–258
Olivares, Ed 105, 149, 209, 221
Olivares, Omar 42, 108, 209
Oliver, Al 69, 158, 257
Oliver, Bob 245
Oliver, Nate 104
Oliver, Reinaldo "Pochy" 205, 206, 224
Oliveras, Francisco Javier 136, 217, 228, 246, 254
Oliveras, Mako 30, 49, 69, 113, 136, 163, 165, 174, 184, 217, 229
Olmeda, José 246
Olmo, Luis Rodríguez 4, 7, 11, 41, 55, 57, 63, 67, 84, 89–90, 97–98, 102, 123, 125, 130, 149, 151–152, 165, 174–175, 192, 199, 205, 209, 211, 247, 251, 258
Omaha (minor league team) 122
O'Malley, Peter 197
Oms, Alejandro 2, 208, 224
O'Neill, Paul 161, 198, 213, 257
Oneonta Yankees (class A team) 207
Oquendo, Ismael 135
Orangegrowers see Hermosillo Orangegrowers
Oriental Grays see Humacao Oriental Grays
Orioles see Baltimore Orioles; Charlotte Orioles
Ortenzio, Frank 245
Ortíz, José "Polilla" 70, 133–134
Ortíz, Junior 136, 201, 209, 217, 245–246
Ortíz, Rafaelito 73, 92–93, 208, 233, 258
Osteen, Claude 199
Osteen, Darrell 245
Otero Suro, Guigo 227
Owchinko, Bob 221
Owen, Mickey 12, 14, 55, 61, 80, 84, 102, 165, 176–177, 203–205, 232
Owls see Nuevo Laredo Owls
Oyler, Ray 178, 211

Pabón, Salvador 141
Pacheco, Edwin 221
Padres see San Diego Padres
Paese, Gabrielle 240
Pagán, José 15, 26, 42, 58, 62, 66, 125–128, 132, 152, 184, 186, 220, 245, 256
Page, Joe 77, 97, 224
Page, Mitchell 229
Pagnozzi, Tom 51–52, 114, 172, 195, 198, 215
Paige, Satchel 2, 4–5, 13, 73–74, 83, 86–87, 91, 93, 98, 139, 147, 182, 208, 210, 233, 247, 254, 256, 259
Palermo, Steve 190
Palm, Clarence 7, 83, 88–89, 115, 248
Palmeiro, Rafael 163, 184
Palmer, Jim 3, 7, 21–22, 165, 167, 206, 238, 254, 258–259
Paniagua, Reinaldo "Poto" 19, 191–192, 196, 200

Paquito Montaner Stadium 10–11, 61, 105, 239, 259
Parque Colón (Aguadilla's Ballpark) 11, 87, 119, 259
Parrilla, Sam 125
Parrish, Lance 7, 26, 227, 251
Partlow, Roy 74, 76, 86, 88, 115, 244, 248, 254
Pascual, Camilo 152, 175
Pastora Milkers (former Venezuelan Occidental League team) 104, 180
Patek, Freddie 69, 158, 257
Patterson, Daryl 95, 158, 254
Paul, Gabe 144
Pawtucket Red Sox (class AAA team) 27
Pearson, Leonard 84, 208
Pedroso, Fernando D. 77, 89, 118, 215, 224, 244, 251
Peña, Adalberto 195
Peña, Orlando 21, 152, 167, 181, 184, 232–233
Peña, Tony 228, 231
Pendleton, Terry 7, 29, 51, 172, 213, 257–258
Pérez, Babel 17, 178, 203
Pérez, Mike 246
Pérez, Tany (Tony) 3, 7, 18, 21, 47, 67, 69, 103, 130, 154, 160, 165, 201, 222, 240, 245, 251, 256
Perfect games (Puerto Rico Winter League) 221
Perkins, William 7, 74, 87, 101, 208, 210
Perranoski, Ron 128
Perry, Alonzo 6, 118, 140–141, 177, 211
Pesante, Demetrio "Menchín" 208, 258
Peters, Gary 181, 258
Philadelphia Phillies 16, 23, 38, 108, 128, 150, 155, 157
Philadelphia Stars 88
Phillies see Philadelphia Phillies
Pichardo, Monchín 229
Pieve, Carlos 44, 195, 200–201
Piñero, Jesús T. (Governor of Puerto Rico) 36
Pioneers see Elmira Pioneers
Pirates see Pittsburgh Pirates
Pittsburgh Crawfords 76, 83
Pittsburgh Pirates 23, 31, 56, 61, 62, 67–71, 125–126, 179, 181
Pizarro, Juan "Terín" 8, 16–17, 19, 21, 47, 58, 60–61, 63, 66–67, 69, 72, 86, 98–100, 103, 125, 130, 132, 151–154, 165–167, 181, 205, 216, 220, 232, 245, 247, 254, 256, 258
Plaskett, Elmo 105, 125
Pless, Rance 231, 244, 251
Plews, Herb 232, 251
Polo Grounds 51, 179
Ponce Cubans (Amateur Team) 118
Ponce de León, Juan (First Governor of Puerto Rico) 37
Ponce Kofresí Pirates 37, 241, 259
Ponce Lions 2, 5, 8, 10–11, 14, 17–18, 20, 25, 32–33, 35, 37–39, 50, 60–62, 65–66, 71, 75–81, 87, 89, 91, 93, 96–98, 100–101, 105–107, 110–111, 117–122, 124, 127–134, 147–149, 156–160, 162, 165–167, 170, 172, 177–179, 181–184, 186, 188, 191, 193–194, 197–198, 202–203, 205, 207–208, 215–216, 221–222, 224, 227, 230, 238–239, 241–247, 255–256, 259
Pont Flores, Rafael 5, 141–142, 179, 187, 203, 231, 258
Poquette, Tom 44
Porter, J. W. 15
Posada, Jorge 246
Powell, John "Boog" 50, 65, 203, 232, 251, 257
Power, Victor Pellot 4, 8, 28–29, 58, 60–62, 72, 92, 94, 97, 102–103, 123, 125, 129, 137, 149, 165, 174–176, 211, 251, 256, 258
Pryor, Paul 64
Puebla (Mexican AAA Summer League) 122
Puerto Rico National (Amateur) Team 71, 104, 199
Puerto Rico 1947 All-Stars 224
Puerto Rico Winter League All-Star games 13, 58, 67, 70–71, 86, 120–121, 135, 151, 168, 221–224
Puerto Rico Winter League All-Star team (postseason) 23, 110, 116, 128, 154, 159, 244–246
Puhl, Terry 159

Queen, Mel 41
Quiñónes, Luis Raúl 137–138, 172, 200, 201, 213
Quiñónes, René 219
Quiñónes, Tomás "Planchardón" 81, 100–101, 215, 239, 254–256, 258
Quirk, Jamie 234

Rainiers *see* Seattle Rainiers
Ramírez, Felo 5, 202
Ramírez, Mario 168, 246
Ramírez, Milton 245
Ramos, Pedro 19, 152, 216
Rangers *see* Texas Rangers
Raymond, Claude 64, 151, 254
Ready, Randy 28–29, 160–161, 172, 213, 251
Reardon, Jeff 26–27, 128, 189, 254
Red Sox *see* Boston Red Sox; Memphis Red Sox; Pawtucket Red Sox
Red Wings *see* Rochester Red Wings
Reds *see* Cincinnati Reds; Mexico City Reds; Waverley Reds
Reed, Rick 189
Refiners *see* Enid Refiners
Rehm, Fred 227
Repoz, Roger 105, 216, 245
Reyes, Carlos 225, 254
Reyes, Napoleón 64
Reynolds, Harold 51–52, 203, 213
Rhodes, Dusty 95
Richert, Pete 42, 128, 254
Richmond Braves (class AAA team) 32
Richmond Colts (minor league team) 2, 84
Rickey, Branch 182
Rickey, Branch, Jr. 56
Riddle, Johnny 12
Ridzik, Steve 14, 59, 254
Riggleman, Jim 165, 173, 195
Rijo, José 227, 230
Ripken, Cal, Jr. 7, 27, 107, 136, 138, 171, 200, 224, 245, 251, 257–258
Rippelmeyer, Ray 149, 254
Rivera, Enrique "Quique" 133–134, 166, 216, 245
Rivera, Florentino 117, 122, 211
Rivera, Germán 63–64, 205–206, 225
Rivera, Germán "Deportivo" 111, 217, 246
Rivera, Jesús "Bombo" 170, 209, 213
Rivera, Manuel Joseph "Jungle Jim" 12, 15, 80, 97, 123–124, 129, 211, 251, 257
Rivers, Mickey 133
Rizzuto, Phil 62, 192, 259
Roberts, Leon 219, 222–223
Robinson, Brooks 192
Robinson, Frank 5, 21–23, 25, 69–70, 96–97, 133–134, 155, 159, 165–166, 188, 192–193, 206, 216, 222, 257–259

Robinson, Jackie 55, 72, 215
Robles, Sergio "Bazooka" 230
Rochester Red Wings (AAA team) 22, 154, 205
Rockies *see* Colorado Rockies
Rodgers, Andre 121
Rodríguez, Chi Chi 41
Rodríguez, Eduardo "Volanta" 160, 169, 209
Rodríguez, Edwin 246
Rodríguez, Eliseo "Ellie" 156, 159, 175, 219, 221
Rodríguez, Gerardo 220
Rodríguez, Henry 230
Rodríguez, Iván 4, 42, 108, 144, 201
Rodríguez, Pachy 199
Roebuck, Ed 3, 41, 254
Rogers, Steve 200
Rojas, Octavio "Cookie" 5, 64, 151–153, 221, 251
Román, Charlie 189–190
Romero Cuevas, Luis 5
Roque, Jorge 238
Rosa, Luis 201
Rosado, Luis "Papo" 217, 221, 246
Rosario, David 246
Rosario, Santiago "Chago" 166, 216
Roseboro, John 128
Rosell, Brujo 2
Roselló, David 221
Rowdon, Wayne 51
Royals *see* Kansas City Royals; Montreal Royals
Royster, Jerry 198
Ruhle, Vern 172, 229
Ruíz, Hiraldo "Chico" 64
Ruth, Babe 2, 72
Ryan, Nolan 219

Sain, Johnny 158
St. Jean (Canada professional baseball team) 122
St. Louis Browns 34, 55
St. Louis Cardinals 12, 16, 19–20, 29, 47, 61, 63, 96, 122, 131, 150, 158, 172, 180–181, 195, 198
St. Petersburg (minor league team) 120
St. Thomas/St. Croix (Amateur) Baseball Team 126
Sálamo, Rafael 61
Salazar, Lazaro 2
Salem (minor league team) 188
Salgado, Marota 238

Sam, Pedro Alejandro 2
Sambito, Joe 254
Samford, Ronnie 46, 57, 60–61, 120, 216, 237
San Antonio (class AA team) 149, 174
San Diego Padres (major league team) 25, 167, 199, 201
San Diego Padres (minor league team) 19, 141, 149
San Francisco Giants 5, 25, 45, 199
San Francisco Seals (minor league team) 83–84
San Juan Metros 35, 39, 52, 94, 115–116, 195–196, 198, 200–201, 204, 217, 229, 243–244, 246–247, 256, 259
San Juan Senators 2–4, 6, 8, 10–13, 20, 23, 29–31, 33–35, 37, 39–41, 47, 53–56, 60–74, 76, 82–83, 85–92, 95, 98, 100–102, 105, 107–108, 111, 113, 117–120, 122–123, 125–132, 134, 137, 139–141, 145, 147–154, 156, 158, 161, 163–164, 167–168, 172, 174–175, 179, 184–186, 191–193, 195–196, 202–204, 207–208, 217, 219–221, 224–225, 230, 235–238, 240–248, 256–257, 259
Sánchez, Celerino 230
Sánchez, Orlando 246
Sánchez, Rey 186, 217, 230
Sanders, Reggie 199
Sanford, Jack 258
Sanguillén, Manny 69, 163
Santiago, Benito 182, 184, 201, 219, 258
Santiago, Carlos Manuel 119, 122, 149, 151, 182, 205–206, 258
Santiago, José G. "Pantalones" 13, 81, 98, 100–101, 198, 215, 224, 255, 258
Santiago, José R. "Palillo" 5, 11, 20–21, 40, 61, 65–66, 69–70, 117, 131–132, 202, 220, 255
Santiago Pérez, Dwight 204
Santiago Stevenson, Dwight 204
Santurce Crabbers 3, 5, 7–8, 10–11, 15, 17–19, 21–22, 25, 29, 31–32, 34–35, 37, 41–42, 46–49, 53–61, 63, 69–77, 81, 84–87, 93–100, 103, 108, 110, 113–115, 120, 122, 125–126, 129, 131–134, 139, 142–144, 146–147, 154–156, 158–160, 162–163, 165–168, 170–172, 174–176, 180–181, 183–184, 186, 191–193, 196–197, 199–201, 205–206, 208, 216–222, 225, 228, 230, 232, 234, 236–238, 240–248, 255–257, 259
Sapperstein, Abe 100
Savage, Ted 68
Sax, Dave 52
Scales, George 77–78, 96, 100, 118, 203, 224
Scantlebury, Pat 118
Schmidt, Kermit 188, 221
Schmidt, Mike 7, 23–24, 43, 71, 104, 133, 209, 251, 257, 259
Schmidt, Waldemar 71, 187–188
Schroll, Al 230
Scott, George 21, 165, 167, 245, 251, 257
Screwball (effectiveness) 16, 94, 96, 102, 137
Scull, Angel 231–232
Sculley, Vin 41
Seals see San Francisco Seals
Seattle Mariners 115
Seattle Rainiers 124
Seaver, Tom 51
Seay, Dick 2, 74–75, 237
Seda, José "Pepe" 90, 208
Sello Rojo (softball team) 53
Semi-Professional World Series 10, 73, 93, 233
Senators see Charleston Senators; San Juan Senators; Washington Senators
Sepúlveda, Rafael "Rafy" 38, 118, 202, 215–216,
Seyfried, Gordon 50, 255
Sharks see Aguadilla Sharks
Sharperson, Mike 134, 174
Shea Stadium 51
Sherman, Darrell 246
Short, Bob 100
Show, Eric 200, 227
Shreveport Captains (class AA team) 198
Siebert, Sonny 18, 182, 255
Sierra, Rubén 4, 8, 72, 109–110, 113, 134, 174, 183, 186, 196, 200, 217, 246, 251, 257
Silver, Roy 246
Silvers, Phil 148
Simpson, Dick 105, 216, 245
Simpson, Wayne 127–128, 157–158, 166, 255–256
Singleton, Ken 69, 156, 158, 251
Sioux City Canaries (minor league team) 61, 127
Sisk, Tommie 67, 255

Sixto Escobar Stadium 10, 37, 47, 56–57, 64, 75, 88, 90, 92, 96, 129, 139, 141, 147, 151–152, 177, 179, 187, 203–204, 220, 225, 231, 232, 259
Skowron, Bill 121, 251
Smith, Dave 172, 245
Smith, Dwight 199
Smith, John Ford 142
Smith, Lee 7, 255
Smith, Lonnie 31–32, 184, 251, 256
Smith, Reggie 131
Smith, Robert G. 255
Smith, Zane 246, 255
Smokers *see* Malboro Smokers
Snider, Van 163–164, 185, 209
Soler Rivas, Rafael 34
Soto Respeto, Francisco 5, 147
Southeast (Puerto Rico Winter League) All-Star Team 86
Sparma, Joe 17
Spencer, Daryl 58
Spikes, Charlie 41, 221
Staehle, Marv 39, 40, 65, 67, 251
Stamford (minor league team) 117
Stanley, Mickey 178, 204, 211, 245
Stars *see* Cuban Stars; Philadelphia Stars
Steinecke, Bill 178–179
Steiner, Mel 64, 187
Stengel, Casey 95
Stennett, Rennie 71, 126, 163
Stock, Wes 192
Stoneham, Horace 56, 96
Strohmayer, John 33, 42–43, 126–127, 235, 255
Sugarcane Growers *see* Los Mochis Sugarcane Growers
Swan, Craig 43, 209
Sweet, Rick 170, 245

Tabler, Pat 18
Taborn, Earl 142, 237
Tacoma Tigers (class AAA team) 49
Talavera, Pepo 143
Talbot, Fred 67, 255
Tars *see* Norfolk Tars
Tartabull, Danny 110
Tartabull, José 110
Tata, Terry 187
Tatum, Ken 182
Taylor, Tony 17, 21, 68, 151–153, 167, 245
Tebbets, Birdie 144

Tenace, Gene 44
Texas Rangers 109, 113
Thomas, Frank 235
Thomas, Gorman 257
Thomas, Showboat 2
Thomas, Valmy 55, 57, 122, 129, 216
Thompson, Ryan 224, 246
Thon, Dickie 8, 26, 28, 89, 94, 108–109, 116, 136–137, 172, 186, 195–196, 200, 202, 217, 219, 228, 240, 245, 251
Thon, Freddie 89, 91
Three King's Day 10, 36, 38, 222
Thurman, Bob 5, 34, 54–55, 57–59, 62, 66, 72, 106, 115, 122, 142, 144–146, 176, 192, 216, 225, 244, 248, 251, 258
Tiant, Luis 17, 18, 33, 101, 104, 133, 136, 182, 200, 230, 232, 255
Tidewater Tides (AAA team) 133
Tigers *see* Detroit Tigers; Licey Tigers; Marianao Tigers; Tacoma Tigers
Timmerman, Tom 20, 42, 255
Timmons, Ozzie 246
Tirado, Jorge "Griffin" 80–81, 215, 239, 258
Tolleson, Wayne 219
Toms, Tommy 45–46, 255
Toronto Blue Jays 111
Toronto Maple Leafs (AAA team) 131
Torres, Miguel Angel 202–203, 236–237
Torres, Rosendo "Rusty" 41, 245, 256
Torres Pérez, Elmo 57
Torrez, Mike 108, 195
Torriente, Cristóbal 2
Torruellas, Billo 83
Trabal, Ismael 52, 87, 202–203, 211, 236, 240
Trappers *see* Edmonton Trappers
Trouppe, Quincy 89, 92, 102, 247
Trujillo, Rafael 48, 121, 181
Truman, Harry S 36
Tulsa Oilers (minor league team) 13, 122
Turley, Bob 7, 13, 39, 74, 98, 103, 255, 258
Twins *see* Minnesota Twins
Twitchell, Wayne 23

Uecker, Bob 44, 64
University of Puerto Rico Baseball Team 94

Valdés, Alfonso 9, 50, 118, 140, 149, 177, 179
Valencia Industrialists (former Venezuelan Central League team) 63, 66, 232
Valentín, Gilberto "Foca" 118, 121
Valentine, Corky 255
Valentine, Ellis 133
Valenzuela, Fernando 162, 228, 231
Valero, Eduardo 2, 224
Valle, Héctor 117, 128–129, 211, 245
Van Harrington, Roland 203
Van Hyning, Bill 204
Van Hyning, Sam, Jr. 3, 240
Van Slyke, Andy 51, 195
Vargas, Hedi 111, 228
Vargas, Juan Esteban "Tetelo" 55, 73–74, 80, 83, 92, 97, 102, 117, 208, 210, 233, 244, 248, 251, 258
Vargas, Roberto 55, 62, 97, 128, 151, 174
Vaughn, Greg 246
Vázquez, Héctor Rafael 202
Vázquez, Juan 126
Vázquez, Pedro 88, 258
Veale, Bob 151
Veeck, Bill 34, 55, 100, 117, 123, 141, 149
Vega, Jesús "Samarito" 128, 219, 256
Vélez, Otto 107, 132–133, 209, 245, 251
Vené, Juan 237
Verdi, Frank 110, 133–134, 157–158, 165, 182–184, 195
Villanueva, Héctor 116, 200, 217, 246, 256
Villodas, Luis "King Kong" 118, 256, 258
Vincent, Al 2
Virdon, Bill 23, 71
Virgil, Osvaldo "Ozzie," Jr. 27, 161
Virgil, Osvaldo "Ozzie," Sr. 12, 22, 120–122, 211
Vuckovich, Pete 258

Walker, Glen 219
Walling, Denny 159, 172, 251
Washington Senators 121, 232
Waslewski, Gary 131
Waverley Reds (Australian Baseball League) 225
Weaver, Earl 48, 96, 116, 154, 165, 188, 193, 206

Wegener, Mike 245
Wendell, Turk 49, 255
Wertz, Vic 36
West, David 217
West, Joe 190
Wetteland, John 174
White, Bill 58, 103, 127
White, Devon 134
White, Roy 19, 96, 105, 216
White Sox see Chicago White Sox
Wilhelm, Hoyt 148
Wilkins, Rick 199
Willard, Jerry 162, 251, 256
Williams, Bernie 186, 209, 217, 230
Williams, Dick 131, 154
Williams, Earl 258
Williams, Gerald 217, 246
Williams, Stan 183
Williams, Ted 142, 179
Williams, Walter 245
Wills, Maury 7, 14–15, 117, 177, 205, 257
Wilson, Artie 6, 115, 117, 140–142, 211, 239, 247–248, 251, 258
Wilson, Earl 62, 105
Wilson, William "Mookie" 27, 128, 224
Wise, Rick 16, 21
Witches see Guayama Witches
Wockenfuss, John 159, 169
Wojey, Pete 14
Wolves see Arecibo Wolves
Working Agreements/Links (Puerto Rico and major league teams) 5, 16–18, 20–23, 25–26, 32, 34, 44, 56, 58, 62, 64–65, 71, 95, 122, 126, 128, 150, 154–155, 157–158, 165, 169, 172, 174–176, 178, 180–182, 192–196, 198–200, 205–206
World War II 9, 12, 36, 100, 144
Worthington, Al 14
Wright, Bill 87
Wright, Clyde 166, 194
Wright, Johnny 81, 215
Wright, Ken 45, 72, 255

Yakima (minor league team) 188
Yankee Stadium 158
Yankees see Carta Vieja Yankees; New York Yankees; Oneonta Yankees
Yawkey, Tom 177
Ydelfonso Solá Morales Stadium 10, 98, 121, 259
Yeager, Steve 228

York (minor league team) 2, 61
Young, Ted 115, 248
Yount, Robin 2, 24–25, 206, 251, 257

Zachary, Chris 33, 255
Zachry, Pat 51–52, 173, 213, 255, 258
Zimmer, Don 3, 40, 57–58, 68, 98, 122, 176, 208, 216
Zimmerman, Henry 1
Zisk, Richard 71, 126, 245, 251
Zorrilla, Diana 192
Zorrilla, Pedro "Pedrín" 34, 37, 53, 59–61, 94–96, 98, 104, 126, 137, 142–143, 147, 175–176, 191–192, 237, 258

www.ingramcontent.com/pod-product-compliance
Ingram Content Group UK Ltd.
Pitfield, Milton Keynes, MK11 3LW, UK
UKHW041926140426
5217IPUK00014B/330